D0327304

DECEIVERS

Exposing Evil Seducers & Their Last Days Deception

First printing: April 2018

New Leaf Press, P.O. Box 726, Green Forest, AR 72638
New Leaf Press is a division of the New Leaf Publishing Group, Inc.

ISBN: 978-0-89221-759-5
ISBN: 978-1-61458-658-6 (digital)
Library of Congress Number: 2018935819

Please consider requesting a copy of this volume be purchased by your local library system.

Printed in the United States of America

Please visit our website for other great titles:
www.newleafpress.com

For information regarding author interviews,
please contact the publicity department at (870) 438-5288.

New Leaf Press
A Division of New Leaf Publishing Group
www.newleafpress.com

Contents

Acknowledgments

As always in a book project, there are so many to thank.

First, I thank our Lord Jesus Christ for the privilege of being allowed to participate in this effort on His behalf.

Although I thank our participating authors in the introduction and conclusion, I also want to note their contributions here. Each brings tremendous knowledge and insight into the areas they cover on this prophetic topic.

To Angie Peters, my long-time editor, who is a daughter in my heart, my thanks and love. As always, she makes the book seamless and as near-perfect as possible.

To Dana Neel, who is daughter-close in every area of my life, my thanks and love.

To Jeanie, a "daughter" who means so much to me, my heart-felt love.

To Todd Strandberg, my partner in raptureready.com, my love and thanks for being a family-close friend and brother in Christ.

To my wife, Margaret, and our "kids," Terry, Jr., Nathan, and Kerry — my love and thanks for always being there, close by.

To everyone at New Leaf Publishing Group, my deep gratitude for all your efforts in bringing this book to publication.

To you, the reader, thanks for picking up and reading this book, which I hope will bless your life in whatever way the Lord chooses.

INTRODUCTION

TERRY JAMES

The greatest of all prophets looked from the mountainside across the Kidron Valley to Mount Moriah. His gaze was unlike that ever cast upon the topography, taking in a prophetic vista unprecedented in breadth and scope.

As He compassionately breathed in the essence of His beloved Jerusalem, God, Himself, pronounced with 100 percent clarity and accuracy the final throes of human history that would precede His Second Coming. He answered His disciples' question about what will mark the end of the age: "And Jesus answered and said unto them, Take heed that no man deceive you. For many shall come in my name, saying, I am Christ; and shall deceive many" (Matthew 24:4–5).[1]

It was the first recorded prophecy Jesus Christ uttered in what is known as the Olivet Discourse. His declaration echoes in cavernous reverberation through the corridors of past ages to our own time. Deception is the order of the day within the 21st-century world.

The deceivers are among us. They, in fact, rule this fallen planet while the wind-up of human history runs its inevitable course. Never have there been prophetic topics more worthy of dissection and analysis than those encapsulated within this book's title.

Authors who agreed to do that dissection and analysis for this volume are far more than merely excellent writers. Each is a widely recognized expert in publishing and broadcasting Bible prophecy. More importantly, each puts the soul-saving gospel message that Jesus Christ is the only way

7

to heaven at the heart of their ministries. Even beyond those credentials they share, each has been granted by the God they serve the dual gifts of spiritual discernment and prophetic insight into the issues and events that flood our daily headlines.

I am most gratified and humbled that they have agreed to take on their various assignments in presenting these chapters. Each one, I earnestly believe, is written with Holy Spirit influence and guidance. Our collective prayer is that you, the reader, will take from the book the things our Lord wants you to discern while life moves forward into the troubling although exciting times just ahead.

In *Deceivers: Exposing Evil Seducers & Their Last-Days Deception,* we have attempted to examine the many facets of today's rapidly degenerating culture — i.e., each chapter looks at a specific, corruptive aspect of life on the planet and in the nation through the prophetic, revealing lens and light of God's Word, the Bible.

We believe that stage-setting for Christ's Olivet prophecy about deceivers and deception is on the front burner of life today. It is altogether fitting, therefore, to assess this particular end-times signal in ascertaining where we might stand on God's prophetic timeline.

End-of-the-age deception has at its black heart increasingly virulent intrusion by the spirit world. This invasion is predicted in the Apostle Paul's prophecy: "But evil men and seducers shall wax worse and worse, deceiving, and being deceived" (2 Timothy 3:13).

Satan, the ultimately evil one, works through human agencies — human beings — to accomplish his nefarious desires. His objective is summed up in one brief and powerful statement of warning by the Apostle Peter: "Be sober, be vigilant; because your adversary the devil, as a roaring lion, walketh about, seeking whom he may devour" (1 Peter 5:8).

So, what do we observe today that shows the devil's use of human agencies to accomplish his intended destruction? His handiwork of seduction and deception is readily manifest in most every area of life at this present hour.

Religious Deception

One of the most blatant displays of Lucifer's deluding assaults is in the arena of theology. While false religions and false belief systems of all sorts are prevalent today, the most troubling such evil comes from within the body of believers. It is, I think, the Laodicean church in the making.

The development of this end-of-the-age church warned about by John in the Revelation exploded on the contemporary scene, I'm convinced, with the Purpose-Driven movement. Its most manifest lie was penned by its key architect, in my view. That lie declared that Bible prophecy isn't relevant and should be disregarded.

According to the author of the movement, like the obstinate members of Christ's body who are opposed to this Starbucks entertainment methodology for seeking out sinners in a "friendly" way, Bible prophecy is a "pillar" of the outmoded way of doing things that should be removed. It just "holds things up" — i.e., Bible prophecy gets in the way of building the mega churches because the subject of Christ's coming again is a downer. It reeks of coming judgment, and we can't have that if we intend to lure the world into the plush sanctuaries of the Laodicean edifices.

Clergy of this so-called enlightened way of "doing" Christianity readily agree for the most part with the present Catholic pontiff on two key tenets of this new *faith* — which, in actuality, is an ancient evil that is again in vogue: (1) there are many ways to God; and (2) today's Israel is not the Israel of the Bible, it is an imposter and it is an occupier of land that belongs to the Palestinians. Besides, the Church has now been given the right to claim all promises given originally to the Jews. They forfeited their rights when they rejected Christ and crucified Him.

The lie is monumental, and people are falling for it by the billions. It is at the heart of the great deception that will bring to fulfillment the prophecy made by the Lord while He sat atop the Mount of Olives: "For then shall be great tribulation, such as was not since the beginning of the world to this time, no, nor ever shall be" (Matthew 24:21).

Societal Seduction

We in America, I realize, are often accused of viewing everything from our perspective only. We think only — the accusation goes — of how America is affected in any given crisis or other situation. This is no doubt a well-founded indictment in many cases. However, in the matter of consideration of how society and culture have come to the low point currently experienced, there is, in my estimation, no better thermometer with which to measure decline than this once-great nation.

"Make America Great Again" is a familiar slogan. We heard it over and over again during the 2016 presidential campaign. We continue to hear it on an almost daily basis.

In my opinion, this was indeed once a great nation. But it was not made so because we were a people especially disposed to comport ourselves in saintly ways. America was a great nation because God, Himself, set it upon a solid foundation of biblical construction. He did so through inspiring the Founding Fathers, in presenting this phenomenal experiment in liberty, to employ Judeo-Christian precepts.

I say all that to say that because the United States was so founded, thus it could be considered a once-great nation, and we can legitimately use America to gauge how precipitously has been the fall into evil spawned by satanic engineering.

Following World War II, America seemed to reach its zenith — although, like any human entity or endeavor, it was far from perfect. The nation certainly far surpassed any in history as far as technological achievement. It also was a church-going, praying, family-togetherness country that held to biblically oriented principles for the most part.

Everything seemed to change when a certain point was reached. I believe that point was when the higher education system — the university — was sufficiently infiltrated by anti-God, anti-Christian thought. It was a process that began much earlier — in the late 19th century and even before.

By the time of the presidential election of 1960, America had turned the corner and headed into the free-thinking, philosophical stratosphere of academia. No moral absolutes, values clarification, situational ethics, and the inculcation of evolution as a guiding scientific rationale for living replaced biblical morality. Man, the thinkers of the neo age of enlightenment held, was no longer bound by the chains to a God who, at best, was no more than existential in His interest in the human race.

It was indeed a New Frontier, and the youth, in particular, threw off the shackles, aided and abetted by news and entertainment media. The university scene nurtured the new-found freedom, and the God of heaven became increasingly irrelevant.

The deception had set in, and the deceivers soon were in every direction one looked. Society and culture moved firmly into the grip of New-Age, "Aquarian" thought, feminism, and the *new morality* of the "if it feels good, do it" philosophical mantra. America did a nosedive into immorality, despite everything on the surface looking as if the New Frontier of John F. Kennedy would be the pathway to Utopia.

November 22, 1963, ended the euphoria, but the break from the bonds of Judeo-Christian morality was complete. Just as many within

America cut God loose, it seemed that the Almighty removed to a degree His protective, guiding hand. The president was assassinated, and at later dates, so were Dr. Martin Luther King Jr. and Robert F. Kennedy. While the youth in Berkeley and other places turned into flower children and/or departed in other ways from formerly moral precepts, Lyndon Johnson's Great Society and War on Poverty began the process of bankrupting America while creating a welfare class that has grown more and more addicted to largess issued from U.S. taxpayers. More than $22 trillion has been spent on welfare since Johnson's War on Poverty began. The national debt continues to grow exponentially minute by minute.

Vietnam took more than 50,000 American lives, and wars and rumors of war have grown in ominous reminder of Jesus Christ's prophecy as part of the Olivet Discourse.

Satan, the grand deceiver, continues to mesmerize much of the American populace. We have watched people — particularly the youth — of America become convinced by Lucifer's minions that marriage between man and man or woman and woman is the same as marriage between man and woman.

Now you can be whatever gender you wish to be, no matter what your birth certificate says about your sex. Good is called evil and evil good. The reprobate mind of Romans chapter 1 is now the norm more than the aberration.

Satanic rage against anyone who opposes his global agenda to bring all into a new world order is front and center each and every hour in news headlines. His deceivers — his minions both human and demonic — are busy building upon his deadly blueprint to bring about the destruction of America and the world.

The Apostle Paul's forewarning of the coming end-times deception and delusion that appear to be just ahead are ringing like alarm bells in spiritually attuned ears:

> For the mystery of iniquity doth already work: only he who now letteth will let, until he be taken out of the way. And then shall that Wicked be revealed, whom the Lord shall consume with the spirit of his mouth, and shall destroy with the brightness of his coming: even him, whose coming is after the working of Satan with all power and signs and lying wonders, and with all deceivableness of unrighteousness in them that perish; because

they received not the love of the truth, that they might be saved. And for this cause God shall send them strong delusion, that they should believe a lie: that they all might be damned who believed not the truth, but had pleasure in unrighteousness (2 Thessalonians 2:7–12).

The authors of *Deceivers: Exposing Evil Seducers & Their Last-Days Deception* have done masterful jobs of bringing to light the delusion taking place in this nation and world. My prayerful hope is that you will receive the same degree of understanding and inspiration from the book as I have during my reading of these chapters while in the process of working on this project. May the Lord bless while you proceed.

Endnotes:
1. Unless otherwise noted, Scripture in this chapter is from the King James Version (KJV) of the Bible.

CHAPTER 1

Religionist Deceivers Rampant

JAN MARKELL

Before I expound on the topic assigned to me by Terry James, let me give you a bit of background information. About a year after I was saved at age 11, I got involved in a strong church in the Minneapolis area. I didn't know a lot about church before that. Because I lived just a few doors down from this church, I was there frequently and soon the youth group became a big part of my formation into a Christian adult.

This evangelical church had no apostasy. As a matter of fact, its goal was to teach against apostasy and all false teaching. Some called this church a bunch of narrow fundamentalists, but looking back, I am glad they took such a strong stand on all theology that was not sound. That prepared me for a lifetime of ministry; the ministers and teachers there taught me to keep an antenna up at all times. Little did I know that as I moved on further and further into the end times, false teaching would become the new normal.

An ominous warning is found in Ezekiel 33:6:

> But if the watchman sees the sword coming and does not blow
> the trumpet and the people are not warned, and a sword comes
> and takes a person from them, he is taken away in his iniquity;
> but his blood I will require from the watchman's hand.[1]

We are all watchmen. Some are super watchmen, as that is just their calling. *None of us want the blood of false teaching on our hands.* At least I surely don't!

The Bible makes it clear that, near the time of Christ's return, apostasy will rage:

> But the Spirit explicitly says that in later times some will fall away from the faith, paying attention to deceitful spirits and doctrines of demons (1 Timothy 4:1).

> For the time will come when they will not endure sound doctrine; but wanting to have their ears tickled, they will accumulate for themselves teachers in accordance to their own desires, and will turn away their ears from the truth and will turn aside to myths (2 Timothy 4:3–4).

But I am not sure that anyone during the time when these were written could imagine just how serious the issue of false doctrine was to become.

In 2001, I began a national radio ministry. It was Christian talk radio that would eventually air on more than 800 radio stations across North America. It would also become a popular podcast destination. I quickly realized that I had a responsibility to talk to this radio audience and school listeners on just what theological minefields they should avoid! I felt I even had to name the blatant false teachers who were devouring the sheep.

Those who long for the truth loved this, but many others felt I was causing trouble and division. I was even blocked from some networks I wanted to air on, as they suggested such name-calling was not wanted. *What a dilemma. In order to hold to truth, I would be banned from some outlets that had listeners who wanted the truth!*

I feel every believer needs to heed Matthew 7:15–20:

> Watch out for false prophets. They come to you in sheep's clothing, but inwardly they are ferocious wolves. By their fruit you will recognize them. Do people pick grapes from thornbushes, or figs from thistles? Likewise, every good tree bears good fruit, but a bad tree bears bad fruit. A good tree cannot bear bad fruit, and a bad tree cannot bear good fruit. Every tree that does not bear good fruit is cut down and thrown into the fire. Thus, by their fruit you will recognize them. (NIV)

Calling out false teachers is no way to become popular. *One is always calling out somebody's favorite teacher.* Yet, as I went on in ministry, I could easily see that many sheep were being eaten by wolves that were preying on them. The sheep were often undiscerning, easily led, and easily fooled — and they just loved the idea of following a pied piper who was joyfully leading them astray. Some leaders did this intentionally, and others just had bad theology that even they didn't recognize was going to harm the flock.

The Mainline Mistake

More than 100 years ago, mainline Protestants made a wrong turn — actually, a left turn if you will. For generations, the Methodists, Presbyterians, Congregationalists, and others had seen net annual membership gains. But in the early 1960s, their growth slowed down, and soon they began to lose members big time. That decline has continued to the present.

These folks were at one time America's "evangelicals." They chose to follow a liberal, progressive agenda, also called the social gospel, in about 1920. They simply quit teaching and preaching the gospel for social issues and causes. It was their conscious choice to feed the stomach but starve the soul.

Visit any Mainline Protestant church today and you will observe an aging membership unenthusiastically singing old hymns with little enthusiasm for the true gospel. Those who are excited have moved on to evangelical churches. They took their eyes off the prize: the saving gospel of Jesus Christ. These denominations are now slipping into irrelevance but still maintain their focus on social justice, which seems to keep some from permanently closing their doors.

Just about the time they began to decline, interest, attendance, and enthusiasm began to soar for conservative, evangelical denominations. Surely, they wouldn't make the same mistakes, would they?

Don't be so sure! They chose to go down the same path!

Evangelicals Start to Wobble

In the 1980s, I looked forward to the monthly magazine put out by the National Association of Evangelicals (NAE). These publications were very solid. I learned that they had been started around 1942 as a counter to the liberalism going on in the Protestant church. The founders of the NAE were conservative, fundamental, and salvation-focused. They had little time for the social gospel.

However, take a trip over to the NAE website today — and be prepared for a surprise upon seeing the organization's transition over the last 30 years and a shocking deviation from its 1942 founding! You will see an emphasis on poverty, racial reconciliation, environmentalism, human rights, immigration, nuclear weapons, creation care, and prison reform. These subjects are right out of the liberal playbook!

To be blunt, evangelicals are walking down the same gangplank as the liberal mainliners. *They may also drown in the same sea.* In 2011, a resolution by the National Association of Evangelicals (NAE) called for a mutual reduction in current nuclear stockpiles, as well as ratification of the Comprehensive Test Ban Treaty. The NAE resolution states: "With their unique destructive potential, nuclear weapons profoundly threaten the lives and prosperity of future generations, and of all God's creatures."[2]

What does this have to do with the evangelical gospel of salvation? And are these folks delusional enough to suggest that North Korea, Pakistan, Iran, and Russia are going to cut back on their nukes? *Liberalism strikes again!*

As I moved deeper into Christian ministry, I noticed that the solid rock of evangelicalism was moving leftward and toward issues that had nothing to do with eternity — more signs of the coming great apostasy. I was shocked and disappointed. When one group of denominations had already hit an iceberg like the *Titanic* did, wouldn't every other denomination sit up, take notice, and vow to not make the same mistakes?

Apparently not.

New Ways of Doing Church

New ways of doing church were going to stoke the fires inside the evangelical church. These new ways would go by various terms, such as "seeker-sensitive," "purpose-driven," "gospel-lite," "church-growth movement," and many more. None of these movements were very healthy, and they would weaken the Church — and strengthen the apostasy — even more.

Somebody came up with a slick phrase that today's evangelical church is all about "nickels and noses" — in other words, how to fill offering plates and pews. *Certainly all churches do not operate like this, but too many do.*

It would quickly become apparent to me that Satan was making a last-days move to weaken the Church so that end-time Christians would be more vulnerable.

Hipster Church

Why would any church want to abandon senior citizens? Don't they represent stability, and aren't they reliable tithers? But today's church has chosen to target the under-45 age group while abandoning the seniors who will never accept the hipper sermons, gospel rock music, casual dress, and what they might perceive as majoring in minors from the pulpit.

Older folks want to talk current events, Bible prophecy, and even politics. The younger crowd wants to "feel good," have "experiences," and sway to the beat of a drum and bass guitar. In today's church world, the two are having a hard time mixing, and the current Church is consequently taking a pounding.

In some churches, there is watered-down preaching, making the younger sheep ripe for the slaughter; false teaching; gospel-lite messages; and little being taught that will make a difference for eternity.

When I started in ministry, all ages blended and did just fine. By the late 1990s, it seemed that the younger generation called all the shots, and that church leadership caved to them. Senior citizens sat in the church foyer during what amounted to a rock concert during the worship time. They then wandered into the sanctuary just for the weekly message.

How tragic.

A more recent movement that has tapped into this is called Postmodernism, also referred to as the Emergent Church. This movement emphasizes experience over reason, subjectivity over objectivity, spirituality over religion, images over words, and feelings over truth. These are the reactions to modernism and are thought to be necessary in order to actively engage contemporary culture. This movement is still quite new, so there is not yet a standard method of "doing church" among the groups choosing to take the Postmodern/Emergent mindset.

This movement is also all about ecumenism. It stresses unity among many different religions and seems to celebrate Catholicism.

Some 15 years ago, once-solid churches began to target young adults by having a special Emergent service. Windows were darkened, candles were lit, sofas were brought in, and informal "services," very unstructured, were conducted. A Bible likely wouldn't be a part of the worship agenda, but sharing feelings, thoughts, and ideas were. Some of the participants even brought arts and crafts projects to work on during these sessions.

In 2004, *Christianity Today* dedicated an entire issue to "The Emergent Mystique." These churches are a new generation unique in style, leadership, worship, prayer, and more. They are progressive and unbiblical, and almost all are flirting with heresy. Even in my youth, I cannot imagine being attracted to such waywardness.

During an Emergent church service, congregants are more likely to pontificate with peers and would flee from having to sit through a verse-by-verse sermon. If a sermon focused on hell, they would be out the door. Emergent Rob Bell suggests there likely is no hell. These young adults would rather learn that all faiths uniting is just fine, and aligning with Rome might be the best idea they've heard in a long time. Other Emergent/Postmodern fathers include Brian McLaren, Doug Pagitt, and Tony Jones. There are many other leaders in the movement, but these are the most prominent. If one could sum up their belief system in a sentence, it would be that we cannot know absolute truth.

The reliable website *gotquestions.org* says this about this movement:

> The dangers of postmodernism can be viewed as a downward spiral that begins with the rejection of absolute truth, which then leads to a loss of distinctions in matters of religion and faith, and culminates in a philosophy of religious pluralism that says no faith or religion is objectively true and therefore no one can claim his or her religion is true and another is false.[3]

More apostasy running amok.

The Laughing Revival that Wasn't So Funny

Sometime during the 1990s came the "Toronto Blessing" and "Pensacola Outpouring." Good Christian friends of mine considered these streams to be solid and a move of God. What was I missing? I watched clips from the various venues and saw no order, only confusion — and God is a God of order. How could rolling on the floor and barking like a dog be "in the spirit"? What verse in the Bible suggests we act in such insane ways? My Bible tells me to do all things decently and in order (1 Corinthians 14:40).

Others who believed in a similar manner were stressing that we were to get "drunk in the spirit" and laugh uncontrollably. I saw more film clips of people growling, dancing, shaking, and weeping uncontrollably. I realized that another atom bomb had struck the Church, and for better or for worse — likely for worse — it was going to leave its mark. It wouldn't be a healthy one.

I wondered why some "new way of doing church" couldn't come along that was stable and sound. People seemed to be pursuing experiential highs, signs and wonders, and an overdose of emotionalism. None of this was built on the foundation of sound teaching and preaching. It was all experience. Talk about "tickling the ears"!

When You Criticize "America's Pastor"

I was both praised and pounded for suggesting that "America's Pastor," Rick Warren, might be causing damage to the Church. He seriously put down eschatology, saying it would distract people from their purpose. As an author myself, I was intrigued with any book that would sell over 25 million copies, as his *Purpose Driven Life* did. It was clearly a publishing phenomenon. But I'm not sure anybody was prepared for how Rick Warren would introduce a new way of doing church, and it wasn't very healthy. There would eventually be two dozen new ways of doing church, but Warren's seemed to be the first option in the evangelical community.

Warren believes the Purpose-Driven principles are so important and so unique that he asks pastors to lead their congregants with his church programs, messages, worship, and even private devotions for 40 days. Rick Warren gives pastors his 40-day challenge: follow his principles in the purpose-driven formula and your church will get bigger, better, stronger, richer, and more. How did churches grow before his formula came out 15 years ago? Somehow they grew and thrived and never resorted to his new way of doing church. Imagine that!

Suddenly, churches with 100 members have imagined that they would become mega-churches if they followed the Warren formula.

Warren also quoted a number of well-known Roman Catholics, but did not note how they believe and even promote concepts against clear teachings of the Scripture. These quotes include those from Brother Lawrence, Madame Guyon, St. John of the Cross, Henri Nouwen, Mother Teresa, and John Main.

In 2011, he tapped into three men who were not only unsound, but they had some ties to the New Age Movement. Warren went on a weight-loss kick for his entire church by embarking on "The Daniel Plan." To accomplish his personal goal of weight loss and that of thousands of church members, he enlisted the likes of Dr. Mehmet Oz, Dr. Mark

Hyman, and Dr. Daniel Amen. Their books and websites blatantly promote the dark side, including yoga and reiki. Yet Pastor Warren proudly featured them in his pulpit for many weekends of rah-rah cheerleading with healthy weight-loss goals.

One attendee said the event was a "pagan palooza." Apparently, during these sessions on improving health, the leaders conveniently avoided spiritual health! I concluded that end-time apostasy was just going to keep on rolling along like old man river. Or was I just getting hyper-critical? I was beginning to doubt myself! Yet sticking only to the truth of Scripture was getting hard to find. The gimmicks just kept galloping along.

Many smaller churches that went the "Purpose-Driven" route now have closed their doors. Church isn't a formula. It's people meeting together to encourage one another and learn from solid Bible preaching and teaching.

Are Today's "Prophets" Only about "Profit"?

Many scoff at this topic and suggest that today's prophets are strictly about profit. I think many are, but I hate throwing a Dave Wilkerson under the bus. I am not a cessationist, because I have been healed, but when the abuses of those into "signs and wonders" only worsen by the day, many legitimately question those who are leading the movement that boasts of prophets and apostles. They are doing enormous destruction.

This movement gained steam thanks to C. Peter Wagner out of Fuller Seminary some 40 years ago. He introduced what is now called the "New Apostolic Reformation," or NAR for short. Thousands of churches and millions of Christians adhere to unsound teachings presented by Bill Johnson, Rick Joyner, Cindy Jacobs, the late Kim Clement, and many more.

The NAR, as noted on their website, teaches "that God's intended form of church governance is apostles and prophets holding leadership over evangelists, pastors, and teachers." However, this has not been the case for much of church history. But according to the New Apostolic Reformation, God began to restore prophets and apostles over the last three or four decades. "Only now, as the church is properly guided by the appropriate spiritual leaders, can it fulfill its commission."[4]

The NAR states that prophets are extremely important and just as important as apostles. These people have been empowered to receive "new" revelations from God that will aid the church in establishing dominion. According to the New Apostolic Reformation, only prophets and occasionally apostles can obtain new revelations.

I cannot count the number of letters and emails this ministry has received from people who have been duped by two dozen prominent people in this stream of thought and theology.

Just because one embraces a more Charismatic theology does not mean he or she gets into some of the activities promoted by these false teachers. I have been a member of an Assembly of God church that would have nothing to do with such strange happenings. They denounced Todd Bentley, who performed like the charlatan he was in Pensacola, Florida, kicking people with his biker boot and suggesting that was "healing" them. Yet Bentley was honored by many leaders in the New Apostolic Reformation. When he fell from grace due to adultery going on all during his healing rallies, he was "restored" in good faith by NAR leaders Rick Joyner and C. Peter Wagner.

This group is also more experience-oriented and not likely to be wild about expositional teaching.

Many in this stream also embrace Dominion Theology. That is, that the Church truly CAN make the world perfect and that will allow Jesus Christ to return — but to a perfected earth. Such delusion.

So Protestants Are Now Catholics?

In more recent years, I began hearing about mystical Christianity. I learned that many churches, and most of them evangelical churches, were promoting labyrinths, icons, chanting, candles, centering prayer, and contemplative prayer. The latter is a distant relative of Buddhism, so I wondered how much stranger things could get. Protestants began taking on Catholic traditions. They were heralding ancient Catholic mystics. *I guess we didn't need the Reformation.*

Some just called this "the new spirituality," even though they were tapping into practices that were very old — so old that it went back to the desert fathers and borrowed their practices. I could not believe what I was seeing and reading.

These folks all talked about a new kind of meditation that sounded quite dangerous. It did not sound like true biblical meditation, but was more aligned with Zen. The Christian college from which I graduated years ago brought in a Buddhist to encourage the students to zone out and meditate, but not on the Bible!

Men who didn't have sound theology, such as Dallas Willard, Richard Foster, and Thomas Merton, started being quoted in church pulpits. What was going on? The more I looked into these mystics, the more I trembled for the Church and the sheep who were going to be slaughtered and eaten by wolves. There was just no end to the last-days' deceptions.

These mystics thought they could sanctify yoga and decided to call it "Christian yoga." You can't put a smiley face on millions of demons who are a part of the yoga experience, but these folks thought you could!

When Left Isn't Right

The rise of the religious left is simply stunning. Jim Wallis, Tony Campolo, Shane Claiborne, Lynne Hybels, and many more, have convinced two generations that the social gospel is where it is at. It had its modern beginning in the late 1800s, which I referred to when I began this chapter. "It developed as a way to address the various conditions in society that caused suffering among the populace. The belief was, and is, that Christianity will attract followers when it demonstrates its love for mankind. This could be best accomplished by helping to alleviate the suffering of humanity caused by poverty, disease, oppressive work conditions, society's injustices,"[5] and civil rights abuses.

Along with this came the push for "social justice," and that spotlight was turned on the so-called Palestinian people and their perceived plight. Denominations and churches then heavily turned away from support for Israel and God's chosen people. Gone are the days when Israel could count on 100 percent evangelical support.

Criticism was always couched in sentiment that Israel was an "occupier" with no thought given to all the verses about her God-given land.

This, too, is end-time deception.

To be honest, the more I learned about these strange theologies, the more I sensed my world was growing smaller and smaller. I just didn't fit in hardly any of them. Was I just a theological prude who was a purist and a victim of a hyper-fundamentalist orientation when I was young? Or was I a Berean who looked at these theological aberrations and concluded they were a part of the great end-time falling away?

Has Discernment Turned Ugly?

In the early 2000s, many "discernment ministries" began to spring up. They looked at the various new theologies and at some of the old theologies that were getting new life, and became their critics. How refreshing! They named names. But even they didn't get it right 100 percent of the time. It seemed to me that in order for them to get more followers and more "likes," they started to name off good people, calling them "heretics" and "false teachers," even if they were very sound!

Many ministries were harmed by these people who took the call to contend for the faith very seriously, but in my opinion, they took it a step too far. I can't count the number of times that my name and ministry were dragged through the mud. If my theology wasn't being questioned, then those I associated with were targeted with guilt by association.

I recall inviting a popular conference speaker to address my annual conference. He would have the opportunity to address 4,000 people with his cutting-edge message. His reply to me was that he could not associate with me because a ministry leader he admired and followed insisted I was heretical because I supported a popular author. I was speechless. Yes, there is wreckage in the Church, thanks to false teachers, *but now there appeared to be wreckage, thanks to people contentiously contending for the faith!*

Perhaps the end-time character of mankind is simply tanking. It seems to me like love is growing cold (Matthew 24:12), just as sound Bible teaching is disappearing. *This doesn't seem like a good combination.* At the bema seat of judgment, we are not only going to be held accountable for every doctrine we abused, but also for how we abused our brothers and sisters in Christ, for slandering their good character or their reputable name. That is what makes doing what I am now — critically looking at some false streams in the church — so difficult. If I am wrong, I have spoken ill against a brother or sister. That is no better in God's mind than the apostasy that is running amok. *It grieves me that discernment has almost turned as ugly as the false teachings.*

The Greatest Tragedy of Our Day

In the last 20 years, I have received hundreds, if not thousands, of emails, letters, and calls telling me that solid believers cannot find a prophecy-preaching church. I honestly believe that this is a part of the end-time falling away. Their churches may be solid in many ways, but the pastors have concluded that the topic of biblical prophecy is controversial and might scare people away, so they bury it in the attic of the church along with the hymnals from which the congregation used to sing.

The church is no longer excited that the King is coming! A few remnant churches remain, many of which are in the Calvary Chapel stream, that continue to proclaim the news of Christ's return, but their numbers are very few. As a result, those who long for new information on this topic flock to a handful of prophecy conferences around America.

In 2016, my prophecy event drew 6,000 people to a venue of 4,300. Traffic was backed up on Minneapolis freeways heading to the church we rent. Hundreds of people have told me that they cannot find this message in a single church in their community.

No one is asking a pastor to make eschatology the focus of his ministry, but the neglect of prophecy is unconscionable when one-third of the Bible speaks of it and a crown is promised to be rewarded to those who long for His appearing (2 Timothy 4:8).

It is fine that the church has marriage seminars and financial seminars, but it's not okay for it to not take one weekend a year to remind people to get their lives in order, for Jesus is coming soon! Jesus chastised the religious leaders of His day for not knowing the signs of His first coming. I believe He is chastising today's church leaders for a sentiment that seems to say, *"Come, Lord Jesus, but not too soon!"*

There is a lot of blame to go around for this deficiency. It likely starts with our seminaries and trickles down. But the path was paved thanks to the seeker-sensitive movement, the Emergent/Postmodern stream, Purpose-Driven motives, the social gospel efforts, and more.

At the same time, evangelical support for Israel has so tanked that I would have to almost include this as another sign of the great falling away. In my younger years, I recall that evangelical support for Israel was a given. After all, her rebirth was not just the miracle of the 20th century; it may have been the miracle of all time. Yet as I write this, I am aware of the new mood in the Church: to swing support away from Israel and toward those whom it perceives as the persecuted Palestinians — with Israel as the persecutor.

A part of this is born out of the strong appeal of "social justice" among the under-age-50 crowd previously mentioned. And a part of it is due to many voices now speaking on behalf of the Palestinians who, at the same time, denounce Israel as an "occupier." Prominent teachers, authors, radio hosts, and more have done major damage over the last 30 years, including Hank Hanegraaff, Lynne Hybels, Dr. John Piper, Tony Campolo, Jim Wallis, Brian McLaren, Gary Burge, and two dozen more.

How this must grieve the heart of God, who has preserved Israel and the Jewish people because He is a covenant keeper!

So the Church of today is vastly different than the Church of my youth that focused on prophecy, Israel, and eternity-related issues regularly. I truly feel today like a dinosaur — outdated and out-of-step with much of the Church. But is the loss theirs or mine?

Jesus states in Matthew 16 that the gates of hell will not prevail against the Church, but the gates of hell are surely trying to interfere! I know of very few people who are looking for the perfect church, but many are looking for a gospel-preaching church that is excited about the fact that the King is coming. They are looking for a church that will hold to sound doctrine and that will contend for the faith. The options are without a doubt shrinking, but some still remain.

I pray you — and your church — can be a lighthouse as the days shorten to get the gospel to a lost and hurting world.

Endnotes

1. Unless otherwise noted, Scripture in this chapter is from the New American Standard Bible (NASB).
2. https://www.nae.net/nae-board-calls-for-nuclear-weapons-reductions/.
3. https://www.gotquestions.org/postmodernism-dangers.html.
4. https://www.gotquestions.org/New-Apostolic-Reformation.html.
5. https://www.thebereancall.org/content/shameful-social-gospel.

CHAPTER 2

Signs Outshine Satan's Seduction

DR. DAVID R. REAGAN

I grew up in an Amillennial church that spiritualized prophecy. Accordingly, I was taught that we are living in the Millennium now, that Jesus is reigning from His throne in heaven, and that He is never returning to this earth again. Over and over I heard it proclaimed from the pulpit that "there is not one verse in the Bible that even implies that Jesus will ever put His feet on this earth again."

With regard to Jesus' Second Coming, I was taught that one day He would appear in the sky without warning and would take all believers, living and dead, back with Him to heaven. The earth would be consumed by fire and cease to exist. Believers would live forever in heaven as disembodied spirits.

All of this was based, of course, on a spiritualization of what the Bible actually says about the Millennium and the eternal state. Strangely, we were taught that the Bible means exactly what it says about everything except when it is talking about the Second Coming and the events surrounding it. We were told that end-time prophecies never mean what they say because they are "apocalyptic in nature."

I had no idea what the word "apocalyptic" meant, but I believed what I heard from the pulpit, so I assumed it meant that end-time prophecy is indecipherable.

A Stunning Discovery

Then, one day I read the Book of Zechariah and, in the process, I noticed that this so-called apocalyptic book was full of prophecies about the First

Coming of the Messiah, and that all of them had been literally fulfilled. I'm speaking of prophecies like the one that says the Messiah will come humbly on a donkey (9:9) and that He will be betrayed for 30 pieces of silver (11:12–13).

It suddenly occurred to me that if the First Coming prophecies in this "apocalyptic book" meant what they said, then why shouldn't the Second Coming prophecies mean what they say?

And one of those prophecies in chapter 14 says that the Messiah will return to the Mount of Olives, and when His feet touch the ground, the mount will split apart. There it was, as plain as it could be: The Messiah is returning to earth! His feet will touch this earth again! To top it off, verse 9 says that on that day, He will begin to rule over all the earth!

My eyes were suddenly opened to a fundamental truth: "If the plain sense of Scripture makes sense, don't look for any other sense, lest you end up with nonsense." I stopped playing games with God's Prophetic Word, and all of the end-time prophecies began to make sense. I no longer had to spiritualize them to mean whatever my church's doctrine demanded that they meant.

And that applied to the signs the Bible tells us to watch for that will signal the Lord's return. I had always been taught that we could know nothing about the timing of the Lord's return — that His return would be completely unexpected, like a sneak attack.

When our members would attend a Bible prophecy conference and come back talking excitedly about the "signs of the times," they would always be put down with sarcastic derision. "There are no signs!" they would be told in no uncertain words. "The Bible says that the return of Jesus will be a total surprise to everyone. So, forget about the so-called signs and just focus on living for the Lord."

A Satanic Conspiracy

I am convinced that Satan does not want anyone to know anything about the timing of the Lord's return, and I think that is the reason for all the confusion. He doesn't know the timing, but he knows the signs the Bible gives us to watch for, and he is determined to get people's eyes off those signs so that the Church will be filled with ignorance and apathy about the timing of the Second Coming.

Ignorance and apathy both contribute to a lack of preparedness and hope. How can you get excited about an event that you know nothing about? How can you have a strong hope when the Lord's return seems so distant and irrelevant to your life? A sense of the Lord's imminent return motivates holiness and evangelism. Satan hates both.

There is no doubt that Satan has been very successful in convincing Christians, including pastors, that there is nothing we can know about the timing of the Lord's return. That's where I was for 30 years before I began studying God's Prophetic Word.

Another Discovery

So, you can imagine my surprise when I discovered that although the Bible says we cannot know the time of the Lord's return (Matthew 25:13), the Scriptures make it equally clear that we can know the season of His return. Consider, for example, this passage from 1 Thessalonians 5:2–6:

> You yourselves know full well that the day of the Lord will come just like a thief in the night…. But you, brethren, are not in darkness, that the day would overtake you like a thief; for you are all sons of light and sons of day. We are not of night nor of darkness; so then let us not sleep as others do, but let us be alert and sober.[1]

This passage asserts that Jesus is coming like "a thief in the night." But then it proceeds to make clear that this will be true only for the pagan world and not for believers. His return should be no surprise to those who know Him and His Word, for they have the indwelling of the Holy Spirit to give them understanding of the nature of the times.

Furthermore, the Scriptures give us signs to watch for — signs that will signal that Jesus is ready to return. The writer of the Hebrews letter referred to these signs when he proclaimed that believers should encourage one another when they see the day of judgment drawing near (Hebrews 10:24–27). Jesus also referred to the end-time signs in His Olivet Discourse, given during the last week of His life (Matthew 24 and Luke 21). Speaking of a whole series of signs that He had given to His disciples, He said, "When you see all these things, recognize that He [the Son of Man, that is, Jesus] is near, right at the door" (Matthew 24:33).

A Personal Experience

Every time I think of "signs of the times," I am reminded of a great man of God named Elbert Peak. I had the privilege of participating with him in a Bible prophecy conference held in Orlando, Florida, in the early 1990s. Mr. Peak was about 80 years old at the time. He had been assigned the topic, "The Signs of the Times." He began his presentation by observing, "Sixty years ago when I first started preaching, you had to scratch around like a chicken to find one sign of the Lord's soon return."

He paused for a moment, then added, "But today there are so many signs I'm no longer looking for them. Instead, I'm listening for a sound — the sound of a trumpet!"

The First Sign

At the beginning of the 20th century, there was not one single, tangible, measurable sign that indicated we were living in the season of the Lord's return. The first to appear was the Balfour Declaration, which was issued by the British government on November 2, 1917.

This Declaration was prompted by the fact that during World War I, the Turks sided with the Germans. Thus, when Germany lost the war, so did the Turks, and the victorious Allies decided to divide up both the German and Turkish empires.

The Turkish territories, called the Ottoman Empire, contained the ancient homeland of the Jewish people — an area the Romans had named Palestine after the last Jewish revolt in A.D. 132–135.

In 1917, Palestine included all of modern-day Israel and Jordan. In the scheme the Allies concocted for dividing up the German and Turkish territories, Britain was allotted Palestine, and this is what prompted the Balfour Declaration. In that document, Lord Balfour, the British Foreign Secretary, declared that it was the intention of the British government to establish in Palestine "a national home for the Jewish people."

An Evangelical Response to the First Sign

The leading Evangelical in England at the time was F.B. Meyer. He immediately recognized the prophetic significance of the Declaration, for he was well aware that the Scriptures prophesy that the Jewish people will be regathered to their homeland in unbelief right before the return of the Messiah (Isaiah 11:11–12).

Meyer sent out a letter to the Evangelical leaders of England asking them to gather in London in December to discuss the prophetic implications of the Balfour Declaration. In that letter, he stated, "The signs of the times point toward the close of the time of the Gentiles . . . and the return of Jesus can be expected any moment."

Before Meyer's meeting could be convened, another momentous event occurred on December 11, 1917. On that day, General Edmund Allenby liberated the city of Jerusalem from 400 years of Turkish rule.

There is no doubt that these events in 1917 marked the beginning of the end times, because they led to the worldwide regathering of the Jewish people to their homeland and the reestablishment of their state.

Since 1917

Since the time of the Balfour Declaration, we have witnessed throughout the 20th century and continuing to this day the appearance of sign after sign pointing to the Lord's soon return. There are so many of these signs today, in fact, that one would have to be either biblically illiterate or spiritually blind not to realize that we are living on borrowed time.

I have personally been searching the Bible for years in an effort to identify all the signs, and it has not been an easy task to get a hold on them. That's because there are so many of them, both in the Old and New Testaments. I have found that the best way to deal with them is to put them in categories, and in doing that, I have come up with six categories of end-time signs.

1. The Signs of Nature

And there will be great earthquakes, and in various places plagues and famines; and there will be terrors and great signs from heaven (Luke 21:11).

This category of signs has always been the least respected, even among believers. The mere mention of it usually evokes a sneer accompanied by the words, "Come on, what else is new? There have always been earthquakes and tornados and hurricanes."

But those who have this attitude forget that Jesus said the signs would be like "birth pangs" (Matthew 24:8). That means they will increase in frequency and intensity the closer we get to the Lord's return. In other words, there will be more frequent natural disasters and more intense ones.

That is exactly what has been happening. For example, between October of 1991 and November of 2004 — a period of 13 years — the United States experienced:

- nine of the ten largest insurance natural disasters in history
- nine of the ten greatest disasters as ranked by FEMA relief costs

- five of its costliest hurricanes in history
- three of its four largest tornado swarms in history[2]

Keep in mind that these statistics were compiled before the Hurricane Katrina disaster in August of 2005!

2. The Signs of Society

> Realize this, that in the last days difficult times will come. For men will be lovers of self, lovers of money, boastful, arrogant, revilers, disobedient to parents, ungrateful, ungrateful, unholy, unloving, irreconcilable, malicious gossips, without self-control, brutal, haters of good, treacherous, reckless, conceited, lovers of pleasure rather than lovers of God (2 Timothy 3:1–4).

This passage sounds like a typical evening newscast today! Notice the three things it says people will love in the end times: self, money, and pleasure.

The love of self is humanism — the belief that man can accomplish anything on his own. The love of money is materialism. When humanism is your religion, your god will always be money. The love of pleasure is the third love mentioned. This is hedonism, the lifestyle that is always produced by humanism and materialism.

But God cannot be mocked (Galatians 6:7). He therefore sees to it that when people choose humanism, materialism, and hedonism, the payoff is always nihilism, which is a fancy philosophical word for "despair."

Need I emphasize that our world is wallowing in despair today? We live in a society plagued by abortion, homosexuality, domestic violence, child molestation, blasphemy, pornography, alcoholism, drug abuse, and gambling.

Like in the days of the judges in the Old Testament, people are doing what is right in their own eyes, and the result is that people are calling evil good and good evil (Isaiah 5:20).

3. The Spiritual Signs

There are more signs in this category than any other. Many are evil in nature, but there are also some very positive ones.

Negative Spiritual Signs

Concerning the negative signs, a typical passage is the following one found in 2 Timothy 4:3–4:

The time will come when they [professing Christians] will not endure sound doctrine; but wanting to have their ears tickled, they will accumulate for themselves teachers in accordance to their own desires, and will turn away their ears from the truth and will turn aside to myths.

Some of the negative spiritual signs that are specifically prophesied include the following: false christs, cultic groups, heresies, apostasy, skepticism, deception, occultism, and persecution.

The one that Jesus mentioned most frequently was the presence of false christs and their cultic groups (Matthew 24:5, 11, 24). In fulfillment of these prophecies, we have experienced an explosion of cult activity since 1830 when the Mormon Church was founded.

One of the most obvious spiritual signs in America today is the rapidly increasing apostasy in the Church. Even many so-called Evangelical leaders seem intent on getting in bed with the world in order to secure the world's acceptance. Thus, we find former Evangelical churches approving abortion, ordaining homosexuals, and endorsing same-sex marriage. Meanwhile, many of the old-line liberal denominations have continued down the path of rank heresy by denying the fundamentals of the faith, like the virgin birth and the Resurrection.

Positive Spiritual Signs

A. Of the outpouring of the Spirit

But, praise God, we are told that there will be some very positive spiritual signs in the end times. The most important one that is prophesied in many places is a great outpouring of the Holy Spirit (Joel 2:28–29).

This outpouring began at the dawn of the 20th century, and proved to be one of the greatest spiritual surprises — and blessings — of the century. You see, when that century began, the prevailing viewpoint among both Catholics and Protestants regarding the Holy Spirit was Cessationism. This view held that the gifts of the Spirit ceased when the last Apostle died. In effect, it was a belief that the Holy Spirit had retired in the first century.

The 20th century had hardly gotten started when a Holy Spirit revival broke out at a small Bible college in Topeka, Kansas, in 1901.[3] Three years later, a similar Holy Spirit revival swept Wales and began to spread worldwide.[4] Then, in 1906, the Spirit fell with great power on a humble black preacher in Los Angeles named William J. Seymour.[5] The

Azuza Street Revival, as it came to be called, continued for four years and gave birth to the Pentecostal Movement.[6]

B. Of the "early and latter rains"

The Bible prophesies two great outpourings of the Spirit and symbolically pictures them as the "early and latter rains" (Joel 2:23), based on the two rainy seasons of Israel. The early rain occurred at Pentecost in the first century when the Church was established. The latter rain was prophesied to occur after the Jewish people had been reestablished in their homeland (Joel 2:18–26).

The latter rain began with the Pentecostal Movement, just as God began to regather the Jews to their homeland under the visionary leadership of Theodore Herzl. But the rain did not become a downpour until after the reestablishment of the state of Israel in May of 1948, just as prophesied by Joel.

First came the anointing of Billy Graham's ministry in 1949, followed by the Charismatic Movement of the 1960s. Today, most of Christianity, whether Pentecostal, Charismatic, or Traditional, fully recognizes that the ministry of the Holy Spirit is alive and well in Spiritled worship, the continuing validity of spiritual gifts, the reality of spiritual warfare, and the importance of a Spirit-filled life in winning that warfare.

C. Additional positive spiritual signs

In addition to the rediscovery of the Holy Spirit, there are other positive spiritual prophecies being fulfilled today — like the preaching of the gospel worldwide (Matthew 24:14), the revival of Davidic praise worship (Amos 9:11), and the development of Messianic Judaism (Romans 9:27).

Another remarkable positive sign is the understanding of Bible prophecy. You see, the Hebrew prophets often did not understand the end-time prophecies that the Lord gave to them. A good example can be found in Daniel 12:8–9, where the prophet complains to the Lord that he does not understand the prophecies that have been entrusted to him. The Lord's response is, "Don't worry about it. Just write the prophecies. They have been sealed up until the end times."

In other words, the Bible teaches that many of the end-time prophecies will not be understood until the time comes for them to be fulfilled. And that is exactly what has been happening in the past 100 years. Historical developments and scientific inventions are now making it possible for us to understand end-time prophecies that have never been understood before.

Take Israel, for example. All end-time prophecy revolves around the nation of Israel. But how could those prophecies be understood as long as Israel did not exist and there was no prospect that the nation would ever exist again? This is the reason that Hal Lindsey's book, *The Late Great Planet Earth*, became such a phenomenal bestseller in the 1970s. For the first time, it explained the events prophesied in the Book of Revelation in natural terms that people could easily understand.

4. The Signs of World Politics

> You will be hearing of wars and rumors of wars. . . . For nation will rise against nation, and kingdom against kingdom (Matthew 24:6–7).

I taught international politics for 20 years before I entered the ministry full time, so this is an area that is particularly fascinating to me.

The Bible prophesies a very specific end-time configuration of world politics. Israel is pictured as being reestablished (Ezekiel 37:21–22) and surrounded by hostile Arab neighbors intent on its destruction (Ezekiel 35:1–36:7). This, of course, has been the situation in the Middle East since the Israeli Declaration of Independence in May of 1948.

Daniel prophesied that the Roman Empire would be revived (Daniel 2:36–41), something many men — like Charlemagne, Napoleon, and Hitler — tried to do through force. But the prophecy had to await God's timing for its fulfillment, and that came after World War II, with the formation of the European Common Market that has since morphed into the superpower called the European Union.

The Bible pictures a great power located in the land of Magog in the "remote parts of the north." This nation will menace Israel in the end times and will ultimately lead an invasion of Israel together with specified allies, all of which are modern-day Muslim states (Ezekiel 38:1–39:16). Russia, with all its Muslim republics and its Muslim allies, fits this description precisely.

All the nations of the world are prophesied to come together against Israel in the end times over the issue of the control of Jerusalem (Zechariah 12:2–3) — a prophecy being fulfilled today.

The magnitude of warfare in the 20th century is another fulfillment of end-time prophecy related to world politics. The 20th century was one of unparalleled war. Like birth pangs, the frequency and intensity of war increased exponentially. It is now estimated that more people died in wars during the 20th century than in all the previous wars throughout all of recorded human history.

5. The Signs of Technology

> . . . men fainting from fear and the expectation of the things which are coming upon the world; for the powers of the heavens will be shaken (Luke 21:26).

The development of nuclear weapons seems to be foreshadowed by this prophecy in Luke 21 that speaks of people "fainting from fear" due to the "powers of the heavens being shaken."

The incredible carnage of the Seal and Trumpet Judgments portrayed in chapters 6 and 8 in the Book of Revelation indicates that the Antichrist will conquer the world through the use of nuclear weapons. We are told that one-third of the earth will be burned and that one-half of humanity will be killed. Further evidence that this is a nuclear holocaust is found in Revelation 16, where we are told that at the end of the Tribulation, the survivors will be covered with sores that will not heal (Revelation 16:11).

As I pointed out earlier, there are many end-time prophecies that simply cannot be understood apart from modern technological developments. Consider the prophecy in Revelation 11 about the two witnesses who will call the world to repentance during the first half of the Tribulation. When they are killed by the Antichrist, we are told that their bodies will lie in the streets of Jerusalem for three and a half days, and the whole world will look upon them (Revelation 11:9). How could anyone understand such a prophecy before the development of satellite television in the 1960s?

Likewise, how could the Antichrist control all buying and selling worldwide (Revelation 13) without the aid of computer technology? How could the False Prophet create the illusion of giving life to a statue (Revelation 13) without the technology of holograms, virtual reality, and robotics? How could an army of two hundred million come out of the Far East (Revelation 9) before the population explosion that was produced by modern medical technology? How could the gospel be proclaimed to all the world (Matthew 24) before the invention of motion pictures, radio, television, and the Internet? The list goes on and on.

6. *The Signs of Israel*

> It will come about in that day that I will make Jerusalem a heavy stone for all the peoples; all who lift it will be severely injured. And all the nations of the earth will be gathered against it (Zechariah 12:3).

The signs that relate to Israel are the most important of all because the Jews are God's prophetic time clock. What I mean by this is that the Scriptures will often tie a prophesied future event with something that will happen to the Jews. We are told to watch the Jews, and when the prophesied event concerning them occurs, we can be sure that the other prophesied event will also occur.

An example can be found in Luke 21:24, where Jesus prophesied that the Jews would be dispersed from Jerusalem and be led captive among the nations. But then He added that one day they would return to reoccupy Jerusalem, and when this happens, the end-time events will occur that will lead to His return.

There are many prophecies concerning the Jews in the end times, many of which began to be fulfilled in the 20th century, but there are four key ones. The first is their worldwide regathering in unbelief (Isaiah 11:11–12). In 1900, there were only 40,000 Jews in Palestine. By the end of World War II, that number had risen to 600,000. Today, there are more than 6.5 million who have come from all over the world. This means that now there are more Jews in Israel than there are who died in the Holocaust.

The prophet Jeremiah says twice that when history is completed, the Jewish people will look back and conclude that their worldwide regathering was a greater miracle than their deliverance from Egyptian captivity (Jeremiah 16:14–15 and 23:7–8). We are truly living in momentous times!

The second key prophecy concerning the Jews is a natural consequence of their regathering. It is the reestablishment of their state, which occurred on May 14, 1948 (Isaiah 66:7–8).

The third key prophecy is the reoccupation of Jerusalem, which occurred on June 7, 1967, during the miraculous Six Day War (Zechariah 8:4–8).

The fourth key prophecy is the one whose fulfillment we are witnessing today — the refocusing of world politics upon the nation of Israel (Zechariah 12:2–3). All the nations of the world, including the United States, are coming against Israel over the issue of the control of the nation's capital — the city of Jerusalem. The Vatican wants the city placed under its control. The United Nations wants it to be internationalized. The European Union and the United States are demanding it be divided between the Arabs and the Jews. The Arabs want all of it.

The Greatest Sign

And so you have it — six different categories of signs, each category containing many prophecies concerning the end times, all of which are being fulfilled before our very eyes. And yet, I have not mentioned the most important sign of all.

Yes, the reestablishment of the state of Israel is the most important individual sign. It is, in fact, the cornerstone sign of the end times, since end-time prophecy focuses on Israel. But overall, there is a super sign that is more important. It is the sign that can be summed up in one word: CONVERGENCE.

The point is that for the first time in history, all the end-time signs are coming together. Not a single one is missing.

All the pieces of the end-time puzzle are in place for the first time ever. To the non-Christian, the world appears to be falling to pieces due to the exponential increase in immorality and violence. But to the Christian who knows Bible prophecy, the fragmented world scene is understandable, for all the prophesied pieces are falling into place.

What a privilege it is to live in a time when we can see Bible prophecy fulfilled before our very eyes and realize that what we are witnessing is God's proclamation that His Son is about to burst from the heavens. Maranatha!

Endnotes
1. Unless otherwise noted, Scripture in this chapter is from the New American Standard Bible (NASB).
2. Robert Longley, "FEMA's List of Top 10 U.S. Natural Disasters," http://usgovinfo. about.com.
3. Wikipedia, "Agnes Ozman," http://en.wikipedia.org/wiki/Agnes_ Ozman.
4. Wikipedia, "Evan Roberts (Minister)," http://en.wikipedia.org/ wiki/Evan_ Roberts_(minister).
5. Wikipedia, "William J. Seymour," http://en.wikipedia.org/wiki/ William_J._ Seymour.
6. Frank Bartleman, *Azuza Street: An Eyewitness Account* (Gainesville, FL: BridgeLogos Publishers, 2001).

CHAPTER 3

Laodicean Lies

DR. GARY D. FRAZIER

To the angel of the church in Laodicea write:
These are the words of the Amen, the faithful and true witness, the ruler of God's creation. I know your deeds, that you are neither cold nor hot. I wish you were either one or the other! So, because you are lukewarm — neither hot nor cold — I am about to spit you out of my mouth. You say, "I am rich; I have acquired wealth and do not need a thing." But you do not realize that you are wretched, pitiful, poor, blind and naked. I counsel you to buy from me gold refined in the fire, so you can become rich; and white clothes to wear, so you can cover your shameful nakedness; and salve to put on your eyes, so you can see.

Those whom I love I rebuke and discipline. So be earnest and repent. Here I am! I stand at the door and knock. If anyone hears my voice and opens the door, I will come in and eat with that person, and they with me.

To the one who is victorious, I will give the right to sit with me on my throne, just as I was victorious and sat down with my Father on his throne. Whoever has ears, let them hear what the Spirit says to the churches (Revelation 3:14–22).[1]

Political Correctness Will Always Bring Disaster on a Culture Because Those Who Rule Define It!

Could we be living in the Terminal Generation? The pages in this book written by my friends and colleagues should lead us to this unassailable truth. We see the world stage being set in an unprecedented manner that will allow the final prophecies of the Lord Jesus Christ and the ancient prophets as recorded in the Word of God to come to fulfillment. One of those prophecies spoken of in numerous passages reveals the spiritual condition of the Church in the last days. While it is true that Christ birthed His Church and promised that the gates of hell would never prevail over it, He also made it clear that there would be a counterfeit church of apostasy. That is a moving away from His teachings as recorded in the Bible and an acceptance of heresy and deceptive teaching that would lead many astray. Today, we find ourselves surrounded by exactly what Jesus and the Apostles warned us against, and that church is often referred to as the Laodicean church.

As you read the title to this chapter and the Scripture above, you may find yourself like many others who have never heard of Laodicea. No doubt, some who are familiar with the Word will recall that this term identifies a people, a place, a culture, and a church that had a problem. Some may be familiar with the historical significance of this city, while others may recall that the word appears in the final book of the Bible, the Revelation. As you spend the next few minutes reading my thoughts and views, I want to acquaint you with Laodicea. Even though some may have never heard the word, I assure you that each of us has, is, and will continue to be affected by the spirit of Laodicea present with us today.

I often pose the question: How can we know where we are going if we do not know where we have been? Please remember that history does tend to repeat itself. People are born. They grow up. Parents, friends, education, religion, and culture influence each of us. We often fail to stop and ask ourselves a very important question: Why? Why are things the way they are, and is it possible to break the cycle by which people seem to be bound? However, the right question we should be asking is: Why not? Why should things *not* be as they are, since we tend to make the same choices over and over?

In the following pages, I will seek to shed some light on the questions above and offer some very strong suggestions that, if implemented, will affect our lives in a meaningful way going forward.

Laodicea: The Place

While Laodicea is largely unknown to us in the 21st century, it was an important city in ancient times with a rich but turbulent past. The city

THE SEVEN CHURCHES OF
THE BOOK OF REVELATION
Rev. 2-3

was located in ancient Asia Minor, modern Turkey, about 11 miles west of the city of Colosse, and was along a major circular route of cities known today as the Cities/Churches of the Revelation. Founded by Antiochus II of the Seleucid Empire (Greeks) and named after Antiochus' wife, Laodicea, it became a major banking center of immense wealth. Dr. Harold Wilmington writes:

> It was immensely wealthy, graced with resplendent temples and theaters. It was noted for the manufacture of garments from black, glossy wool, and for its hot mineral springs. Perhaps because of its excellent medical school, Laodicea was also famous for its eye salve, called cellyrium.[2]

The largest of three cities in the broad valley area on the borders of Phrygia, Laodicea stood where the Lycus Valley joined the Maeander. Significantly, the western entrance to the city was called the Ephesian Gate. The traveler left the city on the east by the Syrian Gate, for the great road ran to Antioch, where other roads branched to the Euphrates Valley, to Damascus, and to the northeast, where the desert trade routes ran toward the mountains, the Gobi, and the remote lands of the East.

Laodicea was not a natural fortress. The low eminence, on which its Seleucid fortifications stood, might have presented a challenge to invaders, but Laodicea had a serious weakness. The water supply came principally vulnerable aqueduct from springs six miles to the north in the ...tion of Hierapolis. Fragments of the aqueduct can be seen today, the ...duit badly narrowed by thick deposits of calcium carbonate. A place with its water so exposed could scarcely stand a determined siege. The double conduit was buried, but was not a secret that could be kept.[3]

Laodicea: The People

God says, "the love of money is a root of all kinds of evil" (1 Timothy 6:10). The people of Laodicea had the same problem many have had through the centuries: money! Wealth tends to bring independence. Independence promotes an attitude of arrogance and pride. God hates both of these and reminds us often: "Pride goes before destruction, a haughty spirit before a fall" (Proverbs 16:18).

This attitude of arrogance, coupled with nonreliance upon the Creator, would ultimately be the downfall of Laodicea. After becoming a "free city" under Roman rule, in A.D. 60, a terrible earthquake "prostrated the city." The phrase is that of Tacitus, who wrote 50 years later. The Roman senate at the time gave large sums to devastated Asian cities in earthquake relief, but the historian records with surprise that Laodicea refused such aid. It rose again, wrote Tacitus, "with no help from us." However, as God's Word reveals, the judgment of God may be slow, but it is always sure; the Turks and Mongols devastated the city, and today it is nothing more than piles of ruins.

Laodicea: The Problem

To properly understand the "Laodicean lie," we must thoroughly understand the problem. To grasp this, we must step backward to a place called Ephesus, another of the churches of Asia Minor and the first of the seven churches of the Revelation. John would remain in Jerusalem until shortly before the destruction of the Temple in A.D. 70, about 40 years following the death, burial, and Resurrection of Christ, as well as the death of Mary, the mother of Jesus. During those years, the Jerusalem church grew and expanded exponentially. Then, in approximately A.D. 70, the youngest and last living of the Apostles would relocate to Asia Minor to become the pastor of the church in Ephesus. While in Ephesus and prior to his exile around A.D. 95 during the reign of Emperor Domitian, the Apostle would pen the Gospel of John as well as the three epistles of 1, 2, and 3 John.

The church of Ephesus was the first of the seven churches God would speak to through the Apostle John, as recorded in Revelation 2:1–7:

> To the angel of the church in Ephesus write: These are the words of him who holds the seven stars in his right hand and walks among the seven golden lampstands. I know your deeds, your hard work and your perseverance. I know that you cannot tolerate wicked people, that you have tested those who claim to be apostles but are not, and have found them false. You have persevered and have endured hardships for my name, and have not grown weary.
>
> Yet I hold this against you: You have forsaken the love you had at first. Consider how far you have fallen! Repent and do the things you did at first. If you do not repent, I will come to you and remove your lampstand from its place. But you have this in your favor: You hate the practices of the Nicolaitans, which I also hate.
>
> Whoever has ears, let them hear what the Spirit says to the churches. To the one who is victorious, I will give the right to eat from the tree of life, which is in the paradise of God.

Most of us approach every problem in one of two ways: Either we attack the root or the branches. Most often we tend to go after the branches, because that's what we perceive to be the issue. However, the best resolution comes when we discern the root that actually produces the visible branches. Please allow me to illustrate. Recently, we had mushrooms springing up in our yard. We had never had this before. Each week, the lawn guys would mow them down — and within a day or two, they were back. I finally went online and researched the cause and learned that it was simple: overly wet soil produces mushrooms. Once I reduced the amount of watering, the mushrooms were gone. We could have continued to mow the mushrooms down, but we would not have gotten rid of them until we addressed the cause. I could SEE the mushrooms, but not the soil below that was too wet!

God, who is all knowing, always addresses the root problem. In this case, the root problem in Ephesus was they had lost their first love. These people had heard the glorious news of Christ, who had died and risen again. They had learned from the Apostle Paul that the wall between Jews and Gentiles had vanished through Jesus. They had openly given themselves to Christ and had become His faithful, fervent followers. Yet over time, the fire had begun to die. Don't misunderstand: They still went about their normal routines. They gathered for teaching, prayer, and fellowship, but the zeal, the commitment, the fire was diminished and dying more with each passing day. So Jesus called them on it. He pointed out that while they were doing some good things — e.g., not tolerating wicked people and imposters — they, at the same time, were focusing on the branches (the resistance of wicked people) as opposed to the root (leaving their first love).

God warned them that this loss of love for Him would have severe consequences over time. What kind of consequences? They would suffer loss — loss of joy, purpose, love, principles, and a sense of fulfillment. So, the question is: Did they repent (change direction) and return to their first love? Did they do the first things once again? Most would say no! In fact, as the years passed, things grew incrementally worse. Isn't this how it goes? We make a wrong turn, a wrong choice, and instead of immediately turning around, we continue down the road and move farther and farther away from our desired destination.

Down the circular road a few miles lay Laodicea — prosperous, prideful, arrogant, independent Laodicea.

Many scholars today understand the letters to the churches of the Revelation speak to real, geographically locatable churches of the first century. Thousands of visitors have toured the ruins of these churches located in modern-day Turkey. I have personally visited the ruins of Ephesus and Smyrna, as well as Laodicea.

However, these also speak of time periods in Christian history.

Dr. Henry M. Morris writes:

Although it is by no means the dominant theme, there is a sense also in which the seven churches seem to depict the respective stages of development and change of Christ's churches during the ensuing centuries. History has, indeed, shown such a general development through the years, and it is reasonable that the sequential development of the respective exhortations in these messages should be arranged by the Lord in the same sequence. He is not capricious in His selection. There is bound to be some significance in the *sequence* of the seven, as well as in the total. The Book of Revelation — all of it — is said to be prophecy, and if there is any prophecy in it concerning the Church Age, it must be here in these two chapters (chapters 2–3). Further, in one way

(Top photo)
Ancient walkway
through the ruins
of Laodicea
(Shutterstock,
Suzanne Morris)

(Left) The ruins
of Laodicea,
near the modern
city of Denizli
(Shutterstock,
Northern
Imagery)

or another, the last four of the churches are to survive until the
return of Christ (note verses 2:25, 3:3, 11, 20) and this can only
now be fulfilled if these four churches specifically represent stages
of church development which persist until the end of the age
(emphasis mine).[4]

If Dr. Morris and numerous other scholars are correct, and I believe them
to be, then Laodicea is the last of the ages of the Church. In order to
more fully grasp this concept please allow me to list the churches and the
church age they represent.

CHURCH	PERIOD	YEARS
Ephesus	Apostolic	A.D. 30–100
Smyrna	Roman Persecution	100–313
Pergamum	Age of Constantine	313–600
Thyatira	Dark Ages	600–1517
Sardis	Reformation	1517–1648
Philadelphia	Missionary Movement	1649–present
Laodicea	Apostasy	1900–present

As you can see, the final two churches overlap. Today, we have hot-hearted, evangelistic, missionary-minded churches alongside the luke-warm, rich, program-driven, no-need-for-God churches.

So how are we to understand the Laodicean lie of the last remaining years before Christ returns? Ephesus revealed the loss of true love for Christ, which is the personal, daily desire to live for and serve Jesus. Laodicea reveals the neither hot nor cold, ambivalent attitude of man's religion. However, if we were to address the problem of today in just one word, what word would describe our present situation? The word is TOLERANCE! Tolerance takes numerous forms, and as you read, we will highlight three of these in the interest of space.

Laodicean Lie Number One: You Don't Need God!

The message of Laodicea was that God was irrelevant. The people, the church of Laodicea, believed they had the ability to do what they wanted apart from trust in and surrender to the lordship of Jesus. They chose to ignore the fact that the Church belongs to Jesus. He and He alone birthed the church (Matthew 16:18). Paul the Apostle called it the "mystery" of the Church. Paul wrote to the believers in Ephesus, who would read his words and share them with the other churches. The Apostle wrote words such as these in Ephesians 1:15–23:

> For this reason, ever since I heard about your faith in the Lord Jesus and your love for all God's people, I have not stopped giving thanks for you, remembering you in my prayers. I keep asking that the God of our Lord Jesus Christ, the glorious Father, may give you the

Spirit of wisdom and revelation, so that you may know him better. I pray that the eyes of your heart may be enlightened in order that you may know the hope to which he has called you, the riches of his glorious inheritance in his holy people, and his incomparably great power for us who believe. That power is the same as the mighty strength he exerted when he raised Christ from the dead and seated him at his right hand in the heavenly realms, far above all rule and authority, power and dominion, and every name that is invoked, not only in the present age but also in the one to come. And God placed all things under his feet and appointed him to be *head over everything for the church*, which is his body, the fullness of him who fills everything in every way (emphasis added).

It could not be clearer! The Church is not yours, it's not mine, it's not theirs; it belongs to Jesus! The Church cannot function apart from surrender to Jesus and obedience to the Word of God. Over time, we have witnessed the decline of the power, holiness, and authority of the Church. The very thing God complimented the Ephesians for, not tolerating wickedness, the Church today accepts. Why? Ignorance of God's Word and of the nature of Christ! The Word of God is crystal clear with regard to the effects of sin and wickedness. To the Corinthians, Paul wrote:

> *Do you not know that wrongdoers will not inherit the kingdom of God? Do not be deceived: Neither the sexually immoral nor idolaters nor adulterers nor men who have sex with men nor thieves nor the greedy nor drunkards nor slanderers nor swindlers will inherit the kingdom of God. And that is what some of you were [past tense]. But you were washed, you were sanctified, you were justified in the name of the Lord Jesus Christ and by the Spirit of our God* (1 Corinthians 6:9–11, emphasis added).

I'd say that's about as clear as it could possibly be. It is deception to think that the Church can possibly operate in the flesh as opposed to the Spirit of God. When it attempts to do so, it has no power! Are you a part of a true church of Jesus in which a man of God preaches the Word of God to the people of God? A church with power and purpose, where people humble themselves before the Creator God and recognize that apart from Him they can do nothing but fail? Laodicea was not and is not THAT church!

In the 21st century, we are surrounded by organizations that claim to be the Church, but as Revelation 3:20 says: "Here I am! I stand at the door and knock." Jesus is portrayed as being locked out of His Church, and He desires to be let in. While there are many true churches, the numbers of Bible-believing, hot-hearted evangelistic churches are in decline as lukewarm churches permeate the landscape. Let me be clear: God hates this and vomits them out!

In August 2015, Dr. George Barna of American Culture and Faith Institute (www.culturefaith.com) released the results of a survey entitled "God's People Want to Know." This survey revealed 23 areas in which church attendees communicated their desire to know what the Word of God has to say. These were respondents who attended church at least two of four Sundays, yet they were not being taught the basic principles of the Word of God. Shocking but true. Wolves in sheep's clothing fill many of the pulpits across America. God's Word informs us: "By their fruit you will recognize them"! (Matthew 7:16).

Laodicea, like so many churches of today, abandoned the Bible and discipleship for programs and entertainment.

Laodicean Lie Number Two: Unconditional Love and Acceptance!

Ignorance of who God is and what God expects has led many today to embrace just about anything and everything under the falsity of love and acceptance. One of the latest examples of half-truths, which are whole lies, as well as acceptance of sinfulness, comes from the mouth of country singer and mega star Carrie Underwood. Ms. Underwood grew up in Checotah, Oklahoma, a small rural town of about 3,000 residents just off of I-40 between Oklahoma City, Oklahoma, and Fort Smith, Arkansas. The town has about 30 churches. Ms. Underwood let it be known while competing on the hit television show *American Idol* that she was a Christian. After the show, her very first hit was titled "Jesus Take the Wheel." The song spent six consecutive weeks at number one on the Billboard Hot Country Songs list and won single of the year at the 2005 Academy of Country Music Awards. Personally, I loved the song from a sweet Christian girl who was open about her faith in Jesus. However, along the way, something changed. Whether it was due to her ignorance of God's Word or her being deceived, her understanding of who God is and what He demands of each of us was altered. Not long ago, Ms. Underwood shared in an interview with *The Independent* the following:

Our church is gay-friendly. Above all, God wanted us to love others. It's not about setting rules or everyone has to be like me. No. We're all different. That is what makes us special. We have to love each other and get along with each other. It's not up to me to judge anybody.[5]

This is the element of tolerance that God hates! Strong words? Absolutely! God hates lies that deceive, but none are more dangerous than when a church led by a supposed man of God lies about the Word of God. Are we to love everyone? Yes! Are we to accept everyone as created by God and therefore worthy of respect? Yes! Are we to accept a lifestyle of sin and evil? No! Ms. Underwood is either confused or deceived. Either way, it is tragic. Yet, sadly, she is not alone! I could cite example after example of how the corrupt perversion of this world has crept into and gained acceptance in the so-called church. Such a large number of people who claim to be Christian have fallen prey to the idea that love equates with acceptance of anything and everything. I was saddened recently as I read the results of a Pew Research survey from December 18, 2015. Please see and read with a broken heart.

December 18, 2015

Most U.S. Christian groups grow more accepting of homosexuality

By Caryle Murphy

Acceptance of homosexuality is rising across the broad spectrum of American Christianity, including among members of churches that strongly oppose homosexual relationships as sinful, according to an extensive Pew Research Center survey of U.S. religious beliefs and practices.

Amid a changing religious landscape that has seen a declining percentage of Americans who identify as Christian, a majority of U.S. Christians (54%) now say that homosexuality should be accepted, rather than discouraged, by society. While this is still considerably lower than the shares of religiously unaffiliated people (83%) and members of non-Christian faiths (76%) who say the same, the Christian figure has increased by 10 percentage points since we conducted a similar study in 2007. It reflects a growing acceptance of homosexuality among all Americans — from 50% to 62% — during the same period.

Among Christians, this trend is driven partly by younger church members, who are generally more accepting of homosexuality than their elder counterparts. For example, roughly half (51%) of evangelical Protestants in the Millennial generation (born between 1981 and 1996) say homosexuality should be accepted by society, compared with a third of evangelical Baby Boomers and a fifth of evangelicals in the Silent generation. Generational differences with similar patterns also are evident among Catholics, mainline Protestants and members of the historically black Protestant tradition.

At the same time, however, a larger segment of older adults in some Christian traditions have become accepting of homosexuality in recent years, helping to drive the broader trend. For instance, 32% of evangelical Protestant Baby Boomers now say homosexuality should be accepted, up from 25% in 2007.

Regardless of age, seven-in-ten Catholics — whose church teaches that homosexual behavior is "intrinsically disordered" — say that homosexuality should be accepted by society, a 12-percentage-point increase since 2007. Similar jumps have occurred among mainline Protestants (from 56% to 66%), Orthodox Christians (from 48% to 62%) and members of the historically black Protestant tradition (from 39% to 51%).

Most Mormons and evangelical Protestants still say homosexuality should be discouraged by society — in line with the teachings of many of their churches — but 36% of both groups say it should be accepted. Among Mormons, there was a 12-point increase (from 24% to 36%) in acceptance since 2007, and among evangelicals there was a 10-point rise (from 26% to 36%). Jehovah's Witnesses remain perhaps the most opposed of any U.S religious tradition toward homosexuality, with just 16% saying it should be accepted by society.

The trend of growing acceptance is evident across many specific Protestant denominations, including some conservative denominations with official teachings that remain strongly opposed to same-sex marriage. For example, among members of the Lutheran Church-Missouri Synod, the share saying homosexuality should be accepted by society grew by 12 points (from 44 percent to 56 percent) between 2007 and 2014. And although Pentecostals who identify with the Assemblies of God remain largely opposed to homosexuality, 26 percent now say it should be accepted by society, up from 16 percent in 2007. [6]

As we can see, the onslaught from media, education, and the Laodicean churches is negatively affecting our ability to discern between good and evil. I would remind each of us of a great danger. God's Word says, "Woe to those who call evil good and good evil, who put darkness for light and light for darkness, who put bitter for sweet and sweet for bitter" (Isaiah 5:20).

Once the Church begins down the slippery slope of accepting sin, it is only a matter of time before the judgment of a Holy God falls. Watch what happens in the days ahead as culture accepts transgenderism and ultimately moves to the vilest of sexual perversion appealing to the lowest base nature of humanity. When life, created by God, is of little value, then humanity loses its very soul. This is the endgame of Satan (the thief), who comes only to steal and kill and destroy! (See John 10:10.)

Laodicean Lie Number Three: Political Correctness!

The Death of Truth:
When that which was once celebrated is condemned.
When that which was once condemned is now celebrated.
When those who refuse to celebrate are condemned.
— Dr. Al Mohler[7]

The final element of tolerance I want to address is that of political correctness. This term that fills our airways and conversations in the offices and classrooms and dominates the media is in and of itself a lie. No doubt, in ancient Laodicea, people were afraid to speak up for fear of reprisal from the Roman government. Domitian ruled the world's greatest ancient power from 81–96 and was the first of the emperors to demand that he be worshiped as God. Citizens were afraid to speak against him, just as so many today are afraid to stand up and speak out about the evil that surrounds us. Fear of being labeled intolerant, homophobic, racist, misogynistic, or any number of labels slams mouths shut. Yet we are called to speak out against the evil that destroys lives. I have stated on numerous occasions that I do not care about being politically correct. Rather, I care about truth! The fact is that so many Christians are confused and think that because they are not perfect, they must keep their mouths shut. This is exactly what the enemy, Satan, wants us to do. It is true that we will never be perfect, but because we have a new life in Christ, we are in the process of striving to be more like Him with each passing day. Imagine a scale with love on one side and truth on the opposite. If we get too full of truth, an attitude of judgment develops and love suffers. However, if we get too full of love, then we begin to think we must accept anything someone does, and truth diminishes. Therefore, the key is to properly balance love based on truth. Am I right about that? Absolutely! That said, the greatest thing we can do for a perverse, deceived, sinful world is to love them enough to tell them the truth!

As we stand upon the threshold of the soon return of Jesus our King, we must boldly reject the Laodicean lies and intentionally embrace the truth of God's Word. Paul wrote, "Let God be true and every human being a liar" (Romans 3:4).

Every man, woman, and child is born in sin. Man is lost and separated from a Holy God by his sinful nature. Man cannot forgive himself, and as such, cannot save himself. One day, each and every person who has lived on this planet and rejected God's love revealed in Christ will stand before a Holy God and sadly hear these words: "I never knew you. Away from me, you evildoers!" (Matthew 7:23).

But it doesn't have to end this way for you! You get to choose to accept God's offer of forgiveness and become a new creation in Him or reject His offer and be separated from Him for all eternity. We will all live forever, and we get to choose where. I pray you will choose wisely. God loves you and Christ died for you. Trust Him now!

Endnotes

1. Scripture in this chapter is from the New International Version (NIV) of the Bible.
2. Harold Wilmington, *Wilmington's Bible Handbook* (Wheaton, IL: Tyndale House Publishers, 1997), p. 797.
3. W.A. Elwell and B.J. Beitzel, *Baker Encyclopedia of the Bible* (Grand Rapids, MI: Baker Book House, 1988), p. 1307–1308.
4. Henry M. Morris, *The Revelation Record* (Wheaton, IL: Tyndale House Publishers, 1983), p. 48.
5. http://www.digitaljournal.com/article/327199.
6. http://www.pewresearch.org/fact-tank/.
7. Paraphrased from "The Briefing," 02-23-17 by Dr. Mohler, commenting on the process of a moral revolution from British theologian Theo Hobson, https://albertmohler.com/2017/02/23/briefing-02-23-17/ accessed January 5, 2018; and "Marriage Crisis Predated Gay Marriage, Conf. Speakers Say," by Tom Strode, October 28, 2014, in the *Baptist Press*, http://bpnews.net/43609/marriage-crisis-predated-gay-marriage-conf-speakers-say, accessed January 5, 2018.

CHAPTER 4

Cultural Craftiness

DON MCGEE

A nation's culture is its foundation and framework, but a closer look at what influences culture shows it is actually much more than that. Culture is a living entity with a heartbeat and pulse. And as a living entity, it also has a national conscience that can be well or sick, strong or weak, and it can be influenced by the forces of good or it can be deceived by the forces of evil. Thus, in order to determine what has gone wrong with our country, it is necessary to take a look at her national conscience.

All national politicians campaign on the promise to change whatever they believe is wrong about America. Inherent in such a promise is the foregone conclusion that something has gone wrong somewhere along the line — or else why is there a need for change? The problem with the secular, political way of examining our culture is that the focus is mostly upon issues having to do with its facade, thus the conclusions and remedies are not only secular but superficial and impotent.

The core problem with America is spiritual in nature, and spiritual problems tend to manifest themselves in every aspect of society. Our nation's leadership has historically made the mistake of treating those manifestations, while ignoring the real problem. This is the reason almost every political attempt to remedy things has failed miserably, whether social, financial, educational, etc.

Politicians, as well as the majority of their constituents, refuse to accept the fact that our national problems have little to do with politics and almost everything to do with spiritual dysfunction. This truth is vehemently rejected by modern American culture, because it speaks of Judeo-Christian religious influences, and the American people have been deceived into believing that a secular society must not have biblical convictions influencing national policy.

This anti-Christian attitude will not change to any appreciable degree. Prophetic Scriptures show clearly that this world, and that includes our country, will not lend itself to godly influences. In fact, it will become further alienated from God until it gets to the place where He destroys this global system as we know it and gives it over to His own King of kings to rule over it. For one thousand years, the world will benefit under the rule of Messiah. But until that happens, this world will only know spiritual alienation from God and will, therefore, know continued suffering.

Before us is the question about the process that has brought us to this point in our national culture: how has Satan been so successful in deceiving an entire Western culture that was arguably founded within the parameters of Judeo-Christian values?

The answer to that question is many-faceted, but in this chapter the answer will be limited to the apostasy of American culture as it fell away from having biblical principles as its foundation, to the point of having godless ideologies as its foundation. In this chapter, several judicial decisions will be considered, the impact of which have forever changed the landscape of American culture. At the conclusion, we will put it all together in generalizations before considering what all of this means in context of the Bible's prophetic Scriptures.

First, consider a few simple things about our morphing American culture. American culture has changed in many ways in the last 100 years. Some of those changes are the results of evolving industrial and technological advancements, and many of those impact how we relate socially. The interrelationships in a society are some of the first dominoes to fall when that society has been deceived into believing it no longer needs to be undergirded by godly principles.

For example, in the early 1950s, people socialized with their neighbors face to face on a daily basis, because they were routinely outside of their houses most of the time, even in suburbia, and especially in rural areas. Almost every house had a porch, the purpose of which was much more utilitarian than aesthetic. Quite often, there were several rocking chairs on those porches, and it was common for people to visit in the late afternoon and evening while enjoying the cool, quiet respite after the day's activities.

This caused the relationships between people to be more intimate. People were deeply connected with each other's lives. They made an investment in each other, one that was rooted in living principled lives according to a commonly held belief system that formed the framework of their society.

Even the public education systems in many parts of America were very conducive to the stability of society. School principals and teachers knew well the parents of their students, and they often taught two generations in the same family. Parents, children, teachers, and school administrators invested themselves in each other, and together they had a positive, synergistic impact upon their communities.

But along with the vast revolution in digital technology came a dramatic shift in the way people live. People have withdrawn from each other, both literally and figuratively. Not only do many people live today with no front porch, much less a yard measuring more than a few square feet, but they have withdrawn any natural affection for those outside the walls of their houses, high-rise tenements, or apartments.

Today, houses are mostly vacant during the day because both parents work outside the home and their children are at school or at a daycare. When evening comes, families return to a house or an apartment with central heating and air conditioning, making the inside of the house the go-to place for comfort and entertainment. Porches and yards are not even a part of many housing complexes, or, at best, they are there for the sake of appearance only. As a result of those kinds of changes, almost every spare moment is spent inside an enclosed box staring at some kind of electronic device. Neighborly visits are rare and are often viewed as unwanted intrusions. Isolation, except through smartphones and computers, has become the new norm. People are no longer known by way of personal relationships but through technological connections. Social media and texting have taken the place of conversation over coffee. Relationships are therefore superficial, and not always truthful.

Because of this, it is not unusual for people in urban and suburban areas to live in close proximity to others, yet never know each other. At times, those living in such dense but disconnected populations are shocked when a neighbor commits a heinous crime. The often-heard refrain from neighbors to police investigators is, "I never really got to know him, but he seemed like a nice person. I would never have thought he was capable of doing such a thing!"

This kind of culture can, and at times does, lead to callused consciences toward others. The value of others' interests, and even their mortal life, can become cheap in a society where citizens are virtually isolated from each other and who are inwardly focused and void of a biblically based moral structure.

But, American culture has digressed for another reason, and it has little to do with technology and demographics. Rather, it has to do with our culture's outright rejection of any and all claims God has to the way we live. This attitude directly parallels the attitude of the servants Jesus mentioned in the parable He told in Luke chapter 19. It demonstrates not only the culture's rejection of God, but it also betrays the caustic, visceral hatred it has for Him.

Evidence of this floods through our lives. Television talk-show panels are filled with media celebrities whose unashamed purpose is to ridicule God, His Word, and His people. The pinnacle of their 60 minutes of broadcast time is the moment when they can make the most outrageous and vulgar charge against anyone who believes in biblical morality.

Entertainers who are willing to demonstrate the most blasphemous behavior are the ones who garner the most attention. Irreverent behavior is now the key to celebrity success. Interestingly, however, is the fact that their irreverence is always directed toward God, the Bible, and Christians, and is never directed toward Allah, the Quran, or Islamic culture in general.

America's national life, even her national soul, has been degraded by her acceptance of moral practices that have no connection whatsoever to Judeo-Christian absolutes. American culture is no longer immoral; it is amoral. This means that, basically, what is now believed, taught, and publicly modeled before America's children is that there really are no absolutes in life.

A nation without God's absolutes has only one option, and that is to commit national suicide. Trains have rails, ships have rudders, and trucks have steering wheels, because a powerful force without guidance will destroy itself and everything in its path. Some people can clearly see this happening to national America, but the numbers of such discerning people and their influence are waning.

Still, the question remains: How did this happen? The answer: It happened through deception.

The first thing to note is that none of this is an accident. There is both a person and a purpose behind decaying values. The person is a very real being whom the Bible calls Satan, and his purpose is to alienate humanity from God. His assault began with Eve in the Garden of Eden, and it will continue until Jesus casts him into the Lake of Fire.

In the meantime, Satan will use each tool and every opportunity available to him, and presently he has a very effective tool in what might be his greatest and final assault upon the human race. It is his appeal to the base, fallen nature of humanity — and since American culture has rejected moral absolutes, there is no longer a barrier between the sin-inclined human mind and what Satan has to offer. To not have a conscience against adultery, fornication, or homosexuality makes it very easy to get involved in such things. Or, even if not directly involved, the lack of a conscience against these things makes it easy to have an accommodating attitude toward them. It is sometimes difficult to describe the fundamental nature of what has happened. Is it that the base nature and inclinations of humanity have finally gained not only American cultural support but judicial support of depraved lifestyles? Or, is it that America's culture and judiciary are simply following the lead of a society that has thrown off moral standards?

Actually, it is a combination of both. At the heart of dysfunctional American society is the truth that national law absent the Lawgiver is not really law. It is merely a degraded national worldview that is most often rooted in the lowest moral common denominator. The result is chaos, because that which society leans upon for any semblance of stability is a shaky, ever-changing value system.

Biblical truth clearly shows that the fallen Adamic nature of humanity came long before our nation's system of law. And because of this, man's heart is much more inclined toward depravity than toward adhering to a moral law.

America's Founding Fathers put together the U.S. Constitution with the purpose of our citizens being free from an intrusive government. And it would no doubt come as a surprise to those men that such liberties are now being used by depraved minds to destroy the moral fabric of our country under color of law. This is deception on the national level.

Of all the generations in the history of America, it is probable that the Baby Boomer generation has a clearer view than most others of how the nation has been seduced. This generation is old enough to have witnessed some dramatic, pivotal points in our country's direction, and is able, by looking back, to understand their impact upon our modern culture. That is not to say that Satan wasn't hard at work attempting to deceive America prior to 1950, but it is to say that our national soul was far more sensitive to his techniques of deception back then than it is today.

But, many middle-aged Americans of today cannot see this so clearly. They have always lived in a culture that has no qualms about shacking up before marriage, about abortion, about urban violence, etc. And kindergarten children of today are not only being taught that homosexuality is an acceptable alternative lifestyle, but that there is moral equivalence between heterosexual marriage and so-called homosexual marriage. Except for those who cling to biblical precepts, these middle-aged people cannot see the vast contradiction between the social mores of the mid-20th century and those of today.

This does not mean that Satan's seduction of American culture began only as late as the 1950s. But it does mean that the rate of decline has increased greatly since those days. The speed at which morally degrading changes are presented for discussion is astonishing. And once they are in the realm of open discussion, they are quickly labeled as socially acceptable, they are endorsed by society, and they are often finally institutionalized in our culture by judicial decisions. The older population of America can only stand with jaws agape not only at what their society is being deceived about, but at the speed at which it is happening.

We need only go back to the 1960s to see just one of Satan's tactics for deceiving our culture. He has effectively used the impact of U.S. law to weaken and ultimately destroy the framework of America's Judeo-Christian value system. And he is far from being finished.

In 1962 and 1963, two distinct changes happened to the fabric of American society. These were decisions handed down by the U.S. Supreme Court, and because American society was relatively conservative and fundamental in those days, they did not wholly reflect the national spiritual conscience as much as they impacted it.

Satan used a very effective tactic in these cases because they did not impact the adult population to a great degree. He went for the minds of America's children, and he hit his mark. The old adage that catastrophic change in culture is only one generation away is a truth borne out in these cases.

In the 1962 U.S. Supreme Court decision in *Engel v. Vitale*, the high court established a prohibition on what is commonly called state-sponsored prayer in public schools. The argument was that prayer in public schools was in direct violation of the First Amendment, and specifically in regard to the Establishment Clause, whereby the state could not establish a religion. This was called a landmark decision because it overturned lower court decisions that had been legal precedents for years.

The second distinct change came about in 1963 when the Supreme Court decided in *Abington School District v. Schempp* that compulsory Bible readings along with other religious activities sponsored by public schools were also prohibited.

Most people think of the infamous atheist Madalyn Murray O'Hair as the instigator in this legal fight, but the truth is that the O'Hair case of *Murray v. Curlett* was consolidated with the Schempp case. The plaintiff in the case, Edward Schempp, was a Unitarian Universalist and since there were more Unitarian Universalists in the United States than there were atheists at that time, and since they stood together in their grievance, it was decided to consolidate them.

Still, Murray's efforts did indeed contribute to the removal of compulsory Bible reading in public schools, and the impact has been both significant and long-lasting. Further, that decision will probably never be repealed no matter who is president and no matter who is on the high court. It is like the proverbial scrambled egg; it cannot be unscrambled.

Justice Potter Stewart had the only dissenting opinion in the decision. Basically, he said that the Establishment Clause of the First Amendment was not to restrict states in their religious liberties, but to restrict the federal government in any effort to prohibit such religious liberties.

In the years since the Schempp decision, many of its critics have referred to Justice Stewart's opinion. The following quote is an excerpt from it:

> If religious exercises are held to be an impermissible activity in schools, religion is placed in an artificial and state-created disadvantage. . . . And a refusal to permit religious exercises thus is seen, not as the realization of state neutrality, but rather as the establishment of a religion of secularism, or at least, as governmental support of the beliefs of those who think that religious exercises should be conducted only in private.[1]

Many citizens believed strongly that Stewart's opinion accurately reflected the intent of the U.S. Constitution's framers. However, since his was the only dissenting opinion, it is clear that the mind of the

United States Supreme Court was already under attack by Satan's deceitful influence.

It is no doubt true that no Christian wants the federal government to establish a state religion, for who knows what religious contrivance the government would endorse? At the same time, though, no Christian wants the federal court to place restrictions on the free practice of religion.

This case ultimately led to the commonly mistaken idea that the Constitution protects freedom of religion. That is incorrect. It prohibits the government from interfering in the free exercise of religion. There is a big difference between the two in that freedom of religion places no restriction on the private practice of religion, whereas the free exercise of religion places no restriction on the public practice of religion. The former is sometimes found to some degree even in totalitarian regimes; the latter is what the founders wanted in America.

Though the precedent set by this court case is constantly used to undermine Christianity at every opportunity, there seems to be no such restriction of the public practice of Islam, as is evidenced by tax-paid accommodations made to Muslims in publicly owned facilities like airports.

It must also be noted that there are some Christians who look with favor upon the decision because they do not want just any teacher or school administrator teaching the Bible to their children. Most Christians would probably feel the same way, but this was not about a teacher or administrator teaching a Bible class to students. It was about having Bible verses read at the beginning of the school day, and that without commentary.

What must be realized is that the Holy Spirit can do His work in the heart of the student body without human commentary. Who knows how much violence, cheating, etc. could have been prevented or lessened, both on and off campus, in the last 50-plus years by the mere reading of the words of God?

But that does not matter to secularists in modern American culture. The only thing that matters to them is that God has been dismissed from the public arena, never to be allowed to return, consequences be what they may.

There is another factor in considering how American law has negatively impacted American culture, and this one has turned American life on its ear. The American judicial system has much blood on its hands in that it has made legal the murder of children before they are born. Since *Roe v. Wade* in 1973, nearly 60 million babies have been viciously murdered in their mothers' wombs, according to various pro-life organizations.

The great American republic, the world's icon of wealth and power, has been deceived into believing that the heinous shedding of a baby's blood is morally and legally acceptable — not only that, but that such shedding of innocent blood can be done for any reason whatsoever.

Any number of variables are associated with this decision, with an equal number of people involved. But in essence, it focused on Norma L. McCorvey and her two attorneys, Linda Coffee and Sarah Weddington, who filed suit in the state of Texas using an alias for McCorvey, Jane Roe. Dallas County District Attorney Henry Wade defended the state. Basically, McCorvey wanted to abort her third child, but state law would not allow it. Though her child was born prior to the *Roe v. Wade* decision, the eventual outcome of the legal battle was that the Supreme Court ruled that abortion was a fundamental right under the U.S. Constitution.

Though this decision was made all those years ago, the debate has not gone away. A small segment of the American population cannot agree with the shedding of innocent blood, and it recoils at the thought that the Constitution gives citizens a fundamental right to do so.

This is reminiscent of the anti-Semitic 1935 Nazi Nuremberg Laws with which some German citizens disagreed. The strong disagreement with official national policy by a shrinking number of American citizens could be one of the precious few and thin veneers that separates our country from a heavy dose of blazing judgment from God.

On January 26, 2017, the Pew Research Center presented five facts about the abortion issue.[2] Though 37 percent of U.S. adults believe abortion should be wrong in all or most of the cases, 59 percent say it should be legal in all or most cases. The 37 percent is not a large percentage of American adults. Further, it is not conclusive quantitatively because of whatever might define the complex variables in those cases that are not part of those "all or most cases."

Still, we may be reminded that as Abraham pleaded for the Lord's mercy regarding Sodom (see Genesis chapter 18), God promised Abraham that He would not destroy the city if as few as ten righteous people could be found there. The city was so deeply mired in wickedness that there were not ten righteous people there. But the point is that God was willing to hold His hand of judgment for the sake of just ten people.

Yet, we have no promise that God's mercy applies in like manner to an America steeped in paganism. To offer such hope is to specifically speak where God has not specifically spoken. We appeal to biblical principles and we surely must intercede for our country, but to go much further than that might be false assurance.

On a side note at this point, the destruction of Sodom did not come before Lot and his family were removed. To most Bible prophecy students, that act of mercy in itself says much about the removal of the Church prior to the moment God pours out His wrath on this earth in the Tribulation. For that specific assurance we have much biblical basis, for example, 1 Thessalonians 1:10.

There have been attempts by pro-life groups to publish pictures in various venues, including on college campuses, of babies who have been aborted, in an attempt to shock people into sensibility about the facts of abortion. They show graphically that the baby is not a mass of indefinable protoplasm, but is clearly a human. Few things stir the bitter wrath of Planned Parenthood and other pro-death groups like such displays. Why is that so, we might ask?

There might be several answers to that question. But one that must be faced squarely is that a culture that has been deceived into believing abortion is a fundamental right under the U.S. Constitution has also, by that same deception, been hidden from and/or desensitized to the hellish and inhuman barbarism that is part of it.

Though such exposure might have its desired result in some people, the others simply cover their eyes and shout obscenities at those posting the images. They don't want to be reminded of the horrors of abortion; they just want to revel in the unlimited license for the practice of depravity that abortion supposedly offers to a society.

In these Supreme Court cases, it was human beings who made such determinations, and it must be stated clearly that it is the members of the Court who will be held responsible before God as individual human beings. U.S. presidents who have political and moral agendas nominate judges who have similar political and moral agendas. These nominees are then confirmed by U.S. senators who also have similar political and moral agendas. This tells us that such decisions would probably not have been as easily forthcoming if American culture had not already been at least partially disposed toward such decisions as a result of Satan's deception.

Satan has been very successful at deceiving the American public and the American judiciary into believing that before a baby is born, he or she is not a human. He has also deceived us into believing that life is measured by what a person can contribute to the whole of society, a way of thinking that is quickly leading us to the practice of euthanasia by withholding life-saving care for the infirm, whether young or old.

From the abortion decision, it seems possible to chart the trajectory of the American judiciary into the future. If that is true, then it is very likely that in the not-too-distant future, the value of a person's life will be determined by panels of people untouched by the life and love of the one whose future is being discussed.

These decisions show that nothing can sway a person's opinion like attaching to the argument some kind of attraction to their lusts and base inclinations. This is Satan's greatest tool of deception. He used it success-fully in the Garden of Eden, and he is equally successful with it today.

What makes it such a heinous deception within the context of abor-tion and euthanasia is that it is cloaked in the guise of government com-passion for the woman who is pregnant or the family that is "sacrificing so much for the care of the terminally ill loved one." This is intended to assuage any guilt brought on by Christian convictions that a person who is involved might have.

And then came the latest Supreme Court decision that has stripped away any remaining vestige of godliness in the crumbling façade of American culture. This one had to do with so-called homosexual mar-riage, and it forever degraded the God-sanctioned institutions of mar-riage and family.

This decision shows without doubt that American culture is disposed to the lowest forms of degradation, and that the American judicial system is ready to make such dispositions legal. It happened on June 26, 2015, when, in a 5-4 decision, the U.S. Supreme Court made homosexual mar-riage legal in the United States.

In the course of the effort to legalize homosexual marriage, a number of lawsuits had been filed in various jurisdictions in the United States, but the one that the ruling is known by is *Obergefell v. Hodges*. The court ruled that homosexuals have the fundamental right to marry, and that such a right is guaranteed by the Due Process Clause along with the Equal Protection Clause of the Fourteenth Amendment to the U.S. Con-stitution. This decision, too, was a landmark decision.[3]

It was a 5-4 ruling with Justice Anthony Kennedy writing the majority opinion. Basically, it said that bans on homosexual marriage by the states violated the U.S. Constitution. The wording included references to the dignity, autonomy, identity, and beliefs of homosexuals who wanted the blessing of the state upon their union. Kennedy was joined by Justices Ruth Bader Ginsburg, Stephen Breyer, Sonia Sotomayor, and Elena Kagan.

The majority of five justices gave four reasons they ruled in the manner they did, but the fourth reason is the most glaring, due to its utter self-contradiction. The justices said that "marriage is a keystone of our social order" and "there is no difference between same and opposite sex couples with respect to this principle."

Such a statement is such a blatantly outrageous lie that it is difficult to imagine what kind of mortal mind could produce it. Homosexual marriage and "social order" are not and never will be mutually inclusive. Further, no amount of legal jargon will ever make them so. To say that homosexual marriage is no different than heterosexual marriage when it comes to social order is an equally despicable pronouncement. It is a statement rooted in an almost blind rage against God, who created man and woman, who performed the first wedding, and who established the first human home and family.

Chief Justice John Roberts wrote the dissenting opinion, which carries not only great legal weight regarding the argument, but also gives a premonition about the future. In his dissent, he wrote that marriage had always had the universal definition as the union of a man and a woman. He further wrote that the court majority made the decision from the basis of their personal moral convictions rather than from a constitutional basis, and that the majority gave expanded fundamental rights "without caution or regard for history." He also said that the Court's language in the case unfairly attacked those who opposed homosexual marriage. That should come as no surprise whatsoever.

Justice Antonin Scalia labeled the majority opinion this way. He said it diminished the reputation of the Court for clear thinking and sober legal analysis, and that the majority "descended from the disciplined legal reasoning of John Marshall and Joseph Story to the mystical aphorisms of the fortune cookie."

Justice Clarence Thomas issued a dissent that blistered the majority by saying that the ruling "exalts judges at the expense of the people from whom they derive their authority."

Justice Samuel Alito echoed much of the above dissent and more. His most thought-arresting statement is akin to Justice Roberts' opinion. He said, "Most Americans — understandably — will cheer or lament today's decision because of their views on the issue of same-sex marriage. But all Americans, whatever their thinking on that issue, should worry about what the majority's claim of power portends."

But it was Chief Justice Roberts' two warnings about how this decision might be used in the future that should be noted. He said that the majority opinion could very well be used in the future in an argument for the inclusion of polygamy as part of legalized marriage. And he further wrote that this decision will ultimately lead to dire consequences for religious liberty. Justices Scalia and Thomas joined him in his opinion.

Essentially, this decision provides a wider gateway for the deception of national, official America. As Satan serves America's corrupt soul with legal justification for depravity, she greedily ingests it with no thought to societal consequences, and certainly with no thought to national accountability before God.

In this case, the U.S. Supreme Court allowed the proverbial camel to get his nose under the tent. Once this much has been done in order to make legal and socially legitimate such horrific moral and cultural changes, there is no end to what might, and probably will, be done under Satan's mounting influence.

As Christians, we appeal to Scripture for our definition of marriage. God, at the beginning of His creation, said that, because woman was taken out of man, a man shall leave his father and mother and cleave to his wife, and the two shall become one flesh (Genesis 2:23–24). That is it. No other relationship is given among human beings in which their deep emotional and conjugal needs are to be met. It is one man for one woman for life.

For all of civilized history, the practice of homosexuality has been labeled as being ungodly, morally degrading and humiliating, and void of any value to national, social, and familial stability. God condemns it because it is the utter antithesis of His purpose in the creation of man, woman, and the human family. Sodom and Gomorrah were so totally destroyed because of their wanton practice of homosexuality that no remains of those cities and their depraved culture can be found even today (Genesis 18).

But since American culture, now devoid of God's moral absolutes, has been on what might be called an exponential dive into the abyss of depravity, the practice of homosexuality is now on the forefront of progressive human aspirations. Anyone who takes a biblical stand on the issue is ostracized from the mainstream of just about any discipline of study, and that includes progressive and emergent theology.

In the 1970s, the behavioral and social sciences began to define homosexuality as an acceptable and perfectly normal variation in the practice of human sexuality. The American Psychiatric Association formally declassified homosexuality as a mental disorder in 1974, and in 1975, the American Psychological Association did the same. Then, in 1990, the World Health Organization got on board and adopted the same policy. So it is very rare, if not practically impossible, to find someone in the mental health fields today who will agree with the biblical view of homosexuality.

Not only has Satan so fully deceived American culture on this issue, but he has been almost equally successful in his deception of Christianity. His words to Eve in Genesis 3:1 — "Has God said?" (NASB) — are still being whispered into the ears of multitudes of Christians. The evil one knows that if just one, minute seed of doubt about anything God has said can be sown in the human mind, half his battle has been won.

As a result of such widespread deception, the world and our country are not only wanting tolerance of the practice of homosexuality, but are now demanding that everyone everywhere embrace it as being normal. The forces of evil want death to the opposition. They want unlimited access into the minds of America's children, and that includes the children of Christian parents.

Many of those Christian parents are already in a situation in which they have to decide how to educate their children, with any number choosing homeschool. And even that is now a target of the evil one and his minions, which means the battle for control and influence over the minds of Christians' children will soon be at the forefront.

Fairly recent to the cultural battle is the transgender issue. There are many sources on this subject, and each one is no doubt geared to a particular view. Critical at this point is that it impacts who your child will run into in a public restroom, whether at school or at the mall. Further, it impacts who will be your child's teacher, coach, physician, boys' or girls' club leader, etc. This issue is akin to the issue of homosexuality. In fact, it shares many of the same arguments.

In all of this, at the forefront of our belief system must be the biblical view: "God created mankind in his own image, in the image of God he created them; male and female he created them" (Genesis 1:27; NIV). God has not made some sort of genetic mistake whereby society would be confused about whether a person is male or female.

These questions never existed just a few years ago; further, they are not bona fide concerns that demand legal decisions, especially legal decisions that turn the whole moral structure of a society upside down. Satan is deceiving America's culture and legal system into believing it is of utmost importance to make such depraved lifestyles and their associated discussions into legitimate social issues. That is unadulterated insanity.

God does not create people with a condemnable condition and no recourse. The sin nature can be remedied by the atoning blood of Jesus. It is all about a person's choices, and that is where the rub comes in. Most people like their choices, and they simply do not want God involved in their lives at all. For a person or a group to think that an appeal to the court system plus emotional and/or hormonal treatment by someone in the medical field somehow legitimizes their perversion is for them to not know God.

The following are some generalizations that fit hand-in-glove with the above evaluation of Satan's deception of American society.

Two things make deception of a person relatively easy. First is Satan's expert understanding of a person spiritually and emotionally. Second, with that knowledge, he constructs a lie, deception, or scheme that corresponds to that person's makeup. This basic strategy is so effective that it can be used against individuals and groups, whether that group is a family, a religious assembly, or even an entire society.

In an effort to describe the great chasm that separates the cultures of North America from South America, someone once said that the destinies of the two were determined by their early settlers. Those who settled South America were looking for gold; those who settled North America were looking for religious liberty.

If that is true, then things have changed a great deal since the 16th century. Once-noble motivations have been changed into efforts that are, at their very least, less than noble. The wealth of the United States of America, along with her unprecedented liberty that is protected by the U.S. Constitution, are no longer viewed through the lens of Scripture but through the lens of materialism and the satisfaction of base desires.

The culture of modern American society has been transformed (perhaps "degenerated" is a better word) by forces that were unknown by her founders. Of course, those men were aware of nefarious factions within the 13 colonies, but they built into the Constitution certain safeguards that limited the power of the government, thus recognizing the ultimate power of the people to determine how they should live. It would have appalled them to know that the real threat to the nation would essentially come more from her own people instead of an overreaching government, and that those people would energize that threat by using the liberties guaranteed by the Constitution.

What has changed American culture is not the U.S. Constitution. What has changed is the impetus for living life in the conscience of American society. In general, people are no longer motivated by noble desires, but by the appeasement of sordid inclinations — and that applies to all aspects of life, including careers, academics, and recreation.

The question has gone from the disreputable "What are you going to do about my problem?" to the even more disreputable "How can we use our liberty to satisfy our coarse desires without ever being responsible for our actions?" Satan has a tailor-made answer to that question, and that is what makes social degradation a spiritual problem, not a political one.

Attempts at seducing American culture have always been around, but they have never been able to make inroads into our society like during the last several decades. What makes those attempts very easy are the hyper-media and formal government-sponsored education.

By "hyper-media," it is meant that almost all forms of media are now digitalized and instantaneously available for immediate consumption. By "formal government-sponsored education," it is meant that from early childhood through early adulthood, a person is indoctrinated by a system that is not only void of godly influence, but is practically unaccountable to society.

Whereas laissez-faireism is good when it comes to a free-enterprise economy, it is a terrible tool in the hand of Satan, as he uses it to deceive and indoctrinate an entire culture. Our American culture has been turned over to those forces and influences by our simply taking a hands-off attitude about what we allow into our lives through media and what we allow into our minds through education.

Consequences of cultural seduction include the illegitimate birth rate, cohabitation outside of marriage, homosexual marriage, open marriages, etc. These are still cultural anomalies to a few people, but that number is decreasing rapidly. Further, consider the widespread use of once-forbidden profane words. These are now commonly being used by children, they are a regular part of social media, and they have been part of movie scripts for years. When a person takes offense at their use, that person is seen as being out of the norm. Fifty years ago, these things would have been anathema, but today there is little protest.

American culture is a living entity. In a metaphorical way, it eats, drinks, breathes, and reproduces itself, though such reproduction is not always in exact kind. Due to strong influences, it can give birth to a succeeding generation that has little resemblance to what came before. One of those influences for such dramatic change is the American legal system.

It is easy for humanity to be deceived within the context of any culture, but this is especially true in a progressive, Western culture like America's. That is because the very foundation of Western culture is based upon humanity's inherent and strong inclination to pursue, and to place a very high premium upon, human logic. The problem with human logic that is separated from the biblical foundation is that it is constantly spiraling downward in an ever-tightening spin.

From Satan's temptation of our original parents in the Garden of Eden until today, he questions God's commands and God's motives while simultaneously supplanting them with ideas that appeal to human logic or reasoning. Throughout the millennia of man's earthly sojourn, it has been ingrained into his fallen Adamic nature to believe in the ultimate triumph of human reasoning over all obstacles, whether physical or spiritual.

Nothing portrays this more clearly than William Ernest Henley's poem, "Invictus."

> Out of the night that covers me,
> Black as the pit from pole to pole,
> I thank whatever gods may be
> For my unconquerable soul.

> In the fell clutch of circumstance
> I have not winced nor cried aloud.
> Under the bludgeonings of chance
> My head is bloody, but unbowed.

Beyond this place of wrath and tears
Looms but the Horror of the shade,
And yet the menace of the years
Finds and shall find me unafraid.

It matters not how strait the gate,
How charged with punishments the scroll,
I am the master of my fate,
I am the captain of my soul.

Henley was an avowed atheist and was deceived and utterly delusional, as atheists are. He was afflicted with tuberculosis and finally died of the disease at age 53. He lost his only child, a daughter, at age 5. So, for him to have believed he was in any way the master of his fate and the captain of his soul was absurd.

Instead of turning from his atheism and throwing himself upon the mercy of God, he chose to remain an atheist. To turn to God would have given him the hope of the resurrection of himself and his daughter, a hope that would have placed them together for all eternity in God's presence. Because of his choice, it is only his little girl who lives in God's presence. His heart was so deceived by an evil spiritual being that he essentially did not even believe in, he chose bitterness until the very end.

William Ernest Henley is only one among many in the myriad people who have been so deceived, but he represents a growing number in Western culture who have been ensnared. The title of his poem, "Invictus," is Latin for "unconquerable." We might wonder how he feels about it today.

Interestingly, "Invictus" was the poem that mass murderer Timothy McVeigh chose as his final statement before he died in 2001 of lethal injection. McVeigh killed 168 people, 19 of them children, in Oklahoma City in 1995.

Well, a reader might ask, does any of this have any relationship to Bible prophecy? Yes, it does.

We have seen how Satan has used deception in order to bring about cultural change in America, and we can be sure he has nefarious reasons for his efforts. He is not only causing great spiritual damage now, but he is also laying the foundation for even greater deception that will happen post-Rapture.

In Satan's current economy, deception is always more effective than duress. The present cultural deception is being accomplished quite well within a relatively peaceful, free, and open society. This allows it to gestate, so to speak, in preparation for when it will be poured out upon society with full force, absent of any peace and freedom.

An even more potent form of deception will be given to the world when the Church is removed from the earth at the coming of Jesus for her. Such a potent form will be needed because the Rapture of the Church will be of such magnitude that it will eclipse anything that has ever happened before. All stops in deceiving the world will be pulled out as Satan makes his sprint to the end of his conflict with God.

Because there is simply no way to accurately describe the mental and emotional tenor of Western civilization when that happens, it is difficult to imagine the details. But even without details, we can be assured that Satan will take full advantage of the unprecedented situation.

Some people will suddenly disappear from plain sight before the very eyes of their loved ones. The chain of command in the military will be affected with perhaps many disappearing who are in positions of great authority and responsibility. Business and industry will likewise be affected, along with civil government agencies.

These vanishings will immediately cause confusion, and during that confusion, national and international conflicts could ignite. Every nation's leaders will be sitting nervously with their fingers on the nuclear triggers. Domestic emergency call centers will probably be flooded and locked up tightly due to the number of calls exceeding their limitations. From a practical standpoint, emergency call centers will be rendered useless due to call volume. This will bring about chaos and will be very conducive to violent civil unrest.

It might be that individual and community vigilantism will be resorted to in order to protect what local law enforcement will be unable to protect. It seems quite likely that martial law will be quickly imposed in an attempt to bring some semblance of order back into American society.

Though some people will have been taught the truth and will have the presence of mind to think long enough to understand what has happened, most will not have a clue. Chaos and confusion will mark the day, and those are open doors to Satan's deceptive schemes.

People will be desperate for answers and for consolation about their missing loved ones. Based upon Revelation 13, it is reasonable to conclude that Antichrist and his False Prophet will soon enough present deceptive answers to those questions and concerns. He will give them what they most need: consolation due to his presence in the midst of turmoil and the promise that he is able do what is necessary if he is given the means to do it. With their acceptance of his leadership, the stage is set. Most of the world, especially Western culture, will swallow his propaganda hook, line, and sinker.

We cannot know the time frame between the Rapture of the Church and the appearance of Antichrist and his False Prophet, but we do know Satan will exploit the chaos in that time frame to the ultimate degree. It is this gigantic propaganda-feed that will be the greatest deception of Satan's career as the great deceiver.

The people of that day will worship this man. They will reject Jesus, who, out of love, died for the remission of all their sins. But they will accept Antichrist who, out of hatred, will have no qualms about killing them at a mere whim. What better illustrates deception?

People are presently watching as the stone chips — large and small — fall from our culture's foundation. Because they are in a self-imposed bubble of deception, they conclude there is no real reason for alarm.

But whether members of American society like the dramatic changes in our culture in the last several decades or not, we can be very sure about one thing. Each change is a part of Satan's great scheme to deceive the hearts of people, even the elect, and he believes each one brings him closer to having what he has always wanted: to receive worship from and have control over humanity, the supreme love of God's great heart.

Endnotes
1. Richard C. McMillan, *Religion in the Public Schools: An Introduction* (Macon, GA: Mercer University Press, 1984), p. 176.
2. Pew Research Center.
3. *Obergefell v Hodges,* https://www.oyez.org/cases/2014/14-556.

CHAPTER 5

Tracking Truth in Deceptive Times

J. MICHAEL HILE

To many, Satan is a cartoon character or mythological creation that is imaginary and harmless. Of course, the real Satan takes pleasure in this harmless caricature of his persona, for it helps disguise his diabolical plans and keeps most people in the dark concerning his real intentions for them. As long as Satan is not taken seriously, he is able to push his agenda forward without being suspected as the culprit and the cause of many of the world's problems.

The real Satan, however, is very much involved in the deception and seduction of the nations in the world in order to bring in a world government that he will control through "the man of sin," also known as Antichrist. Satan's takeover of the world, and specifically our nation, has been a slow, calculated process that has accelerated rapidly in recent years. Satan uses people, who are his willing accomplices, to accomplish his plans and purposes on earth. People don't realize they are being used by Satan, because they are spiritually blind and do not know or understand the Scriptures, but rather have a secular worldview that excludes God from their thoughts and way of thinking.

Satan has had the destruction of Israel (children of Israel) in his plans since the early days of Moses, Pharaoh, and the Egyptian bondage. Since the United States has been the major superpower in the world since World War II, and we have been the main friend and ally of Israel since her rebirth in 1948, Satan's main goal has been to infiltrate and destroy the United States from within by using leftist, subversive groups to create chaos and anarchy. Satan's multiphase plan has been to destroy Israel by first neutralizing the United States, and that plan is well underway.

The formation of the United States of America was unique in all the history of the nations. God miraculously intervened on many occasions to preserve this nation for its role in evangelizing, disseminating the Word of God,[1] and blessing Israel (John 3:16–21; Matthew 28:18–20; Genesis 12:1–3). Where are we today, how did we get here, where are we headed, what does it portend for America and the world, and is there any hope for the future?

The Foundations of America

The United States was founded by men who respected and embraced the Judeo-Christian values contained in the Bible. Not all of the Founders were believers in the God of the Bible, but they understood that the moral and ethical values contained in the Bible were beneficial in promoting and maintaining an orderly and productive society. George Washington (1732–1799), the first president of the United States, understood the importance of including God in our personal, public, and national affairs: "It is the duty of all nations to acknowledge the providence of Almighty God, to obey His will, to be grateful for His benefits, and humbly to implore His protection and favor."[2]

Many of the early pioneers, who faced daily trials, understood the divine providence of God and depended upon Him for daily assistance. Benjamin Franklin (1706–1790), one of the Founding Fathers of the United States and a leading author, printer, political theorist, politician, postmaster, scientist, inventor, civic activist, statesman, and diplomat, said it well:

> I have lived, Sir, a long time, and the longer I live, the more convincing proofs I see of this truth — that God Governs in the affairs of men. And if a sparrow cannot fall to the ground without his notice, is it probable that an empire can rise without his aid? We have been assured, Sir, in the sacred writings, that "except the Lord build the House they labour in vain that build it." I firmly believe this; and I also believe that without his concurring aid we shall succeed in this political building no better than the Builders of Babel. . . . I therefore beg leave to move that henceforth prayers imploring the assistance of Heaven, and its blessings on our deliberations, be held in this Assembly every morning before we proceed to business, and that one or more of the Clergy of this City be requested to officiate in that Service.[3]

God's blessings upon America are a direct result of the Founding Fathers implementing the principles contained in the Scriptures. As parents passed on these principles to their children, America continued to receive blessings from the Lord. Adhering to the principles in the Bible from generation to generation resulted in many benefits to America, such as building machines to harvest food, make clothing, build vehicles, homes and large buildings; discovering medicines to cure smallpox, rabies, polio, and measles; developing new technologies that produced the microwave oven, handheld calculators, weather satellites, personal computers, the Internet, and cellphones; and coming up with technologies that helped defend the nation and win wars.[4] The United States was the first nation to put a man on the moon and return him safely to earth.[5]

Abraham Lincoln (1809–1865) was an American politician and lawyer who served as the 16th president of the United States from March 1861 until his assassination in April 1865. Lincoln led the United States through its Civil War — its bloodiest war and perhaps its greatest moral, constitutional, and political crisis. In doing so, he preserved the Union, paved the way to the abolition of slavery, strengthened the federal government, and modernized the economy. President Lincoln's respect for God and the Bible was well known: "It is the duty of nations, as well as of men, to own their dependence upon the overruling power of God and to recognize the sublime truth announced in the Holy Scriptures and proven by all history, that those nations only are blessed whose God is the Lord."[6]

The Father of American Scholarship and Education

Another important patriot in the early days of our country was Noah Webster. Noah Webster Jr. (1758–1843) has been called the "Father of American Scholarship and Education." Webster's name has become synonymous with "dictionary" in the United States, especially the modern Merriam-Webster dictionary that was first published in 1828 as *An American Dictionary of the English Language*.

Webster's high regard for the truths contained in the Scriptures found their place in many of the books he published. His blue-backed speller books taught five generations of American children how to spell and read. He was an outspoken supporter of the new constitution, and believed American nationalism was superior to Europe, because American values were superior.[7]

"The moral principles and precepts contained in the Scriptures," Webster said, "ought to form the basis of all our civil constitutions and laws. All the miseries and evils which men suffer from vice, crime, ambition, injustice, oppression, slavery, and war, proceed from their despising or neglecting the precepts contained in the Bible."[8]

Testimony from a Foreign Diplomat

Alexis de Tocqueville (1805–1859), who was a French diplomat, political scientist, historian, and noted French political philosopher of the 19th century, visited America in 1831, traveled widely throughout the country, and took extensive notes about his observations and reflections.[9]

De Tocqueville examined our young national government, our schools, and centers of business, but could not find in them the reason for our strength. Not until he visited the churches in America did he find the secret of our greatness. "America is great because America is good; and if America ever ceases to be good, America will cease to be great."[10] This quote, often misattributed to de Tocqueville, nevertheless summarizes an aspect of what he had found during his visit to America.

The reason America was good during the first half of the 19th century was due to the nation's founding upon Judeo-Christian principles of the Bible (Psalm 127:1). The principles of right and wrong, good and evil, and doing "unto others as you would have them do unto you" are taught in the Scriptures and served as a foundation for the development of the new American government.

The Sovereignty of God and Responsibility of Man in Preserving Liberty

A good number of quotations by the Founding Fathers of the nation show that many of the founders were God-loving, God-fearing, and God-worshiping people who understood the importance of religious liberty and the price paid to acquire and help preserve the freedoms we have today. A few of these remarks are below.[11]

- "While the People are virtuous they cannot be subdued; but when once they lose their Virtue they will be ready to surrender their Liberties to the first external or internal Invader."[12] — Samuel Adams (1722–1803), an early American governor, lawyer, and signer of the Declaration of Independence.

Adams was the second cousin of John Adams, the second president of the United States.

- "Posterity — you will never know how much it has cost my generation to preserve your freedom. I hope you will make good use of it."[13] — John Quincy Adams, an American statesman and the sixth president of the United States (from 1825 to 1829).

- "If you love wealth more than liberty, the tranquility of servitude better than the animating contest of freedom, depart from us in peace. We ask not your counsel nor your arms. Crouch down and lick the hand that feeds you. May your chains rest lightly upon you and may posterity forget that you were our countrymen."[14] — Samuel Adams, known for his great animosity toward England's presence in the colonial affairs.

- "The price of liberty is eternal vigilance."[15] — Thomas Jefferson (1743–1826), an American Founding Father who was the principal author of the Declaration of Independence and later served as the third president of the United States, from 1801 to 1809.

- "My God! How little do my countrymen know what precious blessings they are in possession of, and which no other people on earth enjoy!"[16] — Thomas Jefferson.

The Source of Our Blessings

America has been blessed abundantly in areas of economics, education, technology, food production, energy resources, military strength, and religious freedom. Some may attribute these success stories to hard work, education, and American ingenuity alone without considering God's providence and intervening hand in America's prosperity. That type of attitude, called pride, is what got Satan into trouble, and is also the biggest stumbling block for unbelievers, who resist the grace of God, and carnal believers, who refuse to follow God on a daily basis (Isaiah 14:12–17; Revelation 3:15–19).

Beware lest you say in your heart, "My power and the might of my hand have gotten me this wealth." You shall remember the LORD your God, for it is he who gives you power to get wealth, that he may confirm his covenant that he swore to your fathers, as it is this day. And if you forget the LORD your God and go after other gods and serve them and worship them, I solemnly warn you today that you shall surely perish. Like the nations that the LORD makes to perish before you, so shall you perish, because you would not obey the voice of the LORD your God (Deuteronomy 8:17–20; ESV).

The pride and arrogance that got the children of Israel in trouble after they crossed the Red Sea is the same attitude that will get our nation in trouble if we trust in our own abilities and ignore God (Psalm 20:6–8). The young Hebrew nation was forced to wander in the wilderness for 40 years until that generation had died off (Hebrews 3:7–11). God is sovereign, and "the nations are like a drop in a bucket; they are considered as a speck of dust in the scales; He lifts up the islands like fine dust" (Isaiah 40:15; HCSB).

All the inhabitants of the earth are counted as nothing, and He does what He wants with the army of heaven and the inhabitants of the earth. There is no one who can hold back His hand or say to Him, "What have You done?" (Daniel 4:35; HCSB).

If at any time I declare concerning a nation or a kingdom, that I will pluck up and break down and destroy it, and if that nation, concerning which I have spoken, turns from its evil, I will relent of the disaster that I intended to do to it. And if at any time I declare concerning a nation or a kingdom that I will build and plant it, and if it does evil in my sight, not listening to my voice, then I will relent of the good that I had intended to do to it (Jeremiah 18:7–10; ESV).

The Foundations Begin to Move

The strong adherence to the teachings in the Bible during the founding years of the country began to be challenged during the middle of the 19th century. A new way of looking at the Scriptures began to take root. The traditional view of interpreting the Scriptures "literally" was called "Fundamentalism." Some recent followers of Fundamentalism are Jerry Falwell, James Dobson, Charles Stanley, Adrian Rogers, James Kennedy, R.C. Sproul, John McArthur, David Jeremiah, and Robert Jeffress. Except for parables and figures of speech, where it is important to look for the literal meaning of the figurative language, the Scriptures were taken literally as written. What has been called "The Golden Rule of Interpretation" states: "When the plain sense of scripture makes common sense, seek no other sense; therefore, take every word at its primary, ordinary, usual, literal meaning unless the facts of the immediate context, studied in the light of related passages and axiomatic and fundamental truths, indicate clearly otherwise" (Dr. D.L. Cooper).[17]

The Buffet Method or the Whole Counsel of God?

A new way of looking at the Scriptures called "Liberalism" began to infiltrate some of the traditionally Fundamentalist churches. Many preachers and teachers began to turn away from expounding the truth of God's Word and began to focus on stories, fables, and entertainment (2 Timothy 4:1–4; 2 Thessalonians 2:10–12). Liberalism looked at the Bible as a religious book that contained good principles mixed with myth and errors. Followers of Liberalism would pick and choose the parts of the Bible they liked to interpret literally, much like a restaurant buffet, and ignore or interpret the other Scriptures allegorically.

According to the allegorical method, "the literal and historical sense of Scripture is completely ignored, and every word and event is made an allegory of some kind either to escape theological difficulties or to maintain certain peculiar religious views."[18] J. Dwight Pentecost adds: "It would seem that the purpose of the allegorical method is not to interpret Scripture, but to pervert the true meaning of Scripture, albeit under the guise of seeking a deeper or more spiritual meaning."[19]

During the first half of the 20th century (1900–1950), the Literal approach to preaching the "whole counsel of God," as the Apostle Paul taught, began to take a back seat to watering down the Scriptures and majoring on emotional issues and social problems (Acts 20:25–28). Modern-day adherents to the Liberal view of interpretation include Norman Vincent Peale, Robert Schuller, Rick Warren, Joel Osteen, Joyce Meyer, and many of the feel-good and Prosperity preachers that appear on television. A common link between those who interpret the Scriptures from a Liberal viewpoint is to focus on suffering, poverty, prosperity, emotions, healing, and faith or lack of faith issues, while ignoring the rest of the Bible, especially issues involving our accountability to God and our role in the coming Kingdom of God (Matthew 6:33; Colossians 3:1–4).

Preaching Model Has Changed, Robinson Says

During a discussion following his lectures on preaching at Beeson Divinity School some time ago, Haddon Robinson expressed concern:

> The model for the preacher has changed. Up through the 1940s into the '50s — at least among evangelicals — the model for the preacher was the evangelist. . . . In the late '50s and '60s, the model in many circles became the Bible teacher . . . [corresponding to the emergence of the Bible church movement].
>
> In the '80s to '90s, the model of the preacher (became) the therapist — the task of the preacher is to meet the needs of the converted people who are still secular. . . . Sermons today are much more likely to be topical than expository . . . and many of the materials in the sermon come out of the behavioral sciences. . . . The aim of most sermons today is not to explain the biblical text. The aim of most sermons is to connect with the listeners' felt needs. . . . The Bible is used as a way to get a divine imprint on what is simply good advice.[20]

The Liberalism movement within the Church was a move away from the teachings in the Bible. Under the guise of being "enlightened," "cool," and "in touch" with the needs of both the young people and adults, it was actually a move away from the biblical Scriptures and an embrace of the world's ways and methods (Colossians 2:6–9; 1 John 2:15–17). Francis Schaeffer (1912–1984), an American evangelical Christian theologian, philosopher, and Presbyterian pastor, correctly summed things up years ago when he said:

> Here is the great evangelical disaster — the failure of the evangelical church to stand for truth. The evangelical church has accommodated the spirit of this age. First there has been the accommodation of Scripture, so that many who call themselves evangelicals hold a weakened view of the Bible and no longer affirm the truth of all that it teaches.[21]

The acceptance of the Liberalism movement in the Church prepared the way for rejection of the "creation science" model taught in the Bible and opened the door for acceptance of the "evolution myth" model. Those who chose to reject God and the Bible down through the centuries have had no other recourse than to plead ignorance or put their faith in the "evolution myth" as their answer to the question: Where did man originally come from?

Charles Darwin attempted to answer this question in the last half of the 19th century, and his theory was quickly accepted by the education establishment and forced into the science textbooks in the 20th century. Acceptance of the liberal view of interpreting the Scriptures by many in the churches during the last half of the 19th century (1850–1900) and first half of the 20th century (1900–1950) paved the way for the teaching of evolution in the school's science textbooks, which helped accelerate the expulsion of religious freedom from the government-run public schools.

A Change in Direction of the Country

The movement of America away from its Judeo-Christian values (Old and New Testaments) has been a slow process that began in the 19th century (1800–1900), accelerated quickly during the last half of the 20th century (1950–2000), and continued its rapid onslaught during the early part of the 21st century (2000–date). The changes have occurred primarily in five areas: religion, education, government, politics, and culture. There are secondary factors involved, such as philosophy, ethics, biology, psychology, sociology, law, politics, economics, technology, history, and global considerations, that have contributed to the shift away from a biblical worldview.

A "worldview" is how you view the world based upon your experiences, knowledge, and understanding of the five areas and ten-plus factors listed above. Some people have a "secular worldview" wherein they leave God completely out of their lives and decision-making. Others have a "narcissistic worldview" in which everything that happens is viewed through themselves and how it affects them. Some even dare to have a "satanic worldview" in which they filter their thoughts and actions through the "god of this age" and the "great deceiver's" agenda, which they falsely assume will work to their advantage (2 Corinthians 4:4; Revelation 12:9).

> Beware lest any man [educator, politician, rock star, news anchorman/woman] take you captive through vain and deceitful philosophy [naturalism, materialism, existentialism, pragmatism], after the tradition of men [Marx, Darwin, Nietzsche, Wellhausen, Freud, Dewey, Foucault], after the rudiments of

the world [socialism, evolution, higher criticism, humanism, moral relativism, deconstructionism, collectivism], and not after Christ[22] (Colossians 2:8).

The Acceptance of Evolution Theory in the Classroom

The default position for those who do not accept God's special creation, as explained in the first two chapters of the Book of Genesis, is to believe that man evolved from a lower form of life. Where the first lower form of life came from cannot be answered intelligently, if God is excluded from the conversation. Consequently, a biblical worldview must be included in any rational discussion of life origins.

One of the most damaging assaults on the biblical worldview was put forth by Charles Darwin on November 24, 1859, when he published *On the Origin of Species*, which eventually became the foundation of evolutionary biology.

Within a couple of decades, there was widespread, scientific agreement that evolution had occurred, and Darwin's concept of evolutionary adaptation through natural selection became central to modern evolutionary theory. Creation science, as taught in the Bible, was banned from most science textbooks, and evolution has become the unifying concept of the life sciences.[23] The evolution model is followed in all textbooks in the public schools today, and is the basis for origins of life in most secular, historical, and scientific documentaries.

The movement away from the values espoused in the Bible has been a systematic process, orchestrated stealthily by Satan, using his willful servants, aimed initially at the education system. If you can change the moral values of the children, you can change the direction of society. This assault on the children by the educational elite, through mind control, is well understood by politicians, kings, presidents, and dictators — whether they be good or evil.

> "Freedom is a fragile thing and is never more than one generation away from extinction. It is not ours by inheritance; it must be fought for and defended constantly by each generation, for it comes only once to a people. Those who have known freedom and then lost it have never known it again."[24] — Ronald Reagan, from his first inaugural speech as governor of California, January 5, 1967

"Let me control the textbooks and I will control the state. The state will take youth and give to youth its own education and its own upbringing. Your child belongs to us already."[25] — Adolf Hitler (1889–1945) Führer "leader" of Nazi Germany from 1934 to 1945

"Give me just one generation of youth, and I'll transform the whole world."[26] — Vladimir Lenin (1870–1924), Russian communist head of government from 1917 to 1924

Who Are the Agents of Change?

At the beginning of the 20th century, there were not any large, organized, anti-Christian groups in the United States that were trying to cleanse Christianity from the culture. Today, there are more than two hundred anti-Christian organizations that are deeply intolerant of the Christian religion.

According to Matt Barber, an author, columnist, cultural analyst, and attorney concentrating in constitutional law, and founder and editor-in chief of BarbWire.com:

The Mississippi-based American Family Association (AFA) has developed and released a tremendous resource for the fair-minded American public. It's an interactive "Anti-Christian bigotry map," which identifies more than 200 groups and organizations that openly display bigotry toward the Christian faith.

The AFA has also announced that it will be monitoring these anti-Christian segregationists' activities, reporting on those activities to the general public and further warning the tens of millions of Christian Americans of specifics relative to their radical campaign of religious cleansing.

"The website www.afa.net/bigotrymap [which has been removed or taken down] includes an interactive map that identifies groups whose actions are deeply intolerant of the Christian religion," notes AFA. "Their actions, for example, have endorsed efforts to silence Christians and to remove all public displays of Christian heritage and faith in America."

Among the over 200 anti-Christian organizations exposed by the Christian watchdog group are some of the most strident atheist, humanist and "LGBT" extremist outfits in America.

The ironically named Human Rights Campaign (HRC), for example, is listed among them.

Another of the more high-profile groups listed is the hard-left Southern Poverty Law Center (SPLC). The SPLC's propagandist activities have been linked by the FBI to anti-Christian domestic terrorism (something I long ago predicted would happen). Also on the list are the Freedom From Religion Foundation, the Gay, Lesbian & Straight Education Network (GLSEN), and many more.

"A common practice of these groups is threatening our nation's schools, cities and states," said American Family Association (AFA) President Tim Wildmon. "By threat of lawsuit, they demand that prayer be removed from schools and city council meetings, that Ten Commandments monuments be stricken from courthouses, and that memorial crosses be purged from cemeteries and parks," he added. "Families and businesses that express a Christian worldview on social issues often face vicious retaliation from anti-Christian zealots, and it's time to call them out for their intolerance," urged Wildmon. "Because of anti-Christian bigotry, private business owners have been sued and forced to close their businesses."

AFA is warning Christian Americans to be vigilant in that some associated with the 200-plus anti-Christian groups have actually "committed violent crimes against Christians and faith-based groups," and that "physical and profane verbal assaults against Christians" have been, and continue to be, regularly used as "angry methods of intimidation."[27]

Change does not happen in a vacuum. In other words, the deterioration of our culture and the education system in the United States has not happened without input from groups whose goal has been to change how the children and youth in the country think. There are a lot of subversive groups whose goal is to undermine the Constitution of the United States and the laws passed by Congress, in order to destroy the foundations (biblical values) the country was built upon. One group in particular, the ACLU — American Civil Liberties Union — has done more to destroy the Judeo-Christian value system established by the Founding Fathers than any other organization in the history of the United States. "If the foundations are destroyed, what can the righteous do?" (Psalm 11:3; NASB).

A Brief History of the American Civil Liberties Union

In 1915 the American Union Against Militarism (AUAM) was formed to prevent United States involvement in World War I with Crystal Eastman serving as executive secretary. Roger Baldwin became executive director in 1917. A separate organization, the National Civil Liberties Bureau (NCLB) was established in the autumn of 1917 with Roger Baldwin as director. . . . On Jan. 20, 1920, the NCLB was renamed the American Civil Liberties Union (ACLU) with Roger Baldwin and Albert DeSilver as Co-Directors.[28]

Additional insight is provided by Alan Sears, a former federal prosecutor in the Reagan administration, president and CEO of the Alliance Defense Fund, America's largest legal alliance defending religious liberty through strategy, training, funding, and litigation. He is coauthor with Craig Osten of "The ACLU vs. America: Exposing the Agenda to Redefine Moral Values," which reveals the history behind the ACLU.

One of the great myths of the 20th — and now 21st — century is the belief that the American Civil Liberties Union was an organization that had a noble beginning, but somehow strayed off course. That myth is untrue. The ACLU set a course to destroy America — her freedom and her values — right from the start. From its very beginning, the ACLU had strong socialist and communist ties. As early as 1931, the U.S. Congress was alarmed by the ACLU's devotion to communism. A report by the Special House Committee to Investigate Communist Activities stated:

> "The American Civil Liberties Union is closely affiliated with the communist movement in the United States, and fully 90 percent of its efforts are on behalf of communists who have come into conflict with the law. It claims to stand for free speech, free press and free assembly, but it is quite apparent that the main function of the ACLU is an attempt to protect the communists."

Baldwin openly sought the utter destruction of American society. Fifteen years after the founding of the ACLU, Baldwin wrote:

"I am for socialism, disarmament and ultimately for abolishing the state itself as an instrument of violence and compulsion. I seek the social ownership of property, the abolition of the propertied class and sole control by those who produce wealth. Communism is, of course, the goal."

Earl Browder, the general secretary of the Communist Party of the United States, admitted that the ACLU served as a "transmission belt" for the party. Baldwin agreed, claiming, "I don't regret being a part of the communist tactic which increased the effectiveness of a good cause." Baldwin was a devoted follower of the anarchist Emma Goldman (or "Red Emma" as she was called), who was eventually deported to the Soviet Union in 1919 for her communist activities. Goldman was a consistent promoter of anarchism, radical education, "free love" and birth control. According to an online exhibit of Goldman's papers, her career "served as inspiration for Roger Baldwin, a future founder of the American Civil Liberties Union."

[Crystal] Eastman was a zealous feminist, an anti-war activist, and a great admirer of the Soviet revolution. Of her many leftist friends and associates, Eastman held the highest regard for Planned Parenthood founder Margaret Sanger. According to Eastman, "We [feminists] must all be followers of Margaret Sanger."

Of course, Sanger was a passionate advocate of eugenics — the attempt to improve the human race through selective breeding. Abortion was a primary means to this "improvement," leading Sanger to write, "The most merciful thing that a family does to one of its infant members is to kill it." Baldwin also was a great admirer of the Planned Parenthood founder. He heaped praise on Sanger: "She was a frail, beautiful, unassuming woman. . . . She always had a quiet insistence on the rightness of what she was doing."

This adoration of Sanger set the tone for the tragic history of the ACLU concerning the issue of abortion. To this day, the group fights for the most extreme of pro-abortion positions, including support for partial-birth abortion and opposition to parental consent for minors. But the radical agenda hardly ends there. In his wedding vows, Baldwin called marriage as between one man and one woman "a grim mockery of essential freedom." He added, "The highest relationship between a man and a woman is that which welcomes and understands each other's loves."

The result is that today the ACLU is a leading advocate of same-sex "marriage," and has expressed support for polygamy and polyamory ("open" marriage) as well. The ACLU Policy Guide reads:

> The ACLU believes that criminal and civil laws prohibiting or penalizing the practice of plural marriage [polygamy or polyamory] violate constitutional protections of freedom of expression and association, freedom of religion, and privacy for personal relationships among consenting adults.

While many accept the ACLU as a mainstream organization, their history tells a drastically different story. Instead of being an organization that simply took a "wrong turn," the ACLU has devoted itself from the very beginning to the devastation of America's most cherished traditions, values, and laws.[29]

A Change in the Direction of Education

The ACLU, which has been around for nearly 100 years, has waged war against God, the Bible, and traditional American values from the earliest days of its creation and has been instrumental in helping destroy the foundations of the educational system established by the Founding Fathers of the country more than 200 years ago. Shortly after its inception, the ACLU began challenging freedom of religion issues, which had been historically protected by the Bill of Rights, specifically, the First Amendment to the Constitution. Rather than defending the freedoms contained in the Bill of Rights, as many believe the ACLU does, their goal from the beginning has been to destroy those rights, which the Declaration of Independence clearly states are "endowed by their Creator":

> We hold these truths to be self-evident, that all men are created equal, that they are endowed by their Creator with certain unalienable Rights, that among these are Life, Liberty and the pursuit of Happiness. — July 4, 1776[30]

The First Amendment of the U.S. Constitution:

> Congress shall make no law respecting an establishment of religion, or prohibiting the free exercise thereof; or abridging the freedom of speech, or of the press; or the right of the people peaceably to assemble, and to petition the government for a redress of grievances.[31]

Education is influenced by religion, politics, government, and culture to varying degrees. Due to the breakdown in public education (actually government indoctrination schools), many parents have removed or have never started their children in the public education system. Instead, they have chosen to put their children in private schools (both religious and secular) or homeschool them. The primary reason for this has been the selective removal of God, religion, discipline, and structure from the classroom while substituting sex education, drug addiction, bathroom and shower integration, low academic standards, and other problems.

The judicial system (courts) has incrementally removed First Amendment rights from the public schools and society with help from the ACLU, Freedom from Religion Foundation, and other subversive groups. The following 12 court cases involving freedom of religion issues have greatly damaged or destroyed religious freedoms that were guaranteed by the First Amendment. The federal courts, and especially the Supreme Court, by judicial fiat, have systematically twisted and removed freedoms that were originally guaranteed in the Constitution. The ACLU was involved, either directly or indirectly, in all of these cases, and in many others not listed.

12 Court Cases That Have Helped Destroy Religious Liberty in America

1925 — The Scopes "Monkey" Trial is held (*Tennessee v. Scopes*)[32]

1940 — The Free Exercise Clause is applied to the states (*Cantwell v. Connecticut*)[33]

1947 — The Establishment Clause is applied to the states (*Everson v. Board of Education*)[34]

1962 — Prayer is removed from the schools (*Engel v. Vitale*)[35]

1963 — Bible reading is removed from the schools (*Abington School District v. Schempp*)[36]

1973 — The murder of unborn babies is legalized (*Roe v. Wade*)[37]

1980 — The Ten Commandments are removed from classrooms (*Stone v. Graham*)[38]

1992 — Invocations/benedictions are banned from school activities (*Lee v. Weisman*)[39]

2003 — Sodomy is legalized by the Supreme Court (*Lawrence v. Texas*)[40]

2005 — Display of the Ten Commandments is ruled unconstitutional (*McCreary County v. ACLU of Kentucky*)[41]

2013 — Defense of Marriage Act (DOMA) is declared unconstitutional (*United States v. Windsor*)[42]

2015 — Same-sex marriage is approved by the Supreme Court (*Obergefell v. Hodges*)[43]

Sowing the Wind, Reaping the Whirlwind

How does a nation go from having "one nation under God" in the Pledge of Allegiance and "In God We Trust" on the currency, to a nation that has removed God from its culture? In 1954, in response to the Communist threat of the times, President Dwight D. Eisenhower encouraged Congress to add the words "under God," creating the 31-word pledge we say today, which reads:

> I pledge allegiance to the flag of the United States of America, and to the republic for which it stands, one nation under God, indivisible, with liberty and justice for all.[44]

In 1956, just two years after pushing to have the phrase "under God" inserted into the Pledge of Allegiance, President Eisenhower signed a law officially declaring "In God We Trust" to be the nation's official motto.[45]

Ironically, in just a few short years, our country went from honoring God to dishonoring Him, and from teaching the truths of God's Word to the students to removing God completely from our educational system. It was only one year after President Eisenhower left office in 1961 that the U.S. Supreme Court banned prayer in schools in 1962 and followed that the next year with banning Bible reading in the schools (1963).

A curse seemed to be placed on the United States after the Supreme Court symbolically kicked God out of the American schools. President John F. Kennedy was assassinated later that year, and the United States began a downward spiral spiritually, educationally, culturally, and politically that the country has never fully recovered from: "For they sow the wind, and they shall reap the whirlwind" (Hosea 8:7; ESV).

After the religious principles taught in the schools (prayer and Bible study) were removed from the schools in 1962 and 1963, the birth rates for unwed girls (15–19 years of age) skyrocketed by over 400 percent; the number of sexually transmitted diseases went up by nearly 400 percent; premarital sexual activity increased almost 1,000 percent; rape arrests and aggravated assault arrests increased dramatically; and divorce rates, unmarried couples living together, and adultery greatly increased.

The Scholastic Aptitude Test (SAT), which measures verbal and math skills of prospective college-bound students, has declined dramatically since 1962 after prayer and Bible reading were removed from the public schools. Beginning in the mid '60s, new scoring and testing methods were employed that raised report card grades, but at the same time resulted in student achievement scores falling dramatically (an oxymoron).

Raising the scores and grades of students while simultaneously lowering the standards has confused parents, who think making high grades today is equivalent to making high grades 60 years ago. According to Pew Research, 15-year-old U.S. students tested in 2015 scored 24th in reading, 24th in science, and 39th in math behind other countries.[46] No wonder parents, who are informed about today's public schools, are looking at alternatives for their children.

Before the ban on religious teachings in 1963, the top public-school problems were talking, chewing gum, making noise, running in the halls, getting out of turn in line, wearing improper clothing, and not putting paper in the wastebaskets. By 1985, the top offenses were rape, robbery, assault, burglary, arson, bombings, murder, suicide, absenteeism, vandalism, extortion, drug abuse, alcohol abuse, gang warfare, pregnancies, abortions, and venereal diseases:[47] "Do not be deceived: God is not mocked, for whatever one sows, that will he also reap" (Galatians 6:7; ESV).

A Change in Direction of the Culture

According to historians, we are in a period of cultural change called Postmodernism, which began around the middle of the 20th century (circa 1940–1960).

Prior to that, "Premodernism" existed (up to the 1650s), in which religion and revelation were the motivating factors affecting the culture.

From the 1650s to the 1950s, the culture was characterized by "Reason, Empiricism (observation and experiments), and science."[48]

Postmodernism is a philosophy that believes "absolute truth" does not exist. Postmodernism holds that all truth is relative (relativism), and what is right for one group is not necessarily right or true for everyone. Christianity teaches that sex outside of marriage is wrong, while Postmodernism holds that those rules don't apply to today's society. Consequently, sexual immorality, which is condemned in the Bible, is much more permissive in today's society. What traditional family values considered to be illegal in previous decades, such as lying, theft, or drug use, is not necessarily considered wrong in the Postmodern society.

The Postmodern philosophy, which rejects absolute truth, has led many to reject the Bible. Jesus said: "I am the way, and the truth, and the life; no one comes to the Father but through Me" (John 14:6; NASB). Those who have adopted the Postmodernism philosophy believe there are "many paths to heaven," and that all religions are equally valid (Pluralism). In their opinion, all religion, including Christianity, is reduced to one's own opinion.[49] We are reminded of the Apostle Paul's words about those who had chosen to go their own way and forget God.

> Professing to be wise, they became fools. . . . For they exchanged the truth of God for a lie, and worshiped and served the creature rather than the Creator. . . . And just as they did not see fit to acknowledge God any longer, God gave them over to a depraved mind, to do those things which are not proper (Romans 1:22–28; NASB).

Postmodern thinking has led many to adopt the ways of the world (1 John 2:15–17), which is the same philosophy followed during the days before Israel had a king: "every man did what was right in his own eyes" (Judges 17:6; NASB). Postmodernism has accelerated the decline of the American culture, and it is hastening the dangerous conditions, described by Timothy, that will be present in the world before Christ returns.

> But realize this, that in the last days difficult times will come. For men will be lovers of self, lovers of money, boastful, arrogant, revilers, disobedient to parents, ungrateful, unholy, unloving, irreconcilable, malicious gossips, without self-control, brutal, haters of good, treacherous, reckless, conceited, lovers of pleasure

rather than lovers of God, holding to a form of godliness, although they have denied its power. . . . always learning and never able to come to the knowledge of the truth (2 Timothy 3:1–7; NASB).

Similarities between America and the Old Roman Empire

Bill Federer, an author, lecturer, and noted expert on American history, says there are "ominous parallels with modern America and the Roman Empire." The fall of Rome was a result of both external and internal factors that did not happen suddenly but occurred over an extended period of time. The Great Wall of China along its Mongolian border hindered the warlike Huns from going east, so their barbaric invasions westward forced a "Great Migration" of people and tribes into the Roman Empire.

Federer lists the following factors in the decline and fall of the Roman Empire: open borders, loss of common language, the welfare state, violent entertainment, diminished role of the church, planned parenthood with fewer children, immorality and infidelity, class warfare, taxes, outsourcing, exploding debt and coinage debasement, corrupt politicians, military cuts, and terrorist attacks by barbarians from the outside.

In "Lessons from the Fall of Rome," Federer continues:

> John Stossel, host of "Stossel" on the Fox Business Network and author of "No They Can't: Why Government Fails, but Individuals Succeed," wrote in his article on the fall of Rome (www.johnstossel.com): "Historian Carl Richard said that today's America resembles Rome. The Roman Republic had a constitution, but Roman leaders often ignored it."
>
> Empires do crumble. Rome's lasted the longest. The Ottoman Empire lasted 623 years. China's Song, Qing and Ming dynasties each lasted about 300 years.
>
> We've lasted just 237 years so far. . . . We've accomplished amazing things, but we shouldn't take our continued success for granted. Freedom and prosperity are not natural. In human history, they're rare.[50]

The Fear of the Lord or the Praise of Men?

Dr. Jim Garlow, senior pastor of Skyline Wesleyan Church in San Diego, California, host of *The Garlow Perspective* on more than 800 radio outlets nationwide, and who has appeared on national TV shows on networks including CNN, MSNBC, Fox, and Comedy Central, was asked to speak to local pastors and community leaders for a luncheon and lecture to celebrate Pastors and Ministry Leaders Appreciation Month.

"Pastors tell me they don't want to be political from their pulpits," Garlow told the packed room, "and I ask them, 'does that mean you would not have preached against slavery? Or human smuggling?' "

Pastors and church leaders are afraid to speak boldly about cultural decline from the pulpit because of what is called the Johnson Amendment. When President Lyndon Johnson was still serving in the U.S. Congress, he added an amendment to a bill stating 501.(c)(3)'s could not endorse candidates. For tax purposes, most churches are tax-exempt nonprofit organizations and file a 501.(c)(3) tax form. Because of a misunderstanding of the amendment, 90 percent of the pastors feel they cannot speak on social and political matters without losing their tax status, according to Garlow.

But Garlow stressed that all political and social issues are Kingdom issues. He countered Christians who say they are politically only single issue voters — abortion, or double issue voters — marriage and abortion, but he argued all issues are Biblical. The reason is because God instituted marriage and government from the start. "I'm not asking you to be more political, but to be more biblical. . . . Minimum wage, social security — all are concepts in the Bible, so are national defense and climate change," said Garlow.

Garlow charged that Christians had allowed the enemy to push and silence them.

"Ten years ago, all pastors could have spoken that marriage was between a man and a woman and that would have been OK, now it is too politically incorrect to say that from the pulpit," Garlow said. "The debt would have been spoken about from the pulpit, 'Thou shall not steal . . . from future generations.' Now you never hear biblical references to what's happening in the government."

The speaker belongs to a group of pastors who have submitted their political and cultural sermons to the IRS for years, challenging the IRS to take away their favorable tax status, but the IRS has refused to take the bait, according to Garlow. "The IRS knows the amendment is not constitutional and would lose under court scrutiny. The government does not have a right to dictate what can and cannot be said from the pulpit," Garlow emphasized.

Dr. Garlow cited a Barna Group poll where they asked parishioners in 2014 if they wanted their church to speak on political and cultural issues, 40 percent answered yes. Barna took the same poll in 2015 and found the numbers had jumped to over 50%. People want to hear these topics preached from the pulpits.

"If the pulpit is silent, the pews are silent. The problems we have are spiritual," said Garlow.[51]

The Fear of the Lord

The "fear of the Lord" is perhaps one of the most misunderstood expressions used in the Bible. If you asked several people on the street what "the fear of God" meant, they would probably not have a clue what you were talking about. If you asked some in the Church what it meant, they would probably say: "We need to respect God and honor Him on Sundays by going to church." Understanding and practicing the "fear of the Lord," in reality, opens up access to God's knowledge, wisdom, and understanding in a way that cannot be comprehended by the natural (unsaved) man (see 1 Corinthians 2:14).

The fear of the LORD is the beginning of knowledge: but fools despise wisdom and instruction (Proverbs 1:7).

The fear of the LORD is the beginning of wisdom: a good understanding have all they that do his commandments: his praise endureth for ever (Psalm 111:10).

Get wisdom, get understanding: forget it not; neither decline from the words of my mouth. Forsake her not, and she shall preserve thee: love her, and she shall keep thee. Wisdom is the principal thing; therefore get wisdom: and with all thy getting get understanding (Proverbs 4:5–7).

Trust in the LORD with all thine heart; and lean not unto thine own understanding. In all thy ways acknowledge him, and he shall direct thy paths. Be not wise in thine own eyes: fear the LORD, and depart from evil. It shall be health to thy navel, and marrow to thy bones. Honour the LORD with thy substance, and with the firstfruits of all thine increase (Proverbs 3:5–9).

The LORD taketh pleasure in them that fear him, in those that hope in his mercy (Psalm 147:11).

The fear of the LORD is to hate evil: pride, and arrogancy, and the evil way, and the froward mouth, do I hate (Proverbs 8:13).

By mercy and truth, iniquity is purged: and by the fear of the LORD men depart from evil (Proverbs 16:6).

How long, O naive ones, will you love being simple-minded? And scoffers delight themselves in scoffing, and fools hate knowledge? Turn to my reproof, Behold, I will pour out my spirit on you; I will make my words known to you. Because I called and you refused, I stretched out my hand and no one paid attention; and you neglected all my counsel, and did not want my reproof; I will also laugh at your calamity; I will mock when your dread comes, when your dread comes like a storm, and your calamity comes like a whirlwind, when distress and anguish come upon you. Then they will call on me, but I will not answer; they will seek me diligently but they will not find me, because they hated knowledge, and did not choose the fear of the LORD (Proverbs 1:22–29; NASB).

The "fear of the Lord" requires being a "doer of the Word" and not a "hearer only," which leads you into deception (James 1:19–25). Solomon, who was said to be the wisest person in the Old Testament times (1 Kings 4:29–34; 2 Chronicles 9:1–8; Luke 11:31), summarized his thoughts at the end of the Book of Ecclesiastes.

The conclusion, when all has been heard, is: fear God and keep His commandments, because this applies to every person. For God will bring every act to judgment, everything which is hidden, whether it is good or evil (Ecclesiastes 12:13–14; NASB).

Babylon and the Handwriting on the Wall

There is a time when God decides that a person, city, or nation has passed the point of no return and there is no remedy left. Judah, the Southern Kingdom of Israel, rebelled, and would not listen to the Word of the Lord from the prophets (Zephaniah, Jeremiah). So, because of the hardness of their hearts, the Lord sent King Nebuchadnezzar of Babylon to be his rod of judgment.

The LORD, the God of their fathers, sent persistently to them by his messengers, because he had compassion on his people and on his dwelling place. But they kept mocking the messengers of God, despising his words and scoffing at his prophets, until the wrath of the LORD rose against his people, until there was no remedy (2 Chronicles 36:15–16; ESV).

The word of the LORD came to Jeremiah: Behold, I am the LORD, the God of all flesh. Is anything too hard for me? Therefore, thus says the LORD: Behold, I am giving this city into the hands of the Chaldeans and into the hand of Nebuchadnezzar king of Babylon, and he shall capture it (Jeremiah 32:26–28; ESV).

In 586 B.C., after completion of the 11th year of Zedekiah's reign, Nebuchadnezzar broke through Jerusalem's walls, conquering the city. Jerusalem was plundered, Solomon's Temple was destroyed and most of the upper-class citizens were taken into captivity in Babylon. After King Nebuchadnezzar died, his grandson, Belshazzar, later became king. Belshazzar made a great feast for all his lords and took the gold and silver vessels his grandfather Nebuchadnezzar had taken from the temple in Jerusalem, and gave them to his servants to dishonor.

Then they brought in the golden vessels that had been taken out of the temple, the house of God in Jerusalem, and the king and his lords, his wives, and his concubines drank from them. They drank wine and praised the gods of gold and silver, bronze, iron, wood, and stone. Immediately the fingers of a human hand appeared and wrote on the plaster of the wall of the king's palace, opposite the lampstand. And the king saw the hand as it wrote. Then the king's color changed, and his thoughts alarmed him; his limbs gave way, and his knees knocked together. . . . Then Daniel was brought in before the king. The king answered and said to Daniel, "You are that Daniel, one of the exiles of Judah, whom the king my father brought from Judah. I have heard of you that the spirit of the gods is in you, and that light and understanding and excellent wisdom are found in you (Daniel 5:3–14; ESV).

Then Daniel told King Belshazzar:

". . . you have lifted up yourself against the Lord of heaven. And the vessels of his house have been brought in before you, and you and your lords, your wives, and your concubines have drunk wine from them. And you have praised the gods of silver and gold, of bronze, iron, wood, and stone, which do not see or hear or know, but the God in whose hand is your breath, and whose are all your ways, you have not honored.

"Then from his presence the hand was sent, and this writing was inscribed. And this is the writing that was inscribed: MENE, MENE, TEKEL, and PARSIN. This is the interpretation of the matter: MENE, God has numbered the days of your kingdom and brought it to an end; TEKEL, you have been weighed in the balances and found wanting; PERES, your kingdom is divided and given to the Medes and Persians."

Then Belshazzar gave the command, and Daniel was clothed with purple, a chain of gold was put around his neck, and a proclamation was made about him, that he should be the third ruler in the kingdom. That very night Belshazzar the Chaldean king was killed. And Darius the Mede received the kingdom, being about sixty-two years old (Daniel 5:23–31; ESV).

When the handwriting appeared on the wall in the king's palace in Babylon, it meant that God had numbered the kingdom, and the days of the Babylonian Kingdom had come to an end. It also signaled the end of King Belshazzar's rebellious and riotous reign, as Darius the Mede had Belshazzar killed, and the Medo-Persian Empire took control of Babylon (Daniel 2:32, 39, 8:1–4).

Does Satan Have a Plan to Destroy America?

As stated earlier, Satan's plan is to neutralize or destroy the United States in order to isolate Israel and bring all nations against the land as prophesied by the prophets Joel and Zechariah (Joel 3:2; Zechariah 14:2). The United States currently has four enemies that have vocalized, in the past or in recent times, the desire to destroy this country. They are Russia, China, Iran, and North Korea. There are other countries that have nuclear weapons, who are considered friends, or they are at least not considered an existential threat.

Many may remember the Arab oil embargo during the mid '70s — the long lines and waiting to fill their vehicles with gasoline. A brief history follows:

During the 1973 Arab-Israeli War, Arab members of the Organization of Petroleum Exporting Countries (OPEC) imposed an embargo against the United States in retaliation for the U.S. decision to re-supply the Israeli military and to gain leverage in the post-war peace negotiations.

To complicate matters, the embargo's organizers linked its end to successful U.S. efforts to bring about peace between Israel and its Arab neighbors. President Nixon and Secretary of State Henry Kissinger recognized the constraints inherent in peace talks to end the war that were coupled with negotiations with Arab OPEC members to end the embargo and increase production.

The embargo laid bare one of the foremost challenges confronting U.S. policy in the Middle East, that of balancing the contradictory demands of unflinching support for Israel and the preservation of close ties to the Arab oil-producing monarchies.[52]

From a political and economic perspective, the entrance of the United States into the middle of a decades-long feud between Israel and its Arab neighbors, involving peace negotiations, appeared to be simply problems that could be resolved through normal business negotiations. From a spiritual perspective, this was like a hook being placed in the United States' jaws by Satan to lead this country into a trap that would set up a confrontation between the United States, which the Lord helped establish more than 200 years ago, and the nation of Israel, Abraham's offspring and God's chosen people, which the Lord established more than 4,000 years ago.

Although the United States, overall, has helped the nation of Israel ("blessed Israel"), which is the only democracy (republic) in the Middle East, our actions to force Israel to give back the land they had captured after being attacked by Arab neighbors (Sinai and Gaza Strip) has weakened Israel ("cursed Israel"), and has brought judgment from the Lord upon our nation (see *Eye to Eye* by Bill Koenig, http://www.watch.org/eyetoeye).

Every American president since Richard Nixon has been involved in the Israeli/Palestinian peace negotiations, more or less, for nearly 50 years, with minimal success. The Trump administration, like the previous Obama, Bush, and Clinton administrations, is determined to make the Mid-East peace process a successful part of their presidential legacy. The real danger America faces is angering the Lord to the point that He shortens the days of our nation, like He did with the king of Babylon. If that happens, the United States will be no more, and our absence from the end-time prophecies in the Bible will no longer be a mystery.

Are the Days of America Numbered?

The Lord tells us that the very hairs of our head are numbered, and the days of our life are also numbered (Matthew 10:30; Luke 12:7; Psalm 139:16). God knows the day I will die and the day you will die (Hebrews 9:27). Has God numbered the days of the United States of America? The obvious answer is "yes," since He is all-knowing (omniscient), and there is nothing in the future He does not already know. He declared the end from the beginning, and He declares things to His servants, the prophets, before they happen (Isaiah 46:8–10; Amos 3:7). God gave His servants prophetic messages that are now in the Bible so we can understand what He is going to do in the future (Daniel 12:9–10). The purpose of Bible prophecy is to glorify Jesus Christ. That is why "the testimony of Jesus is the spirit of prophecy" (Revelation 19:10; ESV).

As revealed earlier in the Book of Daniel, God had determined the number of days the kingdom of Babylon would exist, including the day it would end. But He also allowed the number of days of Babylon's existence to be dependent upon the behavior of King Belshazzar (Daniel 5:1–4). Belshazzar knew what had happened to his grandfather, King Nebuchadnezzar, but he still chose to disregard the lessons he had been taught from Nebuchadnezzar's debasing experience with God, and had chosen, instead, to rebel against the God of heaven (Daniel 5:22–23). Therefore, King Belshazzar's rebellious behavior hastened the days of his appointment with judgment, which God had determined beforehand.

Since God has already numbered the days of the United States, are we hastening the days leading to our judgment by kicking Him out of the schools, the courthouses, and the public squares? Does legalizing homosexual behavior, gay marriage, and transsexual behavior hasten our day of judgment? Did the Supreme Court's overturning of the Defense of Marriage Act (DOMA) get God's attention? Just because God does not act immediately does not mean He will not act! The postponement of God's judgment allows time for greater wrath to build up, like an earthen dam that eventually reaches its capacity to hold back the floodwaters (Ecclesiastes 8:11–13; Hebrews 10:30–31).

> But because of your hard and impenitent heart you are storing
> up wrath for yourself on the day of wrath when God's righteous

judgment will be revealed. He will render to each one according to his works: to those who by patience in well-doing seek for glory and honor and immortality, he will give eternal life; but for those who are self-seeking and do not obey the truth, but obey unrighteousness, there will be wrath and fury. . . . For God shows no partiality (Romans 2:5–11; ESV).

Have We Passed the Point of No Return?

While the nations of the world, with the United States taking the lead, are directly involved with ongoing negotiations in the Middle East peace talks to force Israel to accept a diabolical peace agreement that divides their land, those who are negotiating do not realize "they" are messing with "the apple of God's eye." "They" may very well be setting a trap (Luke 21:35) that will lead to "their" own destruction (Zechariah 2:8, 12:1–3; Joel 3:2; Luke 21:34–36; 1 Thessalonians 5:1–3; Revelation 3:10). Are we experiencing the beginning of "birth pangs," and are we approaching the time called in the Bible "the beginning of sorrows" (Matthew 24:8)?

> But of the times and the seasons [of the Lord's return], brethren, ye have no need that I write unto you. For yourselves know perfectly that the day of the Lord so cometh as a thief in the night. For when they shall say, Peace and safety [security]; then sudden destruction cometh upon them, as travail upon a woman with child; and they shall not escape (1 Thessalonians 5:1–3).

Has the United States passed the point of no return? Only God knows! But the days of the United States' existence as a nation, as with Babylon, have been numbered, and the evil judges, corrupt members of Congress, and misguided presidents, both past and present, who have legislated immorality and continue to provoke the God of heaven, are hastening the days of judgment that are quickly coming upon our nation. The time for national repentance is long overdue!

Endnotes

1. Unless otherwise noted, Scripture in this chapter is from the King James Version (KJV) of the Bible.
2. George Washington, https://www.usa.church/us-history-quotes-about-god-and-the-bible/.
3. Benjamin Franklin's Request for Prayers at the Constitutional Convention, http://www.beliefnet.com/resourcelib/docs/21/Benjamin_Franklins_Request_for_Prayers_at_the_Constitutional__1.html.

4. Timeline of United States Inventions, https://en.wikipedia.org/wiki/Timeline_of_ United_States_inventions; Timeline of Medicine and Medical Technology, https:// en.wikipedia.org/wiki/Timeline_of_medicine_and_medical_technology; Timeline of the Evolution of Weapons, https://sites.google.com/site/theevolutionofweapons/ timeline; Timeline of Nuclear Weapons Development, https://en.wikipedia.org/ wiki/Timeline_of_nuclear_weapons_development.

5. Timeline of Space Exploration, https://www.archives.gov/research/alic/reference/ space-timeline.html.

6. Abraham Lincoln, https://en.wikipedia.org/wiki/Abraham_Lincoln.

7. Noah Webster, https://en.wikipedia.org/wiki/Noah_Webster.

8. *The Rebirth of America*, Arthur S. DeMoss Foundation, 1986, p. 32.

9. Alexis de Tocqueville, https://en.wikipedia.org/wiki/Alexis_de_Tocqueville.

10. *The Rebirth of America*, Arthur S. DeMoss Foundation, 1986, p. 32.

11. Paul Mitchell, *Founding Fathers Quotations*, "Were the United States Founded as a 'Christian' Nation?" https://famguardian.org/Subjects/ChristianHeritage/Articles/ FfQuotesChrNation.pdf.

12. Samuel Adams, http://www.conservapedia.com/Samuel_Adams.

13. John Quincy Adams, https://en.wikipedia.org/wiki/John_Quincy_Adams.

14. Samuel Adams, http://www.conservapedia.com/Samuel_Adams.

15. Thomas Jefferson, https://en.wikipedia.org/wiki/Thomas_Jefferson.

16. *The Rebirth of America*, Arthur S. DeMoss Foundation, 1986, p. 24.

17. http://www.messianicassociation.org/ezine19-dc.hermeneutics.htm.

18. J. Dwight Pentecost, *Things to Come* (Dunham Publishing Company, 1958), p. 4.

19. Ibid., p. 5.

20. "Preaching Model Has Changed," https://www.preaching.com/articles/preaching- model-has-changed-robinson-says/.

21. "The Great Evangelical Disaster," http://www.submergingchurch.com/2012/05/03/ the-great-evangelical-disaster/.

22. David Noebel and Summit Staff, "The Worldviews of Destruction in the 20th Century," September 11, 2009, https://www.summit.org/resources/articles/essays/ the-worldviews-of-destruction-in-the-20th-century/.

23. *On the Origin of Species*, https://en.wikipedia.org/wiki/On_the_Origin_of_Species.

24. "Is Freedom One Generation Away from Extinction?" dpatton1, http:// humanevents.com/2009/02/02/is-freedom-one-generation-away-from-extinction/.

25. "Pull Your Kids — Save the Nation," http://www.wnd.com/2012/11/pull-your- kids-save-the-nation/.

26. Vladimir Lenin, https://www.goodreads.com/quotes/106700-give-me-just-one- generation-of-youth-and-i-ll-transform.

27. "Watchdog Group AFA Releases Anti-Christian Bigotry Map," http://www. christianpost.com/news/watchdog-group-afa-releases-anti-christian-bigotry- map-134956/.

28. "A History of the ACLU from 1915 to Present," https://aclu.procon.org/view. timeline.php?timelineID=000024.

29. Alan Sears, "The ACLU's Shocking Legacy," http://www.wnd. com/2005/08/31979/.

30. "The Declaration of Independence," http://www.ushistory.org/Declaration/document/.

31. "First Amendment," Legal Information Institute, https://www.law.cornell.edu/constitution/first_amendment.

32. https://en.wikipedia.org/wiki/Scopes_Trial.

33. https://en.wikipedia.org/wiki/Cantwell_v._Connecticut.

34. https://en.wikipedia.org/wiki/Everson_v._Board_of_Education.

35. https://en.wikipedia.org/wiki/Engel_v._Vitale.

36. https://en.wikipedia.org/wiki/Abington_School_District_v._Schempp.

37. https://en.wikipedia.org/wiki/Roe_v._Wade.

38. https://en.wikipedia.org/wiki/Stone_v._Graham.

39. https://en.wikipedia.org/wiki/Lee_v._Weisman.

40. https://en.wikipedia.org/wiki/Lawrence_v._Texas.

41. https://en.wikipedia.org/wiki/McCreary_County_v._American_Civil_Liberties_Union.

42. https://en.wikipedia.org/wiki/United_States_v._Windsor.

43. https://en.wikipedia.org/wiki/Obergefell_v._Hodges.

44. "The Pledge of Allegiance," http://www.ushistory.org/documents/pledge.htm.

45. President Eisenhower Signs "In God We Trust" into Law, http://www.history.com/this-day-in-history/president-eisenhower-signs-in-god-we-trust-into-law.

46. "U.S. Students' Academic Achievement Still Lags That of Their Peers in Many Other Countries," http://www.pewresearch.org/fact-tank/2017/02/15/u-s-students-internationally-math-science/.

47. David Barton, *AMERICA, To Pray? Or Not to Pray?* (Aledo, TX: WallBuilder Press, 1994).

48. Summary of Premodernism, Modernism, and Postmodernism Epistemology, http://www.academia.edu/1707080/Modern_and_postmodern_ways_of_knowing_Implications_for_therapy_and_integration.

49. "What Is Postmodernism? Discover Why Postmodernism Conflicts with Christianity," Juan Estey, Updated June 17, 2016, https://www.thoughtco.com/what-is-postmodernism-700692.

50. Bill Federer, "Roman Empire: Ominous Parallels with Modern America," http://www.wnd.com/2017/09/roman-empire-ominous-parallels-with-modern-america/?cat_orig=education.

51. Betty Miller, "Silence of the Lambs," http://www.thedesertreview.com/silence-of-the-lambs/.

52. "Oil Embargo, 1973–1974," https://history.state.gov/milestones/1969-1976/oil-embargo.

CHAPTER 6

The Schoolroom Seducers

ISRAEL WAYNE

Many Christians today believe that the public school system in America was originally created by Christians with a Christian intent. It is commonly believed that the public schools were essentially good and positive until perhaps the late 1960s when they began to become more liberal and then sort of lost their way. Today, most Christian parents will admit that the current leftist, liberal/progressive agenda of the *government* school system ("government" is a more accurate term than "public," since the schools are controlled by government-mandated textbooks and standards, funded by government taxation, and regulated by governmental compulsory attendance laws) is no longer Christian, even though many believe it once was.

Let us take a walk back through history to see if this view can be substantiated. Were American government schools originally Christian?

Many of our ideas about education today trace back to the philosophies and ideas of the Greeks. During the Enlightenment, many of the ideas of the Greeks were resurrected and reinfused into Western culture. The Enlightenment was a period in the mid-17th through the 19th centuries when God's revelation, as the basis for knowable truth (epistemology), was replaced by human reason and rationality (humanism). Many doctrines that had been laid out during the Protestant Reformation were rejected by "enlightened" men who believed that we no longer needed God to determine what was morally right or wrong. Philosophers like Voltaire, Hume, Hegel, and Nietzsche (among others) believed that the concept of God was antiquated and needed to be replaced by man-centered ethics.

The Doctrine of Original Sin

A biblical doctrine that was "rediscovered" by the Reformers was the doctrine of "Original Sin." This doctrine posits that people (including children) are not born innately good, but rather are born with an inclination away from God and toward what is sinful and rebellious:

> We all, like sheep, have gone astray, each of us has turned to our own way (Isaiah 53:6; NIV).

> Surely I was sinful at birth, sinful from the time my mother conceived me (Psalm 51:5; NIV).

> The heart is deceitful above all things, and desperately wicked: who can know it? (Jeremiah 17:9; KJV).

> Even from birth the wicked go astray; from the womb they are wayward, spreading lies (Psalm 58:3; NIV).

> Do not be misled: "Bad company corrupts good character" (1 Corinthians 15:33; NIV).

> Foolishness is bound in the heart of a child (Proverbs 22:15; KJV).

> He who walks with wise men will be wise, but the companion of fools will suffer harm (Proverbs 13:20; NASB).

The Apostle Paul taught us:

> Therefore, just as sin came into the world through one man, and death through sin, and so death spread to all men because all sinned — for sin indeed was in the world before the law was given, but sin is not counted where there is no law. Yet death reigned from Adam to Moses, even over those whose sinning was not like the transgression of Adam, who was a type of the one who was to come. . . . For if, because of one man's trespass, death reigned through that one man, much more will those who receive the abundance of grace and the free gift of righteousness reign in life through the one man Jesus Christ (Romans 5:12–17; ESV).

And

> For as in Adam all die, so also in Christ shall all be made alive (1 Corinthians 15:22; ESV).

The reason I bring this up is that this is a major dividing line between those who believe that education should be directed by parents and those who believe that it should be directed by the government. If people are basically good, then they can all work together to create a humanistic utopia here on earth. Consolidation of power is the best future hope for humanity in a humanistic worldview. But if humankind is essentially sinful and wicked at heart, then decentralization of power is essential.

The Bible recognizes the waywardness of children and instructs parents to train them against the way they desire to go, toward the way they should go (Proverbs 22:6).

The famous atheist, Bertrand Russell, who lived from 1872–1970, wrote:

> The change in educational methods has been very much influenced by the decay of the belief in original sin. The traditional view, now nearly extinct, was that we are all born Children of Wrath, with a nature full of wickedness; before there can be any good in us we have to become Children of Grace, a process much accelerated by frequent castigation. Most moderns can hardly believe how much this theory influenced the education of our fathers and grandfathers.[1]

Plato (428–348 B.C.)

In Book V of *The Republic* [457d], Plato outlined a thesis that he believed to be best regarding the upbringing of children. He believed that "children shall be common (property), and that no parent shall know its own offspring nor any child its parent." The idea that children should not belong to their parents, but instead should be raised by "the State," is an idea that goes back to Plato.

He admitted that the idea that children should not be raised by their own parents, but instead should be held as property of the state, was a radical idea that would undoubtedly meet with opposition. He felt, nonetheless, that this was in the best interests of the state, and therefore, ultimately to society, if these outcomes could be achieved.

Long before Darwin and Hitler, Plato envisioned a world where children were raised in loveless institutions and sorted out like cattle to distinguish the weak from the strong (survival of the fittest) to determine those who were fit to serve the purposes of the state, and to identify those who should simply be discarded and eliminated.

[460c] The offspring of the good, I suppose, they will take to the pen or crèche, to certain nurses who live apart in a quarter of the city, but the offspring of the inferior, and any of those of the other sort who are born defective, they will properly dispose of in secret, so that no one will know what has become of them. That is the condition . . . of preserving the purity of the guardians' breed. They will also supervise the nursing of the children, conducting the mothers to the pen when their breasts are full, but employing every device [460d] to prevent anyone from recognizing her own infant.[2]

The dehumanizing of the natural bonds between a mother and child into an impersonal function of the institutional state was a radical concept that seemed so preposterous that no decent, civilized society would embrace it. Yet, this is what we find our own Western culture doing today. Daycare facilities accept infants as young as two weeks old so their mothers can go back into the workforce and serve the purposes of the state, through labor and taxation of their income (while their children are largely being raised by "professionals"). None of this practice is coincidental. The groundwork for such a worldview, which pushes against nature and nurture, was laid by Plato.

John Locke (1632–1704)

John Locke is considered by most historians to be the "Father of the Enlightenment."

Locke denied the doctrine of Original Sin. He believed that children were a *tabula rasa* (a "blank slate," or a "clean slate").

It was John Locke who first argued against "Special Revelation" (how God had revealed His Divine Law in the Scripture) to a reliance almost exclusively on "Natural Law," believing that we could know what was right and wrong from looking at nature and the created order. This is where the concept of certain ideas being "self-evident" largely originated. The Bible, on the contrary, argues that the mind of sinful man is hostile to God. It does not understand God's ways, nor can it do so (see Romans 8:7).

This shift resulted in people seeing children not as rebellious at heart and in need of a Savior, but rather as a kind of blank computer program. Educators believed that since children were born neutral, they should shape them into whatever mold they wanted. This led to many social engineers wanting to get hold of young children for their own ungodly purposes. If you can train the young, you can alter the future.

Jean-Jacques Rousseau (1712–1778)

Globally, no one has influenced education today more than Jean-Jacques Rousseau. He is a fascinating individual who had a phenomenal impact on the world. His writings inspired both the French and American Revolutions. But his writings on education may have had an even bigger impact.

He wrote a series of five books on education entitled *Emile (Treatise on Education)*. Rousseau's view of the child differed somewhat from John Locke. Rousseau believed that children were not merely neutral, but were born innately good. He believed that all persons were morally good at birth, but then they were later corrupted by interfacing with society. So, people are good until they get together, and then they go bad. Or something like that.

Rousseau promoted what some have called the concept of the "Noble Savage." He believed that if a child were left at birth in a jungle or on a deserted island to raise himself with no human interaction whatsoever, he would become the pinnacle of human perfection.

Rousseau put it this way:

> Religion commands us to believe that God Himself, having taken men out of a state of nature immediately after the creation, they are unequal only because it is His will they should be so: but it does not forbid us to form conjectures based solely on the nature of man, and the beings around him, concerning what might have become of the human race, if it had been left to itself.[3]

The problem with Rousseau's thesis, however, was a bit of a logistical one. There were only so many deserted islands on which to abandon newborn babies. So humans must then resort to the second-best alternative for society. If children could not merely raise themselves, they must be raised by the people who know what is best for society. Who are these elite decision makers who understand how to create the right kind of citizens? It was, in his worldview, those who had become elected government officials.

Rousseau boldly advocated for a system of schooling controlled by the government:

> If you wish to know what is meant by public education, read Plato's *Republic*. Those who merely judge books by their titles take this for a treatise on politics, but it is the finest treatise on education ever written.[4]

Not only did Rousseau believe that children should be wards of the state, he lived out the practice. He had a live-in mistress for nine years whom he refused to marry. He brought five children into the world with her, but did not raise any of them. He dropped off each of his children on the steps of a government orphanage and never saw them again. When a reporter asked him years later if they were boys or girls, he heartlessly replied that it had never occurred to him to check the sex of the children.

In Book V of *Emile*, Rousseau referred to the fictional character he created in the book (Emile is a fictional student, and Rousseau is his fictional teacher), and he spoke of whom he felt was really in charge of the child and who should direct his future:

> My business, mine I repeat, not his father's; for when he entrusted his son to my care, he gave up his place to me. He gave me his rights; it is I who am really Emile's father; it is I who have made a man of him.[5]

This question of who owns the children is at the heart of the education struggle. Increasingly, courts affirm the notion that once you drop your child off at a government school, you, as a parent, have relinquished your ability to direct their education.[6]

It is ironic that a man who never taught children personally, never raised any himself, and never even (as far as we know) left about a five-mile radius of the home in which he was born, would somehow have been deemed such an expert on education that his books would change the future of the world. *Emile* was originally burned in Paris and Geneva for being radical, but eventually his ideas found their way into the mainstream teachers' colleges of Europe and America.

Friedrich Wilhelm August Froebel (1782–1852)

Like Rousseau, Froebel never raised a child. Unlike Rousseau, however, he was a teacher. Froebel was a big fan of Rousseau and agreed with him, rather than Locke, that children were born innately good. Froebel also denied the doctrine of Original Sin.

He was teaching young boys (about age 9) as a hired tutor, and was conflicted in his views, because while he believed that these boys had been born "very good" in their nature, he observed that their behavior was very, very bad! He had a difficult time reconciling this. He disagreed with Rousseau on the nature of their corruption, because they were too young to have interfaced with society.

So, like a sleuth in a whodunit mystery, he asked himself who could have had both the opportunity and the motive to turn these good boys into little heathens. The only people who had access to them at such a young age were their parents. Parents were obviously the guilty parties.

The question that plagued him, and the one for which he never found an answer, was why seemingly nice parents would so thoroughly corrupt their child's sense of morality and civility.

Facts being what they were, however, he had no choice but to try to remedy the situation as best he could. He concluded that children needed to be removed from their parents' homes as early as possible to keep them from being ruined by their parents. In 1826, he wrote his most famous book, *The Education of Man*. He advocated for the concept of kindergartens ("garden of children") that was eventually accepted in the Prussian school system and later imported into America (as early as 1856).

All early education programs — Head Start, preschool, nursery schools, etc. — were derived from the concepts promoted by Froebel. The basic thesis is that parents cannot possibly know how to raise their own children and are, rather, a destructive force. They therefore need to be removed from the equation as soon as possible so that government "experts" can salvage the innate goodness of the children before the parents completely ruin them.

Horace Mann (1796–1859)

Eventually, the ideals of the Prussians (Prussia is part of modern-day Germany) came across the pond to America. Horace Mann was raised in a Puritan-dominated area of Massachusetts and was steeped in the Calvinistic doctrine of the depravity of man. However, when his older brother died during a drowning accident in a local pond (after intentionally ignoring the Lord's Day services that Sunday morning), Mann decided, at the age of 13, that he hated God.

Mann's desire was to see Christianity driven from American culture. He embraced a religion called Unitarianism, which teaches that there is no personal God. Rather, there is an impersonal spirit force that unites all the universe as one. He proposed the foundation of what he called "non-sectarian public schools" to replace the local, provincial, parent-funded, parent-directed "common schools."

Mann's goal was to allow a limited amount of religious instruction (i.e., generic Bible reading with no commentary, books from the *Common Book of Prayers*, etc.) — but no specific religious doctrine or dogma was to be taught. The plan was to systematically "boil the frog" slowly, subtly removing religious instruction and activities altogether until a humanistic worldview, completely devoid of Christian influence, would be accepted by the masses.

To ensure that there would be no escapees from this plan, Mann (the first secretary of education in Massachusetts) enacted the first compulsory attendance law there in 1852. This meant that no parents could opt their children out of the government-controlled (and eventually compulsory tax-funded) schools. No exemptions, no excuses. By 1900, the government had an almost complete monopoly on schooling in America.

Mann readily admitted his diabolical scheme: "We who are engaged in the sacred cause of education are entitled to look upon all parents as having given hostages to our cause."[7] Mann agreed with Froebel that children were not sinners, but were, in fact, morally good. Their goodness, however, was spoiled by spending too much time with their parents. He admitted that the act of taking young children from their parents and acting *in loco parentis* (in place of the parents) was rather extreme, but he felt that it was a lesser evil than leaving children with their parents. He confessed, "[A] parent may so corrupt the constitution of his child to render poison a necessary medicine."[8]

Protestant churches, for the most part, were eager to sign up for this, because they believed that it would prevent Roman Catholics from taking over the community-led common schools and turning all their children into Catholics. The Catholics, of course, were not happy, because they wanted their children to grow up and embrace their specific religious ideologies. They were the first group to break ties with the government schools and seek to opt out of compulsory attendance laws (see *Pierce vs. Society of Sisters*, 1925).

Mann's utopian vision was for there to be a melting pot of all religious ideologies into one universal religion of human goodness and decency (apart from Christ). This is the view now being promoted by New Agers and globalists through our government school system. It can never work, because we can't have ethics and goodness if there is no universal moral standard by which to judge right and wrong. Without a recognition that there is a higher moral law (that can come from God alone) to which all humans are accountable, we can never have unity or morality.

Karl Marx (1818–1883)

Many do not realize that Karl Marx was one of the most influential thinkers in shaping the form and structure of government-funded schooling. Our American schools have been heavily influenced by his ideology. In the *Communist Manifesto*, Marx made these bold assertions:

> Do you charge us with wanting to stop the exploitation of children by their parents? To this crime, we plead guilty. But, you say, we destroy the most hallowed of relations, when we replace home education by social.[9]

To destroy the family and break the allegiance of children to their parents, Marx was willing to destroy what he referred to as a holy (hallowed) relationship, merely to advance his cause of promoting economic socialism/communism.

The tenth plank of the Communist Manifesto is: "Free education for all children in public schools. . . . Combination of education with industrial production."[10]

The schools, per his vision, would not be parent-controlled and parent-funded, but would, instead, be controlled by the State. Marx's vision was accepted in many nations, including the former Soviet Union, which became a big influence on American schools during the National Education Association (NEA) leadership tenure of John Dewey in the 1920s and '30s.

Charles Darwin (1809–1882)

No one has shaped the world of science more than Charles Darwin. Sadly, when people raised with Christian influence go bad, they tend to go very bad! We see this with Mann, Marx, Dewey, and many others. Darwin at one point in his youth studied the Bible and was influenced toward a biblical view of design and creation, but eventually allowed the influences of "free-thinking" secularists to turn him toward a naturalistic worldview, one that did not correspond with biblical truth.

It is often suppressed in government schools, when studying Darwin, that the original title of his book (published in 1859) was quite racist: *On the Origin of Species by Means of Natural Selection, or the Preservation of Favoured Races in the Struggle for Life.*

It was the worldview of Darwinism (that the universe created itself without God, and all human history is the struggle of the survival of the fittest) that has resulted in the murder of tens of millions of people (born and unborn) since the publication of his fateful book.

Originally, evolution was not allowed to be taught in government schools. But after the Scopes trial in Dayton, Tennessee (argued by William Jennings Bryan for the creation perspective, and the first-ever case introduced by the American Civil Liberties Union, argued by Clarence Darrow), the tables were turned. Today, the law does not allow either biblical creationism or Intelligent Design to be taught in government schools.

This issue of evolution has been one of the most significant factors driving churched youth away from the Christian faith. They have been taught that the Bible is indefensible, and that modern science has proven wrong the "superstition" of the ancient biblical writers. The ministry of biblical creation and Christian apologetics is an extremely important endeavor in today's world.

William James (1842–1910)

Pragmatism is the philosophy that "whatever works is right," "the ends justify the means," and "it doesn't matter how you do something, as long as you get it done." This is a prevailing view practiced by many in our age, but it was popularized by William James, a founder of modern-day psychology. He wrote several books, including some for teachers, in which he pushed the idea of pragmatism as the primary methodology of the American classroom. In one essay to teachers, he wrote: "Education, in short, cannot be better described than by calling it the organization of acquired habits of conduct and tendencies to behavior."[11]

I do not see "reading, writing, and arithmetic" being promoted here. What James was promoting was social engineering. These radical, leftist "progressives" wanted to shift America away from a Christian worldview to a humanistic, socialistic one. Behavioral psychology became popular as experts conducted studies and research to see how students could be conditioned to accept information from their teachers without question.

Peer pressure was encouraged, as classes were formed of 30 to 40 students all the same age. The intent was to create peer dependency so that students would be too afraid to break rank with the others. Once the "herd" was created, all the teacher had to do was learn how to be a good facilitator, infiltrate the herd, and suggest change on the basis of "fun" and doing "what feels good to you." In this way, they could lead the entire student body in a revolutionary direction against the values of their church, parents, and grandparents.

Ivan Pavlov (1849–1936)

A man who is well known but not fully understood by most college graduates is Ivan Pavlov. The Russian scientist, who was inspired by Charles Darwin, won a Nobel Prize in 1904 and wrote a book entitled *The Conditioned Reflex* in 1926. Most famous for his research on dogs, one of Pavlov's experiments involved introducing a piece of meat to a dog, simultaneously ringing a bell. He did this each day until eventually the dog was conditioned to associate the ringing of the bell with receiving some meat. After a time, all Pavlov had to do was to ring the bell and the dog would begin salivating in anticipation of a meal that may (or may not) be forthcoming. What many do not realize is that the Soviets were utilizing this kind of "operant stimuli" and behavioristic conditioning, not to learn how to train and manipulate animals to the "correct" behavior, but to learn to control *people* so they would act predictably and without question, just like the experimental dogs and laboratory rats.

As the results of these studies were made public, government schools around the world soon utilized these methods in their classrooms. In fact, whether they know it or not, every student who has ever attended a government school has been a victim of social experimentation utilizing Pavlov's bell. On the first day of school, a teacher would stand in front of the class and say, "English class is now over. Please find your way down the hall to your history classroom." And she would ring a bell. Before long, the students learned to associate the ringing of the bell with the ending of a class, and they no longer needed verbal instructions. They dutifully followed the maze, like good little laboratory rats, to the "cheese" that awaited them in the history class.

Because most people do not adequately study history, we are unaware of how much we are merely pawns in a bigger game being played out by powerful elites on a global scale.

John Dewey (1859–1952)

The man with the greatest influence in the history of American education is almost assuredly John Dewey. Dewey was a socialist, a pragmatist, a signer of the First Humanist Manifesto, a founding member and president of the NEA, a president of the American Psychological Society, and an ardent atheist.

Dewey was not the founder of the Dewey Decimal System (that was a different Dewey), although he is often credited with that achievement. He was a teacher of teachers at Columbia University and wrote many books targeted to teachers and educational professionals.

He was a big fan of the Soviet educational system, and he wanted the United States to emulate the Soviet model. His desire was to see America embrace economic socialism as a worldview. In 1927, he traveled to the USSR with 24 other educators to learn from the Russians how to better teach economic socialism in the American classroom. There was such a synergy between the NEA and the Soviet Union at that time that the NEA invited the USSR to have a booth at their convention. The purpose was to invite U.S. teachers to travel to Russia to learn how to better teach a Marxist worldview in the American schools.

Dewey decided to focus on the methodology, structure, and pedagogy of the school system, and he commissioned a couple of his colleagues at Teacher's College at Columbia University — James E. Mendenhall and Dr. Harold Rugg — to change the textbooks and curriculum. They removed three subjects that had always been taught independently (history, civics, and geography), and replaced them with a brand-new subject that had never been heard of before: social studies. This new curriculum was socialistic at its core. It is estimated that approximately five million American students used this curriculum between 1930–1950 (before parents protested and it was eventually removed, for a time, from the curriculum).[12]

Dewey's goal was to replace Christianity with humanism as the dominant force in American culture. He spoke of his agenda with a religious fervor: "Every teacher should realize he is a social servant set apart for the maintenance of the proper social order and the securing of the right social growth. In this way, the teacher is always the prophet of the true God and the usherer in of the true kingdom of heaven."[13] As an atheist, Dewey didn't believe in the true God of the Bible; instead, he believed in a humanistic utopia, in which humankind was the ultimate source of everything.

Dewey was not alone in expressing these thoughts about humanism as a religion. Joel R. Burnett, another signer of the first *Humanist Manifesto* and an architect of the modern American educational system, wrote this in the humanist publication he edited: "Public education is the parochial education for scientific humanism."[14]

Dewey confessed that the schools were being (and should be) used as machines of propaganda, promoting a radical new Marxist worldview to children. He saw no problem with this, because, as a pragmatist, he believed that any method was valid as long as it brought about the desired result. In his mind, collectivism and socialism were in the best interests of society, so propaganda targeted to young children was perfectly acceptable. He admitted: "[The] propaganda . . . employed is not a private or even a class gain, but is [for] the universal good of universal humanity. In consequence, propaganda is education and education is propaganda."[15]

Further, he wrote:

> The mass of the people is to learn the meaning of Communism not so much by induction into Marxian doctrines — although there is plenty of that in the schools — but by what is done for the mass in freeing their life, in giving them a sense of security, safety, in opening to them access to recreation, leisure, new enjoyments and new cultivations of all sorts. The most effective propaganda, as the most effective education, is found to be that of deeds which raise the level of popular life, making it fuller and richer, while associating the gains as indissolubly as possible with a "collective" mentality.[16]

Dewey was praising Lenin and Stalin's schools, which were supposed to be the great "Messiah" that would rescue our world from hunger, forced labor, and inequality. Dewey saw Russia's model as the hope for our future in America. In truth, Marxism provided nothing of the sort. There was no "classless society." What emerged from Stalin were the executions of untold millions of his own people, slave labor, and indoctrination of the masses into a system that produced poverty and economic collapse.

Dewey recognized that three elements shaped people toward individualistic thinking and away from collectivist thinking: private property ownership, the home, and the church. He saw the schools as a mechanism to destroy these institutions and replace them with a brave new world of socialistic government control. What he proposed is nothing less than social engineering:

> Hence the great task of the school is to counteract and transform those domestic and neighborhood tendencies that are still so strong, even in a nominally collectivistic régime. In order to accomplish this end, the teachers must in the first place know with great detail and accuracy just what the conditions are to which pupils are subject in the home, and thus be able to interpret the habits and acts of the pupil in the school in the light of his environing conditions — and this, not just in some general way, but as definitely as a skilled physician diagnoses in the light of their causes the diseased conditions with which he is dealing.[17]

The Soviet schools advocated monitoring the views and beliefs of parents through spying and reporting of parents, by their own children, to school officials. Dewey was quite comfortable with this approach, as he felt it pragmatically necessary to know what students were learning at home, so it could be counteracted by teachers in the schools.

He continued:

> The knowledge thus gained of home conditions and their effect upon behavior (and I may say in passing that this social behaviorism seems to me much more promising intellectually than any exclusively physiological behaviorism can ever prove to be) is preliminary to the development of methods which will enable schools to react favorably upon the undesirable conditions discovered, and to reinforce such desirable agencies as exist. Here, of course, is the point at which the socially constructive work of the school comes in.[18]

By "physiological behaviorism," Dewey was talking about the kind of research that was done by people like Ivan Pavlov and, later, B.F. Skinner (1904–1990). Their research demonstrated how to condition students and change their behavior to desired outcomes. Dewey believed these more direct and forthright methods of dividing children and parents and pitting children against their parents would yield faster social engineering results.

Religiously Neutral Schools?

There is a great myth, embraced by many, that public schools are religiously neutral. It is believed that they teach neutral facts and information and simply encourage students to make up their own minds based on those facts. In reality, nothing could be further from the truth.

Vladimir Lenin reportedly used the term "useful idiot" to refer to people who would be used in the great struggle for collective change. Many would have no idea what part they played in the social revolution. Lenin made no pretense about government-controlled schools being neutral in any way:

> The school, apart from life, apart from politics, is a lie, a hypocrisy. Bourgeois society indulged in this lie, covering up the fact that it was using the schools as a means of domination, by declaring that the school was politically neutral, and in the service of all. We must declare openly what it concealed, namely, the political function of the school. While the object of our previous struggle was to overthrow the bourgeoisie, the aim of the new generation is much more complex: It is to construct communist society.[19]

He also stated:

> We say that our work in the sphere of education is part of the struggle for the overthrow of the bourgeoisie. We publicly declare that education divorced from life and politics is a lie and hypocrisy.[20]

Adolf Hitler also saw government-controlled schools as a necessary component in his goal to reorient society to his socialist dream. The following is from William L. Shirer's *The Rise and Fall of the Third Reich*:

> [H]e had stressed in his book the importance of winning over and then training the youth in the service "of a new national state" — a subject he returned to often after he became the German dictator. "When an opponent declares, 'I will not come over to your side,' [Adolf Hitler] said in a speech on November 6, 1933, I calmly say, 'Your child belongs to us already. . . . What are you? You will pass on. Your descendants, however, now stand in the new camp. In a short time they will know nothing else but this new community.'" And on May 1, 1937, [Hitler] declared, "This new Reich will give its youth to no one, but will itself take youth and give to youth its own education and its own upbringing." It was not an idle boast; that was precisely what was happening. The German schools, from first grade through the universities, were quickly Nazified.[21]

Peer Pressure and Herds

Why do you think the Hitler Youth committed the atrocities they did? Are Germans inherently more evil than other people groups? To agree with that statement would be to promote the very bigotry we denounce when we condemn the so-called racial profiling of ethnic groups by the Nazis. I don't think they are any different than anyone else. Their educational system was extremely effective in reorienting them into a total commitment to the desires of the Reich.

Why is it that youth go along with the crowd and refuse to say no? I've heard it said that children's sense of self-worth is determined by what the most important and most influential people in their lives think of them. If those people are the parents, the children will be inclined to do what the parents want. If it is their peer group, they will be inclined to do what the peer group wants them to do.

Danish existentialist philosopher Søren Kierkegaard observed:

> Man is a social animal; only in the herd is he happy. It is all one to him whether it is the profoundest nonsense or the greatest villainy — he feels completely at ease with it — so long as it is the view of the herd, and he is able to join the herd.[22]

Influence is gained through two primary means: time and affirmation. For the most part, whoever spends the most time with a child and encourages or affirms him or her the most has the most influence in that child's life. Unfortunately, most parents do not have this influence. They give it away to others and assume that those who have accepted that position have no agenda.

Christian apologist Ravi Zacharias insightfully notes:

> The whole point of state-controlled education is that it gives to the government the power to shape the souls and write on the fresh slates of young hearts. This empowerment is the most important trust given to elected officers and to assume that they accept that responsibility from a posture of neutrality is to live under the most destructive of illusions.[23]

The very creation of the age-segregated classroom, with 30 to 40 students all the same age, was designed to create peer pressure and cultivate an environment in which it would be very difficult for children to go against the views of the herd. Teachers are even encouraged, in their training, to cultivate and encourage this peer pressure. From a popular textbook used in teaching colleges in 2008: "The more learners want to be accepted and respected by peers, the more they will value membership in the 'in' group and be distressed by the ridicule of the classroom."[24]

Peer pressure is a tool to create conformity in the classroom. In 1951, a researcher named Solomon Asch began conducting "conformity experiments" that were later referred to as the "Asch Paradigm." He would create a "control group" in a classroom, where one student did not know that he was part of a research experiment. The students in the class were told to intentionally give the wrong answer to an obvious question to see if the test student would give a false answer (that he knew to be false) just to conform to the views of the group. It was found that the answers of a peer group were, indeed, very powerful in swaying the student's answers (and the larger the classroom, the more controlling the influence). Those experiments were conducted on college students, who believed their grade was dependent on giving the correct answer! How much more influence does the peer group classroom model have on creating conformity for elementary and junior high students, who so desperately want to be accepted by their friends?

Globalism

As time has gone on, modern classroom education has become a recruiting ground for teaching young impressionable minds the doctrines of socialism and globalism. From "America 2000" to "Goals 2000" to "Outcome-Based Education" to "No Child Left Behind" to "Common Core" and beyond, the American government school system is increasingly pushing a globalist agenda. "Agenda 21" and other U.N. programs are progressively being touted in government schools. Control over the schools is shifting from parents to community to county to state to federal to international.

The globalist vision promoted through government schools is not new. Consider what Mr. Joy Elmer Morgan, a former editor for the *NEA Journal*, wrote in a civics book he authored (published by the NEA) in 1941: "The future of America depends simply on . . . building up our schools . . . and on taking our part among the peoples of the world *to build an effective world government*"[25] (emphasis added).

He also published an essay in the *NEA Journal* in January of 1946 entitled, "The Teacher and World Government," in which he proclaimed:

> In the struggle to establish an adequate world government, the teacher . . . can do much to prepare the hearts and minds of children for global understanding and cooperation. . . . At the very top of all the agencies which will assure the coming of world government must stand the school, the teacher, and the organized profession.[26]

In October of 1947, the *NEA Journal* published "On the Waging of Peace" by NEA official William Carr, who stated:

> As you teach about the United Nations, lay ground for a stronger United Nations by developing in your students a sense of world community. The United Nations should be transformed into a limited world government. The psychological foundations for wider loyalties must be laid. . . . Teach about the various proposals that have been made for strengthening the United Nations and the establishment of world law. Teach those attitudes which will result ultimately in the creation of a world citizenship and world government. . . . We cannot directly teach loyalty to a society that does not yet exist, but we can and should teach those skills and attitudes which will help create a society in which world citizenship is possible.[27]

Also consider what Charles B. Pierce, a professor of education at Harvard, told a conference of school teachers in 1972:

> Every child in America entering school at the age of five is mentally ill because he comes to school with certain allegiances to our Founding Fathers, toward our elected officials, toward his parents, toward a belief in a supernatural being, and toward the sovereignty of this nation as a separate entity. It's up to you as teachers to make all these sick children well — by creating the international child of the future.[28]

The leftist, socialist, globalist agenda of the American government school system has only worsened in recent decades. My intent in giving you the history, prior to 1972, is that most Christians think the schools only started to take a liberal bent in the late 1960s. Nothing could be further from the truth. By the 1970s, the proverbial frog had already been boiled slowly. Now we are dealing with LGBT pride months being promoted in schools, transgender bathroom issues, and much more. These issues are merely the tip of the iceberg that lies beneath the surface. The real issue is humanism and the desire of our government educational system to create an environment where humans, not their Creator, are ultimately the final arbiters of right and wrong. It goes all the way back to the original deception in the Garden of Eden, when the serpent told Adam and Eve they could become like God.

It is my sincere hope that Christian parents will seek an education for their children that is rooted in the fear of the Lord (the beginning of wisdom) rather than in the shifting sands of cultural relativism and man's opinions.

Endnotes

1. Bertrand Russell, *On Education, Especially in Early Childhood* (London: George Allen & Unwin, 1926), http://russell-j.com/beginner/ON_EDU-TEXT.HTM.
2. Plato, *Plato in Twelve Volumes*, Vols. 5 & 6 translated by Paul Shorey. Cambridge, MA, Harvard University Press; London, William Heinemann Ltd. 1969; http://www.perseus.tufts.edu/hopper/text?doc=urn:cts:greekLit:tlg0059.tlg030.perseus-eng1:5.460 .
3. Rousseau, *What Is the Origin of Inequality Among Men, and Is It Authorized by Natural Law?* (1754), http://www.constitution.org/jjr/ineq.txt.
4. Rousseau, *Emile (Treatise on Education)*, 1762, http://www.gutenberg.org/cache/epub/5427/pg5427.html.
5. Ibid.
6. See: Fields v. Palmdale School District, 427 F.3d 1197 (9th Cir. 2005). Also: Fed. R. Civ. P. 12(b)(6); Parker v. Hurley, 474 F. Supp. 2d 261, 263 (D. Mass. 2007).
7. Horace Mann, *Lectures on Education* (Boston, MA: Wm. B. Fowle and N. Capen, 1845), p. 18.
8. Horace Mann, *On the Art of Teaching* (Bedford, MA: Applewood Books, 1989), p. 26.
9. Marx & Engels, *The Communist Manifesto* (Chapter II. Proletarians and Communists), https://www.marxists.org/archive/marx/works/1848/communist-manifesto/ch02.htm.
10. Ibid.
11. William James, *Talks to Teachers on Psychology and to Students on Some of Life's Ideals* (New York: Henry Holt, 1925).
12. Augustin G. Rudd, *Bending the Twig: The Revolution in Education and Its Effect on Our Children* (Chicago, IL: The Heritage Foundation, 1957), p. 74–75.
13. John Dewey, Pedagogic Creed statement, 1887 (*School Journal*, Vol. 54, January 1897), p. 77–80, http://dewey.pragmatism.org/creed.htm.
14. Joel R. Burnett, *The Humanist*, 6 (1961), p. 347.
15. John Dewey, *Impressions of Soviet Russia and the Revolutionary World*, 1929, from the chapter "A New World in the Making," http://ariwatch.com/VS/JD/ImpressionsOfSovietRussia.htm#chapter4.
16. Ibid., from the chapter "What Are the Russian Schools Doing?"

17. Ibid.
18. Ibid.
19. Ibid. (A quote of Lenin by John Dewey).
20. V.I. Lenin, from his speech at the First All-Russian Educational Congress, August 28, 1918, *Collected Works Volume XXIII* (1918–1919), p. 215.
21. William Shirer, *Rise and Fall of the Third Reich* (New York: Simon and Schuster, 1960), p. 249.
22. Søren Kierkegaard, *The Last Years: Selections from the Journals 1853–1855* (New York: Harper & Row, 1965), p.135.
23. Ravi Zacharias, *Deliver Us from Evil* (Dallas, TX: Word Publishing, 1996), p. 143.
24. Jeanne Ellis Ormrod, University of Northern Colorado, *Educational Psychology Developing Learners* (2008 Edition), p. 384–386.
25. Joy Elmer Morgan, *The American Citizens Handbook*, (Hugh Birch — Horace Mann Fund, National Education Association, 1941), p. 1.
26. *The Grab for Power: A Chronology of the NEA*, compiled by Dennis Laurence Cuddy, Ph.D., 1993 (Concerned Women for America), p. 3, http://concernedwomen.org/wp-content/uploads/2013/11/nea.pdf.
27. Ibid., p. 4.
28. From keynote address to the Association for Childhood Education International (Denver, CO, April 1972) by Dr. Chester M. Pierce, M.D., professor of education and psychiatry in the Faculty of Medicine at Harvard University, http://eric.ed.gov/?id=EJ064558.

CHAPTER 7

Middle East Misdirection

PHILLIP GOODMAN

The world says the situation in the Mideast is very complex. There are multiple, centuries-old, competing religious, political, and cultural sects, belief systems, and warring factions. But the Bible says the Mideast situation is actually very simple. It is a matter of people choosing to walk in the "darkness" rather than in the "light." This concept is not found in political forums, newsrooms, or even many churches. But it is found in the Bible.

We will look at the Bible's infallible answer to issues related to a single question, rooted for ages in the Mideast, that plagues our political and religious world of darkness: *Where does Israel get its authority, after nearly 2,000 years, to return to its land long since settled by Arabs, and reoccupy it?* Today, the nations are uniting in their hatred for Israel over this question. They wrestle with it to no avail (Zechariah 12:3). As a result, deception runs deep. But the Bible has the answer!

The Door to Deception — Rejection of Jesus Christ, the Son of God

Deception enters the heart and mind of humanity through a single door. Jesus cut to the heart of this truth when, referring to Isaiah's prophecy, He said:

> For a little while longer the Light is among you. Walk while you have the Light . . . he who walks in the darkness does not know where he goes. While you have the Light, believe in the Light,

so that you may become sons of Light. . . . This was to fulfill the word of Isaiah the prophet which he spoke: ". . . HE HAS BLIND-ED THEIR EYES AND HE HARDENED THEIR HEART, SO THAT THEY WOULD NOT SEE WITH THEIR EYES AND PERCEIVE WITH THEIR HEART, AND BE CONVERTED AND I HEAL THEM." These things Isaiah said because he saw His [Jesus'] glory, and he spoke of Him (John 12:35–41).[1]

The shroud of deception by satanic darkness has been the core problem of the whole world since the dawn of creation. From the first four-point lie given by Satan in the Garden of Eden (Genesis 3:1–5)[2] to the final great war of the ages (Revelation 12:7–12), deception has paraded as truth. But deception has been a particularly entrenched plague of the Mideast since the founding of the Islamic religion by Muhammad in the seventh century A.D. Satan is the master of the darkness of deception. Plainly spoken, the Mideast is "in the dark."

Spiritual Darkness — The Cause of Deception in the Mideast

Deception gains its foothold in the denial of Jesus Christ as the Son of God and the Savior of the world.[3] This denial is expressly written in the tenets of the Islamic religion.[4] The "dark-light" of the Quran, the false "holy book" of Islam, is the great deceiver that dominates the lives of the vast majority of Mideasterners. Islam's "dark-light," preached by their mullahs and imams, blinds people to the Light of the World, Jesus Christ. In John chapter 12, Jesus went on to say, "He who believes in Me, believes not in Me but in Him who sent Me. He who sees Me sees the One who sent Me" (John 12:44–45; see also John 14:9).

If the world wants to know what God wants, thinks, says, and does, look to Jesus!

Elsewhere, the Bible — called "a lamp to my feet" (Psalm 119:105) — says that one cannot honor the Father unless one honors the Son (cannot honor God unless one believes in Jesus Christ as personal Savior, Lord, and Light of the World, i.e., John 5:23 and 8:12; Matthew 10:32–33).

Islam has rejected the Light of the World. Since Islamic religion dominates the Mideast, then the Mideast world is without light and is in the dark. To abide in the darkness is to walk in deception. The only remedy for this is to believe in Jesus: "I have come as Light into the world, so that everyone who believes in Me will not remain in darkness" (John 12:46).

The Road to Deception — Rejection of the Abrahamic Covenant

Once one has rejected Jesus Christ as God the Son, then it is a logical and inevitable step to reject the central and powerful covenant God made with Abraham, to whom God gave this unconditional promise:

> I will make you a great nation, and I will bless you, and make your name great; and so you shall be a blessing; and I will bless those who bless you, and the one who curses you I will curse; and in you all the families of the earth will be blessed (Genesis 12:2–3; expansions given in Genesis 13, 15, 17, and 22).

The essence of the Abrahamic Covenant is this:[5]

1. Israel was to be born as an everlasting people from the seed of Abraham (Genesis 12:2, 13:15).

2. The Land of Canaan was to become an everlasting possession of Israel (Genesis 13:14–15).

3. A worldwide blessing would spring forth from the seed of Abraham (Genesis 12:3).

The Abrahamic Covenant, being an unconditional guarantee from the sovereign God, is therefore also a prophecy. That is, it will come to pass. Thus, Genesis 12:2–3 exposes the deception enveloping the Mideast today. Jesus said that God's Word (our Bible) would light up the darkness. This light shines down through 40 centuries, in the covenant God gave Abraham, to expose the deception causing today's Mideast uproar (2 Peter 1:19–21).

When Israel was brought forth out of Abraham's seed as an everlasting people, they were established as God's "chosen" people because of His love for Abraham, Isaac, and Jacob (Deuteronomy 7:6; Romans 11:28). The rejection of Jesus Christ as the Light of the World by Muslims has led to their denial of the light of God's Word, which Jesus said is revealed in the Bible (John 17:17), not in the Islamic Quran (John 12:48). This in turn has led to their rejection of the true revelation of God's covenant with Abraham, a spiritual covenant with real-world effects. This fact eludes the political rulers of our day. This is expressed well by Cal Thomas in a retort to Saudi Arabia's pseudo pro-Western stance:

> Since Saudi Arabia embraces the most extreme form of Islam known as Wahhabism, which dictates that you [Saudi Arabia]

support a worldwide Caliphate and the eradication of Israel and the extermination of Jews, have you received a recent revelation from your God ["Allah"] cancelling that mandate? Now Rex Tillerson [U.S. secretary of state] said that religion has nothing to do with terrorism; It has everything to do with terrorism, and if the media don't understand this, and they accept the [Saudi message given for Western consumption], when they say just the opposite to their own people, then they are falling for a very serious trick.[6]

This denial of the spiritual nature of the deception gripping the Middle East is the blind spot of our time. Be it the misapplication (Islamists, liberal Church) or the supposed irrelevance (by secularists) of the Abrahamic Covenant, both result in the same, fateful, two-fold deception that reigns in the Middle East today.

The Two-Fold Deception — Rejection of God's Chosen People and God's Chosen Land

When the Abrahamic Covenant is rejected, two logical steps follow:

1. Israel is NOT God's chosen people, and, therefore,

2. Israel has NO God-given right to the Land (properly, "Israel"; paganly, "Palestine").[7]

Yet the Bible declares in no uncertain terms that Israel is "the chosen" people of God:

> For you are a holy people to the LORD your God; the LORD your God has chosen you to be a people for His own possession out of all the peoples who are on the face of the earth. (Deuteronomy 7:6)[8]

When the Christian Bible is taken at its plainly stated word, the Jews are the "chosen" people of God. As such, they have been given the land of Israel forever. Consider the literal "eyeball" surveillance Abraham employed as he staked out the physical land in obedience to God's instructions. Did God promise the West Bank ("Palestinian territory") to Israel?

An Ancient Survey Based on Heaven's Instructions

The West Bank land (west of the Jordan River and the Dead Sea) was part of Jordan prior to 1967. In the 1967 War, Israel took control of the West Bank and East Jerusalem (the old city of biblical times). It was inhabited largely by Arabs as part of the kingdom of Jordan. Did the Jews illegally confiscate that now-famous "West Bank" land? Yes — according to the international community. But the Bible says something else!

> [Abram] went . . . to the place where his tent had been at the beginning, between Bethel and Ai. . . . The LORD said to Abram . . . "Now lift up your eyes and look from the place where you are, northward and southward and eastward and westward; for all the land which you see, I will give it to you and to your descendants forever (Genesis 13:2–15).

Abraham was standing between Bethel and Ai, in what today is the West Bank. He was told to look in all directions. The Lord said, ". . . all the land which you see, I will give it to you and to your descendants forever" (Genesis 13:15). These descendants of Abraham are specifically named through his son and grandson, Isaac and Jacob, who gave birth to the 12 tribes of the nation of Israel (Psalm 105:8–11).

How can any church body that claims to be a Bible-believing church or any Bible-believing Christian miss the significance of Genesis 13:14? Does the Lord's command to Abraham to stand on a piece of geographic landscape, to specifically plant his feet between Bethel and Ai, smack dab in the middle of today's West Bank area occupied by the Palestinians, and then to look in all directions to the four points of the compass — mean anything? If not, then welcome to your new membership in the "Replacement"[9] church camp.

But if so, welcome to the shrinking list of those who stand with Abraham, all the prophets and Apostles, and with the Lord Jesus Christ, who implied that, when He returns, He will identify geographic Israel by the "cities of Israel" that existed at His First Coming (Matthew 10:23). Those "cities of Israel" included Bethlehem and Jericho (Matthew 2:1, 20:29), considered Palestinian West Bank territory today.

Yes, take a trip to Israel today, stand between ancient Bethel and Ai (West Bank), look in all directions as far as you can see, and you will see Israel as God sees it. Neither the land — nor God's promises to Israel — have been replaced. The land promises are clear, made plain in many passages such as these:

- They will live on the land that I gave to Jacob My servant, in which your fathers lived; and they will live on it, they, and their sons, and their sons' sons, forever (Ezekiel 37:25).

- . . . dwell on the land which the Lord has given to you and your forefathers forever and ever (Jeremiah 25:5).

These verses and many more like them were part of the covenant given to Abraham, his son Isaac, and his son Jacob, from whom sprang the 12 tribes of Israel, the "chosen people."

Bible-believing Christians and Jews understand this. But the dark shroud of the Muslim religion rejects the "line" of Abraham, Isaac, and Jacob as God's chosen people and transfers the promises to Ishmael, another son of Abraham. Ishmael is the forefather of the Arab nations. With this deceptive backdrop, these Arab nations have been the age-long enemies of Israel. In their disbelief of the Bible, the Jews are not chosen, and Messiah doesn't come through the Jews.[10] To reject Israel as God's chosen people raises the call to "erase Israel from history," which in turn cries out "drive Israel into the sea" — all of which have inspired today's Hamas Charter.

Middle East Deception in Writing — The Hamas Charter

The so-called Hamas Charter (terrorist Muslims just south of Israel in the Gaza Strip) is the embodiment of the Arab-Muslim consensus of anti-Israel deception. Excerpts of the charter represent the heart of the entire Mideastern worldview regarding Israel. For instance:

The Covenant of the Islamic Resistance Movement[11] was issued on August 18, 1988. . . . It strives to raise the banner of Allah over every inch of Palestine. (Article 6)

Israel will exist and will continue to exist until Islam will obliterate it, just as it obliterated others before it. (Preamble) . . .

The land of Palestine is an Islamic Waqf [Holy Possession] (Article 11) . . .

The Day of Judgment will not come about until Moslems fight Jews and kill them. Then, the Jews will hide behind rocks and trees, and the rocks and trees will cry out: "O Moslem, there is a Jew hiding behind me, come and kill him." (Article 7)[12]

There has recently arisen a "revised" Hamas Charter. But it is simply a reworded version of the first one, which remains the "face" of the Middle Eastern stand against Israel.[13]

Middle East Deception in Writing — The Muslim Rewrite of Israel's History

The following article sums up the fanatical drive in the Mideast to revise the actual history of Israel with an "overwrite" that conforms to the Arab claim to the land of "Palestine."

Anything Goes: A Muslim Penchant for Rewriting History

UNESCO has joined up with Palestinian Arab biblical alterations. . . . The core of the conflict is Muslims' persistent efforts to delegitimize the Jewish State by denying Jewish historical existence in Israel, including Judea and Samaria, by rejecting well established facts, and by fighting any archeological attempt to unearth historical evidence linking Jewish life to the holy land.

Palestinian refusal to recognize Israel as a Jewish State is merely a derivative of their fabricated history, designed to establish their rights to the land while denying Israel's right to exist at the same time. . . .

Muslim believers and their children are brain-washed to deny any Jewish roots to "the land of the biblical Muslim ancestors."[14]

This pervasive spiritual darkness that promotes writing Israel out of history as God's chosen people with a claim to a chosen land is seen not only in the Mideast, but also worldwide.

International Deception in Writing — The Nations Rewrite Israel's History

The nations of the world are also complicit in the overwriting of history where it suits their political purposes. First up in the "delete" column is Israel. One prophecy teacher captures the heart of this history-erasure when he perceptively writes:

UNESCO [an arm of the United Nations, in a written resolution] declared that the State of Israel has no right to the city of Jerusalem, their own capital, and that the Jews have no connection to the Temple Mount and to the Western Wall. . . .

The world organization has consistently denied the 4000-year history of the Hebrew nation beginning with Abraham and continuing until now.[15]

"Christian" Deception in Writing — The Church Rewrites Israel's History

Rewriting Israel's history is found not only in the Mideast, but also in Western Replacement Theology, which is a synonym for a rewrite of history. Replacement Theology says that the Church since the days of Christ has inherited all of the Old Testament covenants and promises originally given to Israel, essentially "replacing" Israel, and spiritualizing Old Testament "Israel" to mean "Church."[16] This deception removes two-thirds of the Old Testament from the normal understanding of plain words, and reduces biblical prophecy to a playground for human imagination. Here is just an example of this widespread and growing, satanic-based deception that has arisen to support the "mistreated" Muslim world as they rewrite Israel's history (and the Bible) by writing Israel out of history and out of Bible prophecy.

Brian McLaren, the most influential writer of the Emerging Church Movement, declares,

> ". . . the need to confront the terrible, deadly, distorted, yet popular theologies associated with Christian Zionism and deterministic dispensationalism," which "use a bogus end-of-the-world scenario to create a kind of death-wish for World War III, which — unless it is confronted more robustly by the rest of us — could too easily create a self-fulfilling prophecy.

> "Anglican priest Stephen Sizer, whose church is a member of the Evangelical Alliance and the Willow Creek Association of Churches, summarizes his beliefs presented in Christian Zionism,

> " 'There has only ever been one people of God through history — "the Church"; All biblical covenants are subsumed under one covenant of grace; The Jewish people, as an ethnic nation, have fulfilled their role in history, which was to prepare the way for the Church/Christianity; The Church is the new Israel, enlarged through Christ to embrace all peoples. . . . Christian Zionism [is] biblically anathema to the Christian faith.' "[17]

Therefore, this worldwide spiritual darkness is found not only in the Mideast rewrite of Israeli history, but also in Western Replacement Theology, which itself is a rewrite of Israel's history.[18]

Though today's vast liberal church aids the anti-Israel agendas of the United Nations, the European Union, at times the United States, and all the nations by rejecting Israel's central role in Bible prophecy, there is One who cannot be moved: "I say then, God has not rejected [or replaced] His people [Israel], has He? . . . from the standpoint of God's choice they are beloved for the sake of the fathers [Abrahamic Covenant]; for the gifts and the calling of God are irrevocable" (Romans 11:1, 28–29).

The Christian Gospel — Referenced in the Land Promise

It's clear that the prophecies about Israel won't be rescripted so easily. When God gave Abraham additional detail on the Abrahamic Covenant in Genesis 15, it included the land promise, and Abraham is commended for believing God. The passage says this faith saved Abraham. The New Testament picks up on this and teaches that this is the same kind of faith that saves us when it is applied to Christ (Galatians 3:6–9). That is the gospel. Here is that original statement in Genesis 15:

> The Gospel Part: "Then he believed in the LORD; and He reckoned it to him as righteousness" (Genesis 15:6).

> The Land Promise Part: "And He said to him, 'I am the LORD who brought you out of Ur of the Chaldeans, to give you this land to possess it' " (Genesis 15:7).

> The gospel that saves and the land promise to Israel are linked in the same passage! They stand or fall together.[19]

Thus, the promise to the Jews that they would possess the land of Israel cannot be so easily dismissed in view of the fact that it is linked directly to the gospel in Genesis 15:6–7. Nor can the 1948 rebirth of national Israel in their ancient homeland be denied as a modern-day fulfillment of Bible prophecy. Both facts expose the lie of Mideast deception. Long before 1948, fervent Bible students saw the return of the Jews to the land of Israel coming. They took the Scripture at its literal word, in spite of the divergent headlines of their day. They persisted in their understanding that the Bible declares the Jewish people would one day be brought back to the land of Israel. For example:[20]

> 1669 "The Jews would return to their homeland before their spiritual conversion just before the Second Coming of Jesus Christ."
> — Increase Mather, *The Mystery of Israel's Salvation*, 1669

1860s "But His [Jesus'] answer implies that when the fullness of time was come, national supremacy should be again restored to Israel." — Bishop Edward Henry Bickersteth on Acts 1:6, *The Holy Bible, With a Devotional and Practical Commentary,* by the Rev. R. Jamieson and the Rev. E.H. Bickersteth, London: 1861–65

1864 "The predictions of their restoration are in words as definite only not yet fulfilled. But one closing act . . . is yet wanting to complete the whole. Their restoration is predicted and demanded. Who will stretch out his hand to move the scene and call forth the actors?" — Dr. John Cumming, *The Destiny of Nations,* 1864

1866 "The personal coming of Christ will not take place until the Jews are restored to their own land!" — James Grant, *The End of Things,* 1866

1870s "We cannot help looking for the restoration of the scattered Israelites to the land which God has given to them by a covenant . . . we also look for the time when they shall believe in the Messiah whom they have rejected." — Charles Spurgeon, Quoted in *The Levitt Letter,* January 2013, p. 4–5

1870s "Search it with an honest determination to put a literal meaning on its prophetical portions, and to reject traditional interpretation, and the difficulty will vanish away. . . . Cultivate the habit of reading prophecy with a single eye to the literal meaning of its proper names. Cast aside the traditional idea that Jacob, and Israel, and Judah, and Jerusalem, and Zion must always mean the Gentile Church, and that predictions about the second Advent are to be taken spiritually, and first Advent predictions literally. Be just, and honest, and fair. If you expect the Jews to take the 53rd of Isaiah literally, be sure you take the 54th and 60th and 62nd literally also." — Bishop J.C. Ryle (1870?)

Even the Muslim Quran says the land of Israel was given by God to the Jews:

Bear in mind the words of Moses to his people. He said:

Remember, my people, the favours which Allah has bestowed upon you. He has raised up prophets among you, made you kings, and given you that which He has given to no other nation.

Enter, my people, the holy land which Allah has assigned you. Do not turn back, or you shall be ruined. (Surah 5:20–24).[21]

The facts of Israel's history cannot be reduced to current Islamic diatribe. Some of today's best Islamic scholars occasionally emerge to proclaim the plain meaning of the above passage. Here, the reader will be rewarded to read their quotes in the endnote on this subject.[22]

The Nehemiah Expose

Still, denial and deception continue to accelerate into our day. The latter-day Mideast meltdown is now the new normal. This prompts today's liberal church to denounce Israel as "occupiers" of "Palestine," bemoan the Arabs as victims of Jewish racism, and condemn the "politics of apartheid."[23] The effect is that the Western church has provided both Islam and the Middle East church with a pseudo-moralistic high ground.

But that same liberal church will break out its Sunday school quarterly and recite stories and verses that celebrate the righteous faith of the Jews who returned to the land of Israel from Babylon under Ezra and Nehemiah. What is amazingly hypocritical about this? Those fifth-century B.C. Jews also resettled their land in "settlements," faced the same hatred, endured the same persecution, and struggled against the same land occupiers that modern Jews have faced since they returned in 1948.

Yes, violent opposition to the return of Israel to its land has happened before. But the liberal Church celebrates *that* return of Israel from exile in Babylon and their resettlement of the land of Israel. The parallels of Israel-then and Israel-today is instructive.

THEN: Prophecy of the first return of the Jews to the Land of Israel — "When the LORD will have compassion on Jacob and again choose Israel, and settle them in their own land" (Isaiah 14:1; also see Jeremiah 29:10; fulfilled 536 B.C. to 444 B.C.).

TODAY: Prophecy of today's return of the Jews to the land of Israel — "For I will take you from the nations, gather you from all the lands and bring you into your own land" (Ezekiel 36:24; fulfillment in 1948 and continuing).

THEN: Opposition to the first return of the Jews to the land of Israel — "Now when [the Samaritans], the Arabs, the Ammonites, and the Ashdodites [occupiers of the vacant land of the absentee Jews during their exile years in Babylonian captivity] heard that the repair of the walls of

Jerusalem [by the returning Jews] went on . . . they were very angry. All of them conspired together to come and fight against Jerusalem and to cause a disturbance in it" (Nehemiah 4:7–8).

> Joining Sanballat and the Samaritans from the NORTH, Tobiah and the Ammonites from the EAST, Gashed and the Arabs from the SOUTH, were men from Ashdod, a Philistine city, from the WEST. They all plotted together to attack Jerusalem, apparently from all sides.[24] (emphasis added)

TODAY: Opposition to today's return of the Jews to the land of Israel — Palestinians are the poster people for land rights to Israel. They are supported by the Muslim nations, the United Nations, the European Union, at times the United States, and by a large segment of mainline churches.

For example, this report from *The Times of Israel*, Thursday, July 30, 2015:

> The European Union, United Nations and others [and recent U.S. stated policy] panned the Israeli government for green-lighting construction projects in the West Bank settlement of Beit El and Jewish neighborhoods in Jerusalem beyond the 1967 Green Line boundary. [The U.N. Response]: "We urge the government of Israel to urgently reverse recent decisions and put an end to settlement expansion."[25]

Look at the two prophecies above in light of today's events. Today is not the first time in history that the Jews have returned to the land of Israel. Nor is today the first time in history that there has been fierce opposition to the Jewish return to the land of Israel. We see the fulfillment of God's prophecy — and thus God's will — when we consider that, in both cases:

1) God decreed the Jews would be expelled from the land.
2) God decreed that He would return the Jews to "their/His" land.
3) God brought the Jews back to "settle" their land amid much opposition from the succeeding occupants.

Today's parade of headlines touting opposition to an expanding Jewish settlement of the land highlights it as a "trend" sign proving that God is fulfilling His Word to return the Jews to their ancient homeland in the last days (Ezekiel 36:24), just as He fulfilled His Word in that first return to that same land over 2,400 years ago.

TODAY'S CHURCH CELEBRATES THIS ↓...so...➡➡		WHY DOES TODAY'S CHURCH OPPOSE THIS?	
IN DAYS OF NEHEMIAH "Faith & Courage"		TODAY "a Zionists, illegal land grab"	
Jewish Nation in Land of Israel	1406-586 BC	Jewish Nation in Land of Israel	536 BC-70 AD
Prophecy of Exile	Eze. 12:11-13	Prophecy of Exile	Luke 21:24
Fulfillment of Exile	586-516 BC	Fulfillment of Exile	70 AD-1948
Prophecy of Return	Jer. 29:10	Prophecy of Return	Eze. 36:24
Fulfillment of Return	536-444 BC	Fulfillment of Return	1948-Today
"Settlements " (homes, cities, etc.)	"settle" them in land", Isa. 14.1	"Settlements " (homes, cities, etc.)	Hos. 11:10-11 & Today's news
Opposition to Return	Neh. 4:7-8	Opposition to Return	Today's news

A chart showing on the left the return of the Jews to their land in the days of Ezra and Nehemiah, rightly celebrated from the pulpits of today's liberal church. On the right is the same set of events related to Israel's return to the land today. Since the liberal church has replaced Israel with itself in biblical prophecy, it is in the hypocritical position of condemning Israel today (R) while praising Israel in Nehemiah's day (L) for their resettlement of the land.

This absurd double standard in the liberal church calls for the question: Who among today's church bodies would vote to punish Nehemiah's Israel through economic divestment, and condemn Ezra's and Nehemiah's return to the land of Israel in obedience to God and in fulfillment of His prophecies? Those Jews returned to an occupied and resistant land. Jewish "settlements"? They built them, too!

Nehemiah's God Has Acted Again — Today!

The *same God* has also prophesied today's return to the land (Isaiah 11:11, 43:5–6). That prophecy, too, anticipates Jews returning to an occupied land — this time occupied for over 1,800 years (A.D. 70–1948), inhabited with long-existing Arab houses, farms, and cities. Yet today many church denominations denounce the Jewish "settlements." Didn't God say that *"settlements"* are necessary when He said He will *settle* them in their own land (prophesied both then, e.g., Isaiah 14:1, the return in 444 B.C.; and today, Ezekiel 37:14, NIV, emphasis added). Meanwhile, the hypocrisy within the Church reveals itself when it decrees policies of economic divestiture to punish Israel.

We should celebrate God's fulfillment of His prophetic Word, not resist it in the name of "land-squatting rights" or "political correctness," etc. The same God who fulfilled His promise to twice return Israel to her land also gave us John 3:16 and its promise of salvation to all who believe in Jesus Christ. Both are promises. How can we hold to the one and deny the other?

Proof Israel Is the Chosen People in a Chosen Land

What is the evidence that the Middle East deception is actually that — deception? There are two proofs that the Middle East is wrong — and not just wrong, but in the dark regarding Israel as God's chosen people, and thus Israel's right to the chosen land. The first proof considers the Bible's Messianic teachings. The Messiah is always connected to the land. Messiah will return to the land. He will reign from the land. Messiah will reign over the land (and the whole world).[26] Since Jesus is the Messiah, let us listen to Him:

1. Jesus read the Bible literally, proven by His statement concerning fulfilled and understandable prophecy in Luke 24:27 and 45 (the First-Advent Messianic prophecies had a literal fulfillment, which made them recognizable, and thus understandable).

2. Jesus refers us to "all that the prophets have spoken" (Luke 24:25).

3. Jesus said, "all things which are written about Me" in the Old Testament will be fulfilled (Luke 24:44).

4. In the chronology of those prophecies "written about Me," the Jews are *in the land* of Israel *before* Messiah Jesus returns (Zechariah 12:1–10).

5. Matthew 24:15–21 shows that the Jews are *in the land* of Israel at least three and one-half years *before* Jesus returns.

6. Daniel 9:27 places the Jews *in the Land* of Israel as a political entity capable of being the primary signatory to an international covenant at least seven years *before* Jesus returns.

7. Therefore, taking our cue from Jesus, among "all things which are written about Me," is the fact that the Jews were predicted to "settle" into the land of Israel sometime *well before the return of Jesus*, with "all things which are written about Me" to be fulfilled as the will of God.

The very words of Jesus expose the Middle East denunciation of Israel's right to the land of Israel as a willful delusion. The Light of the world Himself is "a lamp shining in a dark place" on this subject (2 Peter 1:19).

The second proof that exposes the Middle East deception about Israel is the fact that the hand of God has moved in real time like a "wall of fire from Heaven"[27] to both settle and secure Israel in her land. This is an acknowledged fact among Bible-believing scholars, who preach and proclaim the "miracle wars" in Israel's string of victories in the Arab-Israeli wars of 1948, 1956, 1967, 1973, and continuing unto today. Read the story of the miracle wars:

> When analyzing Israel's recent history, we cannot but come to the conclusion that a higher power was involved: The God of Israel . . . Israel [by 1956], it can be said, miraculously developed into a power to be reckoned with in the Middle East. . . . The victory of the Six-Day War [1967] was nothing short of a miracle. — Arno Froese, "The Six-Day War," *Midnight Call*[28]

> The modern history of Israel has been one of constant struggle and miraculous interventions. Against all odds, Israel won the War of Independence [1948] when she was attacked by the combined armies of Egypt, Syria, Saudi Arabia, Lebanon, and Iraq. In 1967, Israel won a stunning military victory over Egypt, Syria, and Jordan in the Six-Day War, recapturing the city of Jerusalem for the first time since the Roman era. In 1973, Israel again was victorious in the three-week-long Yom Kippur War. . . . Scripture proclaims that Israel's future is securely in the hands of God. — Ed Hindson and Thomas Ice, *Charting the Bible Chronologically*[29]

> Against impossible odds, and following 5 wars of aggression against it, the nation survived. One has to call these wars, "miracle wars." God spared His own!... Throughout it all, Israel survived and even prospered. How can this not be the hand of the God of Abraham, Isaac, and Jacob? — Mal Couch, *Revelation Hoofbeats*, Ron J. Bigalke, ed.[30]

God demonstrated to the Middle Eastern nations His wall of security around Israel through multiple miracle wars. The Israel-Arab wars of 1948, 1956, 1967, 1973, and continuing proved the reality of Israel's miracle-war security.

Ezekiel 38:8 says Israel would be "restored from the sword" after 1,900 years of captivity, and God did in 1948. Ezekiel says God would bring the Jews to the "mountains of Israel" where "old" Jerusalem is located, and God did in 1967. Ezekiel says God would bring Jews out of many nations to Israel, and God did, and continues. Then Ezekiel adds a fourth act of God to the list in verse 8: Israel would *at that time* be "living securely." Would God provide the first four conditions, but not this one? Would God return Israel to their land — after 1,900 years — and then say, "You're on your own now"? How absurd! Israel has had miracle-war security since 1948. Randall Price describes how this applies today:

> The people and land of Israel, at the time of [Ezekiel 38:8], are described as those who have been "gathered from many nations" to a land described as having previously "been a continual waste." This land is "now inhabited," was "restored from the sword [foreign domination]," and is now "living securely" (vv. 11, 14) with enviable economic resources (v. 12–13).
>
> All these conditions describe the present state of Israel since 1967 when it occupied the "mountains of Israel" (v. 8, 21, 39:2–3, 17–19).[31]

Would we expect any less from the God who said Israel will last as long as the sun, moon, and stars remain (Jeremiah 31:35–36)?

This "miracle-war security" is God's real-time, hard-copy, sign-to-the-nations "wall of fire" protecting Israel from defeat, destruction, or conquest (Zechariah 2:5). This is the same divine brand of security Israel has had throughout her history, and that which Ezekiel 38:8 prophesied would exist when Israel was miraculously restored to her ancestral land — the physical "mountains of Israel." These miracle wars are actually the proof of Israel's supernatural security. And the supernatural security is the proof of Israel's God-given deed to the land. Today's Middle East deception stands exposed before the throne of heaven in the light of Israel's God-given miracle-war security. The "wall of fire from heaven" is proof that is hard to deny!

Amazingly, the updated, downgraded, humanistic church aids and abets the Middle East deception by declaring Israel's return to the land — wars and all — to be no more than an accident of history. But more amazing is the blind spot even many Bible-believing churches have today to Israel's miracle-war security. Most will excitedly affirm and agree about the "miracle war" part. They fervently preach and proclaim Israel's miraculous victories through its wars against overwhelming Arab forces. But they go blank on the "security" part. They can't see the link between "miracle wars" and "supernatural security," or even agree with the concept of miracle-war security.[32]

As a result, even many Bible-believing churches unwittingly obscure this proof of the glory of God over His people Israel through miracle-war security and its exposé of Middle East deception. Some of them inadvertently advance the denial of Israel as God's chosen people when they sever the miracle wars from the biblical teaching of miracle-war security, and then go silent on God's protective hand over Israel today! They, too, have rewritten Israel's recent history by assigning the events since 1948 to the inconsequential footnotes of history. In so doing, they sideline the "for-all-the-world-to-see" proof of Middle East deception. Yet the question of whose side of the issue God is on according to divine revelation is hammered into history by the stubborn *fact* of Israel's miracle-war security.

Let's examine this difficulty of seeing Israel "living securely" today as prophesied in Ezekiel 38:8–11.

The issue: Since Israel has endured wars and threats and is forced by sworn-enemy states to assume an "armed-camp" state of readiness, how can Israel be "secure" and "at rest" TODAY? Is that really the security anticipated by Ezekiel 38:8 for today? The answer is yes! And the evidence for that is embedded in Israel's history as reported by the biblical prophets. Four examples bear this out, as follow:

1. *During the Exodus*: Israel was "secure" while engaged in multiple wars.
   Today: Israel is in the same condition.
2. *During the Judges*: Israel experienced periods of "rest" while enduring threats and oppression.
   Today: Israel is in the same condition.
3. *During the Reign of Asa*: Israel was "at rest" while maintaining an "armed-camp" state of readiness.
   Today: Israel is in the same condition.
4. *During the Reign of Solomon*: Israel was "secure" while enduring intense border conflict.
   Today: Israel is in the same condition.

Critical to this point is the fact that each of the four conditions of "security" and "at rest" above use the very same words that are found in Ezekiel 38:8–11: "security" is the Hebrew *betach*; "at rest" is the Hebrew *shaqat*.

Let's consider these four biblical-historical conditions for Israel one by one, as they provide an answer for each of the supposed reasons that Israel cannot possibly be secure today.

How can Israel be secure while experiencing *multiple wars*? The answer is found in the Exodus:

> He led them safely [*betach* / "securely"] . . . but the sea engulfed their enemies (Psalm 78:53–54, which refers to the entire Exodus event).[33]

Since the Israelites enjoyed a God-given "[*betach*] secure" condition while enduring the Red Sea entrapment and attack of the Egyptians, and a 40-year Exodus journey marked by six subsequent wars with the Amalekites, Canaanites, Amorites, and Midianites (Psalm 78:51–54; Numbers 14; 21; 31), then the same could be true of the "[*betach*] secure" condition of Israel in the Magog passage of Ezekiel 38:8.

How can Israel be "at rest" while enduring *war after war*? The answer is found in the time of the judges:

> So Moab was subdued . . . under the hand of Israel. And the land was undisturbed [*shaqat* / "rest"] for eighty years (Judges 3:30).

Since the "[*shaqat*] rest" periods of the judges experienced an overlap of periods of oppression, resulting in rest periods marked by the shadow of war (all major chronologies of Judges concede this overlap of rest and oppression periods),[34] then the same could be true of the "[*shaqat*] rest" condition of Israel in the Magog passage of Ezekiel 38:11.

> How can Israel be "at rest" while under a *state of war*? How can Israel be "an *armed camp*" and "at rest" at the same time? The answers are found in the time of King Asa.
>
> The land was undisturbed (*shaqat* / "rest") for ten years during [Asa's] days . . . and there was no one at war with him. . . .
>
> Now there was war between Asa and Baasha king of Israel all their days (1 Kings 15:16, 32).
>
> ...and he built fortified cities...since the land was undisturbed [*shaqat* / "rest"]...gates and bars...[a huge] army (2 Chronicles 14:1–8)

Since the "[*shaqat*] rest" period of Asa was marked by some degree of external enemy border war or cold war (i.e., "war between

Asa and Baasha king of Israel *all their days*; i.e., threats, harassment, and political, economic, or military opposition"),[35] and since there was a massive "armed camp" buildup by Asa during that "[*shaqat*] rest" period (1 Kings 15:16, 32; 2 Chronicles 14:1–8),[36] then the same could be true of the "[*shaqat*] rest" experience of Israel in the Magog passage of Ezekiel 38:11.[37]

How can Israel be "secure" amid constant border conflict with enemy nations? The answer is found in the reign of Solomon:

So Judah and Israel lived in safety [security] . . . all the days of Solomon (1 Kings 4:25).

Rezon. . . . was an adversary to Israel all the days of Solomon, along with the evil that Hadad [Edom] did (1 Kings 11:23–25).

Since the "[*betach*] secure" period that existed *during* "all the days of Solomon" experienced military opposition from enemy states *during* "all the days of Solomon" (1 Kings 4:25 and11:23–25),[38] then the same could be true of the "[*betach*] secure" status of Israel in the Magog passage of Ezekiel 38:8.

The four biblical examples in the chart on the following page provide a solid rationale that *today*:

1. Israel has been under *betach* security since 1948, protected through multiple miracle wars (Exodus example) from the brink of annihilation amid the ongoing shadow of enemy terrorist states (Solomon example).
2. Israel has experienced a series of *shaqat* rests between these wars at a level that has permitted Israel to fortify as an "armed camp" (Asa example) and become a world-class, socioeconomic superstate while under the ever-present shadow (Judges example) of another war.

"Secure" and "at rest" today, Israel awaits its date with glory in the Magog invasion of Ezekiel 38–39. Therefore, the security of Israel today is a sign of the imminent fulfillment of Ezekiel 38.

Let the reader note that we have not given an assessment of current affairs here, but rather, we have given an assessment of the words of Scripture. Scripture often runs contrary to the "current" of current affairs. Yet we cannot be detracted from the anchor of Bible prophecy by

Israel: Secure & at Rest, then & today   SUMMARY GRAPH

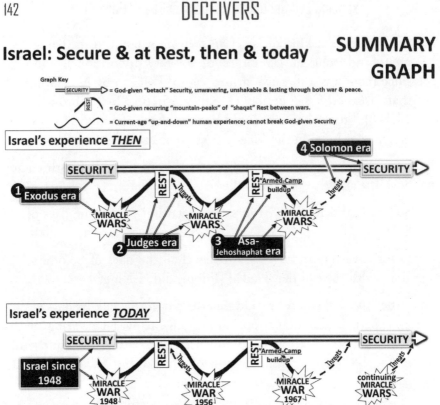

Graph Key

≡≡SECURITY≡≡▷ = God-given "betach" Security, unwavering, unshakable & lasting through both war & peace.

= God-given recurring "mountain-peaks" of "shaqat" Rest between wars.

= Current-age "up-and-down" human experience; cannot break God-given Security

Israel's experience *THEN*

Israel's experience *TODAY*

Four eras of Israel's history where the Bible says that Israel was "secure" and/ or "at rest" while experiencing wars, threats, and oppression. The same Hebrew words describe Israel in the last days in Ezekiel 38:8–11. This shows that Israel today, while in a "secure, at rest" state, could be simultaneously experiencing wars, threats, and oppression.

the winds of current events. Current-event headlines will be drawn, like iron shavings are drawn to a magnet, in the direction of Bible prophecy by the power of prophetic fulfillment ("Truly I have spoken. . . . surely I will do it," Isaiah 46:11).[39]

The Coming "Magog Coalition" — Another Miracle-War Victim

That being the case, let's take a closer look at Ezekiel 38 and 39. This is the "Magog coalition" and the prophecy of its end-time invasion of Israel. Known popularly, but accurately, as the Russian-Islamic invasion of Israel, this prophecy outlines the details of this still-future event. It is the ultimate miracle-war security event. Every sign indicates that it is an imminent event. Every headline shows that the political, media, social, and religious leaders of the world are blinded by their ignorance of this biblical prophecy. The whole world, then, is in the dark about the true nature of events just north of Israel. Here is a summary Scripture of the long and detailed Ezekiel 38–39 prophecy:

> And the word of the LORD came to me saying, "Son of man, set your face toward Gog of the land of Magog, the prince of Rosh, Meshech, and Tubal, and prophesy against him, and say, 'Thus says the Lord GOD, "Behold, I am against you, O Gog, prince of Rosh, Meshech, and Tubal. And I will turn you about, and put hooks into your jaws, and I will bring you out, and all your army, horses and horsemen, all of them splendidly attired, a great company with buckler and shield, all of them wielding swords; Persia, Ethiopia, and Put with them, all of them with shield and helmet; Gomer with all its troops; Beth-togarmah from the remote parts of the north with all its troops — many peoples with you.
>
> Be prepared, and prepare yourself, you and all your companies that are assembled about you, and be a guard for them. After many days you will be summoned; in the latter years you will come into the land that is restored from the sword, whose inhabitants have been gathered from many nations to the mountains of Israel which had been a continual waste; but its people were brought out from the nations, and they are living securely, all of them. You will go up, you will come like a storm; you will be like a cloud covering the land, you and all your troops, and many peoples with you (Ezekiel 38:1–9).
>
> "You will fall on the mountains of Israel, you and all your troops, and the peoples who are with you . . ." (Ezekiel 39:4).
>
> "My holy name I shall make known in the midst of My people Israel. . . . And the nations will know that I am the LORD, the Holy One in Israel" (Ezekiel 39:7).

Now, let's condense this Scripture into a summary statement of these momentous, soon-to-be events: In the latter years, Israel will be supernaturally rescued from the massive invasion of the Magog coalition in an event that will magnify God's name across the world.

Next, let's break the statement down into its major points: when, where, what, who, and why. This will give us a "bird's-eye" view of the prophecy:

WHEN: In the latter years
WHERE: Israel
WHAT: will be supernaturally rescued from the massive invasion of
WHO: the Magog coalition
WHY: in an event that will magnify God's name across the world.

Further, we need to identify the "who" of the Magog coalition:[40]

1. Russia: land of Magog; Rosh
2. Iran: Persia
3. Turkey: Beth-Togarmah; Gomer; Meshech; Tubal
4. Libya: Put
5. Ethiopia/Sudan: Ethiopia
6. the "-stans" (lands): former Russian Republics, Kazakhstan, Tajikistan, etc.

Finally, let us be reminded of our earlier review of Israel's current, God-given miracle-war security, for it is here that we find the two keys to the *timing* of the Russian-Islamic invasion of Israel in these last days in which we live.

1. Ezekiel 38:8: "After many days you will be summoned [to Israel] . . . they are living securely [Hebrew, *betach*], all of them."

This is current-age, God-given *security* (*betach*), a guarantee of divine safekeeping/preservation extending over times of both war and peace. As shown earlier, Israel has been in that situation before, as documented in her biblical history, and Israel is in that condition today.

2. Ezekiel 38:11: "And you will say . . . I will go against those who are at rest [Hebrew, *shaqat*], that live securely."

This is current-age, God-given *rest* (*shaqat*), the "mountain peaks" of *security* (*betach*) that exists between wars, sometimes marked by threats, harassment, oppression, or attacks — and resultant military, armed-camp preparedness. As discussed earlier, Israel has been in that situation before in her biblical history, and is in that condition today.

When, then, will Magog invade Israel? By the criteria not of the breaking news, but of the pages of the Bible itself, modern-day Israel is living in miracle-war security — just as it was in the days of the Exodus, the judges, the early Judean kings, and King Solomon. This miracle-war security has existed since 1948. In addition, the coming invasion against "the mountains of Israel" (Ezekiel 39:2) became possible only since 1967 when Israel captured the mountains on which Jerusalem sits in the Six-Day (miracle) War.

Today, world leaders are deceived by the false prophets of both the East and the West who bluster in harmony that Israel is an illegal intruder in the Holy Land. The Israeli miracle wars of the past 70 years have not persuaded darkened minds that God has declared His hand in the Middle East. These world leaders have no concept of a great prophecy-in-waiting (Ezekiel 38–39). Right before their blind eyes, the Magog coalition has every appearance of mounting the world stage.

The "Magog-Coalition" Will Invade from the North

Scripture is clear that the Russian-Islamic invasion of Israel will come from the North (Ezekiel 38:15).[41] It will involve an air assault "like a cloud" (Ezekiel 38:9), as well as a massive enemy ground force "on the mountains of Israel" (Ezekiel 39:4). Ground troops, in order to come from the north into Israel, must launch their attack out of Syria and Lebanon. Russia will be allied with Iran (Persia) among others as the chief instigator of the invasion. Today, Russia "owns" Syria in that country's civil war, and is firmly planted in Syria, directly *north* of Israel.

Despite Russian President Vladimir Putin's recent order to reduce Moscow's military forces in Syria, two U.S. officials say the opposite is taking place.[42]

The scale and apparent permanence of the massive buildup of the Russian military presence in Syria is detailed in the following report:

Russia's Military in Syria: Bigger Than You Think and Not Going Anywhere

CNN traveled with Russian troops in Syria. The trip demonstrates Moscow's military muscle in the country . . . the Russian military brought more than a hundred international journalists, including our CNN crew, to Palmyra. The trip . . . said a lot about the Russian army's capabilities and the scale of their assets in Syria.

. . . [We saw] at least eight armored vehicles with heavy machine guns, two fighting vehicles and the constant presence of two attack helicopters hovering overhead . . . choppers were switched out several times and the vehicles were shadowed by a variety of gunships, including Mi-28, KA-52, and the modernized Mi-35s. As we made our way across Syria we passed several bases with Russian helicopters along the Western coastline. . . .

Russia [has] deployed dozens of strike aircraft and jet fighters to Syria. . . . Moscow also appears to have built up substantial ground forces in various locations in Syria . . . there were at least several thousand troops on the ground along with modern weaponry and infrastructure. The Hmeymim air base on the outskirts of Latakia . . . is large, modern, and well-maintained.

What's in Russia's military arsenal? . . . Aside from dozens of jets, Russia also has a wide range of combat helicopters, main battle tanks, armored personnel carriers and surface-to-air missile systems. . . . But the biggest surprise was seeing so many Russian ground forces in other places in Syria as well . . . there also are dozens of fighting vehicles and armored personnel carriers stationed at the base. . . . Russia has also deployed a state-of-the-art Pantsir-S1 air defense system that can both launch missiles and fire cannons at incoming planes. . . .

While the exact size of Russia's military presence in Syria is still unclear, the things we saw while embedded with them indicate that it is bigger and more sophisticated than most believe. It does not look like an army that plans on leaving Syria any time soon.[43]

Today, Iran (Persia) is also on the ground directly north of Israel. Iran has created an "arc of influence" rooted in the turf of both Syria and Lebanon. Reuters reports this startling development:

For the first time, Tehran could exert authority over a vast sweep of the Middle East extending through Iraq and Syria into Lebanon — an arc of influence that Sunni Arab powers, particularly Saudi Arabia, have been warning about for years. . . . It would also present a military threat to Israel, through Syria and Lebanon.[44]

Iran's Shia army would extend its arc of influence by implanting forces to "secure ground routes across Iraq and Syria," spanning the entire region north and west of Israel "from Tehran to Beirut."[45] Iran is on a fast track to becoming the powerful Persia portrayed in Ezekiel (as well as Daniel and Revelation)[46] as it nears its goal to build a deliverable nuclear weapon.

Furthermore, Iran (along with Russia and other leader-nations named in Ezekiel 38:1–7), is arming the Lebanese Hezbollah, one of a number of follower nations immediately surrounding Israel not specifically named in Ezekiel 38. These follower nations would undoubtedly participate in the Russian-Islamic invasion of Israel. One report says:

> A leading article published in a Beirut newspaper known for its close ties to Hezbollah has stated baldly that the Lebanese Shia terrorist organization is now being deployed by its Iranian paymasters across the Middle East, warning that Israel can expect "the rain of rockets that will fall in the midst of summer."[47]

A listing of these follower nations, referred to as "many peoples with you" in Ezekiel 38:6 and 9, can be found among those nations that surround Israel listed in Psalm 83:6–8, which would be expected since these nations, along with all of the others listed in Ezekiel besides Russia, are Islamic. Would we expect the "many peoples [nations] with you" to be Finland, Switzerland, or perhaps Brazil? Much more in line with the historic regional hatred that surrounds Israel, they would be the Muslim nations listed in Psalm 83 that continue to surround Israel today. These follower nations will be under the command of leader nations like Persia (Iran).

The threat of Iran to the "north" is such that Israeli President Reuven Rivlin issued the startling warning that "under no circumstances will we allow the establishment of Iranian outposts on our borders. The nations of the world must recognize what is happening and understand the possible consequences."[48]

While the Syrian-Lebanese northern territory is gaining traction as a Magog-Persian military staging platform, the bright spot is the political about-face the United States "seems" (yet to be proven) to have made toward Israel. In a promising upgrade to U.S.-Israeli relations during his state visit to Israel, President Trump made some biblically relevant statements, including the following:

1. About the Jewish people:

    I stand in awe of the accomplishments of the Jewish People, and I make this promise to you: My Administration will always stand with Israel.

2. About Jerusalem:

    Jerusalem is a sacred city. Its beauty, splendor, and heritage are like no other place on earth. What a heritage. The ties of the Jewish people to this Holy Land are ancient and eternal. They date back thousands of years, including the reign of King David whose star now flies proudly on Israel's white and blue flag.

3. About the Temple:

I visited the Western Wall, and marveled at the monument to God's presence and man's perseverance. I was humbled to place my hand upon the wall and to pray in that holy space for wisdom from God.

4. About the Resurrection site of the Savior of the world:

I also visited and prayed at the Church of the Holy Sepulcher, a site revered by Christians throughout the world.[49]

Expressing the hope that the United States has had a genuine turn-about, Israeli President Benjamin Netanyahu excitedly proclaimed in three words, "America is back!"[50]

Could America be in the God-ordained role of a "watchman on the wall"?

On your walls, O Jerusalem, I have appointed watchmen; all day and all night they will never keep silent. You who remind the LORD, take no rest for yourselves; and give Him no rest until He establishes and makes Jerusalem a praise in the earth (Isaiah 62:6–7).

If the United States, which drifted far too close to the "curse" side of the Abrahamic Covenant, continues the course of returning to the "blessing" side of that Covenant (Genesis 12:3), then the promise for this country looks good, according to Jeremiah 18:7–8:

At one moment I might speak concerning a nation or concerning a kingdom to uproot, to pull down, or to destroy it; if that nation against which I have spoken turns from its evil, I will relent concerning the calamity I planned to bring on it (Jeremiah 18:7–8).[51]

Meanwhile, Israel will soon enter an even greater miracle-war security epoch when the Magog coalition implodes on its "mountains" under the "wall of fire from heaven." The Middle East, reveling in its own deception, continues to dwell in the dark. Where, then, does the Bible-believing Church fit in? Turn on the Light! Jesus saves! And thus it is happening, for reports are that not only is Israel living today in miracle-war security, but millions of Muslims are finding Christ in a miracle war against darkness through an eternal relationship with the Light of the World, Jesus Christ.[52] Read this endnote and see how you can enter this eternal relationship with Jesus Christ, the Son of God![53]

We started out with the simple but profound truth behind the deception that blinds the Middle East and its partners in the secular, religious, and political world. In summary, the Mideast and the world have rejected Jesus Christ as the Light of the World. This has led to their rejection of the Abrahamic Covenant as it relates to Israel. This in turn has led to the denial of Israel as God's chosen people. At this point, the next denial comes easily: Israel has no God-given right to the land of "Palestine." Advancing this delusion, the Islamic and pseudo-Christian religions of the East stand in harmony with the Western liberal church that Israel has no God-ordained future. Israel was "replaced" before it ever got started, according to Islam, by the line of Ishmael. Israel was replaced through its unbelief, according to the liberal Western church, by the liberal Western church. Both ignore the testimony of Jesus and the miracle wars of God, which prove that Israel is in its Promised Land as God's chosen people. Bible-believing churches, by their silence, are becoming carelessly complicit in this.[54] Deception, indeed!

But through the light of Bible prophecy, God has already spoken the last word. When Jesus returns to the earth, He will set His foot down not in Egypt, Iran, or Syria, but in the land of Israel — specifically, on the Mount of Olives in Jerusalem (Zechariah 14:4). And who is living in that land today? The Jews, in fulfillment of Bible prophecy. Jesus' first order of business? "All Israel will be saved" (Romans 11:26)!

This ought to tell us something about the depth of the deception in the Middle East today. But it also reveals the ultimate truth about God's "wall of fire from Heaven" safeguard of Israel. Praise God for light and truth and life in Jesus Christ, our safeguard!

Endnotes

1. Scripture in this chapter is from the New American Standard Bible (NASB).
2. Satan's original four-point lie in Genesis 3:1–5 can be paraphrased as such: 1) Your Bible is questionable; 2) death and judgment are an illusion; 3) your inner-eye is your guide to truth; and 4) since your inner-self is God-like, you decide right or wrong, truth, or error.
3. All three major religions whose roots are in the Mideast — Christian, Jew, Muslim — see the coming of a Messiah. The deception is that Jesus is rejected as that Messiah by Jews and Muslims. But the Bible runs a clear genealogical tracer

on Messiah. This literary-DNA-track shows the Messiah would come from the family of Abraham, Isaac, and Jacob (the Jews) — i.e., the 12 tribes of Israel — specifically, the tribe of Judah. This eliminates both the Arabs (descendants of Ishmael, not Isaac), and the Muslims (having no basis in the Jews; "Salvation is from the Jews" — Jesus, John 4:22) as the source of the prophesied Messiah. Jesus, a Jew, fulfilled the Jewish prophecies and founded the Christian Church.

4. For instance, Surah 5:71–75, "The Messiah, the son of Mary, was no more than an apostle." *The Koran*, translator N.J. Dawood (Middlesex, England: Penguin Books, 1974).

5. Tim LaHaye and Ed Hindson, *The Popular Encyclopedia of Bible Prophecy* (Eugene, OR: Harvest House Publishers, 2004), p. 8.

6. Cal Thomas, as quoted on Fox News, "Happening Now," May 26, 2017.

7. In A.D. 135, Roman emperor Hadrian renamed Israel "Palestine" (Latin for "Philistine") after Israel's perennial enemy.

8. The unconditional nature of the promises given to Abraham (the Abrahamic Covenant) can be seen in such passages as Psalm 105:9–10, "The covenant which He made with Abraham. . . . To Israel as an everlasting covenant"; Jeremiah 25:5, "the land which the LORD has given to you and your forefathers forever and ever"; and Ezekiel 37:25 "And they will live on the land that I gave to Jacob . . . they, and their sons, and their sons' sons, forever."

9. The unbiblical teaching that Israel has been replaced by the Church, and thus has no prophetic claim to the Holy Land. This idea has to be force-fed into the Old Testament prophecies by spiritualizing the words to such an extreme that when you read the word "Israel," it actually is supposed to mean "Church."

10. Jesus said that "salvation is from the Jews" (John 4:22), not from the Muslims.

11. Hamas Charter, https://fas.org/irp/world/para/docs/880818a.htm.

12. This is an actual quotation from the second-most-revered Muslim "holy book," the Hadith. The Koran (or Quran) is the first.

13. "In a shift, the new document formally endorses the goal of establishing a Palestinian state in Gaza and the West Bank, with Jerusalem as its capital, as part of a 'national consensus' among Palestinians. While that may be a tacit acknowledgment of Israel's existence, the revision stops well short of recognizing Israel and reasserts calls for armed resistance toward a 'complete liberation of Palestine from the river to the sea.' " http://www.latimes.com/world/la-fg-hamas-charter-20170501-story.html.

14. "Arab Israeli MK, Ibrahim Sarsour (Ra'am Ta'al), has claimed that there was proof in the Quran that there is no Jewish connection to Judea, Samaria and Temple Mount." http://www.israelnationalnews.com/Articles/Article.aspx/14416.

15. Don McGee, Crown & Sickle Ministries newsletter, Amite, LA, July 2017.

16. "While there is much in the Old Testament that speaks of God's promise of restoration of the land to Israel, advocates of Reform (Replacement) Theology believe the Old Testament promises (like the Chosen People) have changed and that God's plan has shifted from the land of Israel to the whole world. Holding to a New Testament priority, Replacement theologians have declared that there is no evidence whatsoever of any promise of Israel's restoration of its land in the New

Testament, and therefore there is no future for Israel as a nation." News from Israel, Midnight Call Ministries, Lexington, SC, Arno Froese, ed., July 2017, p. 11.

17. Paul Wilkinson, as quoted in video, https://amos37.com/what-is-christian-palestinianism/.

18. "World Council of Churches Endorses Palestinian Protests Over Temple Mount Security Measures: July 23, 2017 — The World Council of Churches (WCC) has declared its support for the Palestinian campaign against Israeli control of Jerusalem's holy sites. . . . The WCC is a central promoter of the Christian 'Kairos Palestine' document, which characterizes terrorist acts of 'armed resistance' as 'Palestinian legal resistance,' denies the Jewish historical connection to Israel in theological terms, calls to mobilize churches worldwide in the call for BDS, and compares Israel with the South African apartheid regime."

    (Comment from a perceptive reader: "The same attitude is unfortunately prevalent in possibly a majority of Christian mission groups and denominations that should know better. Definitely a strong delusion and a sign of the times.") https://www.algemeiner.com/2017/07/23/world-council-of-churches-endorses-palestinian-protests-over-temple-mount-security-measures/.

19. This Gospel-Land Promise link in the Abrahamic Covenant is also found in another place, as noted by Arno Froese. "The reason behind Israel taking possession of their land is expressed in Genesis 26:4: 'And I will make thy seed [Israel] to multiply as the stars of heaven, and will give unto thy seed all these countries [Land of Israel]; and in thy seed shall all the nations of the earth be blessed [Gospel].' Taking possession of the Promised Land is one of the conditions for all nations of the earth to be blessed [through the Gospel promise of Salvation in Jesus Christ]," *Midnight Call* magazine, Midnight Call Ministries, Lexington, SC, Arno Froese, ex. ed., August 2017, p. 26.

    Here again, we see the link between the gospel and the land promise to Israel. The link is in no way salvific: salvation is by grace alone, in Christ alone, through faith alone. The "link" is such that, being in the same passage, if the gospel is true, then the land promise must be true also. Otherwise, we decide what is true and pick and choose as we want.

20. Sources from my personal Power-Point presentations, except quote numbers 1 and 6, which are from Paul Wilkinson, *The Church at Christ's Checkpoint*, 2011, document response to Jerusalem conference, Christ at the Checkpoint, Hazel Grove Full Gospel Church, 68 London Road, Hazel Grove, Stockport, Cheshire, SK7 4AF, UK, p. 47.

21. *The Koran*, translated by N.J. Dawood (Middlesex, England: Penguin Books, 1974), p.389–90; Surah 5:21; see also 17:103.

22. "Allah has promised Israel to the Jews — so says Sheikh Ahmad Adwan, a Muslim scholar living in Jordan, who declared on his Facebook page recently that 'Palestine' doesn't exist," http://www.israelnationalnews.com/News/News. aspx/177319.

    In an email from Bible scholar Paul Wilkinson, who has done extensive research on Christian Palestinianism, he quotes Palestinian official Zuheir Mohsen: "The Palestinian people do not exist. The creation of a Palestinian state is only a means for continuing our struggle against the state of Israel and for our Arab unity. In reality, today there is no difference between Jordanians, Palestinians, Syrians, and Lebanese. Only for political and tactical reasons do we speak today about the existence of a Palestinian people."

23. "The Mennonite Church USA voted [recently] to sell its holdings in companies they say are profiting from business in territories occupied by Israel, the latest American Christian group to do so. . . . In previous years, the Presbyterian Church (USA) approved divestment measures . . . the United Church of Christ [has previously voted] to divest from companies profiting from Israel's control of the West Bank . . . the Methodist pension board has barred investment in five Israeli banks," http://www.timesofisrael.com/mennonite-church-usa-votes-to-divest-in-protest-of-israeli-policies/.

24. *The Bible Knowledge Commentary*, John F. Walvoord and Roy B. Zuck, eds. (Wheaton, IL: Victor Books, 1985), Nehemiah 4:7–9.

25. https://www.timesofisrael.com/un-eu-denounce-approval-of-fresh-settlement-houses/

26. Jesus Christ (Messiah) will return to the land of Israel upon the Mount of Olives (Zechariah 14:4); He will reign from Jerusalem over the entire world (Isaiah 2:2–4; Zechariah 13:8–9).

27. "Wall of fire": This is a real term given in Zechariah 2:5 that promises Israel's secure keeping in God's care.

28. Arno Froese, "The Six-Day War," *Midnight Call*, June 2017, Midnight Call Ministries, Lexington, South Carolina, p. 25–27.

29. Ed Hindson and Thomas Ice, *Charting the Bible Chronologically* (Eugene, OR: Harvest House Publishers, 2016), p. 65.

30. Mal Couch, *Revelation Hoofbeats*, Ron J. Bigalke, ed., "Controversy over Prophetic Fulfillment," (Fairfax, VT: Xulon Press, 2003), p. 324.

31. Randall Price, Ezekiel 38–39, *The Popular Bible Prophecy Commentary*, ed. LaHaye and Hindson, p.193.

32. The false assumption of a millennial-level security imposed upon Ezekiel 38:8 and 11 is the basis for rejecting Israel's state of security and rest in that "Magog" passage. This is the underlying error of the popular Psalm 83 theory. This false application of a millennial-level security leads to a logical — but erroneous — conclusion that Israel is NOT secure today. But Israel is not in the millennial age today. Nor is it so in Ezekiel 38. In the millennial age, all war will cease as swords are turned into plowshares (Isaiah 2:4). If millennial-age security were the criteria for a secure Israel in the four examples given in this chapter, then Israel would NOT have been secure during the Exodus or during any of those events, and the Bible would be self-contradictory. The Bible is not self-contradictory, because Israel is in God-given, but CURRENT-AGE, security, both during those events and today. Current-age security means security from defeat, destruction, or conquest. It is not millennial-age security when perfect peace reigns forever. Current-age security and rest is the subject of Ezekiel 38 and the coming Russian-Islamic invasion of Israel — the "Magog" event. For an extensive defense of this much-overlooked biblical teaching on "Miracle-War Security," see the author's linked articles at http://www.bibleprophecyaswritten.com/israel/sumintro14israelsec.html.

33. The entire Exodus event: Note that the context of the *betach* security statement in Psalm 78 includes the first Passover in Egypt (v. 51), the Red Sea crossing (v. 53), and the 38-year wilderness journey; 40 years total, which included numerous miracle wars all the way into the Promised Land.

34. Scholars agree that the sequence of some of the judge periods overlapped, which would require an overlap of "oppression" and "(*shaqat*) rest" periods. For example, "As for the period of the judges . . . the figures in Judges clearly involve several overlappings" (*The Expositor's Bible Commentary,* Vol. 1, Gleason L. Archer, *The Chronology of the Old Testament*, Frank E. Gaebelein, ed. (Grand Rapids, MI: Zondervan Publishing House, 1992), p. 363).

35. Simultaneous "rest" and "war" are stated in the text. While 1 Kings 15:16 and 32 say there was war between Asa and Baasha "all their days," 2 Chronicles 14:1–8 says that during ten years of that period, Asa was in a *shaqat*-rest period. "Throughout [Baasha's] twenty-four-year reign (909–886 B.C.), this king of the northern tribe of Israel waged war with Asa [911–901; thus eight of the ten years of 'rest' included war]." D.A. Carson, ed., *NIV Zondervan Study Bible* (Grand Rapids, MI: Zondervan, 2015), 1 Kings 15:16, p. 634.

36. Simultaneous "rest" and "armed camp buildup" are stated in the text (2 Chronicles 14:1–8).

37. http://www.bibleprophecyaswritten.com/israel/3thekingsshowisraelatresttoday.html.

38. Notice how there was both security and warlike tension "all the days of Solomon." It is clear from 1 Kings 4:25 and 11:23–25 that there were military operations against Solomon, king of Israel, by Hadad king of Edom and Rezon king of Damascus DURING the time Israel lived in safety (Hebrew, *betach*).

39. "Here again, we must emphasize that it matters not who rules which country, what politicians say or don't say, what they do or don't do: The Bible has the last word." Arno Froese, *News from Israel,* July 2017, Midnight Call Ministries, Lexington, SC, p. 21.

40. Mark Hitchcock, *The End* (Carol Stream, IL: Tyndale House Publishers, 2012), p. 294–300.

41. Russia is "the land of Magog" of Ezekiel 38:2. There are two facts that support this: 1) Ancient Jewish historian Josephus says, "Magog founded those that from him were named Magogites, but who are by the Greeks called Scythians" (Josephus, *Antiquities of the Jews*, VI-1); "during the sixth century B.C. [the time Ezekiel was written], the Scythians actually dominated the land that was later to become Russia." *The New Columbia Encyclopedia* (New York: Columbia University Press, 1975), p. 2377; and, 2) the invasion comes out of the "remote parts of the north" (Ezekiel 38:15), and the only vicinity to the remote due north of Jerusalem is Russia.

42. Syria, January 11, 2017, "Russia Steps Up Military Presence in Syria, Despite Putin Promise," by Lucas Tomlinson, published January 11, 2017, FoxNews.com; http://www.foxnews.com/world/2017/01/11/russia-steps-up-military-presence-in-syria-despite-putin-promise.html.

43. http://www.cnn.com/2016/05/09/middleeast/russia-military-syria/index.html.

44. http://www.reuters.com/article/us-mideast-crisis-syria-iran-analysis-idUSKBN143252.

45. https://www.theguardian.com/world/2017/jun/16/from-tehran-to-beirut-shia-militias-aim-to-firm-up-irans-arc-of-influence.

46. Persia (Iran) is symbolized by the "bear" that appears in the last days in Daniel 7:5 and Revelation 13:2.

47. https://www.algemeiner.com/2017/07/10/pro-hezbollah-newspaper-warns-israelis-to-expect-rain-of-rockets/.

48. https://www.worthynews.com/25601-threat-hezbollah-growing-iranian-aid.

49. http://www.israelnationalnews.com/News/News.aspx/230065.

50. http://www.theblaze.com/news/2017/05/22/ready-for-editing-israeli-president-welcomes-trump-america-is-back-again

51. Ultimately, "all nations" (Zechariah 12:3), which includes America, will be gathered against Israel. If the United States is true to its promise of returning to a pro-Israel policy, perhaps God will give this nation another season of blessing before that prophecy comes to pass. (After this chapter was submitted to the publisher, America made the pro-biblical announcement that the United States Embassy in Israel would be moved to Jerusalem. This is a huge step in the direction of realigning a wavering America as a strong supporter of Israel.)

52. http://www.crosswalk.com/blogs/christian-trends/millions-of-muslims-converting-to-christ.html.

53. "What must I do to be saved?" is the question every human on the planet must face (Acts 16:30). The answer that follows is clear: Believe in the Lord Jesus and you shall be saved. Salvation is in Christ alone (John 14:6). Salvation is by grace alone — that is, God gives us salvation, made possible through Christ's death and Resurrection, as a free gift (Ephesians 2:8–9). We receive it by faith alone (John 3:16). If you believe in Jesus Christ at this very moment, before this moment is gone, you will be saved forever and ever. Make your decision now for Jesus. For more information, see, http://www.bibleprophecyaswritten.com/salvationbygrace/oneminutetosalvation.html.

54. The Eastern and Western religions agree in their "replacement" of Israel, albeit by different rationales. The secular-political world finds its moral high ground from this Islam-Church alliance. But they are unwittingly aided in many cases by prophecy-centered, Bible-believing churches. This happens when these churches tone down to a whimper the two compelling proofs that Israel today is the chosen people on God's chosen land, namely: 1) the referral by Jesus to "all that the prophets have spoken" (Luke 24:25); and 2) the powerful hand of God in restoring and preserving Israel through its "miracle-war security" above and beyond all worldly odds. Why is this not preached and proclaimed with power? God did His part.

CHAPTER 8

New World Order Wizardry

DAYMOND DUCK

The word "wizardry" suggests many words and phrases: evil, sin, sorcery, wickedness, witchcraft, black magic, and demonic. Some who have watched magicians on TV might add: skillful, clever, crafty, deceptive, dishonest, fraudulent, fake, scam, lie, lots of practice, and trickery.

These words point to something Jesus told a group of scribes and Pharisees:

> Ye are of your father the devil, and the lusts of your father ye will do. He was a murderer from the beginning, and abode not in the truth, because there is no truth in him. When he speaketh a lie, he speaketh of his own: for he is a liar, and the father of it (John 8:44).[1]

Wizardry on earth began when Satan, the father of lies, deceived Eve in the Garden of Eden (Genesis 3:1–6). God stopped it with the Flood. But it started up again and it will spread until it encompasses the whole world. A famous verse in the Book of Revelation reads:

> And all that dwell upon the earth shall worship him [Satan's world leader called the Antichrist], whose names are not written in the book of life of the Lamb slain from the foundation of the world (Revelation 13:8).

God knew about Satan's deception before He created Adam and Eve. The all-knowing One said, "I am God, and there is none else; I am God, and there is none like me, Declaring the end from the beginning, and from ancient times the things that are not yet done, saying, My counsel shall stand, and I will do all my pleasure" (Isaiah 46:9–10).

God knew that Satan would deceive Eve before He created her. God even decided to provide forgiveness for Eve before she made her first wrong decision. This is where the Lamb that was slain on the Cross (Jesus) comes in.

God wanted Adam and Eve to have dominion over everything on earth, but He knew that Satan would deceive them and seize that dominion (Genesis 1:28). He knew that Satan wants a kingdom and that Satan would replace the rule of Adam and Eve with his own wicked rule (Isaiah 14:12–17).

Satan is a supplanter or a being that trips up and replaces other beings or things. The word "supplanter" comes from Esau's description of Jacob for tricking him out of his birthright and blessing.

Esau asked Isaac, "Is not he rightly named Jacob? for he hath supplanted me these two times: he took away my birthright; and behold, now he hath taken away my blessing" (Genesis 27:36).

"Supplanter" is also used to describe efforts to overthrow or replace kings and kingdoms. Jesus is the coming King of kings and Lord of lords (Revelation 19:16), but Satan tried to trip Him up and take His kingdom by tempting Him in the wilderness (Matthew 4:1–11).

Satan took Jesus up on a high mountain "and sheweth him all the kingdoms of the world, and the glory of them; and saith unto him, All these things will I give thee, if thou wilt fall down and worship me" (Matthew 4:8–9). Satan was trying to oust Jesus and take over His kingdom. He was trying to establish a satanic world kingdom and religion.

There are many reasons God created Adam and Eve: to love Him, to worship Him, to reveal Himself, and more, but one of His greatest reasons must surely be His desire to deal with Satan and the evil one's desire to replace God's kingdom on earth with his own. Behind the scenes of everything that has happened on earth since the days of Adam and Eve is a spiritual war between God and Satan.

This spiritual war raged until the population of the earth was down to just eight people whom Satan had not corrupted: Noah, his wife, their three sons, and their sons' wives (Genesis 6:11–12, 17–18). At that point, God destroyed the world with a Flood. Then, He started all over (Genesis 7:23).

Rebellion, World Government, World Religion, Pagan Deities, Sexual Perversion and Wizardry

> Now these are the generations of the sons of Noah, Shem, Ham, and Japheth: and unto them were sons born after the flood (Genesis 10:1).

The sons of Ham were Cush, Mizraim, Phut, and Canaan (Genesis 10:6). Ham's son Cush begat many sons, including one of special note named Nimrod (Genesis 10:7–8).

Nimrod, a great-grandson of Noah, appears to be singled out because he acquired great power on earth. Notice how quickly this happened. Noah's son Ham survived the Flood by getting on the ark. Shortly after Ham got off the ark, he had a grandson who was a very powerful man on earth.

This was a time when names meant something, and there is some debate about what Nimrod's name meant. Strong's Hebrew Number 5248 indicates that it probably means "rebel." So, Nimrod's name probably means he was a rebel on earth.

The Bible calls him "a mighty hunter before the Lord" (Genesis 10:9). The word that is translated "mighty" is used to describe the giant Goliath that David slew (1 Samuel 17:4). It means that Nimrod was a giant rebel or an unusually powerful rebel who got God's attention not many years after the Flood.

Although the Bible doesn't call Nimrod a king, it says, "the beginning of his kingdom was Babel, and Erech, and Accad, and Calneh, in the land of Shinar" (Genesis 10:10). He was the founder of, and the king or ruler over, many cities in the land of Shinar (ancient Babylonia or Babylon).

Now, when Noah came off the ark, the first thing he did was build "an altar unto the LORD; and took of every clean beast, and of every clean fowl, and offered burnt offerings on the altar" (Genesis 8:20). God had spared the lives of Noah and his family, so Noah was offering sacrifices to that God — and they were sacrifices that we now know speak of the Lord Jesus Christ.

Put another way, the post-Flood world began with the worship of Noah's God, Jehovah. Immediately after the Flood, there was no worship of other gods. And God was pleased with this (Genesis 8:21): "And God blessed Noah and his sons, and said unto them, Be fruitful, and multiply, and replenish the earth" (Genesis 9:1).

The quick appearance of Nimrod's kingdom shows that there was a population explosion: "And the whole earth was of one language, and of one speech" (Genesis 11:1). It also shows that many people settled in the land of Shinar, and Nimrod rebelled against God by urging them to remain in the area and not scatter.

So, they had a choice: obey God or obey their rebellious king.

> And they said one to another, Go to, let us make brick, and burn them thoroughly. And they had brick for stone, and slime had they for mortar. And they said, Go to, let us build us a city and a tower, whose top may reach unto heaven; and let us make us a name, lest we be scattered abroad upon the face of the whole earth (Genesis 11:3–4).

They decided among themselves to do six things: ignore God's instructions for them to replenish the earth, remain in the kingdom, make bricks, build a city, build a tower into heaven, and make a name for themselves.

The Babylonian desire to "build a tower into heaven" shows that they still believed in heaven, but their belief was corrupted because they wanted to ascend into heaven their way. It was most surely inspired by Satan because he would later say of himself, "I will ascend into heaven" (Isaiah 14:13).

Satan was involved because archaeology shows that the Tower of Babel was a ziggurat (a tall multistory temple or place of worship). Approximately 20 ziggurats have been found in the area.

Archaeology also shows that false gods and goddesses were worshiped there and the worship of pagan deities was often tied to sexual perversion. It also shows that astrology was practiced there, along with the worship of the sun, moon, and stars, fortune-telling, and other demonic practices.

The importance of this is essential to the understanding of Mystery, Babylon the Great, the Mother of Harlots, and Abominations of the Earth (Revelation 17:5). Following the Flood, Babel is where false religion first appeared. It is the starting point or the mother of physical and spiritual harlotry (false religion or the worship of many false gods).

The Babylonian desire to "make a name for themselves" was pride. It was an attempt to receive glory for themselves rather than to give glory to God.

So, the people in and around Babel had a powerful, rebellious, proud king who was trying to keep everyone in the area, rule over all of them, and let them change their religious beliefs. With humankind starting to repopulate the earth after the Flood, this was clearly the beginning or the mother of a God-rejecting, one-world government and a one-world religion located in the land of Babylon. Its father is Satan.

More needs to be said about this and that will happen later in this chapter, but at this point, just know that Nimrod prefigured the Antichrist. His power, rebellion, and pride are far more serious than yet said.

But God is not deceived.

> And the LORD came down to see the city and the tower, which the children of men builded. And the LORD said, Behold, the people is one, and they have all one language; and this they begin to do: and now nothing will be restrained from them, which they have imagined to do. Go to, let us go down, and there confound their language, that they may not understand one another's speech. So, the LORD scattered them abroad from thence upon the face of all the earth: and they left off to build the city (Genesis 11:5–8).

God confused the language of these children of men (not these children of God) so that instead of speaking one language, they spoke many languages. This divided them into groups or nations. Then, God scattered the groups or nations all over the earth to repopulate the earth as He originally intended. That temporarily halted Satan's progress toward a global government, global religion, and global capital.

World Government, Spiritual Harlotry, and Deceit Thrived at Babel

Pinpointing some Bible dates is not an exact science, but roughly 1,600 years passed and Babel was back on the scene and thriving as Babylon the empire and Babylon the city. We will check in about 606 B.C., the year that many experts believe the Babylonian empire conquered the Southern Kingdom of Judah (Daniel 1:1–2).

Some call Babylon the most beautiful city man has ever built. God called Babylon the "glory of kingdoms, the beauty of the Chaldees' excellency" (Isaiah 13:19). The city had a double wall around it. The grand entrance was a magnificent gate called the Ishtar Gate.

Ishtar (pronounced "easter") is the name of the Babylonian goddess of fertility, love, war, and sex (the beginning of temple prostitution).

Other decorations included animal figures in the shape of lions, bulls, and dragons that represented other Babylonian gods.

Honoring several gods is clear evidence that the spiritual harlotry (and temple prostitution) that began in the days of Nimrod and the Tower of Babel was alive and well in the Land of Shinar (Babylonia). But there is more.

One of the first buildings inside the Ishtar Gate was the famous Temple of Marduk, the so-called protector god of Babylon (king of the gods, ruler over magic) and supposed husband of a fertility goddess named Sarpanit. The Temple of Marduk was a ziggurat like some of those that were built in the days of Nimrod not far from the Tower of Babel, but it was much more elaborate.

The king of Babylon was a man named Nebuchadnezzar. On at least two different occasions, he had a dream that he didn't understand. The first dream was in the second year of his reign, and he commanded the magicians, astrologers, sorcerers, and Chaldeans to come in and explain it to him (Daniel 2:1–2). The second dream was a few years later and he called in the same groups of incompetent deceivers, but this time he also included a group of soothsayers (Daniel 4:7).

His magicians were skillful in deceit, trickery, illusions, and black magic, etc. His astrologers studied the stars, read horoscopes, and told fortunes. His sorcerers were witches and wizards who cast spells, etc. His soothsayers were like psychics who contacted evil spirits and talked to the dead.

The influence that Satan had upon Nimrod and his followers was stronger than ever in the expanded city of Babylon and the remainder of the kingdom of Babylon. And now the kingdom was dominating the then-known world.

Corrupt Government and Religion Spread Worldwide from Babylon

One only needs to look at part of the second dream that Nebuchadnezzar had and the interpretation of it that Daniel provided to realize this. Nebuchadnezzar said:

> Thus were the visions of mine head in my bed; I saw, and behold a tree in the midst of the earth, and the height thereof was great. The tree grew, and was strong, and the height thereof reached unto heaven, and the sight thereof to the end of all the earth: The leaves thereof were fair, and the fruit thereof much, and in it was

meat for all: the beasts of the field had shadow under it, and the fowls of the heaven dwelt in the boughs thereof, and all flesh was fed of it (Daniel 4:10–12).

Daniel interpreted that part of the dream like this:

The tree that thou sawest, which grew, and was strong, whose height reached unto the heaven, and the sight thereof to all the earth; Whose leaves were fair, and the fruit thereof much, and in it was meat for all; under which the beasts of the field dwelt, and upon whose branches the fowls of the heaven had their habitation: It is thou, O king, that art grown and become strong: for thy greatness is grown, and reacheth unto heaven, and thy dominion to the end of the earth (Daniel 4:20–22).

Daniel told King Nebuchadnezzar he was the tree in the dream. He had become great and exceedingly strong. His greatness reached into the heavens and his kingdom covered the earth.

King Nebuchadnezzar had subdued all of Babylon's enemies. He had built great buildings, many temples, and places of worship, and he had become so wealthy that he now ruled over a world religion and a world government. The way men look at it may cause them to question it. But the way God looks at it is true. Babylon's corrupt government and harlot religion reached into heaven and to the end of the earth. The lies, deceit, prostitution, magic, sorcery, and all the other sins of Babylon had become a corrupt, worldwide phenomenon.

Every World Government and Religion Will End at the Second Coming

But let's go back to Nebuchadnezzar's first dream. It is a timeline of Gentile world governments that starts with Babylon and ends with the Second Coming of Jesus. King Nebuchadnezzar had a dream that he could not understand (Daniel 2). It disturbed him, but he wasn't sure why. He summoned the magicians, astrologers, sorcerers, and Chaldeans who were advising him. They came in and stood before the king.

He told them that he had a dream and was troubled to know what it was. They told him to tell them the dream, and they would tell him what it means. He replied that he could not remember his dream.

Then, he gave them a choice: If they didn't reveal the dream and its meaning, he would kill them and destroy their houses, but if they did reveal the dream and its meaning, he would give them gifts, rewards, and great honor. Neither tactic worked. They simply could not do what he wanted them to do.

King Nebuchadnezzar was furious. He rightly concluded that his advisors had been deceiving him about their abilities. He ordered all of them killed, including Daniel. The young Daniel asked for time to come up with the dream and its interpretation. His request was granted.

He visited his friends Shadrach, Meshach, and Abednego, and asked them to join him in prayer about the issue. The foursome prayed, and later that night, God answered their prayer by revealing the dream and its meaning to Daniel. The next day, Daniel wound up in front of King Nebuchadnezzar.

Time and space doesn't permit this writer to give a detailed exposition of what went on, but basically, Daniel told King Nebuchadnezzar that he had dreamed about a great statue. The statue was a Gentile "timeline" with a head of gold (representing Babylon), chest and arms of silver (representing the Medes and Persians), belly and thighs of brass (representing Greece), legs of iron (representing the Roman Empire), and feet of iron plus clay. It revealed that Babylon would be replaced by a second Gentile world kingdom (the Medes and the Persians), and that one would be replaced by a third Gentile world kingdom (Greece), and that one would be replaced by a fourth Gentile world kingdom (the Roman Empire).

That fourth Gentile world kingdom (the Roman Empire) would break up, but it would eventually come back together and work with others to form one fifth and final Gentile world kingdom. Other Scriptures teach that it will have ten groups of nations (represented by the ten toes on the statue) in it. Each group will be headed up by a king for a total of ten kings, and they will eventually wind up under the domination of a powerful and wicked leader whom many call the Antichrist (Daniel 2:38–41, 7:24; Revelation 17:12).

In the days of these ten kings, Daniel said God will utterly destroy all of the Gentile world kingdoms and set up His own kingdom that will never be destroyed. He will use a Stone to do that, which is a well-known symbol for Jesus — and in this case, it is a reference to the Second Coming of Jesus (1 Peter 2:1–8; Ephesians 2:20).

Notice that the timeline starts with Babylon and leads to the ten kings, the Antichrist, and the Second Coming of Jesus. Ultimately, it will all tie in with Satan worship, world government, world religion, spiritual harlotry, sexual perversion, deceit, and more. The evil that Satan started at the Tower of Babel (astrology, soothsayers, sorcery, world government, world religion, etc.) will continue until Jesus destroys it at His Second Coming.

World Religion Will Get Involved in Idol Worship

Following Nebuchadnezzar's dream about the great statue timeline, roughly 20 years passed and he was still stewing over its implications. He obviously liked Daniel, but he was unwilling to accept Daniel's statement that the kingdom of Babylon would eventually be replaced by another one. He knew the timeline meant that at the Second Coming of Jesus, God will set up a kingdom that will never be destroyed, but he wanted that indestructible kingdom to be Babylon, not a kingdom ruled by Jesus.

He had the same rebellious spirit as Nimrod at the Tower of Babel. He would do things his way, not God's way. Nimrod and King Nebuchadnezzar were both powerful leaders who yielded to the influence of Satan.

So King Nebuchadnezzar built a great statue. But his statue wasn't like the great statue in his dream that had a head of gold (representing Babylon), chest and arms of silver, belly and thighs of brass, legs of iron, and feet of iron plus clay. His statue was made of solid gold from the top of its head to the tip of its toes. It contradicted the prophecies of God in Daniel's interpretation of the dream, and it gave the false impression that Babylon would never be destroyed (Daniel 3:1).

King Nebuchadnezzar scheduled a dedication service and ordered the leaders of the top seven levels of his world government to attend. People gathered from all over the then-known world. The big day arrived, and the crowd assembled in front of the king's gleaming statue of gold. One of the king's heralds made an important announcement for everyone there to follow: when they heard the musical instruments, they were to fall down and worship the statue or they would be cast into a burning fiery furnace (see Daniel 3:2–6).

This is idolatry and a violation of the Ten Commandments (Exodus 20:4–6). It is persecution and a sign of the Second Coming (Matthew 24:9). It is also a precursor to the statue of the Antichrist that the False Prophet will build during the Tribulation Period (Revelation 13:14–18). And it is world religion, because leaders from all over the global kingdom of Babylon attended this worship service.

All of these things prefigure Tribulation Period events and Mystery, Babylon the Great, the Mother of Harlots, and Abominations of the Earth: world government, world religion, idolatry (worship of an image of the Antichrist), and persecution (the death of those who refuse to worship the image), etc. (Revelation 13:15, 17:5).

Rebellion, Sexual Immorality, and Blasphemy Will Fail

Skipping past roughly 40 more years, we come to the last night of Babylon's rule for approximately the next 2,500 years. As we consider another event, keep in mind that Nimrod was a very powerful and rebellious, anti-Jehovah-type figure that got God's attention while he was building the Tower of Babel. God intervened in a dramatic way by confounding the people's languages and scattering them over the earth (Genesis 11).

Nebuchadnezzar's grandson, a king called Belshazzar, was ruling in Babylon. Daniel's interpretation of Nebuchadnezzar's first dream said the kingdom of Babylon, the head of gold, would fall to another kingdom, the chest and arms of silver (Daniel 2:39).

The Medes and the Persians had agreed to unite their armies to conquer Babylon. They had troops stationed not far outside the wall around the wicked city. King Belshazzar felt secure behind that wall. He wasn't afraid of anything or anyone — not anyone in his kingdom, not the army of the Medes and the Persians, not even the God who brought down the rebellious Nimrod.

To show that he feared nothing, the king threw a big party. To demonstrate that he wasn't afraid of God, he decided to send for the vessels that his grandfather Nebuchadnezzar had stolen from the Jewish Temple in Jerusalem when he conquered Judah. He drank wine from them.

This was blasphemy. That Jewish Temple wasn't built to honor pagan gods. It was built to honor Jehovah. The Holy God of Israel had once dwelled there, and those vessels had been set apart for use in worship services that honored Him.

But notice that the penchant for sexual immorality was still alive and well in Babylon. Belshazzar was a polygamist with wives and concubines, and he sent for his harem, so to speak, to come and attend his drunken party (Daniel 5:1–3; Revelation 17:5–6).

As the night wore on, this fornicator (like Mystery, Babylon the Great, the Mother of Harlots, and Abominations of the Earth) began to praise other gods (Daniel 5:4). That is something else that Nimrod did.

Following the Flood, the worship of many gods showed up (or was born) at the Tower of Babel, and this spiritual harlotry will continue into the Tribulation Period.

Drinking wine out of Israel's holy vessels was a big mistake. God has been known to react swiftly, and this was one of those occasions. The Bible says:

> In the same hour came forth fingers of a man's hand, and wrote over against the candlestick upon the plaster of the wall of the king's palace: and the king saw the part of the hand that wrote. Then the king's countenance was changed, and his thoughts troubled him, so that the joints of his loins were loosed, and his knees smote one against another (Daniel 5:5–6).

The sight of the hand that may have written the Ten Commandments on tablets of stone caused the color to drain from the face of this arrogant, rebellious, blaspheming, fornicating king and he went from gulping expensive wine to shaking in his shoes in the blink of an eye.

The trembling king wanted to know what the hand had written. He called upon his always-inept astrologers, Chaldeans and soothsayers, to tell him what was written on the wall, but these nefarious people didn't have a clue. Then the king became even more troubled, and his countenance changed so much that the people around him were astonished.

At the queen mother's suggestion, Daniel was brought in. And to make a long story short, Daniel condemned king Belshazzar's pride, rebellion, his drunken party with his wives and concubines, his idolatry, and the fact that he had not honored the true and living God (Daniel 5:23).

Notice this list of sins. Daniel's condemnation could just as easily be said about the coming Antichrist. These sins will characterize the coming world government and religion. But they will be much more prevalent when that terrible time arrives.

Following Daniel's condemnation, he told the trembling king he had been weighed in God's balances and found wanting. The kingdom of Babylon would be divided and given to the Medes and Persians (Daniel 5:27–28).

Could God really do that? Yes! King Belshazzar didn't anticipate it. He didn't count on God paying attention to his lifestyle. He wasn't expecting God to hold him accountable. But in less than 24 hours, he was dead (Daniel 5:30).

This is the second big intervention of God in taking down a budding world government and religion. He intervened at the Tower of Babel, and He intervened during the reign of King Belshazzar.

These interventions were dramatic. At the Tower of Babel, God confused the languages and scattered the people. At Babylon, God showed the Medes and Persians how to get under the walls to kill Belshazzar.

But there is more. God will intervene a third time, and the rebuilt city of Babylon will be burned by fire in one hour. After that happens, Jesus will sit on the throne and put an end to all of Babylon's sins.

The Rebellion on Earth Is the Result of Satanic and Demonic Activity

The rule of the Medes and Persians didn't stop the work of Satan and his demons at Babylon. In the third year of Cyrus king of Persia, Daniel received a message (Daniel 10:1). Not everyone agrees, but many believe the messenger was probably a very powerful angel or Jesus (Daniel 10:5–6).

Daniel was told that the message was true, and that it involved the distant future (Daniel 10:1). The experience made Daniel weak and caused him to fall to the ground (Daniel 10:8–9). He wound up in a deep sleep with his face to the ground.

A hand touched him and he began to tremble (Daniel 10:10). He got up on his hands and knees. A voice told him to stand on his feet, and he arose, trembling (Daniel 10:11). The voice reminded Daniel that he had been fasting and praying. It said God had heard Daniel's prayers and dispatched him to deliver an answer (Daniel 10:12–13).

The voice said a being called the prince of Persia had interfered with the answer to Daniel's prayer for 21 days. Finally, the archangel Michael intervened. The voice said the message was about Daniel's people (the Jews) and what would happen in the latter days (the Tribulation Period; Daniel 10:14).

This prince of Persia was not a human being. Human beings can't prevent angels or Jesus from delivering answers to prayer. The curtain had been pulled back on an unseen spirit world of fallen angels and demonic spirits working in what was once called Babylon in the latter days.

Paul revealed that believers "wrestle not against flesh and blood, but against principalities, against powers, against the rulers of the darkness of this world, against spiritual wickedness in high places" (Ephesians

6:12). This is what is behind the astrology, wizardry, sorcery, soothsaying, and rebellion.

When the future Gentile world government comes to power, it will do so with the help of Satan. The Antichrist will be a Satan worshiper. He will blaspheme God and persecute those who disagree with him (Revelation 13:1–8).

The Last World Government Will Thrive on Wickedness and Satanic Power

There is more, and this time it comes from a vision that Daniel had about Greece, the belly and thighs of brass on the statue in Nebuchadnezzar's first dream (Daniel 2:32). While Daniel was seeking the meaning of the vision, the angel Gabriel showed up and said, "at the time of the end shall be the vision" (Daniel 8:17). Then he got more specific: "Behold, I will make thee know what shall be in the last end of the indignation: for at the time appointed the end shall be" (Daniel 8:19).

"Indignation" is one of the names of the Tribulation Period. The vision was about something that will happen in the future during the Tribulation Period. Gabriel said:

> When the transgressors are come to the full, a king of fierce countenance, and understanding dark sentences, shall stand up. And his power shall be mighty, but not by his own power: and he shall destroy wonderfully, and shall prosper, and practice, and shall destroy the mighty and the holy people. And through his policy also he shall cause craft to prosper in his hand; and he shall magnify himself in his heart, and by peace shall destroy many: he shall also stand up against the Prince of princes; but he shall be broken without hand (Daniel 8:23–25).

When the Tribulation Period arrives, the wickedness on earth will be great. A ferocious-looking leader called the Antichrist will arise. He will understand sinister words and plots. He will possess impressive power (other Scriptures teach that it will be global; see Daniel 7:23), but it won't come from himself (other Scriptures teach that it will be given to him by Satan; see Revelation 13:2).

The Antichrist will destroy in incredible ways (probably with high-tech weapons). He will succeed in everything he does. He will destroy other very powerful leaders. He will also destroy the holy people (many

Jews and people who become believers during the Tribulation Period). He will cause craft to prosper (cause economic corruption). He will exalt himself. He will use deceptive covenants and peace treaties to destroy multitudes. He will rise up against Jesus (be anti-Christ), and he will perish in a supernatural way (be cast alive into the Lake of Fire; see Revelation 19:20).

All of the characteristics of the Antichrist are important, but this is a good place to take a brief look at just two of them, because they will show up in the coming New World Order (world government). And that is the direction this chapter is heading.

First, notice that the Antichrist will kill many Jews. Concerning the signs of His Second Coming, Jesus warned the Jews:

> When ye therefore shall see the abomination of desolation, spoken of by Daniel the prophet, stand in the holy place, (whoso readeth, let him understand:) Then let them which be in Judaea flee into the mountains: Let him which is on the housetop not come down to take any thing out of his house: Neither let him which is in the field return back to take his clothes. And woe unto them that are with child, and to them that give suck in those days! But pray ye that your flight be not in the winter, neither on the sabbath day: For then shall be great tribulation, such as was not since the beginning of the world to this time, no, nor ever shall be. And except those days should be shortened, there should no flesh be saved: but for the elect's sake those days shall be shortened (Matthew 24:15–22).

The Antichrist will be anti-Semitic, and he will use his world government to try to kill multitudes of Jews.

Second, notice the fact that the Antichrist will cause economic corruption to prosper. He will head up a corrupt global economic system. Some writers call it a corrupt "one world economy." It will involve the tracking of all buying and selling on earth and the death of multitudes (Jews and Tribulation Period believers) who refuse to comply (Revelation 13:16–17).

These two characteristics (the death of multitudes and a corrupt global economic system) and all the others (deception, rebellion, satanic or demonic activity, world government, world religion, etc.) come through loud and clear in Revelation chapters 6 through 19.

Deception

In Revelation 6, it is recorded that the Antichrist will come forth as a rider on a white horse copying Jesus, who is depicted as coming back on a white horse (Revelation 19:11). Antichrist will carry a bow, but no arrows, symbolizing that he is coming forth as a man of peace, but he will go forth conquering and to conquer (Revelation 6:1–2). This is deception, trickery, or dishonesty. It took place at the Tower of Babel, it took place at Babylon, and it is a major subject in Bible prophecy.

Famine

In the same chapter, it is also recorded that a rider on a black horse will come forth with a pair of scales, and the price of food will be extremely expensive (Revelation 6:5–6). It will be a global economic disaster with multitudes starving to death. A corrupt economic system will develop out of it.

Persecution

In the same chapter, we read that multitudes will be slain because of the Word of God and their testimony (Revelation 6:9–11). Nimrod was famous for rejecting the Word of God and the Antichrist will be even worse.

Demons and Torment

In Revelation 9, a star (a "him," perhaps a powerful fallen angel or Satan) will fall to the earth and open the bottomless pit (the subterranean abode of demons; see Matthew 12:40; Ephesians 4:9). It appears that millions of demons will be released to torment people on earth (Revelation 9:1–12). Their leader will be named Abaddon in the Hebrew and Apollyon in the Greek. Who knows? He may even know the prince of Persia.

Babylon's established record of witchcraft, sorcery, and demonic activity will come back on her. God will allow demons to be released from the bottomless pit during the Tribulation Period to torment all who don't have the seal of God on their foreheads. This will include many supporters of the coming one-world government and religion.

Depravity

In that same chapter, John reveals that many people will worship devils and idols, and refuse to repent of their sorcery and fornication (Revelation

9:20–21). Sadly, the tragic Babylonian sins of satanism, idolatry, witch-craft, and sexual immorality on a global scale and at the highest levels of government and religion will require a response from God. The coming world government and world religion will not be headed up by enlight-ened people. They will be headed up by depraved people who have risen to power through deception and the influence of Satan.

The Jewish Temple

In Revelation 11, John was told to measure the Temple and leave out the outer court (Revelation 11:1–2). Many believe this means that Israel will be required to share the Temple Mount and there is little doubt that they will have to share it with Muslims that worship at the Dome of the Rock. It is the result of the Babylonian custom of worshiping false gods and Satan's desire to corrupt or destroy Israel.

Murder

It is written that the Antichrist will kill two powerful men of God whom Christians call the two witnesses (Revelation 11:7). His reason for destroying them will probably be their condemnation of his evil world government, harlot world religion, sinful social positions, and corrupt economic policies.

An Enraged Satan Falls on Planet Earth

In Revelation 12, John revealed a very disturbing event. A great war will break out in heaven resulting in Satan and his fallen angels being cast down to the earth where they will remain for the last three and one-half years of the Tribulation Period (Revelation 12:7–9). Satan will know that his time is short, and he will come down with great wrath (Revelation 12:12), which is what caused John to write, "Woe to the inhabiters of the earth and the sea! for the devil is come down unto you, having great wrath, because he knoweth that he hath but a short time" (Revelation 12:12).

Jews Will Run for Their Lives

The great war that has been going on behind the scenes between God and Satan will turn into a great battle on earth. Satan's first act will be an attempt to destroy Israel, but many Jews will escape into the wilderness, where they will be supernaturally protected by God (Revelation 12:13–

14). Then Satan will focus his evil deeds on the remainder of earth's unfortunate population.

A Satanic World Political Leader and a Resurrection Lie

In Revelation 13, John said the Antichrist will appear to receive a deadly wound that gets healed, and all the world (except for those whose names are written in the Lamb's Book of Life) will worship Satan and the Antichrist. Satan worship and one-world government will literally go global at this time (Revelation 13:1–4, 8).

Total Obedience to Satan Will be Required

Satan will receive a total commitment from the Antichrist. He will influence the Antichrist to blaspheme God, His name, and more (total rebellion against God), and will influence the Antichrist to demand the total obedience of everyone on earth and kill everyone who refuses to give it (Revelation 13:5–10).

A Satanic World Religious Leader

A False Prophet will rise to power echoing the words of Satan. That old serpent will give this False Prophet the same authority as the Antichrist. One of these evil men (the Antichrist) will be a one-world political leader, and the other (the False Prophet) will be a one-world religious leader (Revelation 13:11–12).

False Miracles, Deception, and a Corrupt Economic System

But instead of this False Prophet using his authority to call for repentance and a turning back to God, he will use it to perform false miracles and deceive (lie to) people. He will demand that people worship a statue of the Antichrist (idolatry) and institute a corrupt economic system to track all buying and selling on earth (Revelation 13:13–18).

This rebellion against the true God, worship of Satan (a false god), deceit and lying, idolatry, and economic corruption, etc. began at the Tower of Babel. It continued through the kingdom of Babylon, and it will morph into the New World Order during the Tribulation Period.

Someone came up with the teaching that society rests upon three pillars: politics, religion, and economics. It is amazing that God has presented all three of these pillars in this one chapter, and all of them will be satanic corruptions of what God desires for His people.

God Will Destroy the Corrupt Religious System

In Revelation 17, an angel revealed that God's judgment will fall upon the future one-world religion, and He revealed why it will happen. The very first sin that is mentioned is collusion and fornication (here it refers to the cooperation and religious corruption) between all the Satan worshipers and political leaders on earth. Next is the blasphemy, collusion, and fornication between the religious system (woman) and the Antichrist (beast). Next is the name that God calls this corrupt religious system: Mystery, Babylon the Great, the Mother of Harlots, and Abominations of the Earth. Next is the fact that the false religious system will be involved in the persecution and death of multitudes of people who worship the true and living God. Then we read that the alliance between the corrupt political system and the corrupt religious system will fall apart, with the result being that the global political leaders will destroy the global religious system (Revelation 17:16).

Not all agree, but many students of Bible prophecy believe the name that God calls this corrupt religious system (Mystery, Babylon) links it back to the Tower of Babel and the kingdom of Babylon. The influence of Satan, the rebellion of Nimrod, one world government, one world religion, sexual immorality, astrology, witchcraft, sorcery, deception, lying, and all of those sins that first appeared at the Tower of Babel will go full circle and wind up back at the same place.

That's right! This writer believes that ancient Babylon will be rebuilt and be used as the headquarters of the coming corrupt global religious and economic systems. And think about it: this may be where Satan and some of his demons are located when they are cast down to the earth (Revelation 12:7–9).

God Will Destroy the Corrupt Economic System

In Revelation 18, a different angel addressed the corrupt one-world economic system and its demise. The very first thing this angel said was, "Babylon the great is fallen, is fallen, and is become the habitation of devils, and the hold of every foul spirit, and a cage of every unclean and hateful bird" (Revelation 18:2). "And a mighty angel took up a stone like a great millstone, and cast it into the sea, saying, Thus with violence shall that great city Babylon be thrown down, and shall be found no more at all" (Revelation 18:21).

God Will Destroy the Corrupt Political System

In Revelation 19, it is revealed that God will gather the Antichrist and the world leaders who assist him for a great conflict called the Battle of Armageddon. The Antichrist and False Prophet will be seized and cast alive into the Lake of Fire. Vultures will feed on the bodies of the troops and their leaders (Revelation 19:17–21).

God Will Establish His Kingdom on Earth

In Revelation 20, it is recorded that Satan will be bound, chained, and cast into the Bottomless Pit for one thousand years (Revelation 20:1–3). This will cause a thousand-year halt to the deception, political and religious corruption, etc.

The Stone (Rock; Jesus) that struck the toes of the statue in Nebuchadnezzar's first dream will fill the whole earth (Daniel 2:35). His kingdom will come to fruition on this earth (Matthew 6:10), and Jesus will rule over all the earth (Zechariah 14:9).

Current Events

Now that we know where this great spiritual war began and how it is going to end, it is time to look at some of the things that are happening. The Antichrist can't rise to power until the Rapture of the Church has taken place (2 Thessalonians 2:6–8). It is impossible to know the day or the hour of that, but it is possible to know when it is getting close — and many Christians think it is near (Hebrews 10:25).

World Government

Winston Churchill said, "The purpose of the New World Order is to bring the world into a *world government*."[2] When globalists talk about the New World Order, they mean world government. Most wouldn't admit that is what it means for decades, but since the turn of the century, many no longer try to hide it.

It is common knowledge that creating a New World Order is enshrined in the U.N. Charter. In 1990, former President George H.W. Bush called it the fifth objective of the United States. So, the Bible predicts that a world government is coming, and the U.N. and United States are working together to bring it about.

Globalists have now created the World Bank, the International Criminals Court, the International Monetary Fund, the Bank for International Settlements, the World Trade Organization, the World Health Organization, and the World Court, among others. They have held meetings and pushed through treaties often through deceit (sound familiar?): the United Nations Convention on the Rights of the Child, the U.N. Conference on Environment and Development (Earth Summit), the Convention of Biological Diversity (Bio-Diversity Treaty), the World Conference on Human Rights, the World Economic Forum, the U.N. International Conference on Population and Development, the U.N. World Summit for Social Development, the U.N. World Conference on Women, the World Food Summit, the U.N. Conference on Human Settlements, the Maastricht Treaty, the Trans-Pacific Partnership, and the Paris Climate Accords, just to name a few.

Groups have been established that some conservatives call the "shadow government": the Bilderbergers, the Club of Rome, the Council on Foreign Relations, the Trilateral Commission, the Illuminati, etc. For years, referring to these groups as the "shadow government" would get a person labeled as a "conspiracy theorist." Some members of this so-called shadow government no longer see a need to hide what they are doing, so the label "conspiracy theorist" has just about died out. This signifies that they are confident that the plan to establish a New World Order is succeeding.

There are other signs: The EU has come into being, the U.N. has adopted the 2030 Agenda for Sustainable Development, Pope Francis has called for a world government, U.S. troops have been put under U.N. commanders and forced to wear U.N. helmets, there have been calls for a global identification system, and much more.

The undeniable truth is that these organizations, treaties, groups, and signs are leading to a world government. Power is being concentrated in the hands of a small group of people who agree with the globalists. It will soon be concentrated in the hands of ten globalists that Scripture calls the "ten kings." When the Antichrist (an individual from the bottomless pit; Revelation 11:7) and the False Prophet arrive, power will be narrowed down to the hands of two people. When Satan and his demons are cast down to the earth from heaven, power will be narrowed down to one being: Satan. It is not something that will happen many years in the future. It is something that has already started — and many globalists want to speed it up.

Many globalists ignore the Bible. Many believe their New World Order will make the world a better place. If they can create a utopia on earth or cause the world to evolve into a utopia on earth, they are willing to lie and deceive to help bring it about. In their minds, the society they plan to establish will be so wonderful it justifies whatever they need to do to ensure that it happens.

Many globalists don't see themselves as evil people or people who are rebelling against God. They see themselves as enlightened people who are working to stop war, famine, hatred, discrimination, and diseases. They believe they are going to standardize wages and end war and poverty. They would never admit that they are influenced by Satan or his demons, but they view Christians as narrow-minded, hateful, bigoted, and a threat to global government and global values, so they are willing to pass laws to restrict Christians and to break the bands (laws and values) that tie them to the Word of God.

Many globalists think there are too many people on earth, so they have little or no respect for human life. They fear that the world will run out of resources and there will be violent struggles and war over what is left. Many want to head this off by supporting abortion, euthanasia, and gay marriage. If people need to die to satisfy the globalist utopian mindset, so be it. They think it is for the betterment of humankind.

Since globalists want world government, they don't like words like "patriot" or "nationalism." They don't want to make America great. They want to make world government great. They prefer to call people "citizens of the world," not "citizens of a sovereign nation." They favor open borders (no walls or fences) and no restrictions on immigration. If terrorists cross a border to kill and wound large numbers of people, the globalists close their eyes to it or they use it as an opportunity to pass laws to track the movement of everyone, especially what everyone buys and sells. Christians see this as a direct path to the Mark of the Beast.

World Religion

There is more, but we must move on to something else: If the world is close to a world government, it is also close to a world religion. We will start this subject by focusing on three important signs in this arena.

First, it is widely accepted by the most notable Bible prophecy teachers that the Antichrist will rise to power in a revived Roman Empire

(Daniel 2:42–44, 9:26). The European Union is currently morphing into that, so let's note some facts about the EU's religious views.

In 1950, the EU began to discuss the design of a flag for their group of nations. Some wanted religious symbols on the flag (a cross, a crescent moon, etc.), but the struggle for a flag that would represent the identity and unity of Europe was difficult. The discussions dragged on for about 33 years, with hundreds of proposals being rejected.

In 1983, the European Parliament finally adopted a flag with 12 golden stars in a circle on a blue background. It took another decade or so for various other European groups to accept it, but they finally did.

There is a debate about who really designed the flag, but in 1987, one of the men who worked on it, Arsene Heitz, said the inspiration for the flag was the woman of the apocalypse (the Tribulation Period woman mentioned in Revelation 12:1–2). Mr. Heitz identified the woman as Mary with a crown of 12 stars over her head. Many Christians believe the woman represents Israel (Genesis 37:9–10), but the Roman Catholic Church contends that she represents the Mother of God. People will deny it, but the EU is now linked to the Tribulation Period and false doctrine through its flag.

The European Parliament headquarters, located in Strasbourg, France, meets 12 times a year in a 60-meter tall, unfinished tower simulating Nimrod's unfinished Tower of Babel. As already stated, Nimrod tried to establish a world religion there. Pagan deities tied to sexual perversion were worshiped there. Astrology, fortune-telling, soothsaying, and other demonic practices also occurred there.

Some official EU publications and posters have an artist's portrayal of the unfinished Tower of Babel on or in them. Above the tower is a halo of inverted "eurostars," or stars that are pointing downward. Inverted stars are often associated with witchcraft. The Church of Satan uses a symbol with five stars, one of which is pointing down.

In 1984, a stamp was released with the image of a woman riding a beast. In 1996, a five-euro coin was released with the image of a woman riding a beast. Outside the EU Council Building in Brussels, Belgium, is a statue of a woman called Europa (a pagan goddess) riding a beast. It is impossible to miss the connection of these items to Mystery, Babylon the Great, the Mother of Harlots, and Abominations of the Earth of Revelation chapter 17. These sinister pagan objects reveal much about the religious views of the EU globalist elite that approved them.

A second important sign that reveals the mindset of globalists who are pushing a world religion is the reproduction of the arch at the ancient Temple of Baal in Palmyra, Syria. In the Bible, the pagan god Baal is connected to the horrific sins of child sacrifice and ritualistic prostitution. According to Jesus, there is no difference between the worship of Baal and the worship of Satan and his demons (Matthew 12:24–28; Mark 3:22; Luke 11:18). Why reproduce something that stood at the entrance to a temple that was used for child sacrifice, ritualistic prostitution, and the worship of Satan and demons? Why take a vulgar emblem of sexual sin and Satan to the U.N., New York, London, Dubai, a world government summit, a G-7 summit, etc.? That is what has happened.

The answer is that the leaders of the New World Order have been discussing the need for a human value system, but they have rejected God's value system. They want a world religion that doesn't involve people putting their faith in Jesus. The sexual side of it is rooted in the worship of false gods and goddesses at the Tower of Babel and Babylon. It is setting the stage for the appearance of Mystery, Babylon the Great, the Mother of Harlots, and Abominations of the Earth.

Third, a group of globalists decided to build a chest called the Ark of Hope and display it at the U.N. Their Ark of Hope was constructed according to the same dimensions as the biblical Ark of the Covenant. The Ark of Hope and the Ark of the Covenant both had carrying poles. Those who made the Ark of Hope used those carrying poles to transport it about 350 miles from Vermont to New York City. The Old Testament priests used these poles to carry the Ark of the Covenant when the Hebrews moved around in the wilderness.

But that is where the similarities end. The Ark of the Covenant contained the Ten Commandments, a golden jar filled with manna, and Aaron's rod that budded. The Ark of Hope contains the Earth Charter, a document with ethical principles that often contradict the Word of God, and Temenos Books containing pictures and prayers for a global society (world government), global healing, global peace, etc. The Ark of the Covenant had a mercy seat on top where sacrifices were offered to the one true God. The Ark of Hope has a panel on top with symbols that honor many gods and goddesses. According to those who built the Ark of Hope, a temenos is a magic sacred circle.

This is clearly the spirit of Nimrod (rebellion, worship of false gods, black magic, perversion of the Scriptures, etc.) that appeared at the Tower of Babel, continued in the kingdom of Babylon, and will manifest itself in full strength during the Tribulation Period.

Some say today's society is too enlightened to be involved in black magic. Others know that witches have tried to cast black magic spells on President Trump and his supporters at midnight when there is a waning crescent moon.

Deception

Anyway, if a very powerful, God-rejecting globalist movement is pushing a sinister world government and world religion upon planet Earth, and this is clearly happening, how can they possibly succeed? The answer can be narrowed down to one word: deception.

More than 25 years ago, one of the most powerful globalists on earth, David Rockefeller, said the world needs a global crisis to get everyone on earth to accept a world government. He saw the need for widespread public support for world government, and others agreed. Many believe this was the birth of the great deception that has now morphed into "climate change."

Climate change is just a means to an end, or a created crisis with a hidden agenda. The idea is to convince everyone on earth that the world needs to come together and act as one body, or billions of people will die because global CO_2 pollution is causing storms, droughts, floods, rising sea levels, heatwaves, snow storms, hurricanes, etc. Put another way, it is a scare tactic designed to convince the world that human activity is threatening the very existence of those on earth and is such an enormous problem it can only be solved by global rules and regulations.

Perhaps the most famous and best-known climate-change alarmist in the world is former U.S. Vice President Al Gore. He is an expert at scare tactics. In 2006, Mr. Gore made a movie called *An Inconvenient Truth*. In the movie, he said, "Within the decade, there will be no more 'snows of Kilimanjaro.' " That decade has now come and gone, so it is easy to check the reliability of Mr. Gore's prediction by visiting Mt. Kilimanjaro. Incidentally, take some warm clothes and snow shoes, because there is a lot of snow there.

In 2007–2009, Mr. Gore traveled around the globe saying there won't be any ice at the North Pole by 2013. But instead of telling people this was just his opinion, he said he had scientific data from studies by climate-change experts to back up his claims. Is it possible that one of those experts might be the famous creature named Sasquatch?

Does the Sasquatch statement sound ridiculous? Try this: Mr. Gore once said sea levels are rising so fast that fish are swimming in the streets of Miami. Not long after that, NASA said sea levels have been falling for two years. That is good news. People don't have to worry about stepping on fish when they walk the streets of Miami.

Understand this: God created humans to breathe in oxygen and to give off CO_2. He created plants to do the opposite: Breathe in CO_2 and give off oxygen (a process called photosynthesis). Higher CO_2 levels spur the growth of plants, not the death of plants. It causes the earth to become green with plants, not brown from drought.

Also understand that former vice president Al Gore and many of his allies are hypocrites. On August 3, 2017, it was reported that his house consumes as much electricity in one year as 34 average houses. He wants the average person to consume less energy, but he doesn't practice what he preaches. The goal of the globalists is not to save humankind from global destruction by natural disasters. Their goal is to empower a small group of people to control humankind all over the earth so that this small group of people can make their vision of a utopia on earth a reality. It involves gaining control of the so-called three pillars of society: politics, religion, and the economy.

This is how the globalist scam has been working. Natural disasters are real. It may be a flood in one place and a drought in another; unusually hot weather in one place and unusually cold weather in another. There is no denying that the weather is not always normal all over the world. This has been going on since the creation of Adam and Eve, and it will continue in the future. What is different is the globalists' decision to use this as a scare tactic.

At first, globalists called their scare tactic "global warming." A few cold snaps (which is not unusual) and a lot of ridicule by skeptics caused them to change the name from "global warming" to "climate change." The ridicule that changing the name has caused has been hard to live down. But the necessity of this name change exposes the fraud and lack of true science in the ill-conceived globalist movement.

In fact, it has caused some globalists to give grants to people and groups to produce data to back up their climate-change lie. It has caused globalists to portray scientists who agree with them as highly qualified and intelligent, and to portray scientists who disagree with them as unqualified and unlearned.

Globalists have taken their phony data and called it "settled science," but there is nothing settled about it other than the fact that much of the deception was generated by hired guns, so to speak. Thousands of highly qualified scientists call it "pseudo-science," meaning bogus, contrived, misleading, or not real science. Some refer to it as the "climate-change hoax."

Reputable groups have made studies that document the deception of the climate-change dogma. One study is called "Information Manipulation and Climate Agreements." It was published in the *American Journal of Agricultural Economics* (96 (3), 851–861). Google it. Copies are available.

John Coleman, the highly respected founder of the Weather Channel, referred to global warming as "global-warming silliness." He said the science behind it is fake and it is sheer nonsense.

The U.S. Department of Agriculture (USDA) has even gotten involved. In early August 2017, it was reported that the USDA staff has been directed to stop using the words "climate change" and to start using the words "weather extremes" instead.

Some globalists have admitted that some of their data is wrong. That bothers them, but not enough to switch sides. They cling to their false data and continue to deceive people, because they think their ultimate goal is a good one.

Some globalists appear to be involved in the scam to enrich themselves. Former U.S. Vice President Gore has raked in huge sums of money from speeches, books, a movie, promoting carbon taxes, etc. Many of the things he has said have been debunked, but he continues to say them and the money keeps rolling in.

Some globalists openly support the global-warming hoax, but their actions clearly deny the hysteria that they keep spreading. China and India have both ratified the Paris Climate Change Agreement, and both have criticized President Trump for not signing it. But these two nations are two of the worst greenhouse gas polluters in the world, and they continue to build coal-fired power plants that some think will worsen the situation.

Some globalists have become so involved in this deception that their critics have started calling it a religion. It is not a science, because true science has been rejected. It is more accurately described as a religion. It is a devotion to or a worship of the shared belief that a handful of highly intelligent humans can preserve this earth and transform it into a heaven on earth for like-minded people.

Some globalists have even met with religious groups. They have actively involved religious groups "to help save the world." Christianity is a way of life that trusts Jesus to save the world, but Pope Francis has joined the climate-change cult and elevated it to a priority of his papacy.

This is Nimrod-like devotion: rebellion against the true God that will lead to the worship of Satan. It rejects the idea that God controls the weather and natural disasters (Psalm 104:32, 135:7, 148:8; Nahum 1:3). It rejects the idea that the earth is under a curse because of sin (Romans 8:22–23). It rejects the idea that natural disasters can be stopped by turning from sin and turning to God (2 Chronicles 7:13–14).

It rejects the idea that abortion is murder, because globalists want to reduce the population of the earth to save the planet. It rejects the idea that gay marriage is wrong, because globalists want families to have fewer children and pollute less. It rejects the idea that euthanasia is wrong, because globalists want to preserve resources for other generations.

Some seem to care more about snails, seals, and polar bears than they do about people. They are fanatical and have forgotten about loving others as they do themselves. Never mind if jobs are lost and people don't have enough to live on. Never mind if some are aborting babies as a matter of convenience.

Globalists have projected that the 7.6 billion people on earth today will reach 9.8 billion by 2050 and 11.2 billion by 2100. They believe that this is more than Mother Earth can stand. They have projected that the 962 million people on earth over age 60 today will reach 2.1 billion by 2050 and 3.1 billion by 2100. That is more than they think they can provide for. They want to get control of people's lives and drastically reduce these numbers by controlling fertility rates, birth rates, and death rates.

Child sacrifice in Babel and Babylon have led to an ignorance and disrespect for the value of life all over the world. Some want to terminate the handicapped at birth, etc. Some even want to allow new parents three or four years to decide whether their child should live or not.

Some will argue that calling climate change a religion is wrong. But no less than MIT Professor Dr. Richard Lindzen has called it a religion.[3] And no less than former EPA Administrator Gina McCarthy has admitted that it has become a religion. She has even called it a "politically induced religion."[4]

Notice that the good lady said "politically induced religion." That is what merging world government and world religion will produce: a politically induced religion. And underneath this great hoax is the ever-present father of lies called Satan.

One day, Jesus will come back. He will establish a world government and a world religion to God's liking. Satan will be bound and chained for 1,000 years. Rebellion, lying, deceit, soothsaying, black magic, witchcraft, worship of false gods and goddesses, the persecution of God's people, and other activities and behaviors like that won't be permitted. And sadly, those who are rebelling against Him today will be in torment unless they change before it is too late.

Endnotes:

1. Unless otherwise noted, all Scripture in this chapter is from the King James Version (KJV) of the Bible.
2. Daymond R. Duck and Larry Richards, *The Book of Revelation: The Smart Guide to the Bible Series* (Nashville, TN: Nelson Reference, a Division of Thomas Nelson, Inc.), page cxcii.
3. *Journal of American Physicians and Surgeons*, Fall 2013.
4. Climate Depot, February 9, 2017, http://www.climatedepot.com/.

CHAPTER 9

The Foreteller-Fabricators

NATHAN E. JONES

Her Reward

Sunbeams blazed blindingly though the grand doorway of an opulent Etruscan room, silhouetting the hour-glass shape of a most tall and beautiful woman. Her vigorous youth radiated more brilliantly than the noonday sun. Her lithe form was draped in finery as bejeweled as her marbled seaside villa. Her posture poised as perfectly as an elegant vase.

The maiden inhaled a deep draught of salty air that had wafted in from the Italian Bay of Naples. Brimming with assurance, the noble-woman smiled confidently from her lofty heights overlooking her magnificent city. No city named after the stalwart Roman hero Pompey could ever perish, she thought. Roman might must always prevail, whether the enemy be man or nature. National pride strengthened her fortitude.

But then, another shudder of ground tremors shook her fortitude yet again. Her composure cracked just a little as she attempted to regain her balance.

The warm summer of August in A.D. 79 attracted wealthy vacationers who for centuries had traveled to Pompeii to soak up the sun and scenery in this idyllic jewel of the Mediterranean Sea. That is, until their voyaging ceased. Her vantage point confirmed the beaches were barren. Vesuvius made sure of that. The rumblings of the soaring mountain, clearly visible on the horizon a mere five miles away, rebuked the vacationers to keep their distance and struck terror in the town's inhabitants, causing them to flee. Cowards! As a little girl, she had survived the quake of 63.

This would be no different. And so she, along with the remaining 2,000 out of the regular 20,000 residents the town once held, stayed behind, defiant and unafraid. Well, mostly unafraid.

Her thoughts were interrupted as yet another violent rumbling toppled the mighty god, Apollo, off of his mantle. She turned abruptly back toward the chamber at the sharp cracking sound of the ornate statue shattering into a thousand pieces across the tiled floor. She shuddered visibly at the loss of such an expensive sculpture.

The smashing sound of the statue instantly paled in comparison to what immediately followed. A deafening sonic boom so powerful that she, much like her idol, toppled to the floor. Tearing her eyes away from the broken shards, she twisted her gaze back out of the open doors and witnessed — a nightmare.

Mount Vesuvius had finally erupted! Millions of tons of superheated lava, scorching-hot volcanic gases, grey ash, and rock debris spewed a towering 12 miles high. The blast sent a plume into the sky double the height of the tallest mountain in the world, so high that people could see it for hundreds of miles around. The brilliant sun was blotted into a hazy, blood-red hue. The town plunged into darkness.

Whatever fortitude this brave young woman maintained melted instantly away at the horrific sight. She screamed her lungs out in abject terror.

Time stopped. Over the next 24 hours, the volcanic ash gently falling down like snow calmed the maiden's nerves, all the while deceiving her into complacency. The woman's mind was made up to leave, temporarily, but she just couldn't vacate without taking as much of her great wealth with her as she possibly could. Some vagabond might loot her prized possessions while she was away, she worried. Jittery slaves packed her cart to overflowing as she pointed to this or that valuable and barked out orders.

Despite the frantic packing, no man or beast remained standing as Vesuvius' second blast wave shook Italy to its foundations. The mountain-turned-volcano belched lava as hot as 1,300 degrees Fahrenheit. The surge of superheated poisonous gas and pulverized rock poured swiftly down the mountainside, swallowing everything and everyone in its destructive path.

The panicked slaves instantly dropped their loads and fled in terror through the city's main gate. The woman, focused absently only on her wealth despite the wall of death tumbling toward her, choked back dust to bellow for the slaves to return. Left alone, and unused to manual labor, she grabbed a light silken bag of pearls off of the top of the cart, hiked up her fine robes, and made a mad dash after the slaves.

The earth rocked like a boat in a sea storm and she lost her footing, as well as her bag. The sack of pearls skittered across the ash-filthy ground. The iron gate remained a mere few feet away, but she just couldn't leave the last of her earthly wealth behind. She reached back hungrily toward the bag with outstretched, grasping fingers.

Destiny failed to unite the sylphlike maiden with her beloved possessions. The wall of soot and darkness deluged down upon her like a tidal wave, burying all of Pompeii 16 feet deep under millions of tons of volcanic debris. The opulent city, along with the surrounding 200 square miles, was erased from the landscape.

The noblewoman, along with hundreds of its other naïve inhabitants, remained entombed under the ash for hundreds of years. Not until 1748 did explorers discover the lost city.[1] And what they found amazed the world! Frozen in time, the pumice and ash perfectly preserved buildings, everyday objects, household goods, even food preserves, and most interestingly, skeletons. The remaining inhabitants had been flash-frozen right where they'd fallen, embalmed as if Egyptian mummies.

Excavators marveled at a particularly profound scene. One of the skeletons unearthed was that of a young woman, located so very close to escaping through the city gate. Instead of fleeing away, she had turned toward the town, desperately reaching back for a bag of pearls. Upon looking down at her anguished corpse making its last dying grasp for material wealth, it was said of her, "Though death was hard at her heels, and life was beckoning to her beyond the city gates, she could not shake off their spell. She had turned to pick them up, with death as her reward . . . frozen in an attitude of greed."[2]

The Long War

Greed. It killed the young woman long before the volcano ever did. And, not just her. Greed's victims throughout human history number in the billions.

Greed has been the bane of humanity since the dawn of time, ever since Adam and Eve lusted after the serpent's false promise that if they ate the forbidden fruit they would surely not die, but become like God, knowing good and evil (Genesis 3). And even well before mankind's Fall, up in the angelic realm, greed consumed Lucifer, the magnificent angel of light, who boldly proclaimed in his heart, "I will ascend into heaven, I will exalt my throne above the stars of God . . . I will be like the most High" (Isaiah 14:13–14).[3]

Greed, or avarice as it is sometimes called, is what, exactly? Dictionary.com defines greed as "an excessive, extreme desire for something, often more than one's proper share; an avid desire for gain or wealth."[4] The Roman lyric poet Horace explained that greed encompasses the element of unending dissatisfaction when he philosophized, "He who is greedy is always in want."[5] Author T.F. Hodge explained that greed and ego go hand in hand when he penned, "The ego lusts for satisfaction. It has a prideful, ferocious appetite for its version of 'truth.' It is the most challenging aspect to conquer; the cause for most spiritual turmoil."[6]

If greed belongs to the list of the seven deadly sins, then its cousins — envy, gluttony, lust, pride, sloth, and wrath — are merely different shades of the same, all-consuming self-interest. They combine into the ultimate expression of ego.

Ego unchecked transforms a being from a freeman into a slave. As Jesus Christ taught, "No one can serve two masters; for either he will hate the one and love the other, or else he will be loyal to the one and despise the other. You cannot serve God and mammon" (Matthew 6:24).

Greed and God cannot coexist in a person's heart. The dichotomy will rip a person in two, forcing one to choose a loving master of selflessness or an all-consuming master of self. That spiritual battle raging within the human heart formed the foundation for the long spiritual war the world is now embroiled in — the ultimate Giver versus the ultimate Taker. And in the end, only one shall stand triumphant.

Ego wields as its primary weapon the two-edged sword of deception and self-deception. Often those who greedily lust after God's might, position, and power wrap themselves in the cloak of self-deceived religiosity. They deceive not only others for their own selfish gain, but themselves as well. The Pharisees and scribes of Jesus' day were such men, vainly believing themselves holy and altruistic. Alas, Christ threw their treachery in their faces when He accused:

If God were your Father, you would love Me.... You are of your father the devil, and the desires of your father you want to do.

He was a murderer from the beginning, and does not stand in the truth, because there is no truth in him. When he speaks a lie, he speaks from his own resources, for he is a liar and the father of it. But because I tell the truth, you do not believe Me. . . . you are not of God (John 8:42–47).

Jesus turned up the heat on all the false teachers and false prophets who claim they speak in God's name, as well as the false christs who blasphemously dare to claim equality with God. In truth, these counterfeits exist as "whitewashed tombs . . . full of dead men's bones and all uncleanness" (Matthew 23:27). In the service to the master of greed, some people sink into becoming the most loathsome and detestable of all who self-deceive and deceive others — the "foreteller-fabricators."

In this chapter, we will take a hard look at those deceivers of the false prophet and false christ variety. Looking at the 1st century to the 21st century, these deceivers have served their evil master in their futile pursuit of the great Garden delusion — their egos lust to become gods. We will peek behind the shrouds of some of the cult leaders, who like weeds, have sprung up over the last 2,000 years. We will scratch our heads over the oddity that is the eschatologically confused. And then, finally, we will marvel at the naivety of the eschatologically ignorant. Vital lessons will be learned about how to spot a counterfeit Christ, and how we can apply these truths to our daily lives.

But, first, we must start where Jesus started. We must take a look at yet another tragic story of greed. Let's journey through one of the most dynamic narratives and the greatest series of prophetic revelations found in all of the Bible. The story is called . . .

The Olivet Discourse

The Widow's Mite

One of Jesus' most riveting teachings was recorded in the Gospels in Matthew 24, Luke 21, and Mark 13. Jesus had been teaching from God's Temple in Jerusalem, which overlooked the Mount of Olives. Hence, the sermon has been titled the Olivet Discourse after this pastoral view. As Luke 21:37–38 describes: "And in the daytime He was teaching in the temple, but at night He went out and stayed on the mountain called Olivet. Then early in the morning all the people came to Him in the temple to hear Him."

The narrative opens with a touching little comparison that shines the spotlight on greedy, egotistical deceivers who enshroud themselves in religiosity. While at the Temple, Jesus observed this sharp contrast:

> And He looked up and saw the rich putting their gifts into the treasury, and He saw also a certain poor widow putting in two mites. So He said, "Truly I say to you that this poor widow has put in more than all; for all these out of their abundance have put in offerings for God, but she out of her poverty put in all the livelihood that she had" (Luke 21:1–4).

The story of the widow's mite provides the background to a much larger subject Jesus was about to address. But first, Jesus sets up His teaching by pointing out to His audience an everyday scene of tithing — the masses of Jews flooded the Temple in order to tithe the Temple tax.

The rich were dropping massive bags of loot into the treasury, and likely making a big show of it. Onlookers, including the Apostles, were naturally impressed at the perceived magnanimity.

Not Jesus! He instead focused on a poor woman, who, in her poverty, nobody else would have ever noticed had He not pointed her out. She timidly dropped into the coffers two mites, small copper coins worth a paltry eighth of a cent. And likely, in her humble poverty and out of embarrassment, she attempted to go as unnoticed as possible.

What God Almighty sees, the world does not see. Amount mattered little to Jesus, but rather percent and heart were what drew His interest. For those rich people who gave, some begrudgingly, out of their abundance, they acted as Old Deacon Horner. He sat in a corner, as the contribution box passed by; sweetly content, he dropped in a cent, and said, "What a good churchman am I."[7] But the widow, destined to societal poverty without a husband or son to take care of her, gave all she had to live on. This generous widow presented her gift without withholding herself. She didn't give from the top of her purse, like the parading rich did, but from the bottom of her heart. She loved God and trusted Him to provide for her needs. Now that was a woman of faith!

The Wealthy Temple

After Jesus had dropped this bombshell of profound insight into sacrificial giving, the scene was now properly set to launch an even greater bombshell, at least from a human perspective. From a simple widow unknowingly demonstrating to the world over millennia how God wants His children to give, Jesus was now going to show them how He would be victorious over the great spiritual warfare long being waged against Him by those who greedily covet His position.

The Olivet Discourse does not record how long Jesus' audience pondered the widow. The human mind tends to wander when faced with a revelation too massive for the human mind to fully contain. Likely, only a few minutes passed before Jesus' disciples began to be captivated yet again by the riches they were witnessing. The narrative continues, "Then, as some spoke of the temple, how it was adorned with beautiful stones and donations" (Luke 21:5).

Jesus' disciples must be excused somewhat for being amazed. They were, after all, talking about the Temple. This complex stood as the center of culture for Israel. It was the most beautiful, most ornate, most important building to the Jewish people in the entire planet. Most of Jesus' disciples were small-towners, living in the sticks of tiny 200- to 300-person towns. Imagine spending your entire life living in a one-room house deep in the backwoods. Then, for the first time, you travel to the Big City and ride up the tallest skyscraper. Like the disciples, you'd be like, "Wow! I can't believe this building!"

That was what it was like for the Apostles. These peasants had just arrived at the biggest city they so far had ever seen, filled with commerce and wealth and people. Then they went to the apex of it all — the Temple, God's own dwelling on earth.

The Jewish Temple stood out as the wealthiest of all the buildings in Jerusalem. Located up on Mount Moriah, the very place Father Abraham had nearly sacrificed Isaac, the building was beautifully decorated with panels of cedar and floors of cypress wood. The fixtures were inlaid with gold set to floral designs. The rooms contained marvelous furnishings. The famed and deadly Ark of the Covenant once stood in the Holy of Holies where the *shekinah* glory of God had dwelled.

The magnificence of the Temple building was blinding! Those country boys were naturally awestruck.

The Three Questions

Imagine all the pointing and gaping and *oohing* and *aahing*. And then, somewhere behind the disciples, in a choked but level voice, Jesus quietly says: "These things which you see — the days will come in which not one stone shall be left upon another that shall not be thrown down" (Luke 21:6).

Say, what?! There stood Jesus' disciples, excitedly gaping in awe at the Temple, and Jesus out of the blue basically declared, "None of this will be here much longer. It will all be torn down. Every stone will be thrown away." Just imagine the shock on the disciples' faces! They couldn't believe it. This building was supposed to be the house of God. Why would God abandon His home? The very idea defied logic. After all, throughout Israel's history, the Jewish people believed that as long as the Temple stood, Israel stood invulnerable. And now, Jesus had burst their bubble, and the silence that followed was deafening.

Obviously, the disciples had questions. Some moments later, they finally had built up enough courage to ask Jesus why He said what He did. Likely, all 12 of them started asking at once. Luke 21 parallels Matthew 24 and Mark 13, and when those three chapters are compiled, we discover the disciples asked three questions:

1) When will the Temple fall?

Jesus had just announced that the Temple would be destroyed. So, they first wanted to know, "When, Lord, will this happen?"

2) What will be the sign of the end of the age?

The Son of God had arrived to usher in His kingdom, but was crucified on a cross. With today's hindsight, Christians now know that Jesus' First Coming had only achieved the spiritual aspect of His kingdom — the Church. The world waits for Jesus to return again and usher in His earthly Millennial Kingdom. But, before that, the Church waits for her Lord to return and remove those saved off of this earth and bring them up to heaven in an event called the Rapture. And so, second, Jesus' disciples desired to learn about the signs that would reveal the end of the age, which the Church knows has been the last 2,000 years called the Church Age, which we are living in right now.

3) What will be the sign of Jesus' coming?

And third, this question refers to the setting up of Jesus' earthly kingdom, which will happen upon His Second Coming. Jesus will return after a horrific time of global judgment called the Tribulation. The earth will experience the worst seven-year time period in all of human history.

And so, the disciples had three questions. Jesus' stunning and lengthy answer would shock them more than His statement about the destruction of the Temple.

Prophetic Perspective

Before delving into Jesus' amazing answers to these three vital questions and how His answers encompass the fall of the foreteller-fabricators, we need to learn a little about prophetic perspective.

Near, Far, Farther

Ever watch *Sesame Street* growing up? I did! I loved *Sesame Street* as a child. My all-time favorite character was Grover. The furry, blue guy was my favorite Muppet.

Grover taught children something very important. He taught the concept of near and far. Grover ran far away from the TV and yelled "Far!" Then he trotted very close to the screen and yelled "Near!" Again and again Grover ran and yelled, only to collapse in exhaustion. I laughed every time.

What Grover taught and what prophetic perspective is exactly concerns near and far. Prophecy often contains a near interpretation, which in this case answers the question about when the Temple will fall. History records pointedly that the Temple fell to the Roman legions in A.D. 70. Literally not one stone was left upon another.

But, Jesus also answers the far view concerning what will be the signs at the end of the Church Age. Many, many signs of the end times reveal that humanity has finally reached the end of this age. The time we are living in right now remains very pertinent to the far view.

But then, there is something Grover forgot to teach us, and that's farther. Farther covers the third question concerning the Second Coming of Jesus Christ, when Jesus returns to defeat evil and set up His Millennial Kingdom.

Grover taught one aspect of prophetic perspective: near, far, and farther.

Lesser to Greater

The second concept concerning prophetic perspective can be understood by looking at a woman in labor. Because my wife birthed three children, I now know everything there is to know about giving birth (or so I believe). She told me that when her contractions began, they started out as lesser in frequency and intensity. The contractions began far apart in time, and the pain was weak. But, the closer a woman gets to the birth of the baby, the time between contractions shrinks shorter and shorter, and the labor pains grow greater and greater in intensity.

Jesus, when answering His disciples' questions, taught as the prophets did before Him that the answers to those questions have a near, far, and farther aspect, as well as a lesser-to-greater meaning. In other words, as the signs of the times arrive, and the closer history gets to their fulfilment, the greater, more intense, and more frequent the signs would come.

So, yes, there were many signs that occurred back around A.D. 70 when the Temple finally fell. But, the closer we get to Jesus' return, the greater, more frequent, and more intense the birth pains will strike the world, leading up to the Tribulation and eventual return of Jesus Christ to set up His earthly kingdom.

Prophetic perspective contains the essential concepts of "near, far, and farther" and "lesser to greater." From this understanding, the reader can better understand Jesus' answers to these three critical questions, as well as marvel that we are witnessing His answers being fulfilled in our very day.

Sign of False Messiahs

The Ten Signs

Jesus, in His Olivet Discourse, next provided ten signs that answered the disciples' three questions. I can tell you now, nine of them are absolutely awful. Awful is what one would expect to hear from a Bible prophecy teacher. But, Jesus always speaks the truth, and the signs He gave He felt must be shared. They simply are what they are. Nine of the ten signs cover the worst events that must happen in all of human history. The signs are:

1. False messiahs
2. Wars and revolutions
3. Earthquakes
4. Famines
5. Pestilence
6. Fearful events (social and economic)

7. Signs in the sky
8. The persecution of Christians
9. The fall of Jerusalem

Sign number 10 stands out as the only hopeful sign for the believer in Christ. Hope finds its fulfillment when the baby finally arrives. The birth of the baby ends the labor pains. This "birth" is the return of King Jesus. Humanity must endure the labor pains before we get to the time — the birth — of the full realization of Christ's Kingdom.

The signs of the end times have been covered in another chapter, so let's laser focus this chapter on the first sign — false messiahs. We'll now pick up with Jesus' teaching in Luke 21:8: "Take heed that you not be deceived. For many will come in My name, saying, 'I am He,' and, 'The time has drawn near.' Therefore do not go after them." We read the parallel passage of this statement in Matthew 24:4–5, "Take heed that no one deceives you. For many will come in My name saying, 'I am the Christ,' and will deceive many."

Because of prophetic perspective, we know that Jesus answers the first question concerning when the Temple will fall, but He also explains what the signs of the end of the Church Age will be, as well as the signs that occur before His Second Coming. Jesus covers all three questions with His list of ten signs.

The first sign concerning false messiahs includes false prophets, false teachers, and false christs. These counterfeits stand out as the foreteller-fabricators.

Notice that in His checklist of signs, Jesus lists false messiahs as the very first. He did not just mention this sign once, but three times throughout His Olivet Discourse. False teachers are actually the most prolific end-time sign that Jesus taught. Not only in Matthew 24:4–5 does He mention them, but then in verse 11, He does so again: "Then many false prophets will rise up and deceive many." Again, in verse 24, Jesus warns, "For false Christs and false prophets will rise and show great signs and wonders to deceive, if possible, even the elect." Three times in this passage Jesus stated that false prophets and false christs would come claiming to be Jesus, and they would mislead many people with their heretical teachings.

God Himself believes that false teachers are the number one end-time sign pointing to His soon return. Christians, therefore, should be alert to deception.

Jesus revealed that the closer humanity came to these three prophetic events — the fall of the Temple, the Rapture, and the Second Coming — the more false messiahs, prophets, and teachers would proliferate in frequency and intensity.

The Temple Falls

False teachers and false messiahs have been around for a very long time, even during the first century. Satan works tirelessly, always trying to water down the message of God. Almost as soon as the Good News of Jesus Christ began being proclaimed through the Church, false teachers spewing unbiblical doctrines started proliferating on the scene in an attempt to muddy the doctrinal waters. Let us now address the disciples' first question — "When will the Temple fall?" — and learn about Jesus' "near" answer concerning how foreteller-fabricators would perform as a living sign warning of the Temple's impending destruction.

The Judaizers

One such group of false teachers were (and sadly are still with us today) the Judaizers. They plagued the fledgling Church, denying Christians Christ's grace earned on the Cross by burdening believers under the yoke of living by the obsolete Mosaic Law. The Apostle Paul had some very harsh advice for these false teachers, telling them they should run off and emasculate themselves (Galatians 5:12)! These agitators made the Apostles very angry, for they denied Christ's sacrifice by putting Christians back under a law Jesus had fully fulfilled with His own shed blood.

The Gnostics

Then there were the Gnostics. These deceivers were Greek-learned egomaniacs who believed they possessed superior knowledge about God. To them, Scripture plus their knowledge equaled truth. They also believed Jesus couldn't possibly have come to earth in human form because they shunned the material realm as evil and pronounced everything spiritual as good. They concluded that Jesus' spirit inhabited a body, and then, at the crucifixion, He vacated that body. Therefore, Jesus was never really crucified. By denying the crucifixion, these deceivers denied the very sacrifice that provides mankind salvation from the just punishment for our sins.

Judas the Galilean

Acts 5:37 tells the particular story of a false Christ named Judas the Galilean: "Judas of Galilee rose up in the days of the census, and drew away many people after him." The Jewish historian Josephus added that Judas the Galilean told Jews "that it was shameful for them to be 'consenting to pay tribute to the Romans and tolerating mortal masters after having God for their Lord.' "[8]

Judas was aided by a false prophet named Saddok. This slimy foreteller-fabricator had the gall to claim he was the fulfillment of the Malachi 4:5–6 prophecy that foretold Elijah would precede and announce the coming of the Messiah. Acts reports that these deceivers met their just end, as "he also perished, and all who obeyed him were dispersed" (Acts 5:37). Despite his demise, Saddok's followers went on to found the anti-Roman Zealots, in which Simon the Zealot, one of Jesus' Apostles, once held membership.

Theudas

Acts 5:36 also lists another false christ named Theudas: "For some time ago Theudas rose up, claiming to be somebody. A number of men, about four hundred, joined him." Josephus added that in A.D. 45, Theudas convinced "the majority of the masses to take up their possessions and to follow him to the Jordan River."[9] He claimed that the Jordan would part for them at his command. Embarrassingly, the river refused, and this false christ was slain. Many of his foolish followers paid for their devotion with their lives, and the movement came to nothing.

An Unnamed Egyptian Jew

Acts 21:38 records a Roman commander asking the Apostle Paul, "Are you not the Egyptian who some time ago stirred up a rebellion and led the four thousand assassins out into the wilderness?" Josephus explained that this false messiah "was a cheat, and pretended to be a prophet also, and got together thirty thousand men that were deluded by him."[10] Leading his followers from the wilderness to the Mount of Olives, Josephus reported, "He was ready to break into Jerusalem by force from that place; and if he could but once conquer the Roman garrison and the people, he intended to rule them by the assistance of those guards of his that were to break into the city with him." Of course, Paul assured the commander he was certainly not that charlatan.

These are just a few examples of the fulfillment of the sign of false messiahs, prophets, and teachers leading up to the destruction of the Temple in A.D. 70. Quite a number of foreteller-fabricators greedily hungered for God's power and so deceived many people in the first century, just as Jesus had foretold.

End of the Age

We just looked at the "near" view of Jesus' answer concerning the fall of the Temple. Now let's look at His "far" response concerning the sign of false messiahs in answering the Apostles' second question: "What will be the sign of the end of the age?" This entails the period we live in now called the Church Age, which one day will end with the Rapture of the Church.

According to Watchman Fellowship, a cult-watching website, there are some 1,200 religious organizations and beliefs in the United States and 500 registered cults.[11] Such an astounding number proves we truly are living during a time of prolific false teachings. Satan plots to dilute the truthful teachings of Jesus Christ by drowning His message under the false teachings and half-truths promoted by his demonically charged false messengers.

Because such a staggering amount of unbiblical religions practice out there, we couldn't possibly cover them all here. So, we'll just take a quick survey through some of the most notorious cults and their foreteller-fabricating false messiahs. The term "cult," as Watchman defines it, is "any religious group viewed as strange or dangerous; employing abusive, manipulative, or illegal control over their followers' lives, and exists as a counterfeit or serious deviation from the doctrines of classical Christianity."[12]

Joseph Smith

In 1830, the charismatic Joseph Smith founded the Church of Jesus Christ of Latter-Day Saints, better known as the Mormons. He added a whole other book to the Bible, calling it the *Book of Mormon*. He may have acknowledged that Jesus came in the flesh, but he claimed that Jesus was the spirit brother of Satan! He continued Satan's Garden of Eden lie that one day we are all going to become gods.

Smith even made a number of dated prophetic predictions about men going on mission trips that never happened, churches to be built that never were, and historic battles that never took place. He even claimed that the Native Americans were Jews, which was genetically debunked. Tragically, Mormonism exploded throughout the world, and now as the largest cult, boasts over five million members.

Charles Taze Russell

Next, there's Charles Taze Russell, the founder of the Jehovah's Witnesses. He claimed Jesus is really the archangel Michael, and so denied the Trinity. Russell and his Watchtower Society prophesied that the world would end in 1914, 1918, 1925, 1975, and 1989. Clearly, the world did not end, proving Russell a false teacher.

Jim Jones

Jim Jones claimed to be God, Buddha, and Vladimir Lenin all rolled up in one. Jones took his People's Temple Christian Church devotees down to Guyana to form a town, which he named after himself — Jonestown. In 1978, at this false messiah's command, 914 people drank poison and so committed suicide, as did Jones himself. They followed Jones, believing he was God, but in their last breath, they realized he was of the devil.

José Luis de Jesús Miranda

Miranda made no qualms claiming in 1973 that he had transformed into "the Man Jesus-Christ" incarnate. His Growing in Grace International boasted two million followers across 30 nations. Miranda championed the spirit of the Antichrist as actually a good thing, encouraging his adherents to tattoo their bodies with the Antichrist's number 666. He formed a countdown to June 30, 2012, when he proclaimed the world's governments would usher in his "Government of the 666." Miranda may have died of cirrhosis of the liver on November 17, 2013, but his desperate followers claimed he had instead transformed into the immortal Melchizedek.

Jeane Dixon

Jeane Dixon was a false prophetess who practiced astrology and prognostication, yet claimed her information derived from the Christian God. She uttered many false prophecies, including one that a woman would become the United States president in the 1980s.

David Koresh

David Koresh left the Seventh-Day Adventist Church in 1984 to proclaim his divinity and form the Branch Davidians. He taught that knowing the Seven Seals of the Book of Revelation brought salvation. Though his Waco, Texas, compound was burnt to the ground during a government raid back in 1993, his remaining followers continue to believe Koresh's messianic claims and expect him to be resurrected one day soon.

Sun Myung Moon

Sun Myung Moon taught at his massive South Korean Unification Church that Jesus brought only spiritual salvation, so another savior was necessary to fulfill Jesus' mission, and that man was him. Moon called himself the "Lord of the Second Advent" and believed himself to be the parent of all humanity. Moon's self-proclaimed deity wasn't powerful enough to stop pneumonia, and after a lavishly lived life, on September 3, 2012, he died at 92 years old.

Sergey the Vissarion Christ

Sergey Anatolyevitch Torop, or as his followers call him, the Vissarion, is yet another foreteller-fabricator claiming to be the reincarnated Christ and "He who gives new life." His Community of Unified Faith in Russia boasts membership of around 50,000 adherents spread across 83 communities. There they learn about the importance of vegetarianism, their impending reincarnation, and the coming apocalypse.

Benjamin Crème

Benjamin Crème was the esoteric false prophet for the New Age messiah, Lord Maitreya. He proclaimed in his *The Emergence* newsletter and *Share International* magazine and taught at his North Hollywood Tara Center that Jesus the Christ-consciousness had returned as Maitreya the World Teacher. Universalistic in his doctrine, Maitreya embodies the Imam Mahdi, Krishna, and the Messiah. Crème proclaimed Maitreya as the "Avatar for the Aquarian Age" — that is, until his death in 2016.

We could go on and on through the 1,200-plus modern-day false messiahs and prophets, but instead, please visit Watchman Fellowship's wonderful website at watchman.org. Watchman proves without a shadow of a doubt that today's world has been truly inundated with false messiahs and false teachers. And this is exactly what Jesus said would happen leading up to His rapturing His Church to heaven.

The Eschatologically Confused

The world is clearly barreling headlong toward the Rapture of the Church, for as Jesus warned, false messiahs, prophets, and teachers would proliferate the closer we get to that long-anticipated event. Jesus' number-one sign does not necessarily center on those who greedily deceive themselves and others into believing that they are God Almighty. No, some foreteller-fabricators deceive others unwittingly. The reason? They remain eschatologically confused.

Suffering from Symbolically

The reason these agents of confusion have their Bible prophecy so out of whack is that they are infected by the deadly disease I like to call Symbolically.

Those infected with this inhibitive condition are at first difficult to spot, for they look like any other Christian. Show them a symbol out of everyday life, and they can identify it with ease. But show them a symbol taken from the Bible, particularly Bible prophecy, and the Bible translation portion of their brains are quickly overcome by Symbolically. When it comes to the interpretation of the Bible, patients with this debilitating affliction often struggle over the question, "Should Bible prophecy be interpreted literally or symbolically?"

Those afflicted with Symbolically intentionally spiritualize the Scriptures, choosing whatever interpretation suits their fancy, and then argue automatically that the plain-sense meanings found in the Bible are not their true meanings. Those suffering under this inhibitive interpretive condition may experience . . .

1. A disturbing inability to believe that God knows how to communicate.
2. The compulsive desire to strip Bible verses from their context.
3. Sudden spasms of detective work, searching for hidden meanings.
4. Manic mythologizing of the Genesis creation and Revelation end-times accounts.
5. Delusions of grandeur, playing God by deciding what the Bible truly does or does not mean.

If you, too, suffer from Symbolically, there is hope. Take the fast-acting Golden Rule of Interpretation. Yes, the Golden Rule of Interpretation is the cure that will guide you to a literal interpretation of the Bible. Just generously apply this motto every single time you read the Bible — "If the plain sense makes sense, don't look for any other sense, lest you end up with nonsense" — and you will be cured from spiritualizing Scriptures.

Once Christians apply the Golden Rule of Interpretation, they should keep the Bible study portion of their brains healthy by applying the following eight treatments:

1. The right approach: always approach the Scriptures with a childlike faith and an honest heart.
2. Be filled by God's Spirit: before opening your Bible, ask the Holy Spirit to provide clear understanding.
3. The inspiration of Scriptures: because God Himself inspired the writers of the Bible, accept the truth that what they wrote must be without error.
4. Plain-sense symbols: let the Bible be its own best interpreter as to the meaning of its own symbols.
5. Context, context, context: meanings of words in the Bible should always be determined by their context.
6. The principle of searching: all verses on a particular topic should be searched out, compared, and then reconciled. Never hang a doctrine on one isolated verse.
7. The problem of prefilling: allow that some Bible prophecies are prefilled in symbolic type first before being completely fulfilled later on.
8. Telescoping prophets: understand that prophets often looked into the future and saw a series of prophetic events, not realizing they'd be separated by long time intervals.

There are side effects from using the Golden Rule of Interpretation: a deeper understanding of God, a new appreciation of the Bible, mental acuity, a richer faith, unbelievable hope, spiritual enlightenment, and an inexpressible joy.

So, fight the dreaded Symbolically with the Golden Rule of Interpretation: "If the plain sense makes sense, don't look for any other sense, lest you end up with nonsense." Why live with the heartbreak of confusion? Take the Golden Rule. Because He's worth it!

Harold Camping

Let's now look at some of those eschatologically confused individuals from today who are suffering from Symbolically. Again, they may not be purposefully deceptive, but rather just have their interpretation of the Bible and Bible prophecy so far skewed that what they end up teaching misleads people from the sound, literal interpretation of the Bible. I leave it up to the reader then to decide if that qualifies them as false prophets or not.

The first look is at Harold Camping, president and evangelist of the once-massive California-based radio station, Family Radio, which had broadcast Camping's prophetic messages over 150 radio stations within the United States. Camping, who died of a stroke in 2013, was a classic date-setter. He made a number of calculations that he believed predicted the return of Christ: September 6, 1994, May 21, 2011, and October 21, 2011. The dates passed with no arrival of Jesus Christ, leading Camping to remorsefully repent of his date-setting.

If only Camping had followed the Golden Rule of Interpretation. Instead, he took prophecies that apply to specific historic periods and related them to the end times. He insisted that the Bible is all merely a parable and thus must be interpreted allegorically. He retranslated Scriptures in unorthodox ways in order to give them his own desired meanings. He also obsessively dabbled with numbers. Camping could have spared himself embarrassment and his followers losing all they possessed if only he had taken a literal interpretation of the Bible.[13]

Irvin Baxter

Irvin Baxter Jr. is the founder and president of Endtime Ministries and television host of the internationally broadcast television program, *End of the Age*. Though a wildly popular Bible prophecy teacher, unfortunately for his viewers, Baxter suffers from a serious case of Symbolically. His interpretations of Bible prophecy end up being personal and unique, so much so that no other prophecy teacher is willing to endorse him.[14]

Baxter's prophetic interpretations totally disregard 2 Peter 1:20, which warns "that no prophecy of Scripture is of any private interpretation." His best example of engaging in private interpretation comes when he assigns at leisure one Revelation prophecy after another to historic and modern-day events, such as claiming that the seal judgments began in A.D. 325. He also assigns biblical symbols to modern-day counterparts, such as claiming that the beasts of Daniel 7 are the nations of Great

Britain, Russia, and Germany. He denies that Revelation is written in chronological order, and believes the Rapture and the Second Coming are the same event.

Sadly, the only thing predictable about Irvin Baxter's end-time predictions is that he's scared a whole lot of people senseless.

Doug Bachelor

The Seventh-Day Adventists "denomination" (SDA) was birthed out of the failed Millerite Movement of the 1840s whose leader, Baptist pastor William Miller, prophesied that Jesus would return to earth in 1844, which of course did not come true.[15] Not disheartened by "The Great Disappointment," a small group of Millerites explained Jesus' no-show by doing what all failed prophets do — spiritualizing the prediction. Adventists claim that Jesus instead entered the Holy of Holies in heaven to begin a second stage of His atoning work called the Investigative Judgment, which they claim continues to this day.

Adventists' two main champions over the decades have been the prophetess Ellen G. White, who canonized SDA beliefs in her book, *The Great Controversy* (1888), and Doug Batchelor, today's SDA spokesman on the *Amazing Facts* television program. Almost all of their end-time interpretations revolve around a rabid adherence to Sabbath-keeping.

Still covering for Miller, Adventists claim the end times began in 1844. SDA eschatology virulently opposes the Catholic Church and staunchly adheres to Replacement Theology, claiming the Church has forever replaced Israel in God's prophetic plan. They believe the papacy is the Antichrist. Shockingly, they claim Protestant Christianity is the False Prophet who will use the United States as its enforcer to spark a period of SDA persecution called the Great Tribulation. The persecution culminates in the Battle of Armageddon waged between the true Sabbath-keepers versus Sunday-keepers.[16] You better worship Christ on Saturday and Saturday alone, for if not, to the SDA, you have taken the mark of the Beast and are bound for hell.

Eschatologically Ignorant

As humanity hurtles towards the Rapture of the Church, outright false messiahs and prophets proliferate in frequency and intensity. The Eschatologically Confused abound. And then there are the Eschatologically Ignorant.

These people, pastors often, unwittingly play into the great end-time delusion. For whatever reasons, they just refuse to touch the 31 percent of the Bible that contains prophecy. They fell head-first into the Laodicean malaise Christ warned the churches of in Revelation 3 — the spirit of apathy. This end-time church of Laodicea mentality claims, "We've got it all together, so we don't really need you, God. We are just going to keep on practicing Christianity without Christ, thank you very much." This makes them a pseudo form of false prophets and false teachers by their willing acts of omission.

"Ignorant" can be a harsh word, but for some pastors, it fits. I left a church once because the pastor from the pulpit sneeringly denounced Bible prophecy conferences as "Star Trek Conventions." The congregation whooped approval. And then the pastor went back to his endless use of sports analogies. These scoffers actually fulfill 2 Peter 3:4, which prophesied that in the end times, people would scoff at the very idea of times ever changing. For some, prophecy is just not cool.

Some pastors have been raised by strictly amillennial teachers, believing in no literal, thousand-year reign of Christ coming, and that everything will just pan out in the end. Or they have embraced post-millennialism, a viewpoint that sees the Church conquering the world for Christ and then handing it over to Him upon His return. The Bible teaches neither view, yet many churches are drowning in these errant interpretations.

For other pastors, it's less ignorance and more illiteracy. I feel for those pastors who daily have to deal with their members' marital, employment, and health issues. They're bogged down in daily living, leaving no time for "irrelevant" prophecy. And yet, Jesus will bring all of our heart-wrenching issues to an end upon His return. So then, how can the good news of Christ's return not be relevant in providing the believer hope?

Another reason for the apathy concerning God's prophetic Word is that a lot of pastors just don't know those parts of the Bible. Seminaries have fallen down on the job of equipping pastors in the study of eschatology, leaving these poor ministers ill equipped. Strange end-times viewpoints cross their paths, which naturally confuse and repel them. So quite a number of pastors, whether they are open to Bible prophecy or not, finally throw their hands up and declare, "I can't deal with prophecy right now because I just don't understand it. I'm going to focus instead on what I do understand." So, I will give these pastors some credit.

Regardless of their reasons, spiritual apathy has become the dominant characteristic of today's Western churches, with an even a greater apathy toward God's prophetic Word. At a time when the signs of the times Jesus pronounced swirl about our heads at hurricane strength, the Laodicean church has become Rip Van Winkle.

Second Coming

We have finally reached Jesus' "farther" response when answering the Apostles' third question: "What will be the sign of Jesus' coming?" These signs lead up to His Second Coming at the end of the Tribulation, and they constitute the harshest and most intense of the birth-pain events.

What's most interesting about the sign of false messiahs is that the plethora of false christs, prophets, and teachers will disappear. During the Tribulation, all the foreteller-fabricators of our day will be phased out, boiling down to just two men.

The Antichrist

The Bible calls the ultimate false christ the Antichrist (1 John 2:18). His list of names should strike fear into the hearts of the world's inhabitants: the beast (Revelation 13:1), the man of lawlessness (2 Thessalonians 2:3), the son of destruction (2 Thessalonians 2:3), the despicable person (Daniel 11:21), the willful king (Daniel 11:36), the worthless shepherd (Zechariah 11:17), the insolent king (Daniel 8:23), and the abomination (Matthew 24:15).

Revelation 13 describes this penultimate false messiah as a beast who comes "out of the sea," and Revelation 6 pictures him as a rider on a white horse who sways the world under his power. Daniel 9:26 reveals his origins as rising from "the people of the prince who is to come shall destroy the city and the sanctuary," meaning the Romans who destroyed the Temple in A.D. 70.

The Antichrist's empire will grow to encompass the entire planet (Isaiah 34:2; Jeremiah 30:11; Joel 3:2, 9; Zechariah 14:2; Zephaniah 3:8; and Revelation 14:8, 16:14, and 18:3, 23). The price for finally achieving world domination will be a series of horrific wars that will result in the deaths of a whopping two billion people (Revelation 6). But, this maniacal emperor will act merely as a puppet, for he will be fully possessed by Satan, the prince of this world (John 16:11).

A peace covenant signed with Israel will reveal the Antichrist and mark the start of the seven-year Tribulation (Daniel 9:27, 11:36–39). At the midpoint of the Tribulation, the Antichrist will proclaim himself to be God in the newly built Jewish temple (Daniel 9:27). He will then slaughter both Jews and Tribulation Saints alike in a satanic fury so fierce that if Jesus Christ does not return quickly, this Beast will have devoured all of God's faithful.

The False Prophet

The Antichrist is served by a False Prophet (Revelation 13). All false religions will eventually fold under his command. No more false christs, other than the Antichrist, will be allowed to exist. The final False Prophet will demand that the entire world worship Satan through the Antichrist, or be killed.

The push to form some kind of one-world philosophy grows ever stronger in our day, but it will finally culminate in the False Prophet's harlot religion. He will erect a living image and require all the world to bow down to it. Satan will grant him the ability to perform miraculous signs, such as sending down fire. This lamb-like "beast from the land" will reveal his true colors through his deceptive, dragonesque speech. As his ultimate act of consuming all other religions, the False Prophet will demand loyalty to the Antichrist by forcing all people to take a loyalty mark and worship him alone, or die by beheading.

No wonder that the very first and number-one end-times sign Jesus gave was false messiahs, prophets, and teachers!

Discernment

Because we live in an age of frantic spiritual deception by a ridiculous number of foreteller-fabricators, Moses' advice must be taken to heart. Israel's Exodus leader provided a test for how we can discern false prophets:

> You may say to yourselves, "How can we know when a message has not been spoken by the LORD?" If what a prophet proclaims in the name of the LORD does not take place or come true, that is a message the LORD has not spoken. That prophet has spoken presumptuously, so do not be alarmed (Deuteronomy 18:21–22; NIV).

The prophetic profile for a true prophet of God can be described, as the Apostle Peter did, as "holy men of God spoke as they were moved by the Holy Spirit" (2 Peter 1:21). Their prophecies come true 100 percent of the time, because the origin of their insights is God Himself.

Beware of prophetic predictions that are considered open-dated, meaning prophecies that have no certain time frame in which to be fulfilled. And beware of prophecies that can be self-fulfilling, for they often are not really prophecies at all. Also avoid prophecies that are dependent upon conditions. Only close-dated and unconditional biblical prophetic predictions should be unquestionably accepted.

A second test in discerning a false prophet was provided by the Apostle John (1 John 4:1–3). In order to test the spirits, so to speak, the prophet acknowledged that for Jesus Christ to have come from God, He must have first come in the flesh. A true follower of Jesus acknowledges that the Son of God came to earth as a man and in the flesh.

A virtual potpourri of additional tests abound that help us discern false prophets:[17]

- The prophet cannot also speak in other names such as Allah or Maitreya or Vishnu, but only by the God of the Bible (Deuteronomy 13:1–3).
- The prophet can never tell you that you can be saved by putting your faith in people other than Jesus, such as the Virgin Mary (Galatians 1:8).
- The prophet cannot live a sinful life, but must be committed to holiness (Jeremiah 23:14–15).
- The prophet's followers are never motivated by worldly living, but produce spiritual fruit (Matthew 7:15–16,18; Galatians 5:22–23).
- The prophet ignores self-aggrandizing visions about personal trips back and forth to heaven and hell (Colossians 2:18).
- The prophet calls people out on their sins and pleads for repentance (Jeremiah 23:16–17).
- The prophet is never desirous for money (Jeremiah 8:10–11).
- The prophet never focuses on himself, the Antichrist, or the sensational, but only on Jesus Christ (Revelation 19:10).

Abide by these tests of a false prophet, and you should never fall for the deceptions of the foreteller-fabricators.

Five Applications

We certainly are living in exciting times! When I was a kid, I thought these days were oh so boring. I dreamed of living during the medieval times when I could be a knight and ride my trusty steed. Or I dreamed of living in the Wild West and becoming a cowboy, blazing my guns away at outlaws. Yes, I thought our modern days held little importance.

Then I started studying the Bible, and what a revelation to realize we are living during one of the most exciting times in all of human history! Maybe it's more exciting than most want it to be, but in the end, it will all be worth it. Christians are living in a time when we are going to see our Savior snatch us up in the clouds and take us to heaven. Then, seven or so years later, we will return with Jesus at His Second Coming and witness Him defeating evil and setting up His Millennial Kingdom. How can there be a more exciting time than these days?

Knowing what we now know about Jesus' Olivet Discourse teaching on the sign of false messiahs, how do we apply this epiphany to our lives? Jesus tells us in Luke 21:34–36:

> But take heed to yourselves, lest your hearts be weighed down with carousing, drunkenness, and cares of this life, and that Day come on you unexpectedly. For it will come as a snare on all those who dwell on the face of the whole earth. Watch therefore, and pray always that you may be counted worthy to escape all these things that will come to pass, and to stand before the Son of Man.

We could read Jesus' first nine signs, shakily rub our hands across our forehead, and decide to go out and get drunk as the pagans do. We could decry how awful the world has become, as the apathetic do. Sure, the weight of this world's trials and tribulations remains heavy. Living with devastating earthquakes, terrifying social terrors, frightening signs in the sky, and the horrible persecution of Christians has become standard. These and many other end-times signs are most burdensome to bear.

So, how then, can we live under these crushing terrors? Jesus says, to the effect, "Don't worry. Instead, do these":

1) Avoid Sinning

Don't sin anymore! You, Christian, you were never meant to live a sinful life. Instead, we were meant to be Christ-followers and light-bearers.

Stop whatever you are doing that is sinful. Whatever sins you are holding onto in life, they're not worth it. They extinguish your light.

2) Be Assured that the King Is Coming

Therefore, keep watch! Jesus commanded Christians to keep watch for His return. I have been to churches that didn't give a care that Jesus is coming back. And yet, Jesus commanded His followers to watch. He told us explicitly to keep our eyes watching for His return. That doesn't mean that we should stand outside staring up at the sky all day, but that we should live in anticipation of our King's return.

3) Pray to Escape Evil

We are living in terribly evil times. If you're an American, praise the Lord that you are living in a country that has provided freedom to worship for over 200 years. But we also are offered an endless array of temptations. Pray you will escape those snares.

4) Have Hope in the Rapture

The Apostle Paul told us that the Rapture would happen before the worst time of God's wrath is poured out on the earth (Revelation 3:10). That should provide each of us who knows the Lord as Savior a tremendous hope. We can embrace hope in knowing that Jesus Christ will return.

5) Stand Worthy

To be worthy of escaping God's wrath, the Son of God requires us to accept Him as Savior. We are to give up our sin and turn to Jesus Christ in repentance. We're to pray from our hearts, "Dear Jesus, please forgive me of my sins, and be my Lord and Savior." And, Jesus promises to do just that. He will save us from the Father's judgment for our sins, He will save us from having to live on earth during the Tribulation by first catching us up in the Rapture, and He will save us from the just judgment of hell. Jesus grants new life, a life filled with purpose and hope.

And so, avoid sinning. Keep watch for the return of Jesus Christ. Pray to escape evil. Hope for the Rapture. And, accept Jesus Christ as your Savior. You, too, are now equipped to resist the greedy deceptions of those doomed foreteller-fabricators.

Endnotes

1. "Pompeii," *History,* (2010), http://www.history.com/topics/ancient-history/pompeii.

2. Robert J. Morgan, *Nelson's Complete Book of Stories, Illustrations & Quotes* (Nashville, TN: Thomas Nelson Publishers, 2000), p. 575–576.

3. Unless otherwise noted, all quoted Scripture in this chapter is from the New King James Version (NKJV) of the Bible.

4. Greed, Dictionary.com, *Dictionary.com Unabridged,* Random House, Inc. http://www.dictionary.com/browse/greed (accessed August 31, 2017).

5. "Quotes About Greed," *Goodreads,* https://www.goodreads.com/quotes/tag/greed.

6. Ibid.

7. Eleanor Doan, *Speaker's Sourcebook* (Grand Rapids, MI: Zondervan Publishing House, 1960), p. 109.

8. Flavius Josephus, *Wars,* 2:118.

9. Flavius Josephus, *Antiquities,* 20:97ff.

10. Flavius Josephus, *Jewish War,* 2.261–262[1].

11. Staff of Watchman Fellowship, Inc., "Index of Cults and Religions" (accessed August 2017), http://www.watchman.org/index-of-cults-and-religions/.

12. Ibid.

13. David R. Reagan, "Harold Camping: The Madness of Date-Setting," *Lamplighter,* (accessed August 2017), http://christinprophecy.org/articles/harold-camping/.

14. David R. Reagan, "Irvin Baxter Evaluated," (June 2, 2011), http://christinprophecyblog.org/2011/06/irvin-baxter-evaluated/.

15. David R. Reagan, "Seventh-Day Adventist Eschatology" (accessed August 2017), http://christinprophecy.org/articles/seventh-day-adventist-eschatology/.

16. Ibid.

17. David R. Reagan, "The Danger of False Prophets" (accessed August 2017), http://christinprophecy.org/articles/harold-camping/.

CHAPTER 10

Media Manipulators

TODD STRANDBERG

There can be no doubt that the liberal media is the most powerful tool the devil has at his disposal, guiding and directing world affairs. Liberal-minded people dominate Hollywood, the news networks, and social media. Over 90 percent of the people working in these fields always vote for the Democratic Party.

It is amazing to have newsrooms dominated by radical leftist reporters who overwhelmingly voted for Hillary Clinton. Only about a third of the general population has the same view as the media. The depravity never gets addressed because the liberal media use their influence to protect each other.

When confronted about their liberal bias, major players like NBC, ABC, CBS, CNN, MSNBC, the *New York Times*, and the *Washington Post* would all say, "Well, what about Fox News?" Because one news outlet has a slightly conservative bent, all the other organizations see themselves as a counterweight to what they see as conservative propaganda.

The Fox News network has lost much of its conservative luster. After years of activity by groups like Media Matters, Fox has lost several of its conservative stars. With the ouster of Roger Ailes and the owner, Rupert Murdoch, turning control of the network over to his two left-leaning sons, Fox's future is in doubt.

It doesn't make sense that a billionaire hasn't come along and established a purely conservative network. It would, in such a case, be like a town with 30 hamburger joints having someone come in and build a restaurant with a chicken-based menu. We have a monopoly of these liberal networks because Satan whispers into the ears of men and seduces them into doing things that defy financial logic.

For example, when the *New York Times* and the *Washington Post* were about to fold, two of the richest men in the world swooped in to the rescue.

The devil apparently had to keep his two key beacons of liberal ideology going, because that is how he manages the debased moral status of a society. The average person has no clue who is their senator or what his or her views might be on issues. They blame the president and Congress for their economic and social woes. By the time it comes for a vote on drug laws or some sexual issue, the change in public opinion is what makes it possible for an immoral law to be passed.

The real political power in Washington is on the Sunday talk shows. Do you think the devil would hover over the House and Senate chambers to watch congressional representatives ramble on about a bill that might never come up for a vote? Before the Supreme Court ruled that gay marriage was a constitutional right, it took years of advocacy on the part of the news media to convince people that it's proper to vote for something that was previously abhorrent.

In 1967, CBS news produced a special program called "Homosexual." It was the first network documentary dealing with the topic of homosexuality in the United States. The episode included interviews with several gay men, psychiatrists who thought homosexuality is a mental disorder, legal experts and cultural critics, and it documented a police sex sting. The show was narrated by Mike Wallace, who painted a dark picture of the gay lifestyle. The program reached the following conclusion:

> The average homosexual, if there be such, is promiscuous. He is not interested or capable of a lasting relationship like that of a heterosexual marriage. His sex life, his love life, consists of a series of one-chance encounters at the clubs and bars he inhabits. And even on the streets of the city — the pick-up, the one-night stand, these are characteristics of the homosexual relationship.[1]

It's amazing to see that in 40 years, the liberal media has gone from a standoffish observer of immoral behavior to today, when it has become completely married to the homosexual movement. At the news network, you cannot make a joke or disparaging remark about this form of sexuality. Homosexuals fill the ranks of the news media, and they are in constant contact with gay political and social advocacy groups.

Every day I feel more and more like I'm living in Nazi Germany. What makes it seem this way above all else is the liberal media's fixation on practicing the "big lie" — if you tell a lie big enough and keep repeating it, people will eventually come to believe it.

The Golden Rule of news is dead. We now live in the age of 24/7 propaganda.

Facebook's Stock and the Invisible Hand

What allows the liberal media to be such a perfect fit for the devil is that they both operate the same way. They manipulate affairs without being seen as the manipulator. A perfect example of this is the history of Facebook's initial public offering (IPO).

In the days before Facebook went public, the financial media did not have a negative thing to say about the company. It was praised as one of the leading social media companies in the world. We were told about how everyone connected to this firm had become super rich, and there were wild projections of how Facebook might overtake Microsoft as the company with the highest net worth.

When the stock started trading on May 18, 2012, there was an absolute media circus at NASDAQ headquarters. Reporters told investors that the low quantity of available shares suggested the stock could rise to $60, $70, or $80, and could shoot up to $60 on the first day of trading. Facebook opened at $42, peaked at $45, and then it was all downhill for several months.

The investing community had realized that Facebook had a booming membership, but it lacked the revenue to match the $100 billion stock market capitalization. The liberal media turned on a dime and started blaming foolish investors for buying into the hype. CBS News compared the situation to the dot-com bubble, warning that "you'd think we all would have learned our lesson" from that period of massive overvaluation. The press scorned the stock all the way down to $17.

After the stock drifted in the doldrums for about a year, a new quarterly earnings report showed that Facebook was starting to generate significant ad money off of its various platforms. The financial press was suddenly back in love with the firm; stock traders sent the stock soaring tenfold above its low.

We don't hear about people being tricked by the media into selling their Facebook stock and missing out on huge gains. The press can lead people into making foolish stock trades, but it is never to blame, because the financial reporters can argue that they are just covering the news. It doesn't matter if you have footage of them holding pom-poms, jumping up and down, and saying "buy Facebook." They acquit themselves of any blame by retreating to the notion that they are just the conduit for passing the news on to the public.

Rewriting History

The liberal media isn't satisfied with controlling how people view current events. It is very active in reshaping how historical events are remembered. It's a process that goes on at a constant pace. If history does not support liberalism, then liberals act to change history. The Reagan years are a favorite target of the revisionist liberal media.

In the rewritten version of history, the civil rights era has been the left's most stunning accomplishment. It is a masterpiece of political engineering for liberals to convince the voters that they were the party of civil rights. In truth, the Democratic Party was founded as the original white supremist organization. It was the party of lynching, the Ku Klux Klan, and opposition to every significant piece of civil rights legislation.

In 1957, Republican President Eisenhower sent troops to Little Rock, Arkansas, to escort black students into Central High school. Despite the Supreme Court's decision in *Brown v. Board of Education* that called for desegregation of schools, the state's Democratic governor, Orval Faubus, stood in the doorway to block their entry.

In the 1956 presidential campaign, the Republican platform had endorsed the *Brown* decision. The Democratic platform rejected the ruling. In Congress, 99 members signed the "Southern Manifesto" denouncing the court's ruling. Two were Republicans and 97 were Democrats.

The turning for the Democrats came during the term of Lyndon Baines Johnson. He created the Great Society that bribed blacks into voting for his party. He got the Democratic leadership to go along with him by saying that he would offer those "uppity Negroes" "just enough to quiet them down, not enough to make a difference."[2] The key point of the 180-degree flip was the 1964 Civil Rights Act and the 1965 Voting Rights act. The racist and ever-crass LBJ was overheard on Air Force One telling fellow Democrats, "I'll have them [n-word] voting Democratic for two hundred years."[3]

The liberal media has used the simple strategy of highlighting all examples of Republican racism and downplaying racism on the left.

Every single segregationist in the Senate was a Democrat. Strom Thurmond switched parties in 1964 and became a Republican. This was a big mistake on his part, because he is now the favorite reference name for southern white racism.

The liberal media only has kind things to say about Senator Robert Byrd. There are dozens of office buildings bearing his name. Because he was a legendary Democrat, no liberals are troubled by someone who said:

> I shall never fight in the armed forces with a negro by my side.
> . . . Rather I should die a thousand times, and see Old Glory trampled in the dirt never to rise again, than to see this beloved land of ours become degraded by race mongrels, a throwback to the blackest specimen from the wilds.[4] —Robert C. Byrd, in a letter to Sen. Theodore Bilbo (D-MS), 1944

Byrd was so deep into the Ku Klux Klan that he started his own West Virginia chapter. In 1946, Byrd wrote a letter to a Grand Wizard stating, "The Klan is needed today as never before, and I am anxious to see its rebirth here in West Virginia and in every state in the nation."[5]

However, when running for the United States House of Representatives in 1952, he announced, "After about a year, I became disinterested, quit paying my dues, and dropped my membership in the organization. During the nine years that have followed, I have never been interested in the Klan."[6] He said he had joined the Klan because he felt it offered excitement and was anti-communist.

The press has been able to reverse the racial history of the Republican and Democratic parties by subletting changing how truth is reported. Any news that points to Republicans as being racist was highlighted, and anything racially negative about the Democratic Party went unreported.

The liberal media confront Republicans and say, "Do you condemn racial violence?" This is an offensive question, because it implies that people on the right are guilty of racism. Since there is no such thing as racism on the left, pray for the Republicans who say, "I condemn all forms of racism."

The most irritating tactic by liberal media is using fellow liberals as sources of authority. When leftist author Sam Tanenhaus wrote the cover story, "Original Sin: Why the GOP Is and Will Continue to Be the Party of White People," fellow liberals quoted this opinion piece as the gospel truth.

Jesse Jackson and Al Sharpton are two of the most morally challenged people on the planet. For decades, they used their skin color to shake down corporations and to prostitute themselves out to the media.

The rewriting of history by the liberal media would not have happened if a Republican had stood up to this act of treachery. It occurred because the vast majority were too cowardly in their dealings with the press. The claim of racism is enough to make them back down.

CNN: What Have You Become?

Back in the early nineties, the Cable News Network was the king of news. I remember constantly looking at my watch so I wouldn't miss the "CNN Headlines" at the top of each hour. Today, I would equate watching CNN with wearing bell-bottom pants and platform shoes.

I'm not the only one who has turned away from CNN. Figures from the Nielson ratings agency show that CNN has been in a continuous decline over the past two decades.

At one time, CNN had viewers that numbered into the millions. The network started bleeding when alternative options became available. After Fox News opened its doors in 1996, CNN quickly lost 80 percent of its viewers. The demographic of the nation explains why: sixty percent of the population views itself as conservative, and people on the right are more likely to watch news.

What was CNN's reaction to this mass exodus of conservative viewers? Of course, it became all the more liberal. The few conservatives left at the network were forced out. They did have a brief relapse when they hired Glenn Beck to host a show on its sister network's "Headline News." Beck made his exit when CNN said it was planning to remove one of his nightly telecasts. The financial heavyweight Lou Dobbs left for Fox Business news when it became clear that he was no longer welcome at the network.

One of the most common critiques of CNN's ratings decline by fellow members of the liberal media was that the network is not biased enough in its news coverage. It needs to stop being so fair-minded and start being partial like Fox News. Robert Thompson, professor of television and popular culture at Syracuse University, shared this view in his reaction to CNN's poor ratings. "The biggest problem is inherent in their brand," he said.

"They are trying to stick to old-fashioned, unbiased news broadcasting when their rivals have worked out that to draw an audience when there aren't major stories breaking you need to do the opposite."[7]

Of course, this is pure garbage from the left. If CNN is so unbiased in its coverage, why did so many people leave it at the first chance to get another view of the news? It is like telling people who suffer from obesity that they need to take in more food to lose weight.

CNN has lost more than ratings. It has become so fanatical in its hatred of Trump and conservatives that the network's reputation has been run through a wood chipper. When it tried to blackmail a user on Reddit.com, there was a huge backlash on social media. CNN's willingness to post a blatantly false story has forever branded it in millions of minds as the "Fake News Network."

CNN is still profitable for its parent company, Time-Warner, with profitability largely fueled by the success of CNN International. The network may soon slip into the red as other nations develop their own alternative media.

I have a plan that can save CNN from the ratings doldrums. It should switch to an all-conservative news format. It doesn't even have to change its logo. CNN can become the Conservative News Network. After all, the word "cable" doesn't really fit today anyway, with the advent of satellite TV and the Internet.

What would make the conservative format such a winner is the lack of competitors. There are now more than 1,000 channels for people to choose from. Of all these networks, Fox News is the only one that stands out as being even on the right of the political spectrum. Not everyone at Fox is a red-blooded conservative. Shepard Smith comes across as a closet liberal, and Chris Wallace is registered Democrat, but has a reputation for being fair to both sides.

The rise of a 100 percent, nonliberal news channel would capture a huge audience. I'm sure the executives at CNN would rather put a gun in their mouth than hire someone who appeals to red states. If CNN went to a conservative format, the rest of the liberal media would react as if they had staffed their lineup with convicted pedophiles.

CNN will never follow this winning format because they slavishly follow the agenda set by Satan himself. This world is about to come under new management. There won't be a CNN after the Tribulation, because its target audience will drop to zero.

For though we walk in the flesh, we do not war according to the flesh. For the weapons of our warfare are not carnal but mighty in God for pulling down strongholds, casting down arguments and every high thing that exalts itself against the knowledge of God, bringing every thought into captivity to the obedience of Christ (2 Corinthians 10:3–5; NKJV).

The Power of Search Engines and Social Media

Without a doubt, the craftiest device the liberal media has at its disposal is the ability to manipulate public opinion by judging the value and importance of news. Every single day, millions of events transpire in the world, and the press determines which news items are worthy of major coverage and which ones are not. The liberal media will immediately give top national billing to attacks on abortion clinics, yet leave attacks on Christian churches to coverage by the local press.

Facebook has a major role in disseminating news. The site has sections that list trending news stories, and millions of people get their daily news from this list. Since Facebook is very liberal, the people who compile what qualifies as trend news are very biased to the left.

A decade ago, computers could only assemble very basic lists of information. If you did a search on the word "canary," you would get a list about the bird and the group of islands. Now that computers have begun to think like humans, they can "guess" what type of canary you are researching based on information such as whether your previous searches were for "luggage" or "birdcage."

There is a dark side of computers being able to track and analyze people's activity. If you are looking at voting information, it is very easy for a search engine to feed you articles on the candidate that Big Brother would like you to vote for.

I can't stand the so-called late-night comedians Stephen Colbert and Seth Meyers. I see nothing funny about jokes that are just thinly veiled propaganda. I see these idiots repeatedly on YouTube, which obviously thinks these operatives are so funny that they insist on sharing them with me. I rarely get an unsolicited recommendation to view videos by Christians. Since YouTube tracks my viewing patterns, it should know that liberal garbage is not my taste.

Google has a wide assortment of amazing technology, and I use several of its products. There are two trillion searches each year on half a million Google servers. Google has purchased a dozen companies and has hundreds of patents. Google's brand name alone is said to be worth $200 billion.

Years ago, Google came up with the slogan, "Don't be evil." Because it has grown to have a massive monopoly on search and video, it is very natural for the firm to violate its pledge. Google can block almost any site it wants without most even knowing they are under attack. If you have an account with them, your personal website or video page will rank higher when you do a search than when someone else looks for your material.

Many people have spent years building an audience on YouTube. Most of them depend on ads for their income. I think it is very un-American for Google to come along and decide they are going to pull ads or block your subscribers from accessing a site because it doesn't agree with a company's conservative or Christian agenda. This trend is happening on an ever-increasing scale.

If Google had admitted it was a site exclusively for gay, transgender, atheist, or pro-Islamic content, there would be room for other firms to pop up and fulfill people's hosting needs. Google waited until it was nearly the only game in town before changing the rules.

I think freedom of expression is so vital that antitrust laws should be applied to firms like Google. We did that with ATT, and the smartphone explosion quickly followed. Tech firms use lobbyists to maintain a strong grasp on politicians. It takes a political movement to bust up monopolies.

The Liberal Media Is Your Enemy

Over the years I've been interviewed dozens of times by members of the press. Once the Rapture Ready website stood out from the rest of other prophecy sites, it was natural for reporters to occasionally find an interest in the subject of Bible prophecy.

I've always maintained the reality that each time I was interviewed, I was talking to the enemy. I've only had a couple of interviews in which the reporters were hostile to me. What normally happens is that I get asked a series of polite questions, but then the knife doesn't come out until they post their articles or videos.

When you deal with people who have a political agenda in everything they write about, you have to be very mindful of what you say to them. If I was the ambassador to the Soviet Union during the Cold War, I would say, "Boy, you folks sure have a great space program." The next day, *Pravda*, the Soviet news outlet, would be reporting that I had just admitted to the superiority of Soviet technology.

When Senator Bob Dole ran against Vice President George W. Bush for the 1988 Republican nominations, the key negative attacks against Dole were that he liked taxes and had a mean temperament. I remember the video of Dole running out to the reporters like a little kid to deflect one of these attacks. Dole might as well have been taking a swan dive into a pariah tank; the liberal media used every frame of that footage to attack him. He lost to Bush and likely had no idea how the liberal media was working against him.

The race against President Ford and Governor Jimmy Carter is beyond most people's memory, but recently there was a new perspective on that election. Chevy Chase made an impression of Ford on the original broadcast of Saturday Night Live. In a 2008 interview, Chase said Ford was a "sweet man, a terrific man," but he intentionally worked to make him the butt of jokes just to give votes to Carter:

> It's not that I can imitate him so much that I can do a lot of physical comedy and I just made it, I just went after him. And . . . obviously my leanings were Democratic and I wanted [Jimmy] Carter in and I wanted [Ford] out, and I figured look, we're reaching millions of people every weekend; why not do it.[8]

Ford was obviously clueless to the damage that Chase was causing to his image. He recorded a video for the show, and even met with the comedian. After learning about how Chase put his party membership first, I could never see those old Ford skits the same way.

One of the reasons Trump won in 2016 is that he understood the liberal media was his enemy. He would say something "controversial," and the press would try repeatedly to make him apologize. The other Republicans tried to play nice with the media and got no measure of kindness. The liberal media's mission in life was getting Hillary Clinton elected at all costs.

Jesus said that Satan is the God of this world. He naturally uses organizations like the liberal media to influence society. Because of this evil connection, we need to be on constant guard from allowing the press to shape Christian views:

> Be sober, be vigilant; because your adversary the devil, as a roaring lion, walketh about, seeking whom he may devour (1 Peter 5:8; KJV).

Comparing the Liberal Media's Coverage of Obama and Trump

Obama's Presidency

One of the most destructive factors about the eight-year Obama admin-istration is the protective relationship he established with the liberal media. Every time he did something that was clearly harmful to the best interests of the American people, the press was there defending his actions. Even in cases when people were suffering from some disaster and Obama was on vacation at Martha's Vineyard, the criticism never came from the press. They give this special treatment to all Democrats.

From the moment Obama showed up on the national stage to address the Democratic convention in 2004, the news media fell wildly in love with him. "Obama is a rock star," NBC's Andrea Mitchell exclaimed during MSNBC's live convention coverage back on July 27, 2004. The next morning, ABC's George Stephanopoulos echoed Mitchell's enthusi-asm: "He's the Tiger Woods of the Democratic Party right now."[9]

MSNBC's Chris Matthews had the most famous response to an Obama speech:

> I have to tell you, you know, it's part of reporting this case, this election, the feeling most people get when they hear Barack Obama's speech. My — I felt this thrill going up my leg. I mean, I don't have that too often.[10]

That weird moment occurred during MSNBC's coverage of the Virginia, Maryland, and Washington, D.C. primaries, February 12, 2008.

Most of the praise that has been poured on Obama is cultish drivel:

> Presidential campaigns have destroyed many bright and capable politicians. But there's ample evidence that Obama is something special — a man who makes difficult tasks look easy, who seems to touch millions of diverse people with a message of hope that somehow doesn't sound Pollyannaish. — Associated Press writer Charles Babington in a May 10, 2008, dispatch[11]

The top priority of the liberal media was to help get President Obama reelected. The press used the messiah-like slant to glorify Obama in the 2012 race. MSNBC's Matthews asked this question on his *Hardball with Chris Matthews* program: "Is there going to be a reluctance on the part of the voters and the political community that talks politics as we get into November about dumping the first African-American president?"[12]

Filmmaker Davis Guggenheim demonstrated this mindset when he was asked by CNN's Piers Morgan, "Most documentary makers balance these movies with the negative as well as the positive. What are the negatives in your movie about Barack Obama?" Guggenheim replied, "The negative for me was, there were too many accomplishments. I had 17 minutes to put them all in there."[13]

During the eight years of his administration, our national debt rose by nearly $10 trillion. The price of oil doubled, and Obama has overseen the worst jobs recovery in our nation's history. Even though all these measures are worse than during the Jimmy Carter years, the media set forth the narrative that Obama put America back on the path of prosperity.

I was hardly surprised to learn that *Pravda*, the infamous former Soviet newspaper, had endorsed Obama during his second run for office. The original "pinko-commie" rag gave a nasty jab at Mitt Romney in the following op-ed: "Electing Mitt Romney as the next President of the United States of America would be like appointing a serial pedophile as a kindergarten teacher, a rapist as a janitor at a girls' dormitory or a psychopath with a fixation on knives as a kitchen hand."[14]

It would be the kiss of death for any Cold War candidate to receive this type of praise. If John F. Kennedy had been endorsed by *Pravda*, we would have rejected their advances in the strongest terms. With Obama, Satan could appear and offer his personal endorsement, and it would be reported as a positive thing.

I could write a whole book about why I think Obama was the worst president in American history. He was so detrimental to our nation that it is easy to compile a list of things he was the first president to ever dare to do:

- The first president to preside over a cut to the credit rating of the United States.
- The first president to violate the War Powers Act.
- The first president to be held in contempt of court for illegally obstructing oil drilling in the Gulf.
- The first president to require all Americans to purchase a product from a third party.
- The first president to abrogate bankruptcy laws to turn over control of companies to his union supporters.
- The first president to bypass Congress and implement the Dream Act through executive fiat.

- The first president to order a secret amnesty program for illegal immigrants.
- The first president to demand that a company hand over $20 billion to one of his political appointees.
- The first president to tell a CEO of a major corporation (Chrysler) to resign.
- The first and only president to cancel the National Day of Prayer.
- The first and only president to say that America is no longer a Christian nation.
- The first president to have a law signed by an auto-pen without being present.
- The first president to arbitrarily declare an existing law unconstitutional and refuse to enforce it.
- The first president to tell a company in which state it is allowed to locate a factory.
- The first president to file lawsuits against the states he swore an oath to protect (Arizona, Wisconsin, Ohio, Indiana).
- The first president to withdraw an existing coal permit that had been properly issued years ago.
- The first president to actively try to bankrupt an American industry (coal).
- The first president to surround himself with radical, left-wing anarchists.
- The first president to golf more than 300 separate times during his term in office.
- The first president to hide his birth, medical, educational, and travel records.
- The first president to win a Nobel Peace Prize for doing NOTHING to earn it.
- The first president to be in a continuous state of war throughout his entire presidency.
- The first president to go on multiple "global apology tours."
- The first president to have personal servants (taxpayer-funded) for his wife.
- The first president to keep a dog trainer on retainer for $102,000 a year at taxpayer expense.
- The first president to repeat words in the Quran.

- The first president to say that the Islamic call to worship is "the most beautiful sound on earth."
- The first president to increase the food-stamp spending by more than 100 percent in a single term.
- The first president to conceal food-stamp data from public scrutiny.
- The first president to side with a foreign nation over a U.S. state (Mexico vs. Arizona).
- The first president to (inconceivably) allow Iran to inspect its own facilities.
- The first president to trade five terrorists for a traitor.
- The first president to use the IRS to unfairly target political enemies.
- The first president to terminate America's ability to put a man in space.
- The first president to facilitate the Iranians to acquire nuclear weapons.
- The first president to light up the White House in rainbow colors to honor homosexuality.
- The first president to allow men in women's restrooms and showers.
- The first president to conduct the marriage of two men.
- The first president to actively meddle in an Israeli election.
- The first president to be named by the AP as the least transparent administration in history.
- The first president to develop an openly hostile relationship with the nation of Israel.

The National Security Agency, under former President Barack Hussein Obama, routinely violated the rights of Americans. Thanks to some of the leaked top-secret documents, some of the most serious constitutional abuses by the U.S. intelligence community are only now being revealed.

Obama has left the White House and started working on a series of books that will be pure fluff and will sell poorly, but nonetheless, he will receive multimillion dollar advances for each book. I'm sure he will follow the Clintons' playbook: collecting huge speaking fees for implied lobbying efforts back in Washington.

Nearly a dozen other presidents left office in disgrace because of far more minor misdeeds and, certainly, much less deception. We remember how the president constantly declared his would be an administration that was *transparent*. I think what has allowed Obama to escape justice is our nearness to the Tribulation. Since God is about to judge the whole world, there is no need to discredit Obama with some minor scandal.

> But because of your stubbornness and your unrepentant heart, you are storing up wrath against yourself for the day of God's wrath, when his righteous judgment will be revealed (Romans 2:5, NIV).

Trump's Presidency

The new buzz phrase of the left wing is "Fake News." The defeat of Hillary Clinton is being blamed on websites that are accused of publishing false news stories about her. To preserve the "integrity" of the obviously biased liberal news industry, there is a movement to red-flag all sites that they falsely claim promote hoaxes, propaganda, or disinformation.

The one-sided attack on Trump has backfired on the liberal media. When CNN's Jake Tapper was trying to link Trump to white nationalist leader Richard Spence, the network ran a banner that questioned whether "Jews are people." The backlash against CNN for highlighting a racist statement was so strong on Twitter that Tapper had to return from vacation to apologize for being so callous against Jews.

The next day on CNN, Charles Kaiser used the N-word while allegedly quoting Trump adviser Steve Bannon. He was quickly found to have quoted the wrong person. His use of the word sent the show's host into panic mode:

> All right, gentlemen. We're done. We're done. I appreciate both of your voices. The more I've sat here and listened to the fact that somebody used the N-word on the show . . . it is not okay! It is not okay. Charles Kaiser, I respect you. I enjoy having you on as a guest but . . . not okay. By the way, the claim that Mr. Bannon used the N-word — I've never heard of this. So there's that. Take a break.[15]

When it was weeks away from the day when Donald Trump would take office, the left was using every trick to nullify the 2016 presidential election. First, there was the failed recount effort launched by Jill Stein, an obvious front for the Clinton campaign — in Wisconsin, Michigan, and Pennsylvania. Embarrassingly, that effort actually resulted in a wider margin of victory for Trump, but not before Stein wasted $7 million raised from devastated Hillary supporters.

The second failure was an effort to convince Electoral College voters to become so-called faithless electors by deciding to cast their votes for someone other than the Republican nominee. When the vote was cast, five electors chose not to back Clinton while only two decided not to vote for Donald Trump. I guess threatening the lives of electors was not the way to go.

Their next strategy, more or less from the moment he was sworn in, is to impeach Trump. Trump has already committed a long list of high crimes, according to liberal lawyers who are going over the Constitution with a microscope. Since Republicans control both houses of Congress, the Democrats' dreams of impeachment will have to wait for a future election.

The Women's March that took place the day after President Trump's inauguration is solid proof that the people on the left are being consumed with madness. I think the organizers as well as the participants need to be checked to see if they have that brain-eating amoeba in their skulls.

The gathering was one of the most bizarre and pointless events I've ever seen. One speaker after another endlessly compared Trump to the former leader of Nazi Germany. They said he is Hitler because he acts like Hitler, he does Hitler-like things, and he has a Hitler agenda.

Singer Ashley Judd gave this rambling bit of wisdom to the crowd: "I am not as nasty as a swastika painted on a pride flag and I did not know devils could be resurrected, but I feel Hitler in these streets! Nazi's electro-conversion therapy! Gas chambers! Turning rainbows into suicide!"[16]

This growing madness has motivated some liberals to turn to the devil himself to help them combat Donald Trump. On February 23, 2017, at the stroke of midnight (Eastern Time), witches from around the country cast a collective spell to drive Trump from office. The plan is to continue every night of each waning crescent moon until he is no longer president.

Organizers set up a Facebook page called, "A Spell to Bind Donald Trump and All Those Who Abet Him." The ritual calls on spirits, which include the "demons of the infernal realms," and commands to "bind Donald J. Trump so that he may fail utterly."[17]

The liberal media will use the most trivial and insignificant bits of information against Trump. One headline said: "Donald Trump Doesn't Even Have a Dog — and That Says a Lot About Him."[18] It's true: Trump is the first president in more than 100 years to not have man's best friend at his side. Oh, if only the voters knew beforehand that Trump was a dog hater, they would have voted for Hillary.

I was recently waiting for my food at a restaurant, I read a CNN article that was making a strange comparison between Trump and a Holocaust survivor. At the very least, the writer wanted to paint Trump as a Hitler-like person. The horrors of this poor woman who had survived four concentration camps was being used in trivializing anti-Semitism and racism as it exists today. When I read a similar article by another news outlet, it was clear that the liberal media is working to seduce one of these Holocaust survivors into crying out: "Oh yes, it was bad under Hitler rule, but Trump is much worse."

The difficult thing about writing a chapter about how deceptive and unfair the press has become with Trump is trying to guess how bad things will ultimately get. By the time this book is printed, the liberal media may be openly calling for Trump's head. What the press doesn't understand is that God is in control of all things in this world. If God wants Trump removed from power, there is nothing we can do to save him. If God wants Trump to serve two terms, all the mud-slinging in the world will not matter.

There is much speculation in the Christian community about why God allowed Trump to be elected. I think the Lord's core reason is to expose the evilness of the world system. If Hillary had won in 2016, she would have continued with Obama's destructive policies. With the liberal media attacking as her guardians, much of the public would be ignorant to the danger being inflicted on the nation. I think one of the reasons God put Trump in office is to make it known how the globalist press is battling to enslave the country.

Conclusion

It is vital that Christians and conservatives realize how dangerous the liberal media has become in its deceptiveness — and it's also vital that they take action. If enough people called the press out on its game of bias and manipulation, we could force it to go back to objective reporting.

Unless we act soon, we are headed for a police state in which the media and politicians will work together to prohibit all dissenting opinions. What prevents people from knowing that they live in an authoritarian society is the ability of the media to control the free flow of information.

Christian books are already limited in what markets they are allowed to enter. A growing number of platforms and physical bookstores won't sell anything with an "end-time," "Christian," or "evangelical" label. It does not matter if a book is selling millions of copies. We now live in a world where ideology comes before business.

Since most events don't progress in a constant straight line, there may be a revolt in the near future. My hope is that the liberal media takes a misstep that triggers a huge backlash from the public. Because the average person has become incredibly tolerant of the systematic removal of every truth we once saw as sacred, it's hard to think of something that would turn the tide.

I'm very pessimistic about the future. The press has reached a point of such extreme fanaticism, I don't see how it could be reasoned back to sanity. If we are, as I believe, living in the last of the last days, the situation may be doomed to go from bad to worse. The blessed thing about the Rapture is that when the situation gets hopeless here on earth, the Lord Jesus will come to take us home to heaven.

Now when these things begin to happen, look up and lift up your heads, because your redemption draws near (Luke 21:28; NKJV).

Endnotes

1. Stephen Tropiano, *The Prime Time Closet: A History of Gays and Lesbians on TV* (Winona, MN: Hal Leonard Corp., 2002), p. 11.
2. Robert Caro. *Master of the Senate, The Years of Lyndon Johnson* (New York: Vintage Books, 2003), p. 955.
3. One steward Robert MacMillan. As quoted in *Inside the White House* (1996), by Ronald Kessler, New York: Simon and Schuster, p. 33.
4. https://en.wikipedia.org/wiki/Robert_Byrd.
5. https://www.dailywire.com/news/8696/flashback-bill-clinton-once-justified-robert-byrds-hank-berrien#exit-modal.
6. https://www.thoughtco.com/robert-byrd-kkk-4147055.
7. https://www.newsmax.com/t/newsmax/article/441057.
8. http://edition.cnn.com/2008/SHOWBIZ/TV/11/03/chevy.chase.snl/.
9. https://www.newsbusters.org/blogs/nb/rich-noyes/2017/01/09/farewell-decade-media-drooling-over-barack-obama.
10. https://www.huffingtonpost.com/2008/02/13/chris-matthews-i-felt-thi_n_86449.html.

11. Bernard Goldberg, *A Slobbering Love Affair* (Washington, DC: Regnery Publishing, 2008), p. 87.

12. http://nation.foxnews.com/liberals/2012/04/24/bernie-goldberg-exposes-liberal-skinhead-obsession.

13. http://www.weeklystandard.com/piers-morgan-mocks-davis-guggenheim-for-obama-documentary/article/633359.

14. West, Jonathan. *The Presidential Chronicles: 2010–2012: What Has Actually Been Happening Whether We Like It or Not* (Bloomington, IN: AuthorHouse, 2012), p. 319.

15. http://ew.com/article/2016/11/22/cnn-brooke-baldwin-guest-n-word/.

16. https://www.realclearpolitics.com/video/2017/01/21/ashley_judd_at_dc_womens_march_i_am_a_nasty_woman_a_loud_vulgar_proud_woman.html?src=ilaw.

17. https://extranewsfeed.com/a-spell-to-bind-donald-trump-and-all-those-who-abet-him-february-24th-mass-ritual-51f3d94f62f4.

18. https://www.yahoo.com/lifestyle/donald-trump-doesn-apos-t-143500914.html.

CHAPTER 11

Demon-Conjuring Con Men

DR. BILLY CRONE

A woman went with her husband to the doctor's office and after his checkup, the doctor called the wife into his office alone. He said, "Your husband is suffering from a very severe disease, combined with horrible stress. If you don't do the following, your husband will surely die.

"Each morning, fix him a healthy breakfast. Be pleasant, and make sure he is in a good mood. For lunch make him a nutritious meal that he can take to work. And for dinner, prepare an especially nice meal for him. Don't burden him with chores, as this could further his stress.

[Men, how many of you would like to have this disease?]

"And don't discuss your problems with him, for it will only make his stress worse. Try to relax your husband in the evening by giving him plenty of back rubs. Encourage him to watch some type of team sporting event on television. And most importantly, satisfy his every whim.

"If you can do this for the next ten months to a year, I think your husband will regain his health."

So on the way home, the husband asked his wife, "Well, honey, what did the doctor say?"

The wife simply responded, "You're going to die."[1]

As you can tell, that man has no clue what kind of danger he's in, let alone just how close the instigator of that danger is in proximity to him. Unfortunately, the same thing is happening to the American Church today. Christians are clueless to the dangerous spiritual battle surrounding them as well as to the one who is behind it all. Of course, I'm talking about Satan. Even though the Bible is replete with evidence of his existence and his desire to destroy us, most people today don't even believe he exists, as these statistics reveal:

- Polls tend to show that Americans consider themselves largely a religious people, with something close to 95 percent claiming a belief in God.

- In fact, there are also large numbers of Americans saying that they think that heaven exists, and that angels do, too.

- But in another survey, people were asked whether they thought hell existed as an actual location, "a place of physical torment," and only 31 percent said they thought it did, which means 69 percent said no.

- And as far as so-called American Christians and their belief in Satan, only 35 percent said he is real, which means 65 percent said he's not, he's just "a mere symbol of evil."

- As to the reason why, one researcher stated, "Hollywood has made evil accessible and tame, making Satan and demons less worrisome than the Bible suggests they really are." Further, he said, "It's hard for achievement-driven, self-reliant, independent people to believe that their lives can be impacted by unseen forces."

- In fact, the results may even be worse than that. On the television show, *The View*, Barbara Walters quoted a report from a research group stating, "Only 1% of the youngest adults ages 18–23 has a biblical worldview, which is that the Bible is completely accurate and Satan is a real being. Only 1% of young adults and only 9% of all American adults have a biblical worldview, that is that the Bible is completely accurate which includes Satan being a real being or force."[2]

So now we see upward of 91–99 percent who don't believe in a literal devil. No wonder the Church is getting pummeled today. We have allowed ourselves to become clueless concerning the spiritual warfare we really are in by no longer believing in the enemy's existence. Yet, the sad irony is, the Bible is replete with information about Satan's existence. Old Testament, New Testament — he is mentioned all over the place. Let's take a look at some of that proof:

Genesis 3:3–5: "You will not certainly die," the serpent said to the woman, "For God knows that when you eat from it your eyes will be opened, and you will be like God, knowing good and evil."[3]

1 Chronicles 21:1: Satan rose up against Israel and incited David to take a census of Israel.

Job 1:6–12: On another day the angels came to present themselves before the Lord, and Satan also came with them. The Lord said to Satan, "Where have you come from?"

Satan answered the Lord, "From roaming throughout the earth, going back and forth on it."

Then the Lord said to Satan, "Have you considered my servant Job? There is no one on earth like him; he is blameless and upright, a man who fears God and shuns evil."

"Does Job fear God for nothing?" Satan replied. "Have you not put a hedge around him and his household and everything he has? You have blessed the work of his hands, so that his flocks and herds are spread throughout the land. But now stretch out your hand and strike everything he has, and he will surely curse you to your face."

The Lord said to Satan, "Very well, then, everything he has is in your power, but on the man himself do not lay a finger."

Then Satan went out from the presence of the Lord.

Zechariah 3:1–2: Then he showed me Joshua the high priest standing before the angel of the Lord, and Satan standing at his right side to accuse him. The Lord said to Satan, "The Lord rebuke you, Satan! The Lord, who has chosen Jerusalem, rebuke you!"

Matthew 5:37: All you need to say is simply "Yes" or "No"; anything beyond this comes from the evil one.

Matthew 6:13: And lead us not into temptation, but deliver us from the evil one.

Matthew 13:19: When anyone hears the message about the kingdom and does not understand it, the evil one comes and snatches away what was sown in their heart.

Matthew 16:23: Jesus turned and said to Peter, "Get behind me, Satan! You are a stumbling block to me; you do not have in mind the concerns of God, but merely human concerns."

John 8:44: You belong to your father the devil, and you want to carry out your father's desires. He was a murderer from the beginning, not holding to the truth, for there is no truth in him. Whenever he lies, he speaks his native language, for he is a liar and the father of lies.

John 17:15: My prayer is not that you take them out of the world, but that you protect them from the evil one.

Acts 5:3: Then Peter said, "Ananias, how is it that Satan has so filled your heart that you have lied to the Holy Spirit and have kept for yourself some of the money you received for the land?"

Romans 16:20: The God of peace will soon crush Satan under your feet. The grace of our Lord Jesus be with you.

1 Corinthians 7:5: Do not deprive each other except perhaps by mutual consent and for a time, so that you may devote yourselves to prayer. Then come together again so that Satan will not tempt you because of your lack of self-control.

2 Corinthians 2:10–11: I have forgiven in the sight of Christ for your sake, in order that Satan might not outwit us. For we are not unaware of his schemes.

2 Corinthians 11:3: But I am afraid that, just as Eve was deceived by the serpent's cunning, your minds may somehow be led astray from your sincere and pure devotion to Christ.

2 Corinthians 11:14: No wonder, for Satan himself masquerades as an angel of light.

Ephesians 6:11: Put on the full armor of God, so that you will be able to stand firm against the schemes of the devil (NASB).

2 Thessalonians 2:9: The coming of the lawless one will be in accordance with how Satan works. He will use all sorts of displays of power through signs and wonders that serve the lie.

2 Thessalonians 3:3: But the LORD is faithful, and he will strengthen you and protect you from the evil one.

1 Timothy 3:7: And he must have a good reputation with those outside the Church, so that he will not fall into reproach and the snare of the devil (NASB).

1 Timothy 5:14–15: Therefore, I want younger widows to get married, bear children, keep house, and give the enemy no occasion for reproach; for some have already turned aside to follow Satan (NASB).

2 Timothy 2:26: And they may come to their senses and escape from the snare of the devil, having been held captive by him to do his will (NASB).

James 4:7: Submit yourselves, then, to God. Resist the devil, and he will flee from you.

1 Peter 5:8: Be alert and of sober mind. Your enemy the devil prowls around like a roaring lion looking for someone to devour.

1 John 2:13: I am writing to you, fathers, because you know him who is from the beginning. I am writing to you, young men, because you have overcome the evil one.

1 John 3:8: The one who does what is sinful is of the devil, because the devil has been sinning from the beginning. The reason the Son of God appeared was to destroy the devil's work.

1 John 5:18: We know that no one who is born of God sins; but He who was born of God keeps him, and the evil one does not touch him (NASB).

Revelation 12:9: And the great dragon was thrown down, the serpent of old who is called the devil and Satan, who deceives the whole world; he was thrown down to the earth, and his angels were thrown down with him (NASB).

Revelation 20:1–2: And I saw an angel coming down out of heaven, having the key to the Abyss and holding in his hand a great chain. He seized the dragon, that ancient serpent, who is the devil, or Satan, and bound him for a thousand years.

Revelation 20:10: And the devil, who deceived them, was thrown into the lake of burning sulfur, where the beast and the false prophet had been thrown. They will be tormented day and night for ever and ever.

As you can see, the Bible emphatically declares that a real live devil, Satan, evil one, whatever you want to call him, actually exists. From the beginning to the end, Genesis to Revelation, he's mentioned all over the place. Therefore, how can people, even professing Christians, say he's just "a mere symbol of evil"? In fact, you have to deny what the Bible says in order to deny the existence of Satan — which, last time I checked, is not a good thing to do, especially for the Christian. If I can't take these passages literally that speak of a literal devil, then why should I take anything else in the Bible literally? Maybe Jesus is not the only way to heaven, as the Bible literally says. Maybe God doesn't exist as the Bible literally says. Maybe God doesn't have a problem with unrepentant sin. Maybe there is no hell, and nobody needs to be concerned about it whatsoever. Can I tell you something? That's precisely what the real devil wants people to believe. He's trying to dupe them long enough to reject Jesus so as to join him in the Lake of Fire. That's how evil he really is.

Furthermore, God goes into great detail concerning the character of Satan in the Bible so that we His people are not caught off guard.

The Names of Satan

- Accuser — opposes believers before God — Revelation 12:10

- Adversary — a rival opponent in a conflict — Job 1

- Angel of Light — appears as good when really evil — 2 Corinthians 11:14

- Beelzebub — lord of the flies/dung – Matthew 12:24

- Belial — worthless — 2 Corinthians 6:15

- Deceiver — leads people away from truth and into error — Revelation 12:9

- Devil — one who slanders/falsely accuses — Matthew 4:1

- Enemy — hostile opponent — Matthew 13:28/1 Peter 5:8

- Evil One — intrinsically evil — John 17:15

- God of the World — controls philosophy of this world — 2 Corinthians 4:4

- Great Red Dragon — destructive creature — Revelation 12:3, 7, 9

- Liar — perverts the truth — John 8:44

- Murderer — leads people to physical and eternal death — John 8:44

- Power of this Dark World — creator of dark activity — Ephesians 6:12

- Prince of Devils — commander of demons — Matthew 12:24

- Prince of the Power of the Air — ruler of demonic realm — Ephesians 2:2

- Prince of this World — authority behind our wicked world — John 12:31

- Roaring Lion — vicious animal seeking to devour people — 1 Peter 5:8

- Ruler of this World — the chief leader behind world system — John 12:31

- Satan — incites people to sin and turn away from God — Matthew 4:10

- Serpent — crafty deceiver — Genesis 3:4/2 Corinthians 11:3

- Serpent of Old — the original deceiver in Eden — Revelation 12:9

- Spirit of Those Who are Disobedient — gets people to oppose God's will — Ephesians 2:2

- Tempter — one who solicits people to sin — Matthew 4:3

- Wicked One — evil, corrupt, and morally wrong — Matthew 13:19[4]

Again, the Bible not only emphatically declares that a real, live, actual, wicked entity called Satan, the devil, the wicked one, really does exist, but it also records for us that his character is evil, rotten, and deceptive. Why? Because God loves us and wants us to know what we're up against so that we're not caught off guard. He doesn't want us to get spiritually blindsided.

Now, there's a multitude of ways that Satan is out to destroy us today, including getting us to deny his very existence, but I only have time to deal with one more of those destructive tactics, and that's the media. The Bible describes Satan's fall in Isaiah 14:

> How you have fallen from heaven, morning star, son of the dawn! You have been cast down to the earth, you who once laid low the nations! You said in your heart, "I will ascend to the heavens; I will raise my throne above the stars of God; I will sit enthroned on the mount of assembly, on the utmost heights of the Mount Zaphon. I will ascend above the tops of the clouds; I will make myself like the Most High." But you are brought down to the realm of the dead, to the depths of the pit (Isaiah 14:12–15).

In this passage, the Bible exposes how Satan wanted to be God and to be worshiped like God. But he lost, because the position isn't open, and that's when he went after us, mankind. He hates us. The reason he hates us is because we are created in the image of God, and that's what Satan lost out on. He wanted to be God. He wanted us to worship him as god. He wanted people to reflect his image, not God's. Believe it or not, he's still up to that same evil deed today, and he's using modern technology to get the job done. He's using the power of the mass media to get us, even Christians, to reflect his evil image, his evil character — not the character of God.

The first way he's doing that with the media is by bombarding us with devilish behavior. Over and over and over again, in the media, until we crack, and start to look just like him. That's part of his deceitful character See Revelation 12:9: ". . . who is called the devil and Satan, who deceives the whole world" (NASB).

How does he do this? With the media. The global mass media. He gets people to think that the media has no effect on them when it really does. He deceives them. This is why advertisers spend billions of dollars every year on the media. They know they're going to get their billions of dollars back and a whole bunch more because the media really has an effect on our beliefs, buying habits, and even our behavior. Let's take a look at that power.

The Power of the Media

Calvin Coolidge, the 30th president of the U.S. (1923–1929) stated about the power of media even in his day, "It is the most potent influence in adapting and changing the habits and modes of life . . . affecting what we eat, what we wear, and the work and play of a whole nation."[5]

> TV is not an art form or a cultural channel; it is an advertising medium . . . it seems a bit churlish and un-American of people who watch television to complain that their shows are lousy. They are not supposed to be any good. They are supposed to make money.[6]

> Every day, consumers are exposed to no less than 4,000 commercial messages.[7]

> The name "Hollywood" was carefully chosen as the name for the newly established motion picture industry in the 1920's. In ancient witchcraft, the most powerful wood for a witch or wizard to make a magic wand, was from the Holly tree. Thus, the most powerful magicians always used a hollywood magic wand.[8]

> The average person spends 4½ hours a day watching TV which is enough time to read the Bible 22 times in just one year.[9]

Looks like we're "mesmerized" by the Media and somebody's using it to lead us away from God. I wonder who that might be? Again, it's not just to get us "mesmerized" with it and lead us away from God, it's to get us to act like the devil himself. Here's what he's getting us to put in our brains:

Sex and Violence in the Media

- The average American adolescent will view nearly 14,000 sexual references on TV per year.[10]

- Seventy-five percent of prime-time network shows included sexual content, up 67 percent in one year alone.[11]

- Nearly one-third of family hour shows contain sexual references.[12]

- And it's about to get worse. They're now working on full-blown nudity shows. "Seven . . . shows are being rolled out on cable and satellite channels featuring one central theme: complete nudity"[13] — not just showing nudity here and there . . . that's bad enough . . . but it's complete full-blown nudity all the time.

- MTV has a couple of new shows out. One is called *Virgin Territory*, in which participants are trying to lose their virginity, or what they call the "V-Card." Another show is called Happyland, which features a teen story line that promotes incest. The lead female in the show said, "Incest is hot and we're going to have fun!"[14]

And if you think that's bad consider this: commercials are being aired on TV promoting adultery. *Prime News, CNN, Happening Now* says:

> We certainly don't need commercials to get us to cheat on our spouse. Like this ad campaign by this pro-adultery site, *An Affair to Remember*. But they are out there in-your-face ads and your kids can even see this.
>
> Two couples are getting married, they look so happy. But the next screen shows her with her husband's best friend and he is with some other woman. Or maybe it was her with her co-worker and him with her best friend. The ad says, "Isn't it about time to have an affair, Life is short, have an affair, go to AshleyMadison.com."
>
> Look how happy he is looking up the website and wow she is even happier searching for someone to have an affair with. He can't wait to get into his car to go pick her up and off to the hotel. The music is playing, there's nothing I haven't tried. "Shhhhhh, Ashley Madison." Life is short, have an affair.[15]

That's the tag line for AshleyMadison.com. An online dating service for married people advocating adultery.

- The average American child or teenager views 10,000 murders, rapes, and aggravated assaults per year on television.[16]

- A staggering 80.3 percent of all television programs include acts of violence.[17]

- A child born today will witness 200,000 acts of violence on television by the time he or she is 18.[18]

And the question more and more concerning parents and public officials is this: What is all this viewing doing to them?[19]

Gee, I wonder? But don't worry; we all know the deceitful lie that this has no effect on us whatsoever. It's just entertainment, right? Again, advertisers spent $5–$5.5 million dollars last year alone on a 30-second Super Bowl commercial because we all know they have a lot of money to waste.[20] No. It's because they know it's going to affect our behavior, and it has. Here's a snapshot of some of the ways this devilish media has affected our behavior and gotten us to act like the devil himself.

Sex and Violence in Our Behavior

- Approximately one-third of the entire population of the United States (110 million people) at any given time has a sexually transmitted disease, according to the Centers for Disease Control and Prevention.[21]

- Every single year, there are 20 million new cases of sexually transmitted disease (STD) in America.[22]

- America has the highest STD infection rate in the entire industrialized world.[23]

- The United States has the highest teen pregnancy rate in the entire industrialized world.[24]

- For women under the age of 30, more than half of all babies are being born out of wedlock.[25]

- In the United States today, more than half of all couples "move in together" before they get married.[26]

- The marriage rate in the United States has fallen to an all-time low: 6.8 marriages per 1,000 people.[27]

- And because of that, America has one of the highest divorce rates in the world.[28]

- We also have one of the highest percentages of one-person households on the entire planet.[29]

- One out of every three children in the United States lives in a home without a father.[30]

- 70% of Americans believe there's nothing wrong with divorce.[31]

- 67% of Americans believe sex outside of marriage is perfectly fine.[32]

- 58% of Americans believe having a baby outside of marriage is fine.[33]

- 72% of Americans believe gay and lesbian relations are fine.[34]

- A high school kid took two kitchen knives and went on a stabbing rampage through his school.[35]

- A Florida teen was accused of poisoning a teacher's drink.[36]

- A father allegedly put his six-week-old daughter in a freezer to keep her from crying.[37]

- Three children were left to starve to death while one was chained to the floor.[38]

- A woman was arrested after police say she injected hand sanitizer into the feeding tube of her infant son.[39]

- Florida parents were arrested after abandoning their three kids in the woods.[40]

- A grandmother forced soiled underwear down her 11-year-old granddaughter's mouth.[41]

- A caregiver used a stun gun to punish kids.[42]

- A couple locked their 3-year-old child in the trunk to cure his fear of darkness.[43]

- A mother stabbed her baby in an attempted murder-suicide.[44]

- A woman strangled her newborn son and tossed him in the trash.[45]

- A dad killed his kids and wife "because he didn't have car seats."[46]

- A Texas man was convicted of murdering his neighbors over dog feces.[47]

- A pregnant woman attacked her roommate over butter.[48]

- A North Miami Beach man was fatally shot after a fight over utensils broke out at baptism party.[49]

- A Florida man bit his neighbor's ear off over a cigarette.[50]

- A man stabbed a woman for bringing home pizza instead of a chicken sandwich.[51]

How many of you would say that's some seriously rotten, evil, devilish behavior there? I wonder where it all came from? This is all part of Satan's deceit. He's a deceiver. He gets us to think that the media exists to give us entertainment and fun, when in reality it's his high-tech tool in the last days to get us to emulate his character, not God's. He knows the rule: "Junk in equals junk out." Monkey see, monkey do.

The second way Satan gets us to emulate his character with the media is by bombarding us with devilish practices. I'm talking about the occult. It's bad enough that he uses the media to get us to behave like him, but he uses the same media to get us to engage in his practices as well. That's all part of his lies. That's why he's called the father of them: "You belong to your father, the devil . . . he is a liar and the father of lies" (John 8:44).

This is another one of his biggest lies. He gets us to think his dark occult practices are harmless, when in reality it's evil repackaged — and he's using the media to promote it. Don't believe me? All he's done with just one of his evil practices called witchcraft is change the name to Wicca. That's all he's done. It's just old-fashioned witchcraft, repackaged. Then he makes it appear as if it's something good for the environment, and people — especially teenagers — are falling for it right and left. Witchcraft says that in order to contact the gods and goddesses — which are demons — for personal power, you need to practice astrology, divination, incantations, psychic power, and speaking with the dead. Satan is promoting television shows on these very subjects in the media right now. Shows like *Psychic Hotline*, or *Crossing Over with John Edward*, or the latest one set in New Jersey called *Long Island Medium*. Then there's *Charmed*, and *Twilight*, and the *Harry Potter* series, which are making witchcraft look good, even for kids. Don't believe me? Let's listen to their words. They're more honest than we are.

The Effect of Harry Potter on Kids

J.K. Rowling, the author of the *Harry Potter* series, admitted that she got many requests from children who wanted to attend Hogwarts School of Witchcraft and Wizardry. And we know, from books that are out there and interviews of children, that many kids really wonder at night while they are lying awake if there is a Hogwarts that they can go to.

If you go to the Warner Brothers site, they ask you to enlist in Hogwarts, while there are other sites out there that are pulling in your children who are interested in learning more in various schools of witchcraft and wizardry.

The Association of Teachers and Lecturers tells us, "This goes far beyond a case of reading a Harry Potter story. This represents an extremely worrying trend among young people."[52]

10-year-old Dylan: "I want to go to wizard school and learn magic. I'd like to learn to use a wand to cast spells."

12-year-old Mara: "If I could go to wizard school, I might be able to do spells and potions and fly a broomstick."

11-year-old Jeffrey: "It would be great to be a wizard because you could control situations and things like teachers."

9-year-old Catherine: "I'd like to go to wizard school, learn magic and put spells on people. I'd make up an ugly spell, and then it's payback time."

10-year-old Carolyn: "I feel like I'm inside Harry's world. If I went to wizard school, I'd study everything: spells, counter spells, and defense against the Dark Arts."

13-year-old Julie: "I liked it when the bad guys killed Unicorn and Voldemort drank its blood."

11-year-old Nurya: "The books are very clever. I couldn't put them down. When I was scared I made myself believe it was supposed to be funny so I wasn't too scared."[53]

Very clever, isn't it? Satan is indoctrinating kids into the dark arts of witchcraft through the media, and people don't think it affects them when it does. No wonder he's called the "deceiver." In fact, the kids who grew up watching Harry Potter are now going into the military, and there's so many of them that are now full-blown witches that the military is allowing them to have their own witchcraft services:

Eyewitness News — Ken's 5 reports that Halloween may mean costumes and candy for you and for us, but for those out there that are witches, it is their most sacred holiday.

In San Antonio, there is a Wiccan coven touting the largest weekly service for the study of witchcraft in the world. Where they meet and who is in the class may surprise you. Marvin Hurst has their story.

"Mention the word 'witch' and instantly most conjure a thought of black magic rituals and the belly of seclusion."

"Just keep the line progressing" [says a soldier coming out of the Arnold Hall Community Center in San Antonio, Lackland].

"It's a different picture" [says the reporter].

"My name is Archer, and I am a witch" [says the man in black talking to a room full of soldiers].

"Archer, AKA Tony Gatland, is the high priest of this Coven, a packed house where the basic military trainees are studying witchcraft in his circle" [says the reporter].

"Archer explains, 'When we come over here on a Sunday, often there are three or four hundred.'"

"About 320 [are] this day taking part in Samhain, the witches' New Year celebration on Halloween; they honor the death and rebirth of their god. Trainees literally line up by choice to learn about Wicca."

"One soldier who joined five years ago says, 'There is nothing wrong with Wicca and of course that is why we have this service here.'"[54]

Looks to me like all this media promotion of witchcraft through Harry Potter really does have an effect on people. In fact, so does the *Twilight* series. That's another one. People not only want to become witches, but vampires as well:

> Watching her children in a playground in Guadalajara, Mexico, Maria Jose Cristerna is just an ordinary mom. But with her distinctive look she is likely to attract more attention than from her peers. She's made several dramatic modifications to her body to transform herself into Vampire Woman.
>
> Maria is 98% covered in tattoos, she's also had dental implants to give her fangs and titanium horns placed in her skull. Maria has given up her job as a lawyer to open a tattoo parlor and clothes shop. She insists her life is no different from any other wife and mother.[55]

Yup, all this media and promotion of occult practices with witchcraft and vampirism has no effect whatsoever on people. It's just entertainment. It's no big deal. What's Satan called? The Great Deceiver. But if you don't want to listen to me, then listen to the witches. Even they admit that because of this media promotion of their occult practices, it's got people to no longer be afraid of it, even in the Church.

Quotes from witches and warlocks follow:

- "Fear has gone out of the general public; the craft is more and more acceptable."

- "Paganism has infiltrated the mainstream thought pattern of most Americans today."

- "There is a pagan revival. There are more people practicing true paganism than there are practicing true Christianity."

- "Many people are seeking something apart from Christianity. The thing that attracts young people is the power. And it's immediate power."

- "As you see in the movie *Twilight* the vampire asks the girl he has met if she is afraid of him. Her reply is 'No.' We are conditioned to believe that vampires are more romantic than something to fear."

- "Whenever you drink blood you gain incredible power."

- "Magic is about getting what you want. Magicians are people that get what they want."

- "Slowly but surely the beauty of this is becoming widespread."

- "Psychic vampirism and physical vampirism is a way of achieving power through black magic."

- In the movie, *The Crow*, we see the vampire announcing to the public that he feels it is time to come forward and introduce himself. All the media is there to record the whole production to send to the world.

- A witch proclaims, "I am very proud to be a witch."

- Another says, "We live in a post-Christian era and we are moving toward a neo paganism." And another, "The neo pagan revival has proceeded so rapidly and they have had the cooperation of the media in getting their message spread."

- "They claim that a lot of what they do has been taken over by the Church. The Church has married into occult practices. They no longer know the difference as they become desensitized to the things of evil."[56]

People should be very concerned instead of allowing themselves to become desensitized, because all this media promotion of witchcraft, vampirism, and the occult is designed to destroy you and your family. Also, because of this media promotion, many are saying that Wicca is now the fastest-growing religion in the United States and the second most popular among teens.[57] I wonder why. What's Satan called again? The Great Deceiver. He's got us thinking that the media exists to give us entertainment and fun, when in reality it's his high-tech tool in the Last Days to get us to emulate his evil character, not God's. He knows the rule: Junk in equals junk out. Promote the occult, and people — even Christians — will do so.

The third way Satan gets us to emulate his character with the media is by bombarding us with devilish acceptance. What I mean by that is that he not only wants us to behave like him and engage in his evil practices, but he even wants us to look like him and call him a good guy when he's not: "And no wonder, for satan himself masquerades as an angel of light" (2 Corinthians 11:14).

This is what he's doing with the media today. He's transforming his evil character into an "angel of light" to try to make us to think he's a good guy who's here to help us rather than an evil, satanic adversary with whom we have to deal. Don't believe me? A television program called *Lucifer* is just one of many transforming the devil into a good guy.

In the trailer of the new *Lucifer* show, we find Lucifer driving his hot car down the road. The [narrator of the] clip says, "What would happen if Lucifer quit and moved to the city of angels?" He is no longer the bad guy. Now he brings out people's most forbidden desires.

[The Lucifer character] says, "People like to tell me things, their deep dark naughty desires that are on their minds." At a wedding he asks [the bride], "You're not marrying this human stain. You're not actually in love with him." And she answers, "God no! I can't believe I just said that." [Lucifer] replies, "It must be something about his face."

Another clip: [Lucifer] asks a girl at a bar, "Can I have your autograph?" She asks, "Can I sell my soul to the devil?" Lucifer replies, "So the devil made you do it, did he? The alcohol, drugs, the topless selfies — the choices are on you, my dear."

In another clip: "Someone out there should be punished," [Lucifer] says. Another girl replies, "Stop caring, you are the devil."

And [in yet] another clip: A demon shows up to take [Lucifer] back to hell. The waitress says, "I think you have a visitor." The demon says, "Your return to the underworld has been requested." Lucifer replies, "Let me check my calendar; it says the 7th through never to the 15th of ain't going to happen. How does that work for you guys?"

The demon puts his claws to Lucifer's throat, and Lucifer asks, "Do you think Father is upset now?" The demon replies, "He's not going to be merciful for much longer."

But now he is a good guy, he thinks he should be out there punishing people that are responsible for their wrongdoings. In another clip: A girl asks him, "How can you possibly help me?" He answers, "I have the ability to draw out peoples' forbidden desires."

And the final clip shows Lucifer talking to a little girl asking Lucifer, "What's your name?" He answers, "Lucifer." She asks, "The devil?" He answers, "Exactly."[58]

Nice show for kids to watch. Yes, I'm being sarcastic. But don't you see? Lucifer is just a good guy getting a bad rap from those nasty fundamentalist Christians, when in reality, he's just here to help us and to solve crimes. *Yeah, right.* It would be a crime to believe that lie. But he's not just going after the adults. He's going after the kids as well, with the media trying to get them to think that he's a good guy, too. This is an excerpt from the television program called *Childhood's End*.

As everyone is watching either by TV or congregated in a crowd in the auditorium the speaker comes on and says, "Let the children come forth."

Two small children proceed up the stairs to a bright light that engulfs them.

Everyone watches without making a move. They are mesmerized. The light gets brighter as they try to shade their eyes, but out of the light comes a shadow. As they keep watching, the shadow gets larger and then they see two large, hoofed feet coming down the stairs, with the two small children on each side.

As they get closer to the crowd, they see that the hoofed creature has large wings, horns, and is about eight feet tall. The children are looking up at this creature with smiles on their faces.

He lowers his wings, and as the camera zeros in on his face, the people watching by TV and in the auditorium start gasping and covering their faces. It is the devil.

"Hello," he says. "There is no need to be afraid."

The crowd relaxes.

One couple [is] watching in their living room. [The woman] says, "He was right to hide himself from us. This world will be okay, won't it?" Her husband says, "Yes, I think so."[59]

That's just like those Baphomet statues of Satan that satanists are putting up in our government buildings across America, with kids looking up to him as a source of inspiration. He's a good guy, right? What does the Bible say? He masquerades as an angel of light. He gets people to think he's good when he's not. But don't worry, we know all this media promotion of the devil being a good guy has no effect on us, right? Well, you might want to tell that to this guy:

> This guy wants to look like the devil. His name is Diablo Delenfer, and to complete this dramatic look, he has had his teeth ground to points; he's got his eyeballs tattooed so they are no longer white, they are red.
>
> He's also had his tongue split in half. He has inserted metal balls into his forehead, and he has also [gone] through with an operation to place metallic balls to form a mohawk on the top of his head.
>
> Tattoos cover him head to toe; I guess all he needs now is a pitchfork.
>
> Another piece of interesting information about Diablo is when he goes under the knife, under the needle to get this stuff done, none of it's regulated; it's all classified as body modification, so he does it without the anesthetic. I can't imagine that eyeball procedure was fun.
>
> Diablo Delenfer isn't his real name. He adopted that name while going through all this change. He was born Gavin Paslo. But he got me thinking there are so many other names he could have adopted; he could have gone all the way out and called himself St. Lucifer, Beelzebub (if you open the Bible, that one's in there) or the tempting serpent.
>
> He continues to push forward, coming up with whatever he can to get that look fully completed, and the final step for him is he says he wants a tail. And not just some prosthetic piece you get at the Halloween shop. He wants an organic one. Something that kind of waves behind him. What's he going to do after that? Is he going to get hooves?[60]

What is the spiritually clueless Church saying today? "Don't you know that all this media has zero effect on us? We know the difference. It's all just harmless entertainment." Yet the deceitful, lying, masquerading one knows better. He's using the power of the mass media in these last days as his high-tech tool not only to get young and old alike to accept him as a good guy, but even to want to alter their appearance to look like him. Can you believe this? It is high time we get our heads out of the sand and deal with the spiritual war we are in. We have to wake up and stop being ignorant of the devil's schemes, and cease being brainwashed ourselves by the media. We need to shut this filth off and start emulating God's character and lead the way back. Don't let the enemy get you. Amen?

Endnotes

1. "You're Going to Die" email joke; source unknown.
2. References for people's beliefs about Satan: http://www.nytimes.com/1997/05/10/ us/is-satan-real-most-people-think-not.html; http://www.christianpost.com/news/ most-u-s-christians-don-t-believe-satan-holy-spirit-exist-38051/; and video from The View, source unknown.
3. Unless otherwise noted, Scripture quotations in this chapter are from the New International Version (NIV) of the Bible.
4. Sources for the names of Satan: H. Wayne House, *Charts of Christian Theology & Doctrine* (Grand Rapids: Zondervan Publishing House, 1992, p. 79–80); http:// www.allaboutgod.com/names-of-satan-faq.htm; https://bible.knowing-jesus. com/topics/Satan,-As-Deceiver; https://www.gotquestions.org/names-of-Satan. html; http://www.markbeast.com/satan/names-of-satan.htm; https://bible.org/ seriespage/6-survey-bible-doctrine-angels-satan-demons.
5. http://adage.com/century/rothenberg.html.
6. http://adage.com/news_and_features/special_reports/tv/1960s.html.
7. https://www.redcrowmarketing.com/2015/09/10/many-ads-see-one-day/.
8. http://www.cuttingedge.org/news/n1385.cfm.
9. Billy Crone, *The Character of God — Defeating Practical Atheism* (Morrisville, NC: Lulu Press, 2017), p. 222.
10. https://www.focusonthefamily.com/lifechallenges/love-and-sex/purity/what-your-teens-need-to-know-about-sex.
11. https://www.sagepub.com/sites/default/files/upm-binaries/23151_Chapter_6.pdf.
12. Pastor Lenuf, Pastor Mary E., *Flee from Sexual Immorality* (Lulu.com, 2011), p. 197.
13. https://www.charismanews.com/opinion/heres-the-deal/44802-tv-shows-featuring-nudity-highlight-culture-s-crisis-of-truth.
14. http://deadline.com/2014/07/happyland-incest-mtv-craig-zadan-neil-meron-802510/.
15. Billy Crone, *The Final Countdown*, Vol. 3 (Morrisville, NC: Lulu Press, 2018), p. 136.
16. Estimate by the American Psychological Association; G. Comstock, Ph.D., V.C. Strasburger, MD, "Media Violence: Q & A," *Adolescent Medicine*, State of the Art Reviews, vol. 4, no. 3, October 1993, Philadelphia, Hanley & Belfus, Inc; cited by the Newsletter of the Minnesota Association for the Education of Young Children, November/December 1994. Archived at: https://web.archive.org/ web/19991002034211/http://www.cyfc.umn.edu:80/Documents/C/D/CD1001. html.
17. "Are we selling out our children's minds? Media violence indicated that society values profits over children," by Patricia Peterson. Children Youth and Family Consortium Electronic Clearinghouse. Original URL: http://www.cyfc.umn.edu:80/Documents/ C/B/CB1032.html; archived at: https://web.archive.org/web/19991109114047/ http://www.cyfc.umn.edu:80/Documents/C/B/CB1032.html.

18. "Television & Health," TV-Free America; www.csun.edu/science/health/docs/tv&health.html, accessed 1/23/18.

19. Sources for quotes and information about sex and violence in the media: http://screenrant.com/10-tv-shows-most-nudity/; https://en.wikipedia.org/wiki/Nudity_in_American_television; http://www.vulture.com/2014/08/cable-nudity-countdown-clock.html; https://en.wikipedia.org/wiki/Virgin_Territory_(TV_series); http://www.mtv.com/shows/virgin-territory; http://deadline.com/2014/07/happyland-incest-mtv-craig-zadan-neil-meron-802510/; CNN Broadcast, "Married & Dating? Ad Campaign by Pro-Adultery Site; YouTube Video, source unknown; http://www.cyfc.umn.edu/Documents/H/K/HK1005.html; http://www.cyfc.umn.edu/Documents/C/D/CD1001.html; http://www.cyfc.umn.edu/Documents/C/B/CB1032.html; Ted Baehr, *The Media-Wise Family* (Colorado Springs: Chariot Victor Publishing, 1998, p. 19, 70, 71).

20. https://www.si.com/nfl/2017/01/26/super-bowl-commercial-cost-2017.

21. http://atlanta.cbslocal.com/2014/10/06/cdc-110-million-americans-have-stds-at-any-given-time/.

22. https://www.cdc.gov/std/stats14/std-trends-508.pdf.

23. http://www.nbcnews.com/health/health-news/ongoing-severe-epidemic-stds-us-report-finds-f1C8364889.

24. http://articles.latimes.com/2012/jan/19/news/la-heb-teen-pregnancy-20120119.

25. http://www.nytimes.com/2012/02/18/us/for-women-under-30-most-births-occur-outside-marriage.html.

26. http://www.nytimes.com/2012/04/15/opinion/sunday/the-downside-of-cohabiting-before-marriage.html.

27. https://economix.blogs.nytimes.com/2010/08/28/birthrates-marriage-rates-and-divorce-rates-fell-in-2009.

28. http://www.telegraph.co.uk/travel/maps-and-graphics/mapped-countries-with-highest-divorce-rate/.

29. http://www.ipsnews.net/2017/02/the-rise-of-one-person-households/.

30. http://www.fatherhood.org/fatherhood-data-statistics.

31. https://www.christianpost.com/news/survey-70-percent-of-americans-find-divorce-morally-acceptable-32435/.

32. http://www.gallup.com/poll/3163/majority-considers-sex-before-marriage-morally-okay.aspx.

33. http://www.gallup.com/poll/8839/outofwedlock-births-morally-acceptable.aspx.

34. http://www.gallup.com/poll/1651/gay-lesbian-rights.aspx.

35. http://www.nydailynews.com/news/crime/stabbings-reported-pennsylvania-high-school-article-1.1750425.

36. http://www.sandiegouniontribune.com/sdut-florida-teen-accused-of-poisoning-teachers-drink-2014mar13-story.html.

37. http://www.dailymail.co.uk/news/article-2332522/Man-puts-week-old-daughter-freezer-stop-crying-faces-life-bars.html.

38. http://www.nbcnews.com/NbcNews_2014/news/crime-courts/california-women-arrested-after-3-children-found-starving-1-chained-n59516.

39. http://www.insideedition.com/headlines/11933-mom-who-killed-son-by-injecting-hand-sanitizer-into-his-feeding-tube-gets-40-years.

40. http://abcnews.go.com/US/florida-couple-arrested-abandoning-kids-woods/story?id=22769212.

41. http://cleveland.cbslocal.com/2014/02/01/police-grandmother-forced-feces-covered-underwear-down-11-year-old-granddaughters-mouth/.

42. http://www.clickorlando.com/news/caregiver-used-stun-gun-to-punish-kids-kissimmee-police-say.

43. http://pittsburgh.cbslocal.com/2014/01/24/couple-headed-to-trial-for-driving-with-son-in-trunk/.

44. http://abc7chicago.com/news/police-mom-kills-8-week-old-son-in-apparent-murder-suicide/1511125/.

45. http://www.reuters.com/article/us-usa-texas-infant-idUSBREA0E0WE20140115.

46. http://nypost.com/2014/01/24/dad-killed-kids-after-slaying-wife-because-he-didnt-have-car-seats-for-mexico-trip/.

47. http://www.reuters.com/article/us-usa-texas-murder-idUSBREA081JF20140109.

48. http://www.nbcmiami.com/news/local/Pregnant-Woman-Blames-Hormones-For-Attack-on-Roommate-Deputies-239641111.html.

49. http://www.nbcmiami.com/news/North-Miami-Beach-Man-Fatally-Shot-After-Fight-Over-Utensils-Breaks-Out-at-Baptism-Party-239260151.html.

50. http://www.browardpalmbeach.com/news/florida-man-bites-neighbors-ear-off-over-a-cigarette-6454471.

51. http://www.nbcdfw.com/news/local/Woman-Stabbed-for-Bringing-Home-Pizza-Instead-of-Chicken-239757201.html.

52. http://news.bbc.co.uk/2/hi/in_depth/education/2000/unions_2000/722283.stm.

53. Sharon Moore, *We Love Harry Potter! We'll Tell You Why* (New York: St. Martin's Press, 1999).

54. KENS5 San Antonio news broadcast, "Witches Among Us/San Antonio's Military Witches," YouTube video, source unknown; original URL: http://www.kens5.com/news/No-hocus-pocus-Military-trainees-spellbound-by-Wiccan-faith-176600791.html; https://web.archive.org/web/20121205232657/http://www.kens5.com:80/news/No-hocus-pocus-Military-trainees-spellbound-by-Wiccan-faith-176600791.html.

55. https://www.youtube.com/watch?v=Z127wKKWfXg.

56. Quotes about paganism being on the rise: http://www.youtube.com/watch?v=-6UBO7IOStA.

57. http://www.apologeticsindex.org/w03.html; http://www.christianpost.com/news/online-witch-school-wicca-fastest-growing-religion-59799/; http://thetruthwins.com/archives/the-fastest-growing-religion-in-america-is-witchcraft.

58. https://www.youtube.com/watch?v=X4bF_quwNtw.

59. https://www.youtube.com/watch?v=Rr25OLacsdc&list=PLcbo3s7XSa876YEqrGDa_OMcaGxudu4xS).

60. Excerpts from https://www.youtube.com/watch?v=iLpruZuFQDM.

CHAPTER 12

Interdimensional Deception: Satan Still Demands Blood Sacrifices

GARY STEARMAN

In the UFO world, there is a bizarre ritual. It involves the deaths of many animals, but mostly cattle and horses. When examined, this phenomenon has oddly primitive roots, set within the world of bizarre flying objects and their other-worldly inhabitants.

Any Bible-believing Christian who studies the vast annals of UFO literature will sooner or later arrive at a schism between two poles of understanding. On one side, it is simply unarguable that unidentified flying objects are an obvious and well-documented phenomenon. They are well substantiated and believable. But on the other side of the question, just how is one to fit the myriad weird events of the phenomenon into a theological framework? What does the Bible tell us about the activities of perplexing "ET" visitors? Surprisingly, it speaks with great authority about them.

This is especially true in one particular aspect of UFO study, namely, the widespread mutilation of animals. The occurrence of "cattle mutilations" is a disturbing facet of the UFO puzzle. These now occur all over the world with increasing frequency. The fact that UFOs actually perpetrate these events is beyond doubt. There are too many witnesses to argue otherwise. But what are the intruders doing? Are they using certain animal byproducts for some unknown experiment? Are they, as some have suggested, sending a message to earthlings in the symbolism of ritual cattle slaying? Or are they simply harvesting food?

Since the Bible is divine in its origins and sufficient for the application of truth to any aspect of life, the answers to these and other questions must yield to scriptural analysis. This being the case, the general activities of UFOs and their occupants seem to conform best to the behaviors of fallen angels and demons. Many Christians have collected the evidence that substantiates this case.

And if it is a given assertion that the identity of these interdimensional interlopers is locked into the framework assigned to Satan and his fallen angels, we are forced to a single conclusion — namely, that what they're doing in contemporary times must have its roots in ancient events. That is, since their activities have spanned the panorama of human history, their motives and activities must be the same now as they were in the days of the Old Testament. Their external appearance may have changed, but their basic motives remain the same. This perspective must surely shed some light on the behaviors of these creatures.

Of course, any study of them unveils the topic of human abduction by UFOs — not only the frequency of the phenomenon, but its fiendish purposes. Apparently, there is a human-demon breeding project underway. Some experts in the field say that it is near its goal — to produce a viable human-alien offspring. Once this is accomplished, it remains only for the dark visitors to amass enough counterfeit humans to control the infrastructure of this earthly dimension. Having failed to usurp the kingdom of heaven, Satan is still trying to control the kingdom of earth.

As we have noted in depth on several occasions, Satan and his minions apparently tried to do the same thing in Noah's day, but were destroyed by God in the great Flood. The noted encounter of Genesis 6 between heavenly beings and earthly women produced an accursed offspring.

But the corruption of the human race is far from these visitors' only activity. For reasons that are not yet completely clear, they are also preoccupied with lower forms of animal life here on earth.

There are literally thousands of well-documented cases in which both wild animals and domestic livestock have been abducted and returned after some of their vital parts have been surgically removed. This fact is so repugnant and unbelievable that it is generally dismissed out of hand. Nevertheless, it has been documented beyond a shadow of a doubt. Perhaps the unidentified entities need the organic material from animals for their ongoing projects. But let's go back a few years to the first major incident: "Lady."

For a few months in 1967, an incident in southern Colorado captivated the entire country. Feature writers and press syndicates carried a series of stories about an unfortunate horse, first reported as a male named "Snippy," but later correctly named as "Lady," a female.

That year, a quiet area in the south-central part of the state known as the San Luis Valley was plagued with a rash of UFO sightings. Many of these observations were photographed. The pictures appeared in newspapers and magazines all over the United States and many foreign countries.

Most of the time, the mysterious machines appeared as round or oval lights, silhouetted against the Sangre De Cristo mountains to the east and south, and the San Juan range to the north. But on more than one occasion, they were observed on the ground as well. In these cases, witnesses described them as domed, circular craft, standing on tripod landing gear.

At that time, the area was a sparsely populated basin whose arid terrain was characterized chiefly by the blowing sands of an alkaline soil, scrubby brush, and greasewood trees. Suddenly, the small town of Alamosa lay roughly at the center of a full-blown UFO flap. The clean little town boasted a population of about 10,000 people who were somewhat dubious about their newfound fame. Students at Alamosa's Adams State College took the opportunity to publicize their city's reputation on a blank billboard about seven miles east of town. It read, "Home of Snippy . . . The Flying Saucer Capital of the World . . . Beware of Low Flying UFOs, We May Be Looking for You."

Lady the horse, owned by Berle and Nellie Lewis, had become the victim of a UFO abduction (or so the locals said). The Lewises owned a ranch about 25 miles northeast of Alamosa in the Dry Lakes region at the foot of the spectacular Sangre De Cristo Mountain range.

In October of that year, the animal's remains had been found in a condition so grotesque that there was an instant and universal acknowledgment that her death had not been caused by any earthly action.

First, the flesh and hide had been stripped from the shoulders, neck, and head. No blood or bodily fluids of any sort were found anywhere near the body. Incisions on the body were surgically accurate. Some internal organs were missing. And an autopsy revealed that there was no brain. Somehow — impossibly — it had been completely removed without disturbing the skull. (This is commonly reported in other incidents as well.)

Also, many deep impressions were photographed around the body. Some of them trailed off nearly 500 feet from the body. These "tracks," made by an unidentifiable something, were so deep that they suggested a gigantic presence of some sort. Nellie Lewis told anyone who would listen that she believed Lady was killed by aliens from another world.

This case was the first of its kind to attract national attention. But in truth, there is now much evidence to suggest that our government had been aware of this phenomenon as far back as the early- to mid-fifties. In both 1967 and 1968, the San Luis Valley became a hotbed of UFO sightings. Even the local law enforcement agencies in Alamosa, Mosca, Monte Vista, Hooper, Crestone, and Blanca reported dozens — if not hundreds — of sightings. A good example of a typical sighting was reported in May 1967 by Eleanore Blundell, the wife of a ranger at the Great Sand Dunes National Monument near Blanca.

She sighted a strange craft near the dunes, where it hovered for about ten minutes. An artist, she later painted a picture of the weird craft. She described it as a crescent with little lights. When she sighted the strange object, she had enough time to call several families who lived at the Dunes to watch. All of them reported a beautiful, lighted crescent that had an otherworldly glow.

From then on, the valley became a huge party line finely tuned to detect and watch for UFOs. Residents over the valley's 6,300 square miles kept each other informed on a minute-by-minute basis. For the next two years, they were entertained by the beautiful colors and graceful movements of the unidentified craft. Sometimes they were entranced. But at other times, they were unabashedly afraid of what they saw, particularly when some of their cattle showed up mutilated, like Lady.

In the years since the hapless horse captivated the attention of the media, the mutilation phenomenon has quietly continued. But instead of a few remote and isolated cases, investigators are now reporting literally hundreds of cases.

In the ranchlands of western Washington and Oregon, in Texas and New Mexico, Colorado, and a host of other ranching areas, cattle mutilations have grown so common that they have become an economic detriment. A rancher doesn't have to lose very many cattle before his profit margin is removed. Many of them report losses greater than 10 percent.

Missing Blood

When pressed on the subject, the news media usually pin the blame on some sort of "satanic cult" engaged in a ritual killing. This is an easy connection to make, because the affected animals are typically drained of all blood, and precise incisions have been used to remove the eyes, tongue, ears, genitalia, and often the tail.

However, in thousands of reported cases, no cult group has ever been caught in the act, or even accused. Ranchers have formed all-night watch groups. Even when coordinated with local sheriff's departments and given the use of sophisticated night scopes, they have never witnessed a human intruder.

In one typical case, a prize bull was felled and mutilated within a hundred feet of a ranch house, where the owner and his wife were sleeping with the windows open. The bull had been surgically dissected and many of its parts removed — including many internal organs. The heart had been removed without disturbing the surrounding pericardial membrane. The carcass contained no blood. Nor was there a drop of blood anywhere on the surrounding ground. Losses like this are worth thousands of dollars. Despite great rewards and all-night watches, the phenomenon continues unabated to this day. In fact, the year 2000 witnessed a startling acceleration in the number of reported cases.

A typical incident, like one reported from Durango, Colorado, in September 1998, described a dead cow with large portions of its carcass cleanly excised. It lay in the middle of a clearing, its body surrounded by black, charred earth, suggesting the application of tremendous heat. The cow's heart and several other internal organs were missing, as well as a large part of its posterior hide and musculature.

Cattle, sheep, and — to a lesser extent — horses and wild animals are found dead under similar circumstances. Usually, they lie in a crumpled heap, with many missing parts. Their mutilations are always accomplished with surgical precision. Autopsies invariably report that their wounds display a "cauterizing" effect, suggesting that the incisions involve some sort of heating instrument. Some have suggested a laser or microwave implement.

Common to each reported case is the *complete absence of blood,* either on the animal or the ground surrounding it. No one has yet been able to explain how this is possible. Anyone at all familiar with cattle butchery knows that huge quantities of gushing, splattering blood are involved . . . by the gallon! Yet, *not a single case* of cattle mutilation has demonstrated even a slight bloodstain. And in every case, the carcass is totally drained of blood. As will be seen, this single fact becomes vital to the understanding of what's going on.

It is commonly believed that cattle mutilations are a complete mystery. The general public never reads the reports in which witnesses have actually seen cattle abducted.

One such abduction is graphically described in Linda Moulton Howe's 1998 book, *Glimpses of Other Realities*. She is generally considered the reigning expert on this aspect of the UFO mystery. Her report is quite significant, because it took place in Oregon, one of the current centers of activity.

She reveals that 27-year-old Timothy Fint describes his own abduction from a Portland apartment. He appears to have been taken for the specific purpose of being allowed to witness a cattle mutilation. While resting in his apartment, he was transported to a dark field in the nearby countryside, where he was allowed to see a strange spectacle.

He describes a domed, bluish, glowing disc that hovered above a grazing cow.

> This thing went down the hill a little bit off to my left and hovered above the brownish-red cow. The cow was still eating and didn't even know that the domed thing was there, I guess. All of a sudden, this light beam came down from the blue base of a round, lighted object in the sky, a kind of milky white light that I could see right through. And it came down and surrounded the cow, and the cow started to levitate. The cow went stiff and its head popped up and its eyes were wide open and its tongue was sticking out. And it went up.

At the top of the beam, the cow hung there, and to Timothy's horror, began to be dissected. He heard a sound, which he described as, "a high-pitched zinging sound, like the sound of a power saw cutting wood."

At the same time, the cow uttered a series of blood-curdling screams. As the operation continued, the cow was rotated feet up. The unwilling witness became extremely disturbed:

> I could clearly see that the right side of the cow's face was gone. There was no ear, no eye and the tongue had been removed and it was down to the bone on the jaw. The meat had been removed right down to the bone.[1]

Young Timothy, now himself a victim of interdimensional kidnapping, had for some reason been allowed to witness an event that is often seen by ranchers in their waking state, but for obvious reasons, seldom reported by them. For fear of being branded "crazy," they remain stolidly closed-mouthed. This was true in the case of ranchers who saw things in the Snippy case, and it is true today.

Howe describes the way Dwain Wright of Grants Pass, Oregon, recounted his meeting with a rancher east of Bend while on a hunting trip. He got into a conversation with the old cowboy, who lived in a dilapidated travel trailer near the area where his cattle grazed. While talking, their conversation turned to UFOs. The cowboy asked the hunter an unlikely and riveting question, recorded in the following conversation:

> "Do you believe in flying saucers?" And I said that I did. And he said, "Well, they come across the desert here at night. I want to show you something." He took me to another area and there was a dead bull pressed into the ground as if it had been dropped from a great height.
>
> "How far into the ground?" I asked.
>
> "About half way. The cow was heavy to begin with, but it had to have been dropped a couple of hundred feet." And what I noticed about it is that certain parts of it were missing: ears, eyeballs, sex organs were missing, its anus was also cut out." And the cowboy said, "This is not the only one. There are lots of them like this."[2]

The cowboy went on to describe glowing saucers that came by night and floated cattle off the ground, later dropping them, bloodless and in a mutilated condition.

In this region, ranchers report that it is not uncommon to see cattle in the treetops, hanging twisted, torn, and bloodless.

A recent and well-documented case involved 14 forestry workers in the Mt. St. Helens area of Washington state. It happened in February 1999. It was during the day, as they planted seedlings on a hillside, when they spotted the UFO below them. It was small — about the size of a rectangular parachute canopy. In fact, this is what the workers thought it was, as it descended toward a herd of elk.

Then, it became obvious that it was not a parachute. As it descended to near ground level and approached the herd in "stealth mode," it precipitated a sudden stampede. A lone female became separated from the rest of the animals and was quickly singled out as a target.

As they watched in horrified amazement, the workers saw the elk levitate to the bottom of the craft, which began to climb slowly and laboriously with its load. After almost hitting trees at the edge of the clearing, it began to climb at a 45-degree angle and disappeared into the clouds. The workers agreed to be interviewed by professional investigators, but for obvious reasons, they insisted on maintaining anonymity.

In late 1999, unusual cattle deaths continued to be reported in Oregon, New Mexico, and Colorado. Ranchers are deeply disturbed by all this activity, but are powerless to do anything about it. In the Snohomish region, northwest of Seattle, Washington, dozens of strange animal deaths have been recently reported.

And it is not as though our government is ignorant of these happenings. In the early 1960s, the mysterious ability of UFOs to lift people and animals was described in the literature of various investigations.

Some say the recognized beginning of animal mutilation cases in the United States dates back to 1966. At that time, an Ohio dairy farmer reported that several of her cows had been expertly butchered in part, leaving the bodies bloodless.

However, the real beginning was much earlier. The late Army Lt. Col. Philip J. Corso wrote a best-selling book in 1997 entitled *The Day After Roswell*. In it, he described the U.S. government's knowledge of human abductions and animal mutilations. He asserts that all this was known in the 1950s!

He wrote:

> It was the UFOs, alien spacecraft thinking themselves invulnerable and invisible as they soared around the edges of our atmosphere, swooping down at will to destroy our communications with EMP [electromagnetic pulse] bursts, buzz our spacecraft, colonize our lunar surface, mutilate cattle in their own horrendous biological experiments, and even abduct human beings for their medical tests and hybridization of the species. And what was worse, we had to let them do it because we had no weapon to defend ourselves.[3]

Like other writers who have had experiences with hidden government programs, Corso strongly believes that the "aliens" have made agreements with our political and military leaders. The heart of such agreements offers the aliens freedom of operation in exchange for certain technological advances.

If as we suggest, these "aliens" are the dark forces described in Scripture, these covenants amount to nothing more or less than a pact with the dark side.

Concerning cattle mutilation, Corso writes:

> In the Pentagon from 1961 to 1963, I reviewed field reports from local and state police agencies about the discoveries of dead cattle whose carcasses looked as though they had been systematically mutilated and reports from people who claimed to have been abducted by aliens and experimented on.
>
> One of the common threads in these stories were reports by the self-described abductees of being subjected to some sort of probing or even a form of surgery with controlled, intense, pencil-thin beams of light. Local police reported that when veterinarians were called to the scene to examine dead cattle left in fields, they often found evidence not just that the animal's blood had been drained but that entire organs were removed with such surgical skill that it couldn't have been the work of predators or vandals removing the organs for some depraved ritual.[4]

He even alludes to the famous "Lady" case, saying, "Although the first public reports of cattle mutilations surfaced around 1967 in Colorado, at the White House we were reading about the mutilation stories that had been kept out of the press as far back as the middle 1950s, especially in the area around Colorado."[5]

An Ancient Evil

For the Christian who believes that the Bible is the divinely inspired Word of God, offering an explanation for every aspect of life, there is a strong desire to place these bizarre events into some spiritual context.

The best explanation of the "space aliens" is that they are transdimensional apparitions. That is, their ordinary realm is the dimension just beyond human sight, in which angels and demons fight a perennial battle for control of the spiritual heavens that surround the lives of humans here on earth. Over the eons, the battle has raged back and forth. Paul's description in Ephesians 6:12 says it best: "For we wrestle not against flesh and blood, but against principalities, against powers, against the rulers of the darkness of this world, against spiritual wickedness in high places."[6]

In the New Testament, these dark angels and their demonic hordes are mentioned primarily as spirits in search of incarnation. During His earthly ministry, Jesus cast them out of hapless individuals who previously had no defense against them.

But in addition to "possession," demons apparently engaged in other corrupting activities that affect the daily lives of human beings on a larger scale. The Church does not exist in a vacuum. It is fully immersed in the culture of the old dragon, whom Paul refers to in Ephesians 2:2, as "the prince of the power of the air."

Furthermore, we know that his dark angels are at work as celestial power brokers. They are seen in this capacity in Daniel 10, where the angel who ministered to Daniel related his story of having been impeded on his journey by the princes of the kingdoms of Persia and Greece. These, of course, were the dark angelic princes of Satan.

Only once in the New Testament is an evil angel revealed by name. In Revelation 9, at the opening of the bottomless pit, he is seen for what he really is: "And they had a king over them, which is the angel of the bottomless pit, whose name in the Hebrew tongue is Abaddon, but in the Greek tongue hath his name Apollyon" (Revelation 9:11).

Apollyon, "the destroyer," has waited through the ages for this moment. Now, he can battle humanity face to face, as he and his hordes of followers are released without restraint upon the earth. Prophetically, we may be very near the time of culmination. Perhaps this is a partial explanation of why we're seeing so many strange events now.

In the Old Testament, these dark presences took on the identity of gods and goddesses. There were many of them.

Baal, or "Lord," was the chief deity of the Canaanites. The ongoing struggle between Baal and Jehovah (the Lord) was brought to a dramatic conflict on Mount Carmel under Elijah. There is also an Old Testament reference to Baal as "Beelzebub" — "lord of the flies." (This encounter, in 1 Kings 18, will be described below.) Flies are a metaphor for demons; it would be much better to call him "lord of the demons."

Baal also had his feminine consorts, especially in Ashteroth, the chief goddess of Tyre. In 1 Samuel, chapter 7, the prophet led Israel in a great revival that resulted in the people giving up the evil sexual practices of her worshipers.

Dagon was the chief agricultural god of the Philistines. He was worshiped as the father of Baal. The Ark of the Covenant once destroyed an idol to Dagon in the large temple dedicated to his name (see 1 Samuel 5:2–4). Later, of course, Samson destroyed that temple.

Nebuchadnezzar worshiped Merodach, also called Marduk, the highest god of the Babylonian pantheon.

Molech, god of the Ammonites, conjures up the most horrific images in the Old Testament. Parents sacrificed their children to this god. Both King Ahaz and King Manasseh sacrificed their own children — thrown alive into the idol's burning belly — to satisfy his need for blood.

The Greeks and Romans had their Zeus/Jupiter, Artemis/Diana, and Hermes/Mercury, as well as an abundance of other, lesser gods.

The myriad details of their false worship would take several volumes to enumerate. But it is accurate to say that the activities were clustered around two basic types of activity: blood sacrifice and sexual debauchery, both of which are seen in current abductions.

For the sake of consistency, we must assume that the same dark forces arrayed against the prophets of the Old Testament are the powers in charge of today's mysterious encounters. We must also assume that their behavior — though modified to conform to 20th-century thinking — is very much the same as that described in the Old Testament.

Baal, for example, is frequently referred to in the ancient pagan rituals as, "the rider of the clouds." In this title, we hear ancient rumblings of the "prince of the power of the air." We also note that the powers of today's UFO stories are viewed in exactly the same way. Also, the Baal myth contains many rituals that suggest the events of modern ufology. From the *Zondervan Pictorial Encyclopedia of the Bible* we read:

> Aliyan Baal, [worship of Baal, the Strong] at the height of the summer drought (i.e. when vegetation is dying and the land parched) was slain by Mot (Death). Anath searched for the body with the assistance of the sun goddess, Shapsh. She found it, and through *numerous animal sacrifices (seventy each of buffaloes, neat, small cattle, deer, mountain goats and roebucks)* Baal was restored to life and reigned over Mot, thus assuring life and fertility for the year ahead[7] (emphasis added).

Note the great appetite of Baal for cattle of various kinds. This description is typical of the old gods, who seemed to gain strength from the sacrifices of their followers, who brought various kinds of blood offerings to satisfy their dark and despotic overlords.

In those days, the prophets of the false gods, such as Baal, fought against God's own prophets. In a physical sense, they were acting out the spiritual battle that is waged in the regions of the heavens.

Perhaps the leading example of this opposition is found in 1 Kings chapter 18, where the story of Elijah and the prophets of Baal is recounted. In this famous contest, Elijah challenged his people:

> And Elijah came unto all the people, and said, How long halt ye between two opinions? if the LORD be God, follow him: but if Baal, then follow him. And the people answered him not a word (1 Kings 18:21).

In the events that followed, the prophets of Baal prepared a bullock and then appealed to their gods to receive the sacrifice. The gods remained silent. The pagan prophets worked themselves into an emotional state, dancing, shouting, and even cutting themselves to add their own blood to the sacrifice. But Baal remained silent. From morning to evening they continued. But their god would not answer, even to spite the continuous mocking of Elijah, who taunted them mercilessly.

Then, later in the day:

> And it came to pass at the time of the offering of the evening sacrifice, that Elijah the prophet came near, and said, LORD God of Abraham, Isaac, and of Israel, let it be known this day that thou art God in Israel, and that I am thy servant, and that I have done all these things at thy word.
>
> Hear me, O LORD, hear me, that this people may know that thou art the LORD God, and that thou hast turned their heart back again.
>
> Then the fire of the LORD fell, and consumed the burnt sacrifice, and the wood, and the stones, and the dust, and licked up the water that was in the trench (1 Kings 18:36–38).

The fire of the Lord received Elijah's sacrifice, proving the Lord's superiority to the false retinue surrounding Baal. All his servants were then taken and slain. And the heavens, which had held back the rain so vital to the crops, opened in a great torrent. The Lord, not Baal, brought fertility back to the land.

The Mystery Religion (Obscene Sacrifices)

In the centuries of Greek and Roman ascendancy, the "Babylonian Mystery Religion" flourished throughout the ancient world. It brought together many of the ancient pagan practices into a single, secret practice. Its participants were engaged in a series of initiations, each of which required actions and oaths aimed at keeping the central ritual a deep secret. In fact, its priests were so successful in this enterprise that very little is known of its actual practices.

Like its pagan predecessors, this religion had its basic roots in the myth of Ishtar and Tammuz, the husband and wife who became the origin of the pagan worship of wife/mother and husband/son. Ishtar, the great mother goddess, became the model for all the goddesses who follow. Tammuz appears as the youthful spouse or lover of Ishtar. Tammuz dies, and is cut to pieces by a jealous rival. The goddess searches the underworld for his parts. Upon finding them, she resurrects the reassembled Tammuz.

In Egypt, the myth was repeated in the annual drama of Isis and Osiris. Historian Alexander Hislop writes, "The ordinary way in which the favorite Egyptian divinity Osiris was mystically represented was under the form of a young bull or calf — the calf Apis — from which the golden calf of the Israelites was borrowed."[8]

When Aaron fashioned the golden calf, he was responding to a people who had, in Egypt, learned to believe in the power of sacrificing cattle to certain false gods who would bring them blessing.

In Egypt, Isis was based upon the traditional Astarte, the Ashtoreth of the Canaanites, the Aphrodite and Artemis of the Greeks and Diana of the Romans.

The god Baal, who revealed himself before the Egyptians as Baal, also took on another identity. Later, he became Mithra, the mediator, and the so-called victim-man whose followers labeled him "the savior of all men."

In the Christian era, the ages-old mystery religion was finally crushed by those who believed that it was fit only for destruction. But traces of its sacraments survive in other religions to the present day. Once, in the past, the false gods demanded the blood of cattle for their deceptive and powerless form of redemption. It is a ghastly and repulsive rite — an obscene ritual in which a bull was led onto an iron grate, where its throat was slit. Fresh, warm blood showered into a room below, where worshipers bathed in a putrescent shower that was falsely believed to have regenerative power.

In a strange way, the dark forces of our own day still seem to have the same appetite for cattle. Just as in the days of Elijah — who defeated the priests of Baal 900 years before Christ — the pagan gods still demand their obscene sacrifices. Just as in the prophet's day, they consume cattle and corrupt mankind.

Posing as "ancient astronauts" from elsewhere in the galaxy, they are none other than the gods who once reveled in blood sacrifice and human sexual debauchery.

The latter activity is seen in the phenomenon of human abduction and impregnation, about which we have written at length elsewhere. The former is witnessed with increasing frequency by cattlemen throughout the world.

Elijah's faithfulness was rewarded when the fire of God fell from heaven, licking up every last trace of the bullock and its altar. Doubtless, the prophets of Baal had expected their god to do precisely the same thing. But his power was halted by the superior force of the one true Lord and God.

Today, in a very real sense, UFO observers report the descent of a very real — albeit preternatural — fire that falls from heaven in the form of the UFO phenomenon. They report beams of light that burn vegetation, with the power to lift humans, cattle, and even automobiles! The fires of the ufonauts burn with an evil and frightening glare.

The famous Cash-Landrum case of 1980 offers a perfect example of such fire. Betty Cash and Vickie Landrum of Dayton, Texas, witnessed a fiery UFO, which burned them so badly that they both required lengthy treatment for strange radiation burns. The event produced a series of inexplicable symptoms in the two, resulting in lengthy medical documentation. The "machine" they witnessed produced flaming beams of a type that neither had ever seen. Then, after burning them, their car, and the asphalt pavement, it simply disappeared.

Such blazing power may be suggested by a passage concerning the "beast out of the land," in Revelation:

> And I beheld another beast coming up out of the earth; and he had two horns like a lamb, and he spake as a dragon.
>
> And he exerciseth all the power of the first beast before him, and causeth the earth and them which dwell therein to worship the first beast, whose deadly wound was healed.

> And he doeth great wonders, so that he maketh fire come down from heaven on the earth in the sight of men (Revelation 13:11–13).

Clearly, this beast, who causes all men to receive a mark, has the power to summon the preternatural powers of the heavens. There is very little doubt that this is a reference to the ancient fires of the very demigods who demanded human and animal sacrifice.

Certainly, the ancient bronze effigies of Baal and Molech were stoked with wood to bring physical fires to high heat. But ancient references seem to suggest something more — that their fires took on a supernatural heat, making believers out of those who witnessed it.

The good king Josiah caused such worship to cease:

> And the king commanded Hilkiah the high priest, and the priests of the second order, and the keepers of the door, to bring forth out of the temple of the LORD all the vessels that were made for Baal, and for the grove, and for all the host of heaven: and he burned them without Jerusalem in the fields of Kidron, and carried the ashes of them unto Bethel (2 Kings 23:4).

Furthermore, Josiah commanded that the idols of Molech be broken down so that the pagan fire sacrifices might forever cease. This god, whose very name means "king of sacrifice," demanded the blood of Canaanite and Israelite children. Sometimes, lambs were used. But, like all of the ancient idols, Molech had an appetite for blood. Josiah destroyed the idols of Molech: "And he defiled Topheth [the incinerator], which is in the valley of the children of Hinnom, that no man might make his son or his daughter to pass through the fire to Molech" (2 Kings 23:10).

East and West

Like their Eastern counterparts, the gods of the Western hemisphere had a keen appetite for blood. Quetzalcoatl, the Aztecs' god of creation, was called the "feathered serpent." He was said to be the inventor of agriculture, and patron of learning.

But his worshipers were bloody beyond belief, sacrificing thousands of victims each year to ensure peace, good weather, and successful agriculture.

The Aztecs' sun god and ruler of war was called Huitzilopochtli, a name having the seemingly harmless meaning of "left-handed hummingbird."

Of all the gods of ancient Mexico, Left-Handed Hummingbird had the greatest appetite for human blood. At the time of the Aztec Empire's greatest glory, literally thousands of victims were paraded to his altar every year. There, they had their spurting hearts torn from their bodies.

Such blood sacrifices were typical of the Incas, Mayans, and Aztecs. Their corrupt priesthoods were enriched with gold and the produce of superior agricultural methods. Their sculpture, painting, and architecture were superior. But their culture was drastically weakened by the terrible toll of human blood demanded by their gods.

The foregoing historical notes suggest that blood sacrifice has a high value, indeed. This, of course, should come as no surprise to Christians, who believe in the saving power of the ultimate sacrifice of the Son of God, the Lord Jesus Christ.

But, as we continually observe, Satan always usurps that which God has created for man's redemption. He is the great counterfeiter. The history of the human race emphasizes the fact that there is something very significant about the sacrificial blood of animals and humans (as in the Aztec sacrifices).

From this perspective, the Lord makes a telling statement about blood, as recorded in Leviticus 17:10–14. It contains a truth that is, in many respects, self-substantiating. At the same time, its central message is surely beyond our understanding:

> And whatsoever man there be of the house of Israel, or of the strangers that sojourn among you, that eateth any manner of blood; I will even set my face against that soul that eateth blood, and will cut him off from among his people.
>
> For the life of the flesh is in the blood: and I have given it to you upon the altar to make an atonement for your souls: for it is the blood that maketh an atonement for the soul.
>
> Therefore I said unto the children of Israel, No soul of you shall eat blood, neither shall any stranger that sojourneth among you eat blood.
>
> And whatsoever man there be of the children of Israel, or of the strangers that sojourn among you, which hunteth and catcheth any beast or fowl that may be eaten; he shall even pour out the blood thereof, and cover it with dust.
>
> For it is the life of all flesh; the blood of it is for the life thereof: therefore I said unto the children of Israel, Ye shall eat the

blood of no manner of flesh: for the life of all flesh is the blood thereof: whosoever eateth it shall be cut off (Leviticus 17:10–14).

Certainly, blood contains the living cells that convey life from one part of the body to another. In this day of transfusions and blood drives, its ability to prolong life is well known. Physiologically, it does bring life to the flesh.

To the Israelites, the consumption of blood as food was forbidden. In the United States, it is not our custom to eat blood. But certain cultures have a long tradition of doing so. Some still practice it today.

Scripture clearly teaches the power of the blood atonement. There is a great mystery here. It began after man's sin in the Garden of Eden, when the young shepherd, Abel, "brought of the firstlings of his flock and of the fat thereof" (Genesis 4:4) as an offering to the Lord. This offering of flesh and blood was received by Him.

As many have pointed out, Abel's sacrifice is typical of Christ, the Lamb of God. In John 1:29, He is called, "the Lamb of God, which taketh away the sin of the world."

Abel's offering is in stark contrast with Cain's bloodless offering — the fruit of the ground. Over and over again, we are told that only in blood is there power to make atonement for sin, and only in the blood of Christ is man's sin finally blotted out.

Being justified freely by his grace through the redemption that is in Christ Jesus: Whom God hath set forth to be a propitiation through faith in his blood, to declare his righteousness for the remission of sins that are past, through the forbearance of God (Romans 3:24–25).

In the final analysis, only the blood of Christ could satisfy the holy requirements of God the Father.

There is a power in the blood that God placed there at the creation. It seems beyond the present level of human comprehension to understand this power. But we are to respect it.

Certainly, Satan knows of the power of blood sacrifice and has consistently attempted to take command of it. Through ages of pagan idolatry, he has solicited the false blood sacrifices of millions of deceived supplicants. In Babylon, Persia, Greece, and Rome, as well as the primitive cultures of the Western hemisphere, myriad false blood cults have risen, then sunk to shameful self-destruction.

And now in the medium of "scientific" 20th-century culture, Satan seeks the very same blood offering. Only this time, his representatives are masquerading as space aliens when they come to take their blood sacrifices.

They brazenly come as ambassadors from a faraway, superior culture. Posing as our overlords and keepers, they take their gruesome human and animal toll. It is probably better not to know what it is that they do with the stolen blood of cattle, sheep, and goats. Doubtless, their activities are vile, corrupt, and impure, to say the least. They are taking unclean and sinful offerings.

Endnotes

1. Linda Moulton Howe, *Glimpses of Other Realities, Vol. II* (New Orleans, LA: Paper Chase Press, 1998) p. 167, 170.
2. Ibid., p. 170.
3. Philip J. Corso, *The Day After Roswell* (New York: Simon & Schuster Inc., 1997) p. 292.
4. Ibid., p. 197.
5. Ibid. p. 199.
6. Unless otherwise noted, Scripture in this chapter is from the King James Version (KJV) of the Bible.
7. *The Zondervan Pictorial Encyclopedia of the Bible* (Grand Rapids, MI: The Zondervan Corporation, 1975, 76) Vol. 1, p. 432.
8. Alexander Hislop, *The Two Babylons* (Neptune, NJ: Loizeaux Brothers, 1943) p. 45.

CHAPTER 13

The Israel Revilers

JIM FLETCHER

The room is perhaps smaller than photographs suggest, but the history of the place looms large. A large portrait of early Zionist leader Theodor Herzl dominates from the wall behind the dais, where on May 14, 1948, the state of Israel was born.

Independence Hall, Tel Aviv.

Just steps from the beach (in the vicinity of the drama that played out in the Book of Jonah), the unassuming building is, oddly, not a popular stop for Christian tourists. Yet the place pulsates with history and Bible prophecy fulfilled (Isaiah 66:8).

Independence Hall's relative obscurity today is symbolic of the level of knowledge in the American Church regarding the specialness of Israel and the Jews.

To put a different spin on the famous maxim from screenwriter William Goldman, "Nobody knows anything."

Biblical illiteracy in America is at an all-time high, as all polling suggests. One has only to watch one of the "man on the street" interviews to see the knowledge base, especially among Millennials, is abysmal.

Somehow — the reasons are many — generations of churchgoers grew up hearing little or nothing about Bible prophecy and the role of the Jewish people in history, especially their role at the end of history.

Today, it is my contention that pro-Israel support in the American Church is poised to go right off a cliff within the next generation. No less than the director of Christians United for Israel, David Brog, has said as much. That is sobering coming from the head of the largest grassroots pro-Israel group around.

British scholar Paul Wilkinson is the first, I believe, to coin the term "Christian Palestinianists" to describe those who embrace the Palestinian narrative. This view used to be exclusively the domain of mainline churches and many Catholic sources.

It is now raging throughout Evangelicalism.

My awakening accelerated a half-decade ago.

O Little Town of Bethlehem

When I was in high school in Oklahoma City, we were all by our lonesome out on the prairie, in the southwest part of town. Those were the years in which Barry Switzer's Sooners were rolling across opponents and dominating college football, using their vaunted wishbone offense like the fast-moving tumbleweeds that dot the area.

In those days, it was hard to imagine the land was anything more than a backwater and a place for scrub brush.

Fast-forward a few decades. I am standing in the vast parking lot of the corporate headquarters for Hobby Lobby. It is right across the street from my old school!

The retail chain is swimming in money, and the Green family is deeply into funding Christian ministries around the globe. Mart Green, founder of Mardel Christian Stores and former chairman of the board at Oral Roberts University in Tulsa, has also funded EGM Films, which in 2010 produced *O Little Town of Bethlehem.*

Supposedly a film about peacemakers in the Holy Land (featuring an Israeli, a Muslim, and a Palestinian Christian), *O Little Town of Bethlehem* was a hit piece on Israel. All three people featured leaned toward the Palestinian view of the conflict, which says that the "Occupation" is the chief villain, and the Palestinians are oppressed by the Israelis.

The film was screened at scores of Christian college campuses. It was featured even in *Charisma* magazine!

I attempted many times to interview Green (even meeting him by chance in airports and hotel lobbies!), but he never agreed to be interviewed. I wanted to ask him his views of Jews and Israel, but curiously, he demurred.

Green was also part of "Empowered 21," a who's who of Pentecostals globally. In 2012, an event was held at Regent University, in which *O Little Town of Bethlehem* was screened and featured a talk by Sami Awad, a self-professed Palestinian Christian from Bethlehem. Awad is from the

Awad family that runs Bethlehem Bible College, which for 30 years has promoted the PLO narrative that the Occupation is responsible for the evil in the region.

A press release from the Institute on Religion & Democracy (IRD) described the gathering thusly:

> Often identified as strong supporters of Israel, Pentecostal Christians are now being targeted by anti-Israel activists from the Evangelical Left.
>
> Meeting March 1–4 in Virginia Beach, Virginia, the Society for Pentecostal Studies is jointly gathering with Empowered 21, a group of Pentecostal ministry leaders. Themed on "peacemaking and social justice/righteousness," this year's gathering will feature presentations by academics with anti-Israel views, as well as a screening of "Little Town of Bethlehem," a film with a subtle anti-Israel message aimed at usually pro-Israel evangelicals.[1]

Mark Tooley of the IRD had this to say:

> The Evangelical Left is eager to dissuade Pentecostals, Charismatics and Evangelicals from their traditional support for Israel.
>
> Although some Pentecostals rely on their end-times teachings to buttress support for Israel, many (including the vast majority of American Evangelicals) support Israel because it is a democratic ally surrounded by hostile dictatorships.
>
> The inclusion of several speakers to conduct workshops around themes of liberation theology, which emphasizes Jesus Christ as a political revolutionary rather than an atoning savior, is distressing.
>
> Almost certainly the vast majority of Pentecostals reject these leftist and anti-Israel themes. But just as in the old-line Protestant denominations decades ago, often church academics pursue political fashion at the expense of faithfulness to their own church.[2]

Why would a mainstream (and influential) family like the Greens promote anti-Israel rhetoric?

Curious indeed.

They are far from alone in evangelical circles featuring leaders who are stepping away from supporting Israel.

Lynne Hybels' Mysticism

In 1975, a young Chicago couple decided to canvas neighborhoods to find out what "people wanted" in a church. This was the beginning of the "Seeker-Driven" model for doing church. Today, from Rick Warren's empire in southern California to Andy Stanley's Seeker-Driven model in Atlanta, the "Church Growth" plan for "growing" churches dominates.

Bill and Lynne Hybels started it.

A few years before his death, Noah Hutchings at Southwest Radio Church showed me a stack of letters he'd received from church members all over the country. Each described the takeover of their church by the Seeker-Driven, "Purpose-Driven" model (they go by many names, but all have the same format).

He had enough material to write a book, so he did (*The Dark Side of the Purpose-Driven Church*).

Noah understood exactly what was happening. He knew that pastors who bought into Rick Warren's Purpose-Driven stuff would present the plan to the church as a "new vision." If anyone balked, they would be marginalized and, if necessary, shown the door. Many thousands of Bible-believing Christians around the country have experienced painful and disheartening departures from churches they have called home for generations.

The Hybels have been major drivers behind the Seeker-Driven movement, and Lynne Hybels in the last few years, as she moves more to the left, has taken up Palestinian advocacy as a cause. This she disguises as being "Pro Peace, Pro Palestinian, Pro Israel," but it is decidedly anti-Israel. I've heard her speak on the subject, accusing Israel of everything from occupying Palestinian land to rationing Palestinian water.

To her credit, in the spring of 2015, Hybels traveled with a group of women to Iraq, to give a voice to embattled, persecuted Christians in the Middle East. This was no small effort or feat, given the savagery of Islamic terrorists rampaging through the region.

I believe Lynne Hybels came to this position after her descent into mysticism more than 20 years ago.

Since the '70s, Lynne Hybels and her husband have been mentored by people sympathetic to the Palestinian Narrative, including Dr. Gilbert Bilezikian. In October 2008, she attended a conference in Amman, Jordan, led by Arab Christians from "Jordan, Lebanon, Egypt, Iraq, and the West Bank."

Since that time, Lynne Hybels has been very active in promoting the so-called Palestinian Narrative, which points to Israel as an occupier of Arabs. The narrative is classic PLO (Palestine Liberation Organization) propaganda, but Hybels' networks allow her the luxury of promoting this worldview — couched in the language of "nonviolent resistance" — which is also shared by Millennial influencers such as Donald Miller and Cameron Strang.

Both Miller and Strang have accused Israel, in print, of war crimes, including the harvesting of organs from Palestinians, and outright murder of Palestinian women and children by the IDF (Israel Defense Forces). To date, Miller in particular offers no documentation for his allegations.

At the leadership conference known as Catalyst Dallas in the spring of 2014, conference organizers made available a booklet titled *Known*, in which various celebrity evangelical leaders pontificated on all sorts of topics. Hybels' contribution is a highly revealing personal journey into mystical spirituality.

Two things stand out about Hybels' worldview, based on the article (titled "Enough"): (1) her embrace of mysticism and shedding of biblical Christianity should be overwhelmingly alarming to evangelicals, and (2) because of her belief that she is helping her mystical god remake the world, one can now see why she applies leftist principles to solving the Arab-Israeli conflict.

From her essay, "Enough":

IN MY EARLY FORTIES I EXPERIENCED A CRISIS OF FAITH. The Christianity I'd grown up with was about being good and working hard and following the rules in order to placate an angry God. It was about being an athlete winning the prize and a solider [sic] advancing the work of the Kingdom, thereby avoiding hellfire and damnation. A sensitive little girl, I took it all to heart and did my best. But after nearly four decades of striving to earn God's love, I was exhausted. God had become a burden I no longer had the energy to carry.

So I quietly turned my back on God. For quite some time, I was content to have no god, but eventually God's absence began to feel like a void. Thus began my journey from the god of my childhood to a God expansive and untamed enough to embrace my adult life.[3]

This led Hybels to read mystics like Thomas Merton and Thomas Keating.

In short, Lynne Hybels' path to paganism makes it easy to see why she views the Bible (and Israel) the way she does. By spiritualizing the Bible and making large chunks of it myth, she simply doesn't believe in Israel's biblical right to the land. She is not biblical in her thinking at all.

And the Willow Creek Association she and her husband crafted is perhaps the most influential group in the evangelical world.

Southern Baptists Aren't Immune to Propaganda

For generations, scores of Southern Baptist churches and pastors (along with many in the Pentecostal world, particularly the Assemblies of God) were staunch supporters of Israel and Bible prophecy.

I grew up SBC, and the Hal Lindsey view of Bible prophecy dominated. Conferences and sermons were constantly shaped around the view that Jesus could return at any minute. The glorious hope of the Rapture was everywhere.

That was then.

For many years, Dr. Richard Land led the SBC's Ethics & Religious Liberty Commission (ERLC).

Land is pro Israel.

From its website, the ERLC exists for the following reasons:

> The Ethics & Religious Liberty Commission is an entity of the Southern Baptist Convention. The ERLC is dedicated to engaging the culture with the gospel of Jesus Christ and speaking to issues in the public square for the protection of religious liberty and human flourishing. Our vision can be summed up in three words: kingdom, culture and mission.[4]

In 2013, Land ran afoul of the PC police when he expressed views about the Trayvon Martin case that didn't sit well with left-wing forces in the SBC, who have since shown their true colors by pandering to radical minorities.

Land was subsequently removed as president of the ERLC and replaced by the urbane, younger Dr. Russell Moore.

Moore, from Biloxi, Mississippi, worked for Democratic congressman Gene Taylor prior to entering the ministry. It appears that he was always much further to the left politically and theologically than his predecessors, though Moore would dispute this.

From smiling photo ops with Barack Obama, to softened stances on immigration and homosexuality, to his relentless bashing of Donald Trump for a year, Moore is a "new" kind of Southern Baptist leader.

Unfortunately, operating from a multimillion-dollar war chest, with offices in Nashville and Washington, Moore is able to advance what I believe is a stealth agenda to reshape the SBC fundamentally — much like his friend in the White House did to the country from 2009–2017.

With regard to Israel, it is clear that Moore is not a classic SBC prophecy student or Israel advocate. In fact, his description of Jesus Christ in a *New York Times* op-ed is quite telling:

> The man on the throne in heaven is a dark-skinned, Aramaic-speaking "foreigner" who is probably not all that impressed by chants of "Make America great again."[5]

Huh?

Jesus Christ is a Jew, born into an ethnic Jewish family, in a Jewish town, in the first century. Why would Moore describe Him in such a bizarre fashion (notice, too, that it gave Moore an opportunity to push his immigration views, which are essentially open borders)?

A clue comes in Randy White's piece on Moore's Israel views:

> When Moore writes about Israel, it is often with a negative tone. He says things like, "Israel's American critics on both the left and the right of the political spectrum have been frustrated by what they consider to be the political carte blanche given by evangelicals to the Israeli state." He goes on to say, "it is rather obvious that contemporary evangelical support for Israel draws its theological grounding from the dispensational/Bible conference tradition, not from the Reformed/Princeton tradition." As you read his works, Moore is clearly not a fan of this dispensational/Bible conference tradition. He is, however, an avowed covenant theologian, and he says that such theologians "have maintained that the church, not any current geo-political entity, is the 'new Israel,' the inheritor of all Israel's covenant promises." (This is, by the way, a perfect definition of replacement theology.)

> If there is any good news in Moore's position on Israel, it is that "Evangelical public theology would be in error, however, if it sought to remedy past errors by abandoning support for Israel." I hope you note that evangelical support in the past has been built

on "errors." It would be a mistake to remove this support, but Christians should ground such support in a quest for geo-political stability and peace in the Middle East, not in the "Thus saith the Lord" of the prophecy charts.

My word to Southern Baptists who may hope for a powerful pro-Israel denominational stance coming from the ERLC: Good luck! There is no hint Moore would allow it. My prediction is subtly anti-Israel messages or Israel-phobia. Moore is too much the politician to throw Israel under the bus, but he is not a supporter of Israel as a modern Jewish state unless it serves the purposes of the new Israel's expansion and well-being.[6]

This is chilling!

Further, Moore's backing led the ERLC to support an amicus brief that would allow a mosque to be built in Bernard's Township, New Jersey. Laurie Cardoza-Moore (who heads Proclaiming Justice to the Nations) took note of Russell Moore's odd priorities:

> Cardoza-Moore adds that Moore and the ERLC, meanwhile, have said nothing after the Obama administration's controversial actions against Israel at the UN Security Council in recent weeks.
>
> Israel has alleged that the United States not only abstained — allowing the anti-Israel resolution to pass — but worked behind the scenes to co-author the resolution and push for a vote.
>
> A search of the ERLC website by OneNewsNow produced no results for "Israel" or "UN Security Council" during the closing weeks of December.
>
> There were also no press releases nor published statements by the ERLC after the Obama administration's abstention, OneNewsNow found.
>
> "Why has the ERLC been silent on that issue?" Cardoza-Moore asks of the controversial UN vote. "But they want to support and build Islamic centers that preach and teach jihad?"[7]

Don't hold your breath, though, waiting for Russell Moore to respond. Although he endured some significant pushback after the 2016 presidential election and has kept a somewhat lower profile, his powerful friends in leadership within the SBC will ensure that he keeps his post, from which he can undermine Israel, Bible prophecy teaching, and wider social issues.

Welcome to the 21st-century Southern Baptist Convention.

Pentecostals and Palestine

My late friend and mentor Dr. David Allen Lewis was an Assemblies of God evangelist for a half-century. He was also the greatest champion for Israel I've ever known.

David often told the story of hearing the radio announcement of Israel's founding on May 14, 1948. This larger-than-life Christian Zionist would weep when telling the story, for his family had alerted him through the study of Scripture that Israel's regathering would certainly happen.

"I was privileged to live in that time," he would say.

Just after the Six-Day War in 1967, David began taking Christian tour groups to Israel. Something a lot of people don't know is that he was also an early pioneer in Arab-Israeli dialogue. He even accepted the peace treaties with Egypt and Jordan, saying, "A cold peace is better than no peace." He was not a rigid ideologue when it came to the realities of the present situation in the Middle East.

At the same time, his love for the Jewish people was boundless.

I well remember my first trip to Israel, in 1998. David was my guide! It was a wonderful, life-changing moment, capped by our hour-long interview of Ariel Sharon in Tel Aviv.

Sadly, as David entered Glory in 2007, a movement was well underway within Pentecostal circles to undermine Israel and support the Palestinian narrative that Israel is a brutal occupier of the hapless Arabs.

Paul Alexander, a young professor from the Palmer Theological Seminary at Eastern University (the same institution where anti-Israel activist Tony Campolo taught) wrote a blog post in 2012 in which he referred to Jesus Christ as "the Palestinian Jew."[8]

Due to his radical statements about other subjects, the Assemblies of God (AG) in 2013 revoked his ministry credentials. It was a courageous act by the AG leadership, but I maintain that as the older generations die off, activists like Alexander will be welcomed back into the fold.

Note a web response from a supporter of Alexander, after the AG acted:[9]

I'm thankful fo[sic] Dr. Paul too. If it were not for his courage and willingness to the gospel in away[sic] that is not white and not male, than[sic] I would not be a believer today. I am a United Methodist Pastor an[sic] member of SPS. I grew up AG, attended AG College and was credentialed AG. I also lost my faith in the AG. Paul helped me see that God was more than any white mans[sic] interpretation. God bless Paul Alexander! And God d**n close minded, raced white, sexed male oppressive systems of coercion like the Assemblies of God!

Wow. This pitiful person, invoking the gospel but "damning" God Himself, is a prototype — I mean this seriously and sincerely — of the new Millennial who identifies in some way as Christian.

The Social Gospel is being advanced in these circles like a speeding train, and millions are hopping onboard.

One of the hallmarks of the Christian Millennials being targeted by anti-Israel forces is a repudiation of Israel and Bible prophecy.

Men and women with Pentecostal roots, like Alexander, Jonathan Martin, and *Relevant* publisher Cameron Strang are fast-tracking a total transformation of next-generation leaders.

Targeting Millennials

You need to know that dark forces are mobilizing in astonishing ways to overturn evangelical support for Israel. This is a story so deep and vast that many people I discuss it with are distressed.

A very highly placed Christian advocate for Israel told me "if something isn't done to reverse this trend, in ten years it will be all over." He was referring to Christian Millennials, particularly on college campuses. Anti-Israel fervor is that intense.

And this was four years ago!

Strang Days

One must begin to "discover the networks" as David Horowitz would say, to begin to understand the leviathan-like network that seeks to harm Israel in the evangelical community.

In the 1970s, Pentecostal journalist Steve Strang launched *Charisma* magazine. It is the leading periodical in that community. Though different tracks of evangelicalism would disagree with aspects of theology appearing in the pages of *Charisma*, Strang however did always produce a pro-Israel slant to articles.

As a prime example, though, of the deep cultural shifts that have already taken place within evangelicalism, Strang's own son, Cameron, has moved sharply to the left.

His *Relevant* magazine claims a digital and print footprint of more than seventy *million*. Now consider that the left-leaning slant inside the magazine is greatly influencing next-generation leaders. Consider an article that appeared in the magazine in 2009. Titled "Israel's Reprehensible Organ Program,"[10] the short piece linked to another article that alleged Israel Defense Forces (IDF) troops were harvesting organs from dead Palestinians. The distortion of the real story further demonized Israel among Millennials.

Oddly, *Relevant* didn't start out this way. In a December 19, 2005, article that can only be described as advocating the pro-Israel editorial views that characterized his father's magazine, Cameron Strang's views were more traditional:

> After thousands of years of dispersion and intense, concentrated persecution, the Jewish state of Israel exists anew. After walking around with a target on their back (or a star on their front) since time immemorial, the Jewish people make their home once more in the exact same place their culture was born. Many younger generations take for granted the simple fact that Israel shows up on a map, failing to recognize the miraculous events that revived this country and this people from literal near-death.[11]

I can trace the sharp turn in attitudes about Israel to the 2010 release of anti-Israel films *O Little Town of Bethlehem* and *With God on Our Side*. This fits with the change in editorial policy for *Relevant*, where it regards Israel (and Bible prophecy, which the magazine's editors love to mock).

Cameron Strang began taking trips to what he calls "Israel/Palestine" with people like Lynne Hybels and popular author Donald Miller (*Blue Like Jazz*). There, they met with the PLO and other Palestinian propagandists, including those who identify as Palestinian Christians. The sadly predictable results can be seen in the propaganda that these Millennial leaders circulate about the Arab-Israeli conflict.

In a November 19, 2012, blog post, Miller accused Israeli troops of the most outrageous things, including war crimes.

Miller wrote the following:

> We spent much of our time in the West Bank, interviewing Palestinian leaders. The stories we heard were heartbreaking. We had dinner with a woman whose mother was killed by Israeli guards after placing a rose on a tank. She was gunned down while sitting with her husband on their front porch later that week. We met

with the assistant to the mayor of Bethlehem, a Christian man whose twelve-year-old daughter was killed sitting in the backseat of the family car while driving through an Israeli checkpoint.

Israel gives most Palestinians fresh water once each week, water they store in tanks on top of their homes. On the other side of the wall, within a hundred yards, Israeli children swim in personal swimming pools. In Gaza, Israel also rations their food, allowing only so many calories per human being. The Palestinians have no port, no trade and no way to get out except through illegal tunnels into Egypt, tunnels Israel allows in order to stay off a humanitarian crisis.[12]

What? Israel troops murder Palestinian children? Israel rations the daily caloric intake of Gazans? What kind of madness produces lies like this?

I attempted many times to ask questions of Miller on these subjects, but he always refuses. As does Cameron Strang.

In a 2014 cover story, Strang used *Relevant* to push a pro PLO view.

In his recent *Relevant* article, "Blessed are the Peacemakers," publisher Cameron Strang states "many are beginning to believe it is possible to be authentically pro-Israeli, pro-Palestinian and pro-peace." However, one of his concluding statements in the article, which appeared in the March/April issue of the magazine, demonstrates the very one-sided approach of this article — an approach that reveals a false pretense behind his claim to be both pro-Israeli and pro-Palestinian. Strang writes:

To remain a democratic state that is Jewish in character and majority, Israelis must find a way to acknowledge Palestinian demands for sovereignty in a portion of the historic land of Israel. And in order for Palestinians to achieve dignity and freedom, they must either be allowed to create their own state in a portion of historic Palestine or be given equal civil and political rights in Israel.[13]

In spite of his claim to be pro-peace, pro-Palestinian and pro-Israeli, Strang places all the responsibility for a successful peace process on the Jewish State. He says Israel "must find a way to acknowledge Palestinian demands" and Palestinians "must be allowed to create . . . or be given. . . ." At no point in the article does Strang judge the Palestinians responsible for anything. According to his definition of what it means for the

Jewish state to remain a democratic state, Israel must do all the giving. And apparently, if Israel would just do what Strang says they should do, there would be peace.

I attempted to interview Cameron Strang about his one-sided article, but he declined. I hope you can see that such journalists are not really journalists at all. They are advocates. Left-leaning advocates.

Social Media

Social media is a key place to understand just how networked and vast the anti-Israel community is. For example, if you look at the Twitter account of leftist activist Shane Claiborne, you will see several examples of anti-Israel folks, along with agendas to overturn capital punishment, etc.

I previously mentioned Jonathan Martin. A former pastor from North Carolina, Martin is now a writing and speaking gadabout. While he was still a pastor, he hosted the producers of the film *With God on Our Side*, and has written from a pro-Palestinian slant on his blog.

Cleverly, he associates not only with mainstream evangelicals, but also with leftists like Brian McLaren and Rob Bell. Recent photos from his social media sites show Martin posing with the folks from Hillsong, former Hillary Clinton running mate Tim Kaine, former Obama staffer Josh DuBois, Word-Faith guru Steven Furtick (officially pastoring a Southern Baptist church plant in North Carolina), homosexual-affirming blogger Jen Hatmaker, and Shauna Niequist, daughter of Bill and Lynne Hybels.

Are you beginning to see the reach of these networks?

Although the members of this leftist network advocate for many causes, they are unified in their dislike of Israel.

The Future

Finally, it is with alarm that many of us have followed the Calvary Chapel movement after the death of founder Chuck Smith in 2013.

Let me state at this point that there remain many, many great CC pastors and churches. The problem has arisen with the ascension of Smith's son-in-law, Brian Brodersen, to the leadership role within the association.

By networking with church-growth gurus like Rick Warren, Brodersen has departed from the strict teaching of Scripture that has long characterized Calvary Chapel. Even before Smith's death, cracks appeared.

In 2013, North Coast Calvary Chapel hosted a panel discussion featuring pro-Palestinian activists Lynne Hybels, Sami Awad, and Mae

Cannon (of World Vision). This caused a firestorm within the CC family, and Smith denounced it, along with influential pastor Jack Hibbs.

Although the incident blunted efforts to infiltrate Calvary Chapel directly with the Palestinian narrative, the networks I've mentioned ensure that such influence will continue to be felt.

What this means is that there is no "safe place" for pro-Israel, pro-Bible prophecy evangelicals to go, in terms of completely escaping this corrosive worldview. Point being: Your children and grandchildren are being targeted by pro-Palestinian activists, and so it behooves you to learn as much as you can to counter this deadly teaching in your own home.

New Testament prophecy points to an end game that features apostasy in the Church. That day is already here.

Hold on fast to the truth, and oppose the Israel revilers wherever you find them.

To God be the glory.

Endnotes
1. http://www.christiannewswire.com/news/9602218969.html.
2. Ibid.
3. Lynne Hybels, "Enough" in *Known*, a booklet available at the 2014 Catalyst Conference, Dallas, TX.
4. https://erlc.com/about.
5. Russell Moore, "A White Church No More," *New York Times*, 5/6/2016, p. A25.
6. https://randywhiteministries.org/articles/what-southern-baptists-can-expect-from-russell-moore-and-the-erlc/.
7. http://www.christianitytoday.com/news/2017/february/southern-baptists-back-away-from-backing-mosques-imb-erlc.html.
8. http://balfourpost.com/the-palestinian-jesus/.
9. https://juicyecumenism.com/2014/02/10/paul-alexander-dismissed-from-assemblies-of-god-clergy/.
10. http://www.pre-trib.org/articles/view/opposing-joshuathe-modern-evangelical-war-on-israel.
11. https://relevantmagazine.com/god/deeper-walk/features/977-israel-why-you-should-care.
12. http://storylineblog.com/2012/11/19/the-painful-truth-about-the-situation-in-israel/.
13. https://relevantmagazine.com/god/worldview/blessed-are-peacemakers.

CHAPTER 14

From Deception to Deliverance

ERIC BARGER

Introduction

Greetings! As some readers may know, I am the founder and president of Take A Stand! Ministries based in the Seattle, Washington, area. Since 1983 we've crisscrossed North America presenting Take A Stand! Seminars in both conferences and local churches. The seminars and the ministry specialize in topics pertaining to biblical apologetics, the examination of current events, and Bible prophecy, both past and future. The ministry represents a mix of teaching and evangelism, with a healthy dose of exhortation and encouragement.

We've produced many resources, including books, booklets, and video projects. Along the way, I've hosted my own radio program for two extended periods of time, and during the past several years it's been my honor to regularly cohost *Understanding the Times Radio* with my friend and sister in the Lord, Jan Markell. I'm now also addressing issues and presenting interviews on our Take A Stand! TV broadcast seen weekly.

In this chapter, I'll be discussing some of the deceptions facing Christians in these last days. I hope to arm readers with information taken directly from our ministry archives that could prove crucial for those in the reader's sphere of influence. I also want to speak directly about various aspects of the ministry of apologetics and discernment that I believe are directly related to the prophetic end times. I'll close by weaving in part of the account of how God cleansed us and then began to call us into this ministry. Hopefully you will be challenged, perhaps convicted, and also inspired as you read. That's a tall order, but with God's help all things are possible! So, without further delay, let's begin exploring from deception to redemption.

About the Word "Deception"

Over the years I have occasionally witnessed God orchestrating the use of a particular topic, word, or phrase in my life as a way of confirmation that He is speaking specific direction into my life and our ministry. Sometimes this occurs through situations or experiences and other times by sheer frequency. It has taken place in conversations with those in our ministry's leadership, my family, or my peers, and is either preceded or followed by something from His Word.

Though it is not particularly unusual for those of us who participate in the ministry of apologetics and discernment, there have been numerous times over the months before this writing when the word "deception" has arisen very specifically, causing me to take special note. Through message titles and topics, in articles, and in interview discussions, the very word itself has become like a drum beating louder and louder, as if to make certain I couldn't miss the point. So you can imagine that when Terry James asked me to contribute a chapter to this book on the topic of deception, I immediately knew that God was in it and that I wanted to be a part of it.

Could it be that God by His Holy Spirit is now trumpeting a widespread warning to His people? I believe He is indeed doing just that as He sends men and women with a fresh urgency to alert His Bride. Considering the many scriptural warnings concerning the rise of evil opposition toward the end (2 Timothy 3:1–5; 1 Timothy 4:1; Matthew 24:12), it is not hyperbole to believe that the Evil One is scheming with new strategies or revising old ones to more effectively infiltrate individuals, households, and particularly our churches. Oh, that we would have eyes opened and ears attuned to God in this hour!

Deception in the Culture

> And as he sat upon the mount of Olives, the disciples came unto him privately, saying, Tell us, when shall these things be? and what shall be the sign of thy coming, and of the end of the world?
>
> And Jesus answered and said unto them, Take heed that no man deceive you (Matthew 24:3–4).[1]

Here the disciples inquired of Jesus what the signs of His coming and the end of the world would be. He answered by giving an extensive list of specific issues and events that would mark the last days. But before doing so, note how the Lord began His response: "Take heed that no man deceive you."

Think about that. Jesus was speaking to His trusted inner circle who had given up everything to follow Him. They were sold out to Him and completely convinced of His messiahship. They were there when He fed the 5,000, healed the sick, cleansed the lepers, and raised Lazarus from the dead. Yet as Jesus began to address the end times, He cautioned His faithful followers to first beware of deception. If that was His first concern for those eyewitnesses of His glory, how much more are those words a warning for us as we approach the most troubling era in mankind's history?

No doubt the biblical end times are going to be replete with deception. Deception's origin extends back to the Fall of mankind in the Garden of Eden (Genesis 3). Indeed, deceivers have often taken center stage as deception has played an incalculably destructive role and has been a reality throughout human history. It is a character flaw in our fallen Adamic nature. The ugly byproducts of deception are evident everywhere we turn as the earth continues to suffer the effects of what Lucifer accomplished with Eve. Of course, this will continue until the Lord Jesus sets up His Millennial Kingdom.

As evil as deception is in all its many forms, it is safe to say that what is ahead will be a period unlike any other. We can see the crescendo of deceit happening now. Have you noticed in just the last few short years how the citizens of supposedly civilized societies now interact? Decency is disappearing, and dialogue and decorum are things of the past. For all the positives the Internet has brought us, one huge negative is that now in social media, anyone can say anything to anyone or about anything — with complete anonymity. Debate is nearly a thing of the past, whether in a chatroom or on college campuses. With the mob mentality, factions now simply shout down those with views they find repugnant. In fact, Millennials have been taught that they have a right not to hear or be offended by ideas they find upsetting! Are we training them for life in the real world, or for a la-la land comprised of safe zones, puppy dogs, and color crayons where no one challenges them? What a ridiculous use of tax dollars.

Trust and honor are waning, and it's taking a toll — but, frankly, I believe we're seeing just the beginning. We've all watched as politicians apparently can't help but turn any situation into a news bite with a goal of denigrating their opposition and often employing deception in the process. Deception and its main attribute, lying, have become normal and even acceptable to some. The condition of our society's moral compass is evident when we champion those who are, in reality, the best deceivers.

We have also witnessed that some in the media aren't satisfied with simply reporting what is happening in our world. Now they have inserted themselves into the stories they cover. With once-hidden biases exposed, some reporters and journalists brazenly twist facts to achieve desired political outcomes. This includes the deception of incorrectly reporting details, or simply omitting vital information that would undermine their viewpoints. Perhaps the most unseemly facet of this wave of "fake news" is fictitious accounts reported to the public as fact. Though retractions often follow, corrections never have the impact of the original false allegations. It is no wonder that public confidence is shaken in the media's ability to accurately report events. Journalism's "sacred trust" is now found riddled with deception. This has taken an ugly toll on consumers. The results are confusion, disappointment, defensive skepticism, and growing cynicism as many information sources we trusted not long ago are now proved questionable at best.

Reports of the latest scandal seem to break every day, sometimes nearly every hour. With claims of sexual harassment erupting throughout every area of the culture, no one seems completely sure about whom to trust at any level. Who will be the next villains, and from what arena of the culture will they come? Musicians and entertainers have long been known for their escapades. The most powerful within the entertainment world have now been outed as predators. Sports stars, some of whom refuse to show honor and allegiance to the country that has provided them great opportunity for status and great wealth, are regularly exposed as abusers. While fans adore their God-given talents, too many of the famous have proven that money and fame are not fixes for what ails the human heart. All of this and so much more rock society. Almost everyone wonders: *Who can we trust?*

Many of the accused claim innocence. In reality, some may instead be victims. Once a claim of such activity is made, it often doesn't matter whether what is alleged is true. The stigma of the accusation is sometimes enough to ruin a life. Those who do accuse falsely, whether as a political tool, a vendetta, for their 15 minutes of fame, or for some other sad or sordid reason, are deceivers of the highest order.

Some wonder how and why this cascading breach of trust is resonating throughout the world. We are reaping what we have sown, but we haven't identified the root of the problem or embraced the only solution, which is a return to God. Stop and consider what has happened here in America over just the past 60 years. It started when God and His Word were put aside like worn-out relics and declared unwelcome in our schoolrooms. The non-constitutional fallacy of "the separation of church and state" evicted God as evolution became the substitute. The ideal of the family unit has splintered. Marriage has been forsaken and redefined. Narcissism has become normal. Right and wrong are continually stretched and confused as absolute truth is widely reviled. What was immoral not long ago is now acceptable. It is every person for himself; whatever feels good, do it.

However, this new "freedom" absent of absolute morals and faith comes with a price. Most people are shocked by and appalled at every new sexual scandal, but wasn't it the promotion of the perverse and sensual that enticed and gave license to the Harvey Weinsteins and Matt Lauers of the world to act as we understand they have? They and many more were deceived by their position and power and were overtaken by their lusts. But the same society that gasps as its heroes are seen for what they are gave license to free love and sex as a sales tool. Just the two words "Victoria's Secret" say it all.

Is it any wonder that several states have legalized recreational marijuana and others will do likewise in the coming months? We have a genuine epidemic of heroin use, and more prescription drugs are now being manufactured than at any time in history. With all this new "freedom," mankind isn't satisfied and certainly is not happy. Without God at the center of his or her life, no one will be truly happy. Determined to go it on their own, people are bent on groping in the dark, yet deep inside, we know something is missing. Satan is going to take care of that in the very near future. As the culture disintegrates, unrest is growing. The threats to our world have probably never been greater, even when Adolf Hitler and Emperor Hirohito were making their run at planetary domination. All that is happening now is serving to desensitize and crack open the door for an eventual supernatural character who is coming to rescue us . . . or so it will appear. Though the world will perceive the Antichrist as its "messiah," he will embody the very epitome of deception. The slickest and most demonically empowered person to have ever lived will possess deceptive abilities like no other in history.

As we speed into the end days, no nation on earth will be immune to the growth and expanding effects of deception. I think it is safe to say that the increase of deception will take a toll on every facet of society, including the Church.

As we live in frail bodies with a fallen nature constantly vying for control, we understand that there is no perfect immunity from deception's reach. Some people may be tempted to give up hope if a trusted friend or Christian leader falls into deception. Some Christian leaders could also be tempted to throw in the towel if deception makes a victim of one of their role models, peers, trusted friends, or leaders in their church.

Situations like these are some of life's most bitter tragedies that some among us never get over. I think it's wise to buttress ourselves, at least in general terms, against these sorts of disappointments. However, I caution that we not do so out of paranoia. It is a main attribute of the Church to follow the biblical model of restoration when others in the Body of Christ fall, and that is what we must do. The point is that the days ahead promise to be a time of great deception and disappointment, and if Satan can use disappointment as a means of pulling down others who are being affected by the deception that's overtaken another, then of course he won't hesitate to do so.

We should guard against fatalism during these days in which we live. I need to remind you that just because some event or problem is prophesied for the end times doesn't mean that we should throw our hands up and say, "Oh well, it was going to happen anyway; there's nothing I can do about it — no big deal." The task for us as Christians is to stand against evil whenever and wherever we see it raising its ugly head. That is one of the attributes of true Christianity. It is what Jesus did, and it is what the disciples did. It is what the Early Church did, and it is certainly what the apologists of the Early Church did in what is known as the Age of the Apologists (A.D. 2nd–4th century). I pray that individually and together, our lives will be a bright light in the midst of deception's darkness as we watch and wait for the Lord to return.

Deception of the Cults

Deception can take on many forms and can be disseminated many ways. Perhaps the Enemy's most effective deceptions are those that lead humans away from truth but are cloaked in a benign, even innocent, package. Satan's ability to deceive humans would have been considerably hampered throughout history were he to knock on our doors and appear as he really is. Even in our day, when there is an escalating fascination with overt evil, most unbelievers would want little to do with what the Evil One is peddling if he came without a disguise. Even though our discussion here is focused on religious deceptions, consider this: If a philosophy, practice, amusement, or activity appears harmless and nonthreatening, yet is sent with the intention of harm or of enticing us to contradict God's Word, then wouldn't that be a more effective tactic for the powers of hell than something that was obviously evil? Walking in godly discernment, through knowledge of the Scriptures, can help us detect and expose various traps that come cloaked with innocuous facades. "And no marvel; for Satan himself is transformed into an angel of light. Therefore it is no great thing if his ministers also be transformed as the ministers of righteousness; whose end shall be according to their works" (2 Corinthians 11:14–15).

Take the broadcaster and popular personality Glenn Beck, for example. There are many cultural issues about which believers might find complete concurrence with Beck, such as abortion, freedom of speech, and religious liberties. However, as a Mormon, Beck is governed by a different set of spiritual doctrines and beliefs. One major example is that Mormonism presents a "different Jesus . . . a different kind of Spirit . . . and a different kind of gospel" (2 Corinthians 11:3–4; NLT). While Beck may be completely correct concerning particular issues, when he speaks of spiritual matters, look out! He and others belonging to the LDS Church commonly attempt to present Mormonism as just a slightly more enlightened and perhaps quirky Christian sect. Mormonism's founder, Joseph Smith, surely didn't see the religion he founded that way. He claimed that when he inquired of God as to what church he should join, he was told that all churches were apostate, the people in them were deceived, and their pastors were "hirelings of Satan."[2] Since Beck's "Jesus" was a man who became a god and this same transformation that Mormonism advertises can happen to any human, it is clear that Beck's "Jesus" is not and never has been the biblical Jesus Christ, but is instead one of many look-alike imposters. While Beck may be completely sincere when he speaks of spiritual matters, we need to be clear that whatever he might suggest is not coming through the inspiration of the Holy Spirit, but instead from a counterfeit spirit impersonating the authentic Spirit of God. I understand that may be a tough pill to swallow for Beck fans. However, those we look to for spiritual advice and what creeds they keep are very serious matters. Eternity could hang in the balance. It should also matter that ignorant and uninformed Beck listeners are being fed cultic ideas in the name of Christianity. Though these listeners may not fall into Mormonism's trap, perhaps through their attraction to Beck and their lack of understanding of the Bible, they'll simply see little if anything wrong with the LDS Church, even though it is a sure ticket to eternal hell and not to eternal godhood.

Upon reading the previous paragraph, some will immediately become upset that I would say such things. How could I pick on Glenn Beck? He claims to be a Christian! However, for all that we might find to appreciate in Beck, such as his boldness or his positions on political or social issues, we cannot discount the spiritually deadly nature of Mormonism and simply give him a pass.

Though, like Beck, modern Mormons have adopted the tactic of presenting their religion as just an enhanced or advanced Christianity, Mormon doctrine hasn't changed, nor has the Mormons' outlook on non-Mormons. In fact, when addressing the 171st Semiannual General LDS Conference in October 2001, Gordon B. Hinckley, president, prophet, seer, and revelator of the LDS Church from 1995 until his death in January 2008, made that clear to the assembled crowd, saying, "Those who observe us say that we are moving into the mainstream of religion. We are not changing. The world's perception of us is changing. We teach the same doctrine."[3]

Hinckley, remembered as the LDS' "mainstreaming" president, along with missionary trainer Robert Millet, are responsible for the evangelical "speak" employed by thousands of bike-riding LDS missionaries we encounter at our front doors today. The LDS Church now carefully trains its missionaries on what they themselves should know and on how to respond to questions about longstanding LDS doctrines. Just a couple of those long-held beliefs should cause biblically literate Christians to pause before they consider anointing the "new" Mormonism as acceptable for Bible-believers.

One of those doctrines would be the aforementioned godhood for mankind — perhaps the main spiritual selling point of their sect. Often illustrated in what LDS folks refer to as a "couplet" made famous by the fifth prophet, seer, and revelator of the Church, Lorenzo Snow, it says, "As man now is, God once was: As God now is, man may be."[4] This, known as "The Law of Eternal Progression," is precisely what Joseph Smith Jr., Brigham Young, and every LDS head to the present day have believed. In fact, on April 4, 1844, in the now-famous King Follett discourse, Smith stated that God was a man like us. The official LDS Church magazine, *Ensign*, reprinted Smith's sermon in April 1971. That in itself appears to indict Mormonism as polytheistic (*p:* "many," and *theos:* "gods"), but elaborate and misleading apologetics have been constructed to appear to "correct" this and other criticism coming from those outside the Mormon Church.

Whether Mormonism teaches that man becomes god in the same sense that Jehovah is God, with the same understanding, intelligence, abilities, etc., or simply that Christians become heirs of eternal nature and given glorified bodies as the Bible teaches, there is another issue that cannot be ignored: Mormonism declares that mortals attain this promised new eternal state of being. Everyone interested in ministering truth to LDS folk should understand what Mormonism teaches this process entails.

In his book, *Mormonism and the Nature of God: A Theological Evolution, 1830–1915*, Kurt Widmer, a recognized authority and instructor of religions at the University of Lethbridge, Lethbridge, Alberta, Canada, states on page 6 that "Joseph Smith taught that humans can become joint-heirs with Christ and thereby inherit from God all that Christ inherits. . . ." Sounds reasonably orthodox so far, right? However, Widmer accurately continues, "if they are proven worthy by following the laws and ordinances of the gospel (of Mormonism)."[5] Widmer's statement correctly enumerates something that forever separates Mormonism from Christianity. It is, of course, the assertion that a human's good works have anything whatsoever to do with authentic, biblical salvation. In fact, this is also the case when one examines religions around the world, both large and small in number. Works are important — but are not required in order to attain salvation. No good deed or work, no matter how great in number, can atone for our sins and give us right standing before God. We cannot work to become saved. Instead, Christians "work" *because* we are saved.

Mormonism panders to the part of our fallen Adamic nature that tells man, "If I'm just good enough, God will accept me." I'm not sure there is a cult anywhere that doesn't adhere to this abomination. The cult of liberalism in the mainline denominations, operating as if they were Christian, does this far and wide. Most readers know that "faith *plus* works" was a central cause of the Protestant Reformation 500 years ago. Catholicism continues to present a hopeless works-based salvation to millions daily. Regardless of all other dogma, "faith and faith alone" is the single doctrine that forever separates biblical beliefs from the world of cults and religions. "For by grace are ye saved through faith; and that not of yourselves: it is the gift of God: Not of works, lest any man should boast" (Ephesians 2:8–9).

Mormonism teaches that people must prove themselves worthy through strict adherence to the edicts of the LDS Church. This process, called *exaltation*, means that humans can literally become gods through the atonement; thus, "god" is a term for an inheritor of the highest kingdom of God. Exaltation, through human effort and the LDS teaching of man becoming a god, obviously acknowledges the existence of many gods, but holds to the idea that no matter how many humans become gods, there is still only one supreme God who is ruler over life in this universe. This idea is known as monolatry and, though it is clear to ascertain in LDS teaching, Mormon Church authorities such as Bruce R. McConkie have vehemently defended their views as completely monotheistic!

The leaders of the modern Mormon Church set out to deceive anyone they, through their missionaries, come into contact with. It is biblical Christians who have the remedy for the spiritual sicknesses of the cults. We must be ready to give every man, woman, boy, and girl an answer for the real hope that lives within us (1 Peter 3:15). We must be equipped to expose and refute the works and doctrines of darkness (Ephesians 5:10–11). If we do not know our Bibles and have at least a framework of what the aberrant religions prevalent in the regions where we live believe, then the possibility exists that we or our loved ones could more easily be deceived into following their disastrous paths.

Deception in the Church

Since the days of the Apostles, then fresh out of the Upper Room, the Church has been the object of attack from the outside world, from individuals within, and from the powers of hell. While Christianity as a whole is targeted by Satan's forces, of particular interest are those set on following God's Word. No wonder, for what military commander sends his forces to retake ground already under his control? The primary enemies of the powers of darkness have always been those dedicated to serve the Lord and who are focused on winning the lost. Robbing hell of all the victims we possibly can is the crux of the believer's mandate. In waging spiritual warfare against the Body of Christ, Satan has consistently sown the seeds of deception in our midst. Though he can't know the specific outcome, as he does not know the future, the devil understands human nature and is aware of our individual strengths and weaknesses. Wherever we allow him room to operate, he sets up camp to distract us from our mission. When we entertain deception and veer from Scripture, we allow evil to advance.

Most seasoned Christians understand that Satan seizes every opportunity he is given. One avenue he doesn't miss taking advantage of is working through human ignorance. Paul stressed this point in writing to the Corinthian church. Speaking about the critical area of forgiveness, the Apostle stated, "Lest Satan should get an advantage of us: for we are not ignorant of his devices" (2 Corinthians 2:11). Paul made the point of how vital obedience to the will of God is and how issues such as forgiveness play into our own spiritual safety and peace. He closed the thought by warning that ignorance of Satan's traps and operations gives the Enemy opportunity and places him in a position of superiority. If we open a door, the devil is more than willing to oblige — and it's not always sin on our part that gives him room to operate. Our unawareness of his strategies can be just as profitable for the powers of hell.

The Lost Art of Discernment

My wonderful friend, the late Jim Spencer, who was a terrific thinker and writer ministering on discernment issues, once remarked to me the simple yet profound truth that "discernment appears to be at an all-time low in the Church." That was 15 years ago. Jim was correct then, and what he said is certainly accurate now. One unfortunate scenario in the modern Church is an unquestionable lack of discernment regarding spiritual issues. I believe this is partially due to a generally inadequate understanding of the lifelong spiritual conflict that every human being faces in simply living in a fallen world. In my book, *Disarming the Powers of Darkness*,[6] I discussed how teaching about the spirit realm has fallen out of favor in our pulpits. In today's user-friendly church setting, there is a general unwillingness to address anything pertaining to the demonic realm. Sadly, this has become the case even among some in what would be considered strong Bible-believing circles. Additionally, in the postmodern generation, there is a general unwillingness — nearly a disdain by some — to accept the Bible's teachings from cover to cover as supreme authority. The postmodern age group trusts little, or so we are told. To their detriment, many postmodern people in our churches seem more interested in debunking the claims of past generations and unchaining themselves from absolute truth whenever possible. They insist Christianity is acceptable only on their terms, "their" way, but with little if any thought to the tragic outcome and, yes, prophetic fulfillment their desires are bringing about.

With this new "pick and choose" attitude concerning what is acceptable to this generation, the Church is already reaping a harvest of disturbing, even cultic, ideas on which many are now basing their spirituality. While a resemblance to Christianity may still be present and the moniker of "evangelical" may still be uttered, the doctrines and practices that have knit believers together for centuries are now unraveling day by day. And why is that? Because a sort of perfect storm exists within this growing group of people in our midst who are demanding change and abandoning absolutes. The day is approaching — or has, traumatically, already arrived for some of us — when postmodern adherents will outnumber traditional Bible-believers in many churches. As this happens, unless there is a sovereign move of God, many of those who do not respect or believe the Bible are sure to become the next generation of leaders. This aberrant movement inside evangelicalism has advanced, at least to some extent, because the Baby Boomers either couldn't discern the deception that was being invited in or were, for various reasons, unable to call it what it is: cultic.

Understand that, though the word can be a caustic firebrand, using the word "cultic" is an accurate spiritual descriptor, as I will demonstrate in the paragraphs below. By definition, in this context, first and foremost, a cult teaches or ascribes to doctrines other than, in addition to, or in subtraction from the central or essential doctrines of Christianity as taught in the Bible. When it is suggested that some once-trustworthy schools and seminaries or denominations and fellowships from recent years have theologically cracked, some substantially, those loyal to particular organizations recoil. I can tell you from personal experience that it has been a game of "kill the messenger," regardless of the facts. Others remain in denial and just can't bring themselves to believe that anything such as I'm suggesting could have transpired or been introduced in their own local churches. However, if we compare what is happening now far and wide in both large and small congregations with the beliefs of just one generation ago, when evangelicals in overwhelming numbers proclaimed the historic, biblical doctrines of the faith, it is clear that evangelicalism is in the midst of radical, cult-like change.

As one influential advocate of the current cultic transformation wrote, "Now, some five hundred years later [after Luther], even many of the most die-hard Protestants among us have grown suspicious of 'Scripture and Scripture only.' We question what the words mean — literally? Metaphorically? Actually? We even question which words do and do not belong in Scripture."[7] What is happening is very clearly yet another assault on the authority of the Bible.

The Postmodern Rejection of Truth

Can anything be more disturbing than to witness the very core of the faith disintegrate as those charged with defending biblical truths give way to cultural whims and the allure of increased attendance? We've been notified that unless *we* change, then the postmoderns simply won't come. We're told that evangelicals could surely compromise to save a fight and be less rigid. The gurus of church growth have opined that if we want to fill our church buildings, then Christianity's message and methods must be transformed into a more acceptable, user-friendly, feel-good model. Entertainment for all who come is mandatory, we're told. Those entertaining best on Sundays will get the biggest crowds. And above all, a positive message — *free from teaching or even any mention of issues such as sin, Satan, demons, hell, judgment, holiness, worship, or end-times prophecy* — is the ticket to attract the unchurched. What is not being said is that by allowing these unbiblical desires to dictate what is presented as Christianity we are effectively handing control of the Christian message over to a generation taught to believe that nothing is absolute — including the Bible. How insidious.

I want every church where the authentic gospel is preached to be full. But are we ministers charged with accountability to the message of the Bible or to the size of the crowd? I shudder to think of the reception that some who stand in pulpits offering partial, redefined, or culturally acceptable messages may receive when they stand before God. Those concerned about offending individuals with biblical yet culturally awkward themes will themselves be judged by the words of the Book they found fault with while claiming to represent the God of its pages!

Another often-ignored truth is that as the Church Age comes to a close, the Bible indicates that the Body of Christ will become as a remnant. I realize it's another negative truth, but the study of Bible prophecy indicates that the Church, the real, born-again Christians, will shrink drastically in number as we approach the close of the age. The "feel-good" churches appear as if they represent a great victory in marketing strategy, but are many authentic converts to the faith being made and properly discipled? Church leaders determined not to scare or offend those who might happen by for some Sunday morning entertainment should instead consider whether they are helping prepare their congregations for the projected troubling days ahead. Sermonettes modeled after Joel Osteen's surely don't provide sound preparation for life as we approach the end of the age. Neither does the Emergent Church.

Enter the Emergent Church

The title "Emergent Church Movement" (also known as "Emerging") takes its name from the concept that the culture has experienced great change and that a new Christianity must now emerge in response. A "new" Christianity? But how? What would that look like? The term "Emerging Church" was first coined in 1997 by members of what was then known as the Young Leadership Network. This occurred during meetings to discuss why the postmodern age group appeared to be absent in many churches. According to some who were involved, the talk at first focused on what aesthetic changes or shifts in music and presentation would appeal to the missing postmoderns. However, the discussion quickly moved to the doctrines and beliefs of the faith and identified them as the culprits responsible for the postmodern rejection of Christianity. With very little resistance to the idea, these disgruntled and obviously ungrounded folks deduced that it was the Church that had to change. That was a tragic mistake based on monumental deception with little or no discernment. Many issues are negotiable, but the Bible and its essential doctrine cannot be.

As time passed and their own popularity grew, emergent leaders began casting doubt on biblically founded beliefs such as God's eternal judgment upon individuals because of sin, the existence of hell, and whether salvation might also be available to others apart from faith in Jesus Christ. In short, doctrine became anathema, a dirty word, as popular teachers such as Brian McLaren, Tony Jones, and Rob Bell began seeking a dissolution of "cold, hard fact" in favor of a "warm, fuzzy subjectivity," all supposedly to reach the postmoderns. In my pamphlet, "How to Spot the Emergent Church in YOUR Church,"[8] I identify six attributes that separate Emergent thought from orthodox Christianity. They are:

- Experience over reason
- Spirituality over doctrine
- Images over words
- Feelings over absolute truth
- Earthly justice over salvation
- Social action over eternity

Key Emergent leaders indicated that evangelicalism and fundamentalism had failed them and that, like it or not, they were intent on revolutionizing Christianity. They began by de-emphasizing doctrine and quickly started changing definitions to match their ideas — even though they weren't sure exactly what they believed. To that point, emergent Tony Jones stated in a PBS television special on July 15, 2005, "The emerging church is a place of conversation and dialogue and movement. Where that's going to go, we don't know. We're figuring this out together. We don't have an agenda of what it looks like at the end of the road. We just want to gather up people who are on this road, who want to go together on it."[9]

But wait! How can anyone lead who doesn't know where he or she is going? Perhaps a better question is: Who would want to follow them? More important is to note that the historic position of biblical Christianity is that ABSOLUTE TRUTH, SALVATION, and DIRECTION come from the Bible. However, Emergent ideology is in direct opposition, stating the goal for life is based upon a set of EXPERIENCES in a never-ending CONVERSATION on a JOURNEY without a specific DESTINATION!

I wonder how many previously unchurched or biblically ignorant teens and young adults have followed this cultic model? Emergent leaders have reduced Christianity to a set of values apparently applicable to this life only. The hope of salvation and eternity as well as the horror of hell are conveniently missing. These ideas aren't just heretical. They are damnable!

Like those who want to revise history, Emergent leaders are free to proclaim their teaching to be Christian and even evangelical but, in fact, it is at best an earth-based religion loosely formed on Christian concepts. These rogue religionists should just be honest and admit that what they are proclaiming is NOT Christianity!

Serving as the "theologian in residence" at Minnesota's Solomon's Porch (led by Emergent teacher Doug Pagitt), Tony Jones has become known as the primary theologian of the Emergent Church. So, what theology does Jones embrace? Though the quote from the PBS television program I cited seems to say he's not quite sure, he's been an outspoken advocate of the lesbian, gay, bisexual, transgender (LGBT) community and gay marriage. In fact, Jones waited to marry his second wife in solidarity with the gay community until Minnesota ended the prohibition of same-sex marriage.[10]

As for Doug Pagitt, who is perhaps more influential than Jones, the Solomon's Porch website[11] identifies the group as a "Holistic Missional Christian Community." At Solomon's Porch, Pagitt is director of "Gatherings, Spiritual Formation and Community." Pagitt's wife, Shelley, is leader of their yoga sanctuary, which features classes such as "Family Yoga," "Kundalini Yoga and Gong Bath," "Restorative and Guided Relaxation," and "Yoga Mala," which follows the teachings of Ashtanga Yoga Master Sri K. Pattabhi Jois, one of the key 20th-century Hindu yogis responsible for exporting yoga to the West.[12]

After examining this movement for more than ten years, I can safely say that Emergent ideas, beliefs, and practices are far more cultic than orthodox, as the Emergents have consistently chosen mystic ideas that more closely align with New Age philosophy than biblical Christianity.

The word "emergent" is a term that many of us still use to identify this aberrant religious movement. However, many Emergent leaders have stopped using the word and have begun disavowing it. This is directly related to the success that many of us who are apologists for the Bible have had in effectively exposing the Emergent Church and its leaders. It is now the responsibility of Bible believers to recognize and expose Emergent error when we encounter it, no matter what it may be called.

The deconstruction of 2,000-year-old Christianity has been underway for some time. However, as I have mentioned, hardcore postmodern leaders gained a voice and have become increasingly insistent that the Church change and conform to their culture — or else. Now we seem to have hit a tipping point. If congregations were to retain or regain the coveted postmodern-age people, they are faced with a pivotal question: Would the churches stay with the Bible, or would they amend virtually anything needed to have peace and harmony with a generation demanding change? Of course, not all postmodern-age kids bolted over to the side of their peers, and not every church acquiesced to the demands of some who were barely out of youth group. But unless those in leadership in any given congregation were solid Bible believers and dedicated to the idea that, regardless of what may come, the Bible and the doctrines of the faith were off-limits to change and nonnegotiable, then they were in immediate or eventual jeopardy.

Considering that surveys, polls, and personal experience indicate that the Church in general is in a dreadful place when it comes to biblical literacy, I fear that many churches may have but a handful of faithful adherents to the Scriptures. Can they stave off the mounting assault on biblical Christianity — and, if so, for how long? Those refusing to give in are in many cases treated as Stone-Age Neanderthals and quickly marginalized when they dare ask the wrong questions.

I wish I had more confidence that pastors, including professing evangelicals, would serve as a last line of defense against the burgeoning postmodern takeover. However, after years of church-growth materials, "seeker" seminars, and "Purpose-Driven" ideas, a diminishing percentage of clergy might put a clamp on those determined to transform the Church into a social justice network based on yoga classes, walking the labyrinth, and the mystical spirituality of Meister Eckhard, Henri Nouwen, Thomas Keating, and Thomas Merton. After all, if William Paul Young's *The Shack* — which clearly teaches reconciling universalism — could become the #1 best-seller among Christians in 2008–2009, then one must wonder what else is possible in modern Christianity.

The remnant Church must resolve that nothing will impede our clear, unreserved, and uncompromising presentation of the Word of God. Anything else is deception.

The Ministry of Discernment

A Crucial "Word"

When I accepted Jesus Christ and became a Christian, I was nearly 30 years of age. My wife had come to Christ two years before me and, though I didn't vocalize it in those days, I couldn't help but notice as God radically transformed her life. That transformation was a direct result of what God's Word was doing in her life. As Terry James has asked me to do, in the next section, I'll include part of the story of our transition as God moved us "from rock to Rock."

Immediately after I was saved, I began to read, learn, and memorize passages from the Bible. The effect this discipline had on my life, my behavior, my family, my occupational decisions — *every facet of my life* — was immediate and profound. Along with millions of other people, part of my testimony is that the Word has a revolutionizing, supernatural effect on the mind (Romans 12:1–2) and the heart (Psalm 119:11). In that early season, very little else mattered. My life had been radically changed, and I just wanted to serve the Lord. I simply couldn't get enough of the Word of God.

Now, well into my fourth decade as a believer, I have become concerned as I've seen the Bible slowly slip down the list of priorities in the lives of many Christians. I hope this isn't the case in your life, but it is indeed taking place around us. It is no coincidence that we are also seeing the moral, spiritual, and cultural lights of Planet Earth dimming and the time of Jacob's Trouble drawing near. No matter what the conditions around us may be, it is great comfort to remember that the Word of God is the only trustworthy standard of truth, and it remains potent to revolutionize any life. So, here are a few words concerning the ministry of discernment.

Be Dedicated to Uphold the Scriptures

You must be confident of what you believe — regardless of what ministry God may call you to — and be certain your beliefs are in harmony with the Scriptures!

"The Word" about "The Word?":

- Psalm 119:105: Thy word is a lamp unto my feet, and a light unto my path.

- Psalm 119:11: Thy word have I hid in mine heart, that I might not sin against thee.

- Matthew 5:18: For verily I say unto you, Till heaven and earth pass, one jot or one tittle shall in no wise pass from the law, till all be fulfilled.

- Matthew 24:35: Heaven and earth shall pass away, but my words shall not pass away.

- Psalm 119:89: For ever, O LORD, thy word is settled in heaven.

- Matthew 4:4: But he answered and said, It is written, Man shall not live by bread alone, but by every word that proceedeth out of the mouth of God.

The Bible refers to Jesus as the living Word of God. John begins his Gospel with "In the beginning was the Word, and the Word was with God, and the Word was God" (1:1). Verse 14 continues, "And the Word was made flesh, and dwelt among us, (and we beheld his glory, the glory as of the only begotten of the Father,) full of grace and truth."

The popular gotquestions.org website brings clarity to what John writes in these passages. It states, "for his Jewish readers, by introducing Jesus as the 'Word,' John is in a sense pointing them back to the Old Testament where the Logos or 'Word' of God is associated with the personification of God's revelation. And in Greek philosophy, the term Logos was used to describe the intermediate agency by which God created material things and communicated with them. In the Greek worldview, the Logos was thought of as a bridge between the transcendent God and the material universe."[13]

The point here is that Jesus and the Word of God are inseparable. Jesus *IS* the Word of God incarnate. The Word of God simply must be our standard, and though the Bible doesn't answer every question one might have, it represents exactly what God wanted humanity to know and understand. Christians — and in this case, those called to apologetics ministry — can never waver from the firm foundation of the Bible lest we do a disservice to the One who paid the penalty for us.

Finally, Revelation 19 paints a vivid picture of the King of kings leading the armies out of heaven en route to defeat the Beast and False Prophet at the end of the seven-year Tribulation. Verse 13 dramatically refers to Jesus as "The Word of God"!

Lest anyone get the impression that the Old Testament is somehow less important for believers or that only the New Testament is valid for us, we need only consider the earthly ministry of Jesus. The Lord's constant referral to the Old Testament carries a weight nothing else can match. It displays the Master's complete trust in its accounts and accuracy. When Jesus walked in human form, He never brought any Old

Testament passages or stories into question. Instead, by His own teaching, Jesus authenticated the divine origin and the theological and historical reliability of Genesis through Malachi.

Here are just a few of dozens of examples wherein Jesus validated people and accounts that many vainly seek to dispute or discredit today.

Abel — Luke 11:51

Noah — Matthew 24:37–39; Luke 17:26–27

Abraham — John 8:56

Sodom and Gomorrah — Matthew 10:15, 11:23–24; Luke 10:12

Elijah — Luke 4:25–26

Elisha — Luke 4:27

Daniel's status as prophet — Matthew 24:15

Jonah — Matthew 12:39–41; Luke 11:29–30, 32

Moses — Matthew 8:4, 19:8; Mark 1:44, 7:10

Genesis 1 and 2 — Matthew 19:4–5; Mark 10:6–8 (creation, traditional marriage, etc.)

Know That You Are Called

Most important for Christians who wish to enter the ministry of apologetics is to be certain that this ministry is where God wants them. In these last days, every biblical believer must understand and operate in a certain degree of apologetics. However, no one should call himself or herself (by human intellect or emotions) into the ministry of apologetics. It is a particularly treacherous spiritual minefield. But if God has called you to it, *then welcome aboard!*

How will you know that you are "called"? You will know (1) through the Word, (2) by His Holy Spirit, and (3) by the confirmation of seasoned spiritual leaders such as your pastor, etc.

There has always been a need, but with the escalating confusion of our times, the work of discerning Christians and apologetics ministries are sure to have a great and vital impact in the days ahead.

Put Yourself to the Test

We should constantly subject our beliefs, ideas, and attitudes to the test of Scripture (1 Thessalonians 5:21–22; 2 Corinthians 13:5), asking God to correct whatever He desires in us. It is easy to become extremely focused on exposing "the unfruitful works of darkness" (Ephesians 5:11). This is indeed a good thing, providing that whatever you are exposing really is a work of darkness. However, you can be carrying out that good work *but also be caught up in doing so with a completely wrong attitude.*

Be Prepared to Be Misunderstood, Abandoned, Rejected, and Ridiculed

It's a fact that those who point out practical and doctrinal error are not received with open arms in the Church today.

I realize how uninviting and negative that sounds, but there should be no expectation of teddy bears, puppy dogs, and fuzzy feelings here. Today's apologists find themselves facing off with every imaginable ideology, including atheists, Satanists, Islamists, and any number of special interest and social justice storm troopers who see Christianity as their main foe. Perhaps most disheartening, however, is the rising opposition created by the sweeping left turn that many once-evangelical denominations, seminaries, and churches have recently made. *Could this possibly be the worst deception facing us today?* I'd be hard pressed to find another more troubling . . . and damaging.

The Evangelical left values cultural acceptance and champions the politically correct (PC), misguided virtue of tolerance. In doing so, they acquiesce to pluralistic universalism and reject the Great Commission that Jesus gave His Disciples and Church in the period between His bodily Resurrection and ascension (Matthew 28:19–20).

One of the main tenets of this current wave of PC fascism is that all religious views must be validated and that absolutely no one claim that any belief system is supreme to any other. Because biblical Christianity rightfully stands opposed to these edicts, they now whisper their mockery and shun Bible believers as "radicals." What is truly disturbing is that this movement has within it numerous individuals and groups claiming to be "Christian," and "evangelical" to boot! Don't be shocked when these apostates claim that we, who trust and follow the Scriptures, are nothing but a "cult" and that they are the true and "tolerant" Christians. It's coming.

From Deception to the Kingdom

You have read a little about the ministry of discernment and apologetics and just a few of the challenges that the remnant Church is facing today.

However, 40 years ago no one could have convinced me that I would spend the second half of my life dedicated to serving God and defending His Word.

As you are about to read, my one and only goal was to play secular music and chase the dream of producing hit records. However, God had other plans. In fact, when I was baptized as an infant (something I do not believe in but obviously had no control over), the pastor handed me back to my grandmother, bent over, and whispered in her ear, "This boy is destined to be a preacher." My grandmother held that as a secret in her heart, not telling me until I had been in the ministry for almost ten years. Make no mistake: Satan heard those words that were uttered back then. His plan for my life was anything but the ministry.

The following contains excerpts from my testimony, "How I Came from Rock to Rock." Let it challenge you and also encourage you. If God can save me, He can save anybody. So please don't give up praying for anyone. There are many around us just like I was, and our job is to trust that He can and will do the miraculous and change the lost — who appear to be so far away — for His glory.[14]

Like most of you reading this, I was raised going to church. As a child, I attended St. Paul's Methodist Church in my hometown of Parkersburg, West Virginia. My grandparents, who had taken on the responsibility of raising me, sent me faithfully to Sunday school. I took part in the usual activities such as church plays, camps, and various Vacation Bible Schools. I was not a bad kid. I didn't cause a lot of trouble and just fit into the crowd. If you had asked me if I were a Christian, of course I would have answered "yes." I heard all the great Bible stories, learned about the Bible's characters, and had some general understanding of the Christmas and Easter stories. But to my remembrance, no one ever explained to me in a way that I understood that becoming a Christian was not a set of church activities, charity, or good works. Those things are all *proof* of one's salvation and relationship with God, but are in no way the *means* by which to be saved. Though I would have claimed to be a Christian and did all kinds

Eric Barger, 9 years old

of Christian things, like so many who have an unbiblical concept of Christianity, I did not possess the authentic salvation experience needed to cross the line between "lost" and "saved." I had never trusted Jesus as the Lord and Savior of my life, but instead had fallen into the pattern of doing church stuff. So let me be clear about what I wish someone would have communicated to me so long ago — church membership, trying to be good, and doing nice things are fine; but, like baptism, those things do not gain us admittance into God's heaven. It is faith in Jesus Christ as our only Savior and acceptance of what He did for us on the Cross of Calvary, *and nothing else,* that can cleanse and bring us assurance of eternity in the presence of the Lord. I truly wish I would have understood this at a young age. It would have saved me from much heartache and would have radically altered the path of my life.

Early in my life, it became evident that I had musical talent. By age ten, I had begged my grandmother for a guitar and began taking lessons. But I learned the songs I wanted to play, by ear, directly from the records I had purchased.

In those days, the music being produced, and the lifestyle and attitude being advocated by the musicians, was vastly different from those popular today. Then, the most rebellious song on the radio was Leslie Gore's "It's My Party and I'll Cry if I Want To"! It all seemed so harmless, but little did we know where the music revolution was going to take us. There were no songs glorifying drugs, the occult, murder, gangs, sexual acts, or rape. In the 1950s, record companies, the media, and the public at large would have shunned any group or artist who glorified Satanism or suicide in their music. They would have found no audience. Yet today, themes like this garner those responsible various esteemed artistic awards, loving accolades from large fan bases, and of course, lots and lots of money.

I was first actually paid for playing music when a local disc jockey hired my band, "The Echoes," to play at an area teen dance. That was in early 1963 and I was only 11 years old. By the fall of 1964, our band was busy just about every weekend playing dances and parties. Getting up to go to church on Sunday morning quickly became a thing of the past. After all, how could my grandparents expect me to do that since I had been out late the night before entertaining somewhere? To say it frankly, since they had become less dedicated to church as I had grown older and since our home was at best a minimal witness for the Lord, I was allowed to slide and was not told that I had to attend church. Now don't miss this — you see, if Satan can separate a person from any sort of Christian fellowship, then he has accomplished a real coup in their lives. He is continually working to undermine and destroy God's will and purpose for each and every life. As long as I was in church, there was always the possibility that I might have heard the gospel presented in such a way that the Holy Spirit would have convicted me. I might have turned my life over to Him before the world, the flesh, and the devil could get a paralyzing hold on me. But without any influence from Christians and only the fleeting memories of Sunday schools from years gone by, Satan had me right where he wanted me, ensuring that I would fall for his plan for my life instead of discovering what God wanted.

A major part of hell's plan for me began to unfold on a Sunday night in February 1964, when I first saw the Beatles. Watching their performance on the "Ed Sullivan Show" was a turning point for me, and probably for thousands of other aspiring young musicians. I said, "That's what I want to do. I want to be a musician for life." Little did I know what that was going to mean for me.

By the time I turned 16, I was playing in the largest party bar at Ohio University six nights a week. I was popular and financially successful for my age. My high school English teacher even told me that I was making more money each week than she was! I grew up too fast and I was growing up without godly guidance, having elected to follow the morals and lifestyles of my musical heroes. In short order, I had thrown off the upbringing that my grandparents had tried to give me, exchanging it for sexual experiences, drugs, and the rock-'n'-roll lifestyle. The idea of going to our little church seemed "weird," and "old-fashioned" — in short, a waste of time. I gave it little or no thought as I soon had my eyes firmly planted upon my selfish desires and myself as the ultimate center of my universe.

Please don't misunderstand me. I am extremely grateful for my grandparents and what they did for me. They loved me and provided for me in every way they knew how. They did not neglect disciplining me when I needed it. But as I grew older, so did they, and though they were aware of some of the unsavory changes taking place in my life, I understand now that they were lost as to know just what to do with me. It is certain that the biblical value system, which parents should employ, was sorely missing in our home. This is in no way a knock on my grandparents' character or upon their earnest desire to see me grow up right. However, one cannot teach what one does not know, and as I look back. it is apparent to me that instead of growing closer to God, our entire family moved further away.

My grandmother had tried to deal with me, but I was out of control and not willing to listen much to what she or my grandfather had to say. I know I grieved them greatly in those days and only wish I had come to my senses in time to get things right with my grandfather before his death in the early '70s. By hiding my sin, in particular the drug use, they really knew relatively little of what was really going on in my life. It wasn't until years later that I allowed the truth

Eric Barger on stage at the Paramount Theater, Seattle, Washington, circa early 1970s

to surface of how my teen years were spent with a joint in my mouth as I experimented with my newfound promiscuity. Life for me was the ultimate in "doing your own thing" — a prescription for certain disaster.

Some may wonder, "What's wrong with that? We live in a free society. Besides, everybody's doing it!" I understand that rationale. I felt that way for many years, living in my "do your own thing" existence. I couldn't see what harm could come from getting all of the self-gratification possible. After all, it was my life.

At 17, with one girl pregnant and my 23-year-old girlfriend very upset, I split for the West Coast. That was where it was all happening: success, possible stardom, fame, and fortune. And for me, it would be a fresh start. But nothing in my life really changed except the scenery. By 21, I was playing regularly in Seattle area recording studios and nightclubs. Playing lead guitar and doing most of the arranging for the groups I was in, my songs were full of lyrics about love, but I didn't have a clue about what that word really meant.

Life had become one big "high." Sex, drugs, and rock 'n' roll were all I really cared about. Traveling with my band and living with one girl, while spreading myself around to any willing groupies and taking mind-expanding MDA, psychedelic mushrooms, and LSD became my daily staples. All the while I was after the elusive record contract that would enable me to "make it" in the music business. I was searching for reality in Eastern mysticism — something we now call "New Age." I had a lingering affair with a bona fide practicing witch who dabbled in candle magic and astrology. I wanted to know why I existed and where I was going, but my very existence was distorted and the forecast for my future was at best "cloudy with limited visibility."

With my search for reality at a dead end, I found myself burnt out, disillusioned, and in a fog, I left the group and invested what I had into a recording studio. It was there that I found the most success by worldly standards. From that first small studio, I moved through several others and finally became the studio manager for what is now advertised as one of the largest state-of-the-art recording complexes on the West Coast. I had found my niche. I had a gift for hearing sounds and arranging music. Future Grammy Award winners Kenny G, the metal group Queensryche, and others were regulars there. I had my own production company, a Lincoln Continental (gained in a failed record deal), and more money than sense. I was on my way — to what, I didn't know, but I was going!

I continued to play in a local bar with friends "just for the party." That group was called "The Sin City Ramblers." With all of my apparent successes, I had actually hit the bottom . . . thinking I was heading for the top.

It was at this point in my life that I met Melanie. At first, she was destined to be no more than just another notch on my belt, another sexual trophy. But I really began to feel something different for her. After knowing her for only three weeks, I moved out of my girlfriend's house and did what I always said I'd never do — I got married!

Melanie and I had a lot in common. She had a library of reference books on witchcraft and the occult. We were both into partying, drugs, and rock 'n' roll. What else was there? In my confused mind, life was complete. But the bliss didn't last. It wasn't long before Melanie found that I couldn't be satisfied with just her. The scars of a life without morals were deep and impossible to change — or so I thought. Each day at home was a fight. Since I never knew what responsibility truly was, I ran to the things that made me feel good: my studio and my cocaine.

Eric and Melanie's wedding photos

Marriage just didn't fit in my plans. Though we had eloped in what I thought was true love, the daily responsibilities of a committed life together hindered me. But as far as I could understand what love was, I loved Melanie. What was I to do? I see now that I really loved the convenience of marriage, but had no understanding of the respect and care that comprises authentic unconditional love.

We tried marriage counseling, the secular brand. After two visits, we both agreed that was a dead end. So, on we went — drugging and drinking and partying and bickering.

One day during a heated argument, Melanie threw a two-inch thick phone directory of yellow pages at me. I had made a smart comment about getting our lives straightened out through a marriage counselor. Shaking off being nailed in the back of the head with the Yellow Pages, I picked them up, shook them at her, and for reasons unknown to me, I said, "But it's gotta be a Christian marriage counselor."

She screamed, "You figure it out; you *@&$%!!" and slammed the bedroom door, locking it for the night.

The next morning, I opened those same Yellow Pages to "religious counselors," closed my eyes,

Eric Barger in his first studio
in the mid-70s

and jabbed my finger at the page. The phone rang and a man answered, "Good morning, God bless you." The number I had called — *at random, or so I thought* — was that of a real-live, Bible-believing, Christian minister who counseled people from the office of his real estate firm.

I explained that my wife and I had "problems" and we needed a counselor. In the back of my mind I kept thinking, "She is the one who needs help, so I'll get this counselor so she'll get off my back and leave me alone!" What I didn't realize was how desperately I needed help too, as well as did our daughters, having been raised in an ungodly environment where drugs ruled from behind closed doors and rock 'n' roll was the master of ceremonies.

During that first conversation with the counselor, he asked if we were Christians. I said, "Oh sure. We were both baptized in the Methodist church when we were babies" (her in Iowa and me in West Virginia). Besides, I was thinking, what did he think we are? We weren't Hindu or something and we lived in America. Of course we're Christians!

The counselor knew just by the way I had answered the questions that he'd asked that I didn't have any notion of who God was, and surely didn't have a personal relationship with His Son. To my knowledge, that was the first occasion in my adult life when I had communicated about anything the least bit theological with a born-again Christian. In all the nights I had performed in bars and concert halls, and on the many occasions I had traveled and conversed with people, I never recall *anyone* ever evangelistically sharing the salvation message of new life through Jesus Christ with me. I had once even been hired to help write, record, and perform in a live presentation of a Christian "rock opera" in which I played the part of the Apostle Peter no less! Yet, if anyone ever actually did challenge me about my need to know Jesus personally, it doesn't come to mind at all. What a tragic and telling indictment against the church in America.

Ted, the counselor, would eventually counsel Melanie and me separately or together over 50 times. It was during these sessions that he kept suggesting something that I didn't understand or want: that I "take responsibility in our home." He also kept talking about the Bible — I knew only as a "good book." For though I called myself a "Christian," I knew nothing about God.

After just two or three sessions with Ted, I began making up any excuse possible to get out of going to see him. However, Melanie kept going and was genuinely seeking and receiving help. She was immediately drawn to his presentation of Scripture. I, however, felt very uncomfortable and wanted no part of this business. I know now that while she was being drawn by the Holy Spirit that God was also after me, but I wasn't at all willing or ready — yet.

I came home from the studio one evening in my usual state of being loaded on drugs to find a Bible sitting on the coffee table. I thought, "Well, isn't that nice . . . as long as Melanie doesn't get weird with it."

She got weird.

Melanie began to read the Bible, and supernaturally God slowly drew her to faith in the Jesus that the pages revealed to her. She stopped being my drug partner. Our $500–$1,000 a week habit was now mine alone. Her speech changed. She stopped smoking, drinking, and partying. She was different. But my life was still on a downward spiral that came to a head when she cajoled me into going to a counseling session. When Ted asked in closing, as he always did, if either of us wanted to "receive Jesus as savior," Melanie said yes. With huge tears flowing down her cheeks, he led her line-by-line in a prayer of commitment. I watched as my wife made an open confession of her faith. But I determined that no way was He getting me!

I had long since disdained the counseling, but now she had "flipped out" and become a "Jesus freak." I'd had it. I promptly packed a bag and left her for several days, but as time passed I missed her and our girls, and I was getting tired of sleeping on the floor at the recording studio. So back I came to find that her witchcraft books were gone — not because a well-meaning Christian had advised her to throw them out, but because God had already dealt with her heart that she only needed ONE book. She had also discovered "Christian" music, and I had to admit that it was indeed pretty good. It had life and was a far cry from what I had always thought church music was. I had always thought that Christian music was an organ playing in a minor key that made you cry or feel depressed.

There was one more change. Over the span of just a few days, she had become like the Apostle Paul's sister! But when she realized that preaching at me was not going to facilitate any change, she started loving me unconditionally, which was nearly unbearable. It was then that I began to feel an inkling of what I now understand to be the drawing of the Holy Spirit as He began wooing my heart. Still, I rejected God. Though He was showing me close up in Melanie what He can do to cleanse and restore a life, I was deeply entrenched in my hopeless condition.

Weeks passed, then months. We were still together, in theory, but it was anything but happy or peaceful. Melanie read her Bible and attended a Bible study group and church services, while I plunged deeper into cocaine and my work. She was going to heaven, while I was going to Hollywood! I had lost my drug buddy and partner in perversion, but I was still determined to follow "my dream," regardless of what it cost or where it led.

Then, one Friday night, Melanie discovered my car close to a girlfriend's house. Though she didn't catch me there, I knew I'd been caught by the note she left on my windshield. That night I did as much coke as I ever had, throwing me into a state of hyper-paranoia. I spent the next day in a hotel room trying to "come down." The coke had taken me into a new level of experience, but not a good one. I couldn't stop shaking, and my worst fear was realized when I found my dealer had run out of the white powder I craved.

Melanie spent that day praying and crying to God for direction. She and our counselor had prayed together on the phone at 1 a.m., "God . . . whatever it takes . . . GET ERIC!"

Sunday was a cold, rainy Seattle day. Melanie went to the bookstore to find something that would give her peace. Finding nothing on "peace," she walked out with *Racing Toward Judgment* by prophetic author David Wilkerson. Reading it entirely, her mind had been diverted from dwelling on me. For all she knew, I could have been dead by then, but she was comforted with the peace that only knowing God can give.

My memory blurs on the actual chronology of events from those days. Concerning what happened that night, Melanie has had to help me accurately reconstruct this story. She says that in my drunken state, I came through our front door screaming obscenities at her. Just as had been my habit, I began blaming her for all our problems. This is often the kind of demented psychology that individuals execute on others, when they are themselves unwilling to take responsibility for their own failings. At some point I simply sat down on the floor and passed out. Two hours later I came to with perhaps the worst drug and alcohol hangover of my life. I hadn't slept in three days, had overdosed severely, and had been drinking heavily for most of that period. All I had on my mind was finally ending our ruined marriage — the reason I had come back to our house earlier that night.

I climbed up onto the couch where she had been sitting quietly praying for me. Confused and depressed, I was trying to muster up some sort of cowardly courage to inform her that, after throwing the word "divorce" at each other in our fights month after month, I was finally going to do it. It was at this point that I picked up the book that was lying there between us. In my nervousness, I simply flipped *Racing Toward Judgment* open to page 60. There on the left side of the page, underlined with my wife's pen from just hours before, were three words: "GOD HATES DIVORCE!"

It was then — at the lowest state of my life — that I finally reached out to God.

I fell on the floor and burst into tears. My wife began to cradle me in her arms. I know now that through her, Jesus was hugging the adulterous, abusive, drug addict. I genuinely pleaded with God (and my wife) to forgive me. I'd said I was sorry to her before, but only because I had been caught. This time however, I had hit the bottom and I really meant it. I was finally crying out to the God who I had heard about in that Methodist Sunday school two decades earlier, and who had radically transformed my wife, delivering her from the same pit that He was now pulling me out of.

I was forgiven right there of every evil thing I had ever done. How am I sure? Because the Bible promises that "whosoever shall call upon the name of the Lord *shall be saved*" (Romans 10:13, emphasis added). You might ask, "But how can you trust the Bible?" One simple thing separates the Bible and Christianity from every other religion: the historical fact that Jesus Christ died and rose from the grave. I had searched enough for "inner enlightenment" to know that the answer to life didn't lie inside of me or in the teaching of dead sages.

For the first time, I had an inexpressible feeling of wholeness and value. I was clean. I was saved! And although I never checked into a drug or alcohol rehabilitation center, I miraculously never experienced any withdrawals from the years of substance abuse. God's Holy Spirit came and did it all!

My prayer is that you won't have to "hit the bottom" on your way to what you think is the top. You

Eric and his wife

don't have to. How tragic that so many people have to get to their very lowest place before they look around and realize the mess they are in and that they can't solve it alone.

Though many people comment to me that we have a "great" testimony, I really wish my story were much different. I wouldn't wish what Melanie and I experienced all those years on anyone. More than once I have wrapped my arms around my now-grown daughters and asked their forgiveness for the things I did during their formative years, most of all for just neglecting to be a good, loving dad.

Some "church people" hear a story like ours and think, "My, they really needed God. Isn't it nice that they got straightened out?" But you need to understand that each and every person needs the same cleansing experience from life's sins that Melanie and I received.

As human beings, we share in common the fact that we have each sinned (Romans 3:23). Yet many want to rationalize that they are surely better than most and believe that God must grade on a curve, sending only the *really* bad people to hell. But as much as some want to believe so, that is not what the Bible teaches. God does not judge arbitrarily. It is a lie of Satan and part of our flawed human thinking to believe that God will accept us just because we're good and kind or that any good works we could accomplish can save us eternally. The fact is there is *nothing* — no good deeds or human works — that we can ever do that can save us (Ephesians 2:8–9). To believe that we can redeem and then save ourselves is a deception that will take millions of people on a one-way trip to hell (Romans 6:23). But you don't have to go there, and God has provided a way out!

Because of God's great love for us, Jesus Christ came to earth and sacrificed Himself for us. He took our place and paid the penalty for each and every one of our sins. He died and resurrected, and in doing so, He triumphed over death, hell, and the grave. He has already paid the price for you to enter God's Heaven forever. All you have to do is first ask Him for forgiveness, and then decide to repent, that is, turn from your sins and follow Him with all your heart.

He didn't come to spoil your fun or ruin your life. Jesus came to provide us with abundant life (John 10:10). He offers real, lasting peace and joy for our lives on earth and for all eternity! The joy and peace of knowing Him is the greatest high I've ever known. This is NOT "religion." This is a personal relationship with the Creator of the universe!

So, we are all faced with a choice. What will YOU do with Jesus? The Bible implores us not to put it off. Jesus is waiting on your decision now, but He won't be for long. He's coming back for His people, those who have put their trust in Him by faith (1 Thessalonians 4:13–18). A convergence of biblical signs announcing His arrival is all around us. These clues indicate that His return for the Church could be anytime. It is imminent. Please consider as well that none of us have any guarantee of another day or even another heartbeat. What would happen if your life were suddenly taken? Where would you be for eternity? Remember, as I said before, there is a line to cross from being "lost" to being saved. Have you crossed it yet?

Call out to Him today, even right now. Simply and sincerely pray something like this: "Lord Jesus, please forgive me for all of my sins. Change my life and give me peace. I accept You as my Lord and Savior. I believe that You died in my place on the Cross 2,000 years ago and by faith I receive Your salvation — not based on my goodness or actions but on Your blood shed for me. Please fill me with Your Holy Spirit and give me eternal life. Thank You, Lord. Amen."

If you've prayed that just now, you may not fully understand it. You may not "feel" anything. Understand that just saying those words alone cannot save you nor can just repeating them transform you. However, I can tell you without a shadow of a doubt that if you ask Jesus to forgive you by faith — and you mean it from the depths of your heart — He will answer that prayer! He will truly become your "Rock." If you ask Him to save and change you, He has promised that He would never reject you (Matthew 28:20). If you've asked Him by faith, He'll make you a new creation — with a fresh start on life (2 Corinthians 5:17–21).

To find out more, get a Bible (start by reading in the New Testament, perhaps the Book of John), begin talking with God in prayer, sharing with Him your needs, joys, sorrows, etc. It's also important to find a Bible-believing church, where God is worshiped and honored and where the Bible is taught without compromise. Then as you grow in Him, and remain faithful to His word, watch what God will begin to do in your life. He has a great plan for you because He loves you! If we can help you in any way, please let us know. God bless you!

Endnotes

1. Unless otherwise noted, Scripture in this chapter is from the King James Version (KJV) of the Bible.

2. http://www.watchman.org/articles/mormonism/mormon-temple-ritual-changes/.

3. https://www.lds.org/ensign/2001/11/living-in-the-fulness-of-times?lang=eng.

4. https://www.lds.org/manual/teachings-of-presidents-of-the-church-lorenzo-snow/chapter-5-the-grand-destiny-of-the-faithful?lang=eng.

5. Kurt Widmer, *Mormonism and the Nature of God: A Theological Evolution, 1830–1915* (Jefferson, NC: McFarland, 2012), p. 6.

6. Eric Barger, *Disarming the Powers of Darkness* (Abbotsford, WI: Aneko Press, 2016).

7. Phyllis Tickle, *The Great Emergence* (Grand Rapids, MI: Baker Books, 2012), p. 46.

8. www.ericbarger.com/spot.pdf/.

9. http://www.pbs.org/wnet/religionandethics/2005/07/08/july-8-2005-the-emerging-church-part-one/11744/.

10. http://www.patheos.com/blogs/tonyjones/2013/11/11/im-getting-married-again/.

11. http://www.solomonsporch.com.

12. http://www.yogasanctuarympls.com.

13. https://www.gotquestions.org/Jesus-Word-God.html.

14. This section contains excerpts from Eric's testimony, "How I Came from Rock to Rock." Copies are available to read, download, and freely distribute at www.ericbarger.com, copyright 2017, Eric Barger.

CONCLUSION

TERRY JAMES

Spiritual darkness pervades the planet. Its opaqueness obscures the profoundly troubling things actually taking place while we move through daily life in the incremental seconds we have been granted. That is why it is necessary to present a volume like the one you've just read.

Unless one is spiritually attuned to the massive delusion being designed and implemented by the ultimate enemy of mankind, there is no way out of the maze the devil has perpetrated. Each author of *Deceivers: Exposing Evil Seducers and Their Last-Days Deception* has provided clarification about these evil days that each of us must traverse. Again, I thank each of them for contributing to understanding these times so near the end of the age.

The road ahead is pocked with dangerous pitfalls. It is necessary that those who are part of God's family follow His roadmap in order to avoid the dangers. That roadmap is provided in clear, easy-to-understand, divine direction: "Trust in the LORD with all thine heart; and lean not unto thine own understanding. In all thy ways acknowledge him, and he shall direct thy paths" (Proverbs 3:5–6).[1]

Mankind's chief adversary has lined all pathways through life on earth with deceptive, deluding landmines. These deadly spiritual booby traps are enticing allurements to even the most savvy Christian. Those who lack Holy Spirit insight into the many snares the devil sets haven't a chance to escape their inevitable doom.

Jesus points to the only guide through life's seductive quagmires: "I am the way, the truth, and the life: no man cometh unto the Father, but by me" (John 14:6).

Jesus Christ, the Son of God, comes to reside within each and every individual who believes in Him for the salvation of his or her soul. God, the Holy Spirit — the Third Person of the Godhead — indwells and enlightens the believer's pathway. No matter how perilous or dark the pathway, Christ within the believer assures that God's sons and daughters find their way home to heaven.

There are many, many seducers and deceivers on that pathway that leads to God the Father, as the authors of this book have well delineated. We don't have to look very long to see the perils of these troubled times. Our hourly news tells just how fraught with treachery are all facets of life on this fallen planet.

Our authors have thoroughly covered those various pitfalls of deceit. I will add my thoughts in bringing this book to its conclusion by looking at what I believe is Satan's grand scheme of deception for building his Antichrist world order.

We will consider in more detail here things wrapped up in my words offered in the book's introduction.

To repeat: *Satanic rage against anyone who opposes his global agenda to bring all into a new world order is front and center each and every hour in news headlines. His deceivers — his minions both human and demonic — are busy building with his deadly blueprint to bring about destruction of America and the world.*

The rage that followed the 2016 presidential election campaign, in my view, illustrates the point. Never in America's history has there been such total anger leveled at the winner as when Donald J. Trump unexpectedly, stunningly, won the presidency. The almost insane rage continues to the time of this writing.

Deception and outright fabrication of false news stories by what were once considered trusted news media assail Trump's presidency hourly. The youngest adults among us — the so-called Millennials — dumbed-down by seductive American and world history revisionists within educational institutions, fall victim to Satan's blueprint.

Globalism offered as the only hope for humanity is the monumental deception of this late hour. And, at globalism's center is the grand lie that seals the deal for that young demographic.

"Global warming" — a phrase deceptively altered now to be termed "climate change," because "global warming" has been proven to be a thoroughly refuted hoax — is, the deceivers say, destroying the planet. To save Mother Earth, we all must agree to come under the auspice of those who know best — the global elitists of the Al Gore type.

America, the Millennials and the rest of us are told, is the hang-up to implementing plans that will save the planet from ruin.

America, the most advanced, materially blessed nation to ever be upon the earth's surface, must lead the way in cutting back on carbon emissions. We must redistribute the wealth of the United States to the other nations of the world less fortunate. All must be made equal so the planet can achieve equilibrium — be put back into balance, ecologically, economically, and in all other ways.

The planet, because of America's wanton domination of the earth's resources of the carbon-based sort, is destined to become uninhabitable at some point. The United States is the culprit, so it must be governed by the so-called international community. Our nation's vast wealth must be taken by carbon taxes or by however necessary in order to rectify things.

This hoax was outed through an article written by a top weather official who blew the whistle.

John Coleman, founder of the Weather Channel, wrote an article in which he called the idea of man-made global warming "a scam:"

> It is the greatest scam in history. I am amazed, appalled and highly offended by it. Global Warming; It is a SCAM. Some dastardly scientists with environmental and political motives manipulated long term scientific data to create in [sic] allusion of rapid global warming. Other scientists of the same environmental whacko type jumped into the circle to support and broaden the "research" to further enhance the totally slanted, bogus global warming claims.
>
> Their friends in government steered huge research grants their way to keep the movement going. Soon they claimed to be a consensus. Environmental extremists, notable politicians among them, then teamed up with movie, media and other liberal, environmentalist journalists to create this wild "scientific" scenario of the civilization threatening environmental consequences from Global Warming unless we adhere to their radical agenda. Now their ridiculous manipulated science has been accepted as fact and become a cornerstone issue for CNN, CBS,

NBC, the Democratic Political Party, the Governor of California, school teachers and, in many cases, well informed but very gullible environmental conscientious citizens.[2]

At the heart of this attempt to seduce the world into accepting that man is the equivalent of a hurtful, unwanted infection within the ecosphere is the master deceiver, Lucifer. He still intends to usurp the throne of God as recorded in Isaiah 14:14, even if only an earthly throne.

The election of Donald J. Trump, an avowed anti-globalist, anti-climate change proponent and America-first advocate, has thrown Lucifer's minions, both demonic and human, into a frothing-at-the-mouth fit. The Washington, D.C., establishment, itself governed by the globalist cabal, in my view, is doing all within its dark power to bring this presidency down.

Government insiders, news and entertainment media, and all other globalist-oriented forces are arrayed to accomplish the task. Most of all, the powerful money brokers of the world pull the levers, I'm convinced, at the behest of Lucifer. We are indeed in the struggle the Apostle Paul describes: "For we wrestle not against flesh and blood, but against principalities, against powers, against the rulers of the darkness of this world, against spiritual wickedness in high places" (Ephesians 6:12).

Despite the deceivers, the deception, the seductiveness that surrounds this generation as mankind moves to the end of the age, we who are in God's family have the *blessed hope* (Titus 2:13). Jesus Christ is the same today, yesterday, and forever. He will never leave or forsake us.

We are instructed to do the following by the Lord Jesus, the Creator of all that is: "These things I have spoken unto you, that in me ye might have peace. In the world ye shall have tribulation: but be of good cheer; I have overcome the world" (John 16:33).

Endnotes

1. Unless otherwise noted, all Scripture from this chapter is from the King James Version (KJV) of the Bible.
2. American Thinker Blog: Weather Channel Founder: Global Warming "Greatest Scam in History" by Rick Moran, November 08, 2007.

Terry James

Terry James is author, general editor, and/or coauthor of more than 30 books on Bible prophecy and geopolitics, hundreds of thousands of which have been sold worldwide. He has also written fiction and nonfiction books on a number of other topics.

Terry James

Rapture Ready . . . Or Not: 15 Reasons Why This Is the Generation That Will Be Left Behind (New Leaf Publishing Group, 2016) is his latest book release. His next upcoming release for 2018 is *Essays in Apocalypse* (New Leaf Publishing Group).

He has had books published by houses such as the Penguin Group (E.P. Dutton), Harvest House, and others.

James is a frequent lecturer on the study of end-time phenomena and interviews often with national and international media on topics involving world issues and events as they might relate to Bible prophecy. He is partner with Todd Strandberg and is general editor in the www.raptureready.com website, which was recently rated as the number-one Bible prophecy website on the Internet. The website has more than 25,000 articles and much more material for those who visit the site.

He writes a weekly commentary for the website, in which he looks at current issues and events in light of Bible prophecy. James speaks often at prophecy conferences. He is a member of the Pre-Trib Research Center, founded by Dr. Tim LaHaye. His personal blog is terryjamesprophecyline.com. He lives with his wife, Margaret, near Little Rock, Arkansas.

Dr. David R. Reagan

Dr. David Reagan is a native of Texas. He received his undergraduate degrees in government and history from the University of Texas at Austin. His graduate degrees were all earned at the Fletcher School of Law & Diplomacy in Boston, Massachusetts, a graduate school that is owned and operated jointly by Harvard and Tufts Universities.

After teaching international law and politics for 20 years, in 1980 he decided to step out in faith and establish Lamb & Lion Ministries. The ministry is dedicated to teaching the fundamentals of Bible prophecy and proclaiming the soon return of Jesus.

He is the host of the ministry's television program, *Christ in Prophecy*, which is broadcast both nationally and internationally. He and his wife, Ann, have been married 57 years. They have two daughters, four grandchildren, and two great-grandchildren.

David Reagan

Lamb & Lion Ministries
PO Box 919, McKinney, TX 75070
www.LambLion.com
972-736-3567

Jan Markell

Jan Markell is the founder of Olive Tree Ministries, headquartered in suburban Minneapolis, Minnesota. She has a national radio program now airing on 840 Christian radio stations called *Understanding the Times* and hosts one of the largest prophecy conferences in North America, with an average attendance of 5,000. Markell has authored eight books and has produced many DVD teachings.

Jan Markell

In 2017, Dr. David Reagan included her in a book recognizing Christian leaders, citing her as one of America's most important prophetic voices to America.

Olive Tree Ministries
P.O. Box 1452, Maple Grove, MN 55311
Website: www.olivetreeviews.org

Dr. Gary D. Frazier

Gary D. Frazier

Dr. Gary D. Frazier is executive vice president of United in Purpose, a cultural change ministry. Further, he is a member of President Trump's Faith Advisory team. He is also the founder and president of Discovery Missions International, a nonprofit organization birthed to equip believers through travel to Israel and promoting Christian support of the State of Israel and its biblical right to exist in their God-given land. Frazier has traveled to Israel and the Middle East more than 100 times, and tens of thousands of believers have made his *Walking Where Jesus Walked* journey.

Previously, he has served as a Southern Baptist pastor as well as associate teaching pastor at Prestonwood Baptist in Plano, Texas, with his good friend, Dr. Jack Graham, and speaks weekly across America on the subject of biblical prophecy and culture.

Dr. Frazier is the author of 14 books: *Miracle of Israel, Hell Is for Real, It Could Happen Tomorrow, The Great Divorce, Signs of the Coming of Christ, The Glorious Appearing, The Divine Appointment,* and *America at the Tipping Point* to name a few. He is also a contributor to the *LaHaye Prophecy Bible* and *The Prophecy Encyclopedia.* He has appeared on numerous TV and radio programs as well as on the documentaries *God vs. Satan* and *The Apocalypse Code* on the History Channel, and was featured in *Vanity Fair.*

Frazier attended Criswell College, Southwestern Seminary, and received an M.A. and a Ph.D. from Louisiana Baptist University. He received an honorary Doctorate of Humanities from Liberty University as well as an honorary Doctorate of Divinity from International Seminary.

On the fun side, Frazier is a multiengine IFR pilot and an avid golfer as well as the father of four and grandfather of eight. He and his wife, Sandra, live in Colleyville, Texas.

J. Michael Hile

Michael Hile

J. Michael Hile is president of Signs of Our Times, a biblically based research ministry. A former research and development chemist for Johnson & Johnson, petroleum analytical chemist, and environmental scientist, Hile holds degrees in zoology and chemistry from the University of Arkansas. He was director of the Arkansas Bureau of Standards for several years and served as president and chairman of the board for the Southern Weights and Measures Association. He also served on the executive committee for the National Conference on Weights and Measures.

Hile is author of *Timeline 2000,* which discusses several of God's time cycles in the Bible and contemporary history, and was a contributing author for *Piercing the Future, Prophecy at Ground Zero,* and *The Departure,* edited by William T. "Terry" James. Hile wrote a "Signs of the Times" column on current events for a weekly Christian publication for several years, and currently teaches a senior adult Sunday school class in Cabot, Arkansas. Hile and his wife, Joyce, have four grown children and 14 grandchildren.

Don McGee

Don McGee

Don McGee, founder and director of Crown & Sickle Ministries, is a Vietnam War veteran and retired Louisiana state trooper. He was a pastor for 12 years, and since 2002 has been an evangelist whose focus is exclusively on Bible prophecy. He and his wife, Valerie, live in a rural area near Amite, Louisiana. They have two grown children and three grandchildren.

Israel Wayne

Israel Wayne is an author and conference speaker and Director for Family Renewal. He is author of a number of books, including: *Questions God Asks, Questions Jesus Asks,* and *Education: Does God Have an Opinion?* He is the site editor for ChristianWorldview.net (www.FamilyRenewal.org).

Israel Wayne

Phillip Goodman

Phillip Goodman is the founder and president of Bible Prophecy As Written, a Bible Prophecy ministry dedicated to encouraging and strengthening faith in Jesus Christ. He is the Bible teacher on the television program *Bible Prophecy As Written,* and 24 bi-weekly *Prophecy Retreats.*

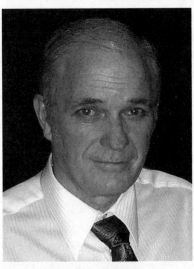

Phillip Goodman

Phillip is the author of *The Assyrian Connection,* which develops the outlines of the final world empire and the origins of the Antichrist, and *The Sequence of End Time Events,* as well as many booklets and DVD programs on Bible prophecy. He has shared space with some of the world's best prophecy experts as a contributing author to the books *Piercing the Future, Prophecy at Ground Zero, Revelation Hoofbeats, One World, Frightening Issues, The Departure, The Lawless One,* and *Living On Borrowed Time.* Phillip is a regular guest on radio and television, and sponsors the annual Mid-America Prophecy Conference, a non-speculative presentation of Bible Prophecy "As Written" (Matt. 4:4) with Jesus Christ at center stage (Rev. 19:10); for this reason it is one of America's premier Bible prophecy conferences. He and his wife Mary, who was born and raised in Bethlehem, Israel, have four sons.

Daymond Duck

By God's grace, Daymond Duck is a graduate of the University of Tennessee in Knoxville, the founder and president of Prophecy Plus Ministries, the best-selling author of a shelf full of books (three have been published in foreign languages), a member of the prestigious Pre-Trib Study Group, a conference speaker, and a writer for raptureready.com. He is a retired United Methodist pastor, has made more than 300 TV appearances, and has been a member of the Baptist church in his hometown since 2006. He can be contacted at duck_daymond@yahoo.com

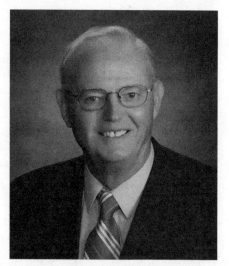

Daymond Duck

Nathan E. Jones

Nathan Jones serves as Associate Evangelist and Web Minister for Lamb & Lion Ministries. He can be found co-hosting the ministry's television program Christ in Prophecy, growing and developing the Web Ministry at www.lamblion.com, authoring books such as 12 Faith Journeys of the Minor Prophets, blogging daily on The Christ in Prophecy Journal, discussing current events on the Christ in Prophecy Facebook Group, producing video Q&As such as The Inbox, being interviewed on radio programs, speaking at conferences and churches, and answering Bible-related questions sent in from all over the world.

Nathan E. Jones

A life-long student of the Bible and an ordained minister, Nathan graduated from Cairn University with a bachelor's in Bible, attended Southern Baptist Theological Seminary, and received his Masters of Management and Leadership at Liberty University.

Todd Strandberg

Todd Strandberg is the founder of www.raptureready.com, the most highly visited prophecy website on the Internet. He is a partner in the site with Terry James. The site has been written about in practically every major news outlet in the nation and around the world. Founded in 1987 when few websites existed, Rapture Ready now commands the attention of a quarter million visitors per month, with more than 13 million hits registered during most 30-day periods.

Todd Strandberg

Strandberg is president of Rapture Ready and coauthor of *Are you Ready Ready?* a Penguin Group book under E.P. Dutton imprint. He has written hundreds of major articles for the site, which have been distributed in major publications and websites around the nation and the world. He writes a highly read column under the site's "Nearing Midnight" section. Strandberg created "The Rapture Index" — a Dow Jones-like system of prophetic indicators — which continues to draw the attention of most major news outlets.

Dr. Billy Crone

Billy Crone is the senior pastor of Sunrise Bible Church in Las Vegas, Nevada. He is married to his lovely wife, Brandie, and they have two wonderful children, Rebecca and Billy. Crone is a gifted author, counselor, conference speaker, and teacher, a frequent guest on radio talk shows and television programs, and serves as a speaker at numerous Bible prophecy conferences around the world. He addresses thousands

Billy Crone

of people across the United States as well as an international community of over 200 countries. He has appeared in the Christian movie *Standing Firm*, and has produced a multitude of documentaries, including his latest work in progress, *The Road to Eternity* series.

Gary Stearman

Gary Stearman

From 1983 to the present, Stearman has pastored Grace Fellowship, a Bible Church in Oklahoma City. He also serves as president of Prophecy Watchers, a television and Internet video prophetic ministry. Over all these years, he has been devoted to deep investigation and application of God's truth as fully expressed in His divinely ordained Scripture. Having written counseling manuals and hundreds of articles on prophetic interpretation, edited two books, and authored a third called *Time Travelers of the Bible*, he is deeply conscious of the critical nature of our current social frenzy.

Stearman believes that we are now living in an era of amazing prophetic significance. He views the Bible as explicit and authentic . . . to be taken literally. "It speaks of our era," he says, "when, as prophesied, the dark spirits of old are beginning to openly reveal themselves, driving society in numerous ways. Some masquerade as beneficent social reformers, taking humanity into what they see as a progressively improved future. Others present academic regimens that will end up controlling humanity through deceptive socio-scientific developments. Many people are in league with the occult 'principalities . . . powers and rulers of the darkness' spoken of by the Apostle Paul in Ephesians 6:12. In our 'sci-fi' culture, they often present themselves as ambassadors from outer space, who have traveled here from distant places to help humanity. Some inhabit unsuspecting human beings, as the driving force behind progressive philosophies. We live in an age of incessant lying, which is consistently exposed by the Bible."

Stearman notes that "for many years, presently culminating in my work at Prophecy Watchers, I have been led to expound upon biblical prophecy as the only hope for the individuals in this world. My expectation and goal is that many will listen and heed the call of salvation through the finished work of Jesus Christ.

"These are the last days, and just as foretold, we have entered the era of counterfeit spiritual phenomena, led by 'the prince of the power of the air' (Ephesians 2:2). The old gods, who have plagued men in ages past, are finding new strength in hundreds of apostate societies. It is in times such as these that our Lord has promised His return to judge the world."

Jim Fletcher

Jim Fletcher is a popular blogger (*Jerusalem Post*, RaptureReady, WND, Beliefnet) and author. His specialty is Bible prophecy and Israel. Jim has a BA in journalism and lives in northwest Arkansas. He can be reached at jim1fletcher@yahoo.com.

Jim Fletcher

Eric Barger

Eric Barger is the founder and president of Take A Stand! Ministries headquartered in the Seattle, Washington, area. He is the author of numerous books and has produced dozens of videos detailing various aspects of the Cults, the Occult, World Religions, Current Events, Bible Prophecy, and today's Entertainment Industry all in the light of a biblical worldview. Since 1983, he has traveled extensively across the United States and Canada defending the faith and presenting the Take A Stand! Seminar series. Eric also serves as the co-host of *Understanding The Times Radio with Jan Markell* and hosts *Take A Stand!* TV

Eric Barger

weekly. Please visit www.ericbarger.com for more information.